Neurobiology of
Sleep and Memory

ACADEMIC PRESS RAPID MANUSCRIPT REPRODUCTION

Proceedings of a Conference held in Mexico City in March, 1975

Neurobiology of Sleep and Memory

EDITORS

RENÉ R. DRUCKER-COLÍN

Departamento de Biología Experimental
Instituto de Biología
Universidad Nacional Autónoma de México
México, D.F., México

JAMES L. McGAUGH

Department of Psychobiology
School of Biological Sciences
University of California
Irvine, California

ASSOCIATE EDITORS

Robert A. Jensen and Joe L. Martinez, Jr.

Department of Psychobiology
School of Biological Sciences
University of California
Irvine, California

ACADEMIC PRESS   New York   San Francisco   London   1977
A Subsidiary of Harcourt Brace Jovanovich, Publishers

LRk HhtHv

ACADEMIC PRESS, INC.
111 Fifth Avenue, New York, New York 10003

United Kingdom Edition published by
ACADEMIC PRESS, INC. (LONDON) LTD.
24/28 Oval Road, London NW1

Library of Congress Cataloging in Publication Data
Main entry under title:

Neurobiology of sleep and memory.

    Papers presented at a conference held in Mexico City
in March 1975.
    1. Sleep--Physiological aspects--Congresses.
2. Memory--Physiological aspects--Congresses. 3. Brain
chemistry--Congresses. I. Drucker-Colin, René Raúl.
II. McGaugh, James L. [DNLM: 1. Memory--Congresses.
2. Sleep--Congresses. 3. Neurophysiology--Congresses.
WL108 N495 1975]
QP425.N46   612'.821   77-1300
ISBN 0-12-222350-0

Contents

List of Contributors

BARRETT, TERRY R., Department of Psychology, University of Colorado, Boulder, Colorado 80302

BLOCH, VINCENT, Département de Psychophysiologie, Laboratoire de Physiologie Nerveuse, Centre National de la Recherche Scientifique, 91190 Gif-sur-Yvette, France

BOAST, CARL A., Department of Neuroscience and Center for Neurobiological Science, College of Medicine, University of Florida, Gainesville, Florida 32610

BOHUS, B., Rudolf Magnus Institute for Pharmacology, University of Utrecht, Utrecht, The Netherlands

DEMENT, WILLIAM C., Sleep Disorders Clinic and Laboratory, Stanford University School of Medicine, Stanford, California 94305

DE WIED, D., Rudolf Magnus Institute for Pharmacology, University of Utrecht, The Netherlands

DRUCKER-COLÍN, RENÉ R., Departamento de Biología Experimental, Instituto de Biología, Universidad Nacional Autónoma de México, México 20, D.F., México

DUNN, ADRIAN J., Department of Neuroscience, University of Florida College of Medicine, Gainesville, Florida 32610

EKSTRAND, BRUCE R., Department of Psychology, University of Colorado, Boulder, Colorado 80302

FERIA-VELASCO, ALFREDO, Departmento de Investigación en Medicina Experimental, Instituto Mexicano del Seguro Social, México 7, D.F., México

FERNÁNDEZ-GUARDIOLA, AUGUSTO, Unidad de Investigaciones Cerebrales, Instituto Nacional de Neurología, S. S. A., México 22, D. F., México

GIACOBINI, EZIO, Laboratory of Neuropsychopharmacology, Department of Biobehavioral Sciences, University of Connecticut, Storrs, Connecticut 06268

GOLD, MARK S., Department of Neuroscience and Center for Neurobiological Science, College of Medicine, University of Florida, Gainesville, Florida 32610

GIUDITTA, ANTONIO, International Institute of Genetics and Biophysics, Naples, Italy

GUILLEMINAULT, CHRISTIAN, Sleep Disorders Clinic and Laboratory, Stanford University School of Medicine, Stanford, California 94305

HENNEVIN, ELIZABETH, Département de Psychophysiologie, Laboratoire de Physiologie Nerveuse, Centre National de la Recherche Scientifique, 91190 Gif-sur-Yvette, France

HOBSON, J. ALLAN, Laboratory of Neurophysiology, Department of Psychiatry, Harvard Medical School, Boston, Massachusetts 02115

JACOBS, BARRY L., Department of Psychology, Princeton University, Princeton, New Jersey 08540

KASTIN, ABBA J., Veterans Administration Hospital and Department of Medicine, Tulane University School of Medicine, New Orleans, Louisiana 70112

KESNER, RAYMOND P., Department of Psychology, University of Utah, Salt Lake City, Utah 84112

LECONTE, PIERRE, Département de Psychophysiologie, Laboratoire de Physiologie Nerveuse, Centre National de la Recherche Scientifique, 91190 Gif-sur-Yvette, France

LOZOYA, XAVIER, Division of Neurophysiology, Scientific Research Department, National Medical Center, Instituto Mexicano del Seguro Social, México, D.F., México

McGINTY, DENNIS J., Neurophysiology Research, Sepulveda Veterans Administration Hospital, Sepulveda, California 91343

MAIER, WILLIAM G., Department of Psychology, University of Colorado, Boulder, Colorado 80302

MORGANE, PETER J., Worcester Foundation for Experimental Biology, Shrewsbury, Massachusetts 01545

MOSKO, SARAH S., Department of Psychology, Princeton University, Princeton, New Jersey 08540

REES, HOWARD D., Department of Neuroscience, University of Florida College of Medicine, Gainesville, Florida 32610

ROJAS-RAMÍREZ, J. A., Departamento de Farmacología, Facultad de Medicina, Universidad National Autónoma de México, México 20, D. F., México

RUTIGLIANO, BRUNO, International Institute of Genetics and Biophysics, Naples, Italy

SANDMAN, CURT A., Department of Psychology, Ohio State University, Columbus, Ohio 43210

SANDOVAL, MARÍA-ELENA, Departamento de Biología Experimental, Instituto de Biología, Universidad Nacional Autónoma de México, México 20, D. F., México

SASSIN, JON F., Departments of Medicine and Psychobiology, University of California, Irvine, California 92717

SIEGEL, JEROME M., Neurophysiology Research, Sepulveda Veterans Administration Hospital, Sepulveda, California 91343

SPANIS, C. W., Department of Biology, University of San Diego, San Diego, California 92110

STERN, WARREN C., Worcester Foundation for Experimental Biology, Shrewsbury, Massachusetts 01545

TAPIA, RICARDO, Departamento de Biología Experimental, Instituto de Biología, Universidad Nacional Autónoma de México, México 20, D. F., México

TRAVERSO, RENATO, International Institute of Genetics and Biophysics, Naples, Italy

TRULSON, MICHAEL E., Department of Psychology, Princeton University, Princeton, New Jersey 08540

URBAN, I., Rudolf Magnus Institute for Pharmacology, University of Utrecht, Utrecht, The Netherlands

VAN WIMERSMA GREIDANUS, TJ. B., Rudolf Magnus Institute for Pharmacology, University of Utrecht, Utrecht, The Netherlands

VELAZQUEZ, XAVIER, Division of Neurophysiology, Scientific Research Department, National Medical Center, Instituto Mexicano del Seguro Social, México, D. F., México

VERZEANO, MARCEL, Department of Psychobiology, University of California, Irvine, California 92717

VITALE-NEUGEBAUER, ANNA, International Institute of Genetics and Biophysics, Naples, Italy

WEITZMAN, ELLIOT D., Department of Neurology, Montefiore Hospital and Medical Center, The Albert Einstein College of Medicine, Bronx, New York 10467

WEST, JAMES N., Department of Psychology, University of Colorado, Boulder, Colorado 80302

ZORNETZER, STEVEN F., Department of Neuroscience and Center for Neurobiological Science, College of Medicine, University of Florida, Gainesville, Florida 32610

Foreword

Sleep and memory are clearly important processes in the integration of human nature. While animals, in particular the higher mammals, are capable of storing information and display sleep and waking cycles, such processes are of a different level of complexity in human beings. Memory is essential for all human social behavior. Examination of memory function is fundamental to the evaluation of psychic integrity in cases of mental disturbance. There appear to be at least two kinds of memory in human beings: (1) long-term memories, which are deeply rooted and slowly forgotten, and (2) memories that are labile and easily forgotten. These different kinds of memories are differentially affected by aging, cranial trauma, and drugs.

The analysis of human memory process has clarified some of the characteristics of the contents of memory. One type of memory is concerned with acquired knowledge such as memories of mathematics or physics. The other type of memory involves uniquely personal experiences. These two types of memory are affected differentially by pathological conditions.

The papers in this symposium provide new insights into the basic neurobiological processes underlying the storage of different kinds of memories. The papers are of particular interest because they deal with relationships between two basic bodily processes, sleep and memory. Sleep does not appear to interfere with memory. On the contrary, sleep appears to aid the fixation of memory of recent experiences. Studies of sleep deprivation indicate that many kinds of behavioral disturbance can be produced by prolonged sleep deprivation. The sleep–memory relationship seems to be fundamental for the preservation of personality with all of its characteristics. The interdisciplinary study of sleep and memory should not only provide an understanding of these basic processes but should, in addition, help to clarify the neurological bases of disorders of sleep and memory as well as certain forms of mental illness.

Guido Belsasso, Director General
Mexican Center for Studies on Drug Dependence

Preface

Perhaps it is only too fitting to have a meeting such as this one in Mexico, because it seems as though some of our Mexican forefathers had pertinent things to say about modern neurobiological problems. For example, Toltec mythology suggested that vegetative functions are under volitional control, thus anticipating recent work on the voluntary control of autonomic functions. Certainly more pertinent to this symposium was their suggestion that during the resting of the body, perhaps meaning sleep, the mind and memories continue to work. The Toltec mythologists suggested that during sleep the mind works more lucidly for the concerns of the spirit than it does during wakefulness.

The Toltecs were not the last people to suggest that memory processes are active during sleep. The view that sleep—and particularly dream sleep—is important for the storage of recent experiences has been suggested by both laymen and scholars. While the role of sleep in memory has been studied intermittently for several decades most of what we know has been discovered only in recent years. The papers in this symposium provide a systematic summary of the major facts and theory concerning the fundamental neurobiology of sleep as well as the role of sleep in the formation and functioning of memory. While it is clear that progress is being made in understanding the nature as well as neural bases of both sleep and memory, it is also clear that we have much yet to learn. We hope that this symposium is a step toward providing answers to the questions raised by Toltec mythologists.

Acknowledgments

This symposium was supported by the National Science Foundation, Consejo Nacional de Ciencia y Tecnología, and the Centro Mexicano de Estudios en Farmacodependencia. We thank Drs. Robert Jensen and Joe Martinez for their extensive help in editing the manuscripts. We thank Deanna Neal for attending to the countless details in preparing the manuscripts for publication. We especially want to express our thanks to her for giving the book her meticulous attention and us her unbelievable patience and good humor.

THE BLOOD-BRAIN BARRIER AND ITS IMPORTANCE
IN THE STUDY OF THE MECHANISMS OF SLEEP AND MEMORY

ALFREDO FERIA-VELASCO

*Departamento de Investigación en Medicina Experimental
Instituto Mexicano del Seguro Social
México 7, D. F., México*

The aim of this paper is to discuss the concept of the blood-brain barrier and its importance in a) designing experimental models to study the basic mechanisms of sleep and memory, and b) in the interpretation of the effects that various pharmacological substances have upon these closely related basic functions of the nervous system.

There are numerous theories to explain the mechanisms of sleep (King, 1971). In this communication I will mention only the humoral theories, since they are closely related to the blood-brain barrier phenomenon. Légendre and Piéron (1910, 1911, 1912) found that when dogs were deprived of sleep for a few days, there appeared in their cerebrospinal fluid a substance which, upon injection into a non-deprived dog, promptly induced sleep. These investigators called that substance "hypnotoxin" and the effects were only observed when it was directly injected into the cerebrospinal fluid and not when the administration was intravascular. The substance could not be dialyzed and it was destroyed by heat and by the action of some oxidizing agents. Pappenheimer and co-workers (Pappenheimer, Miller, & Goodrich, 1967; Fencl, Koski, & Pappenheimer, 1971) repeated these experiments using more precise techniques for the atraumatic collection of large volumes of cerebrospinal fluid from goats. They reinvestigated what they called the "Piéron phenomenon" observing that cerebrospinal fluid from goats deprived of sleep for 72 hours produced profound sleep when injected into cats or rats. Upon partial purification, the substance seemed to be a peptide with a molecular weight of between 1,000 and 2,000 daltons; again, the principle had to be administered directly into the cerebrospinal fluid and not intravascularly. Based upon carefully performed experimental works, various authors have since postulated the existence of substances which are released to the interstitial space in

the brain parenchyma during sleep, and then pass to the cerebrospinal fluid (Drucker-Colín, 1973, 1974; Drucker-Colín,
Rojas-Ramírez, Vera Trueba, Monroy-Ayala, & Hernández-Peón,
1970; Drucker-Colín, Spanis, Cotman, & McGaugh, 1975). Other
authors have shown that these substances pass to the blood
stream, from which they can be recovered. When administered
to awake animals these substances will induce sleep (Monnier
& Hatt, 1971; Monnier & Hosli, 1964; Monnier & Schoenenberger,
1974). Whether these substances are causative of or result
from the physiological mechanisms involved in sleep is at
present unknown. In these cases, the recovered substances
appear to be peptides and are effective when administered into
the cerebrospinal fluid or directly into the brain parenchyma
in certain specific areas. No effects are seen when the
principles are injected intravascularly.

Furthermore, other humoral theories to explain the
mechanisms of sleep posit a role for neurotransmitters or
modulator substances such as serotonin, catecholamines, and
acetylcholine (Drucker-Colín, Rojas-Ramírez, & Rodríguez, 1971;
Jouvet, 1969, 1972; Radulovacki, 1974). Melatonin, synthesized in the pineal gland by influence of the environmental
lighting conditions, appears to play a role in sleep mechanisms
(Antón-Tay, Chou, Antón, & Wurtman, 1968; Fernández-Guardiola
& Antón-Tay, 1974). Numerous substances regulate the biosynthesis and/or degradation of neurotransmitters. It is also
of fundamental importance to consider the blood-brain barrier
phenomenon and the various factors involved in maintaining
the concentration gradients of those substances between the
blood and the interstitial fluid in the central nervous
system.

The humoral aspects involved in the basic mechanisms of
learning and memory are less understood than those involved
in sleep. However, it is known that numerous pharmacological
agents affecting sleep have marked effects in the processes
of learning and memory (Bloch, 1970; Dismukes & Rake, 1972;
McGaugh, 1973; McGaugh & Gold, 1974). Whether the agents
themselves produce these effects directly or indirectly by
modifying the access of other substances to the brain parenchyma is not well understood.

THE BLOOD-BRAIN BARRIER

The blood-brain barrier is a phenomenon by which certain
molecules pass from the blood to the brain interstitial space
at a lower rate than that observed for the same substance at
the same blood concentration and during the same time interval in other vascular territories. This concept gains

importance when we consider the permeability restrictions to the brain parenchyma for some pharmacological agents and toxins (Edström, 1964; Prockop, Schanker, & Brodie, 1962; Rall, 1971). Although there are numerous studies dealing with various aspects of the blood-brain barrier, neither its anatomical representation nor the precise transport mechanisms for all substances are well known at present.

Most areas of the brain show the phenomenon of selective permeability. However, there is no restriction on substances passing into the perivascular space in some structures of the central nervous system. Some of these structures are the area postrema, choroid plexuses, the interpenduncular tubercle, the subcomissural organ, the pineal gland, the meninges, the neurohypophysis, some hypothalamic areas, and the supraoptic crest (Dempsey, 1968; Dobbing, 1961; Wislocki & Leduc, 1952). The morphological structure of the blood vessels in these areas differs from that in areas where there is a limited passage of some substances from the blood to the brain interstitial space (Figures 1 and 2).

TISSUE LOCALIZATION OF THE BARRIER PHENOMENON

There is general agreement that the restriction mechanisms for the passage of substances from blood to brain parenchyma are located at the capillary wall and the perivascular processes of astrocytes. Much controversy has been generated when researchers have tried to localize the precise site of the barrier. Some authors have postulated that the vascular endothelium is the site of the barrier (Broman, 1955; Friedeman, 1942; Jeppsson, 1962), whereas others claim that the perivascular astrocytic processes regulate passage from blood to brain parenchyma (De Robertis, 1962; Dempsey & Wislocki, 1955; Ishii & Tani, 1962). Van Breemen and Clemente consider two restriction thresholds, one at the endothelial lining and the other at the cell membranes adjacent to the perivascular space (Van Breemen & Clemente, 1955). Other postulated elements involved in the phenomenon are the capillary basement membrane (Dempsey & Wislocki, 1955), the amorphous material at the perivascular space (Hess, 1962), electrostatic forces (Friedeman, 1942), and the metabolism of brain tissue elements (Dobbing, 1961; Herlin, 1956; Yamamoto, 1959).

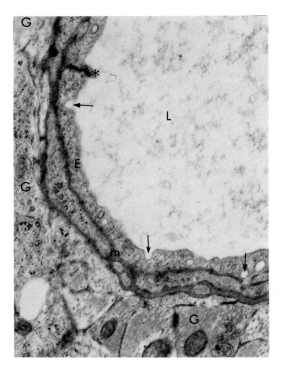

Fig. 1. Electron micrograph of part of a blood capillary in rat motor cortex. The endothelial lining appears continuous with a small number of pinocytotic vesicles (arrows). L=Vascular lumen; m=basement membrane; asterisk= endothelium intercellular cleft; G=glial processes. Uranyl acetate and lead citrate stains. (17,000 X)

TRANSPORT REGULATION FROM BLOOD TO BRAIN PARENCHYMA

The transport regulation of various substances from the blood to the brain interstitial space depends mainly upon three groups of factors: a) those related to the substance itself; b) those related to the brain tissue elements; and c) those related to the brain physiology.

As to the substance itself, the permeability rate depends upon its liposolubility, its ionization rate at physiological pH, its molecular size, and its binding to proteins. Liposoluble substances rapidly diffuse to the brain, whereas the moderately liposoluble substances and those partially ionized at a physiological pH, diffuse at a lower rate

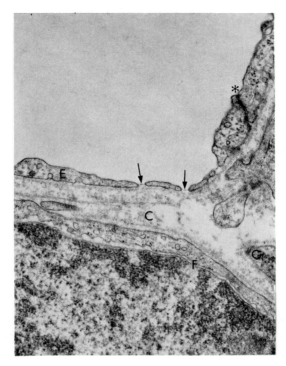

Fig. 2. Portion of a blood capillary in pineal gland
where the endothelial cell (E) appears fenestrated (arrows).
C=collagen fibers in loose perivascular connective tissue;
F=portion of a fibroblast; G=glial process; asterisk=endo-
thelium intercellular cleft. Uranyl acetate and lead citrate
stains. (23,000 X)

(Rall, 1971). For a non-liposoluble substance totally ionized at pH of 7.4, such as acetanilide, sulfaguanidine or
N-acetyl-4-aminoantipirine, the permeability coefficient
(blood-brain parenchyma) is very low (Rall, 1971). An exception to this is the small group of compounds which are ac-
tively transported to the brain tissue elements, such as some
sugars and some amino acids (Fishman, 1964). However, there
are important differences in the active transport of the latter substances. This has been demonstrated in relation to
the selective passage restriction of amino acids supposedly
involved in neurotransmission: namely, glutamic acid, as-
partic acid, γ-amino butyric acid and glycine (Yudilevich,
De Rose, & Sepúlveda, 1972).

As to the *tissue elements* in relation to the blood-brain
barrier phenomenon, it is necessary to consider the morphological characteristics of the blood vessels, which in the
brain are different from those in the rest of the body. In
those areas possessing blood-brain barrier, the capillaries
are of the non-fenestrated type, with thick endothelial layer
and small amounts of cytoplasmic vesicles in the endothelial
cells (Figure 1). The intercellular cleft appears to be im-
permeable to non-liposoluble substances, even to those of
very low molecular weight (Feria-Velasco, in preparation;
Reese & Karnovsky, 1967). In the areas where there is no
blood-brain barrier, the blood capillaries are fenestrated,
with thin endothelial lining and permeable intercellular
clefts (Figure 2) (Dempsey, 1968; Wislocki & Leduc, 1952).

The capillary-glia interphase may also be of functional
importance in regulating the passage back and forth between
the blood and the brain interstitial space, thus maintaining
the concentration gradients for some substances (Pappenheimer,
1966).

Regarding the factors related to *brain physiology,* it is
important to consider the metabolic activity and requirements
for certain physiological substrates in mechanisms influencing the passage rate of certain substances from the blood to
the brain parenchyma. This may be the case for some ions
(Dobbing, 1961; Herlin, 1956), glucose (Fishman, 1964) and
some amino acids (Yudilevich, De Rose, & Sepulveda, 1972).

MORPHO-PHYSIOLOGICAL CORRELATIONS

Relationships between physiological and morphological
findings are clearest for the non-liposoluble substances and
those completely ionized at physiological pH. Two types of
morphological studies have been carried out in this respect:
a) those using electron microscopy techniques to examine the
structural configuration of brain capillary elements (Delorme,
1972; Karnovsky, 1967); and b) those introducing tracers of
various molecular weight before examining the samples with
the electron microscope (Feria-Velasco, in preparation;
Johansson, Olsson, & Klatzo, 1970; Olsson & Hossmann, 1970;
Reese & Karnovsky, 1967).

In various vascular territories, the non-fenestrated capillaries behave toward water and small non-liposoluble substances as if they had pores or clefts of 5 to 6 nm width,
permitting a rapid passage of water and small molecules from
the blood to the perivascular space. The physiologists have
called it a "small pore system" (Landis & Pappenheimer, 1963;

Pappenheimer, 1953). Based upon correlative ultrastructural and physiological studies, these "small pores" appear to be the intercellular clefts at the capillary endothelium (Karnovsky, 1967, 1968). On the other hand, large non-liposoluble substances (above 100,000 d molecular weight) pass from blood to the perivascular space through what physiologists call a "large pore system" (Grotte, 1956; Mayerson, Wolfram, Shirley, & Wasserman, 1960). According to ultrastructural studies using tracers of large molecular weight vesicular transport appears to be involved (Bruns & Palade, 1968; Palade & Bruns, 1968; Renkin, 1964).

Employing tracers of low molecular weight in the central nervous system, some authors have concluded that the morphological substrate of the blood-brain barrier to small non-liposoluble substances is the intercellular cleft at the vascular endothelium (Karnovsky, 1968; Reese & Karnovsky, 1967). In our laboratory, injecting ferrocyanide into the cerebrospinal fluid in anesthetized animals and perfusing the brain with small radicals and ions via the carotid arteries, we have not been able to observe passage of such small substances from the blood to the brain interstitial space (Figures 3 and 4) (Feria-Velasco, Note 1). In an area where there is no blood-brain barrier (the pineal gland), the radicals and ions injected into the blood stream passed to the intercellular space and combined with the ferrocyanide injected into the cerebrospinal fluid. It could be visualized in the electron microscope as an electrodense precipitate (Figure 5). These results find support in the freeze-fracturing studies of Connell and Mercer which demonstrated that in the intercellular clefts of brain capillaries there is a tight junction evidenced by the characteristic linear pattern of intramembranous globular particles (Connell & Mercer, 1974). As mentioned before, the passage of non-liposoluble substances from the blood to the brain parenchyma should be by means of active transport mechanisms, in part regulated by the brain metabolic conditions and the physiological requirements of substrates by the brain tissue elements.

In conclusion, we can say that the blood-brain barrier is part of the rather complex brain-barrier system which involves passive passage mechanisms and active transport processes in order to maintain the brain interstitial fluid in optimal conditions of composition and concentration.

It is important to note that the various factors involved in the maintaining of the concentration gradients between the blood and the brain interstitial fluid have to be taken into account when designing experimental models to study the basic mechanisms of sleep and memory, as well as in the evaluation of their results.

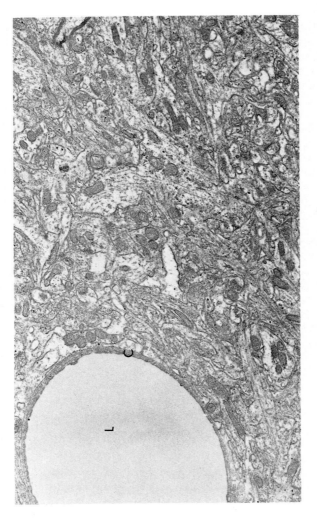

Fig. 3. Panoramic electron micrograph showing part of a blood capillary (C) in cat parietal cerebral cortex. In this experiment, sodium ferrocyanide was injected into the lateral ventricle and copper sulfate was perfused intravascularly. No dense precipitate is seen within the lumen (L) or in the perivascular space. Unstained section. (8,500 X)

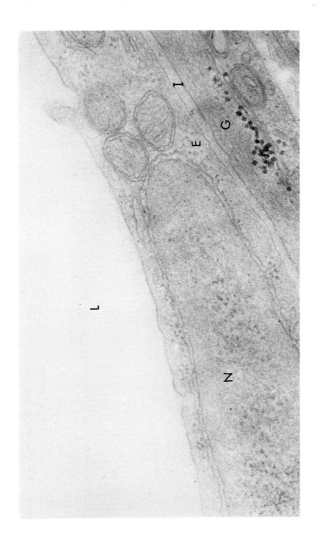

Fig. 4. High magnification of a blood capillary in cerebral cortex of a cat injected with ferrocyanide into the lateral ventricle and further perfused with copper sulfate via carotid arteries. No dense precipitate is observed at the vascular lumen (L), nor at the perivascular interstitial space (I). N=nucleus of the endothelial cell (E); G=glial process. Lightly stained section with lead citrate (45,000 X)

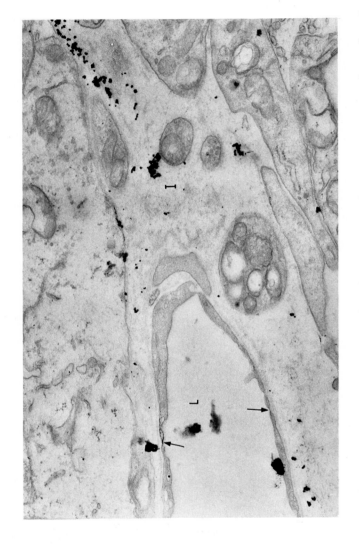

Fig. 5. Portion of a blood capillary in pineal gland from a cat treated as in Figures 3 and 4. Coarse electrondense precipitate of copper-ferrocyanide is seen in both the vascular lumen (L) and the perivascular interstitial space (I). Arrows=endothelial fenestrae. Un-stained section (23,000 X).

REFERENCE NOTE

1. Feria-Velasco, A. Further studies on the blood-brain barrier to low molecular weight substances. Ultrastructural cytochemical study. Submitted for publication, 1976.

REFERENCES

Antón-Tay, F., Chou, C., Antón, S., & Wurtman, R. J. Brain serotonin concentration: Elevation following intraperitoneal administration of melatonin. *Science*, 1968, *162*, 277-278.

Bloch, V. Facts and hypotheses concerning memory consolidation. *Brain Research*, 1970, *24*, 561-575.

Broman, T. On basic aspects of the blood-brain barrier. *Acta Psychiatrica Neurologica Scandinavica*, 1955, *30*, 115-124.

Bruns, R. R., & Palade, G. E. Studies on blood capillaries. II. Transport of ferritin molecules across the wall of muscle capillaries. *Journal of Cell Biology*, 1968, *37*, 277-299.

Connell, C. J., & Mercer, K. L. Freeze-fracture appearance of the capillary endothelium in the cerebral cortex of mouse brain. *American Journal of Anatomy*, 1974, *140*, 595-599.

De Robertis, E. Some old and new concepts of brain structure. *World Neurology*, 1962, *3*, 98-111.

P. Différenciation ultrastructural des jonctions ercellulaires de l'endothélium des capillaires ncéphaliques chez l'embryon de poulet. *Zeitschrift Zellforschung und Mikroskopische Anatomie*, 1972, 571-582.

E. W. Fine structure of the rat's intercolumnar ercle and its adjacent ependyma and choroid plexus, special reference to the appearance of its sinual vessels in experimental argyria. *Experimental ology*, 1968, *22*, 568-589.

Dempsey, E. W., & Wislocki, G. B. An electron microscopic study of the blood-brain barrier in the rat employing silver nitrate as a vital stain. *Journal of Biophysical and Biochemical Cytology,* 1955, *1,* 245-256.

Dismukes, R. K., & Rake, A. V. Involvement of biogenic amines in memory formation. *Psychopharmacologia,* 1972, *23,* 17-25.

Dobbing, J. The blood-brain barrier. *Physiological Review,* 1973, *41,* 123-134.

Drucker-Colín, R. R. Crossed perfusion of a sleep inducing brain tissue substance in conscious cats. *Brain Research,* 1973, *56,* 123-134.

Drucker-Colín, R. R. The possible nature of sleep inducing brain perfusates: Their relationship to seizure inhibition. In R. D. Myers and R. R. Drucker-Colín (Eds.), *Neurohumoral Coding of Brain Function.* New York: Plenum, 1974.

Drucker-Colín, R. R., Rojas-Ramírez, J. A., & Rodriguez, R. Serotonin-like electroencephalographic and behavioral effects of quipazine. *Federation Proceedings,* 1971, *31,* 317.

Drucker-Colín, R. R., Rojas-Ramírez, J. A., Vera-Trueba, J., Monroy-Ayala, G., & Hernández-Peón, R. Effect of cross-perfusion of the midbrain reticular formation upon sleep. *Brain Research,* 1970, *23,* 269-273.

Drucker-Colín, R. R., Spanis, C. W., Cotman, C. W., & McGaugh, J. L. Changes in protein levels in perfusates of freely moving cats: Relation to behavioral state. *Science,* 1975, *187,* 963-965.

Edström, R. Recent developments on the blood-brain barrier concept. *International Review of Neurobiology,* 1964, *7,* 153-190.

Fencl, V., Koski, G., & Pappenheimer, J. R. Factors in cerebrospinal fluid from goats that affect sleep and activity in rats. *Journal of Physiology,* 1971, *216,* 565-589.

Fernández-Guardiola, A., & Antón-Tay, F.   Modulation of
    subcortical inhibitory mechanisms by melatonin.   In R. D.
    Myers and R. R. Drucker-Colín (Eds.), *Neurohumoral Coding
    of Brain Function.*   New York: Plenum, 1974.

Fishman, R. A.   Carrier transport of glucose between blood
    and cerebrospinal fluid.   *American Journal of Physiology,*
    1964, *206,* 836-844.

Friedeman, U.   Blood-brain barrier.   *Physiological Review,*
    1942, *22,* 125-145.

Grotte, G.   Passage of dextran molecules across the blood-
    lymph barrier.   *Acta Chirurgica Scandinavica* (Suppl.), 1956,
    211, 1-38.

Herlin, L.   On phospate exchange in the central nervous system
    with special reference to metabolic activity in barriers.
    Acta Physiologica Scandinavica (Suppl.), 1956, *37,* 127-186.

Hess, A.   The ground substance of the central nervous system
    and its relation to the blood-brain barrier.   *World
    Neurology,* 1962, *3,* 118-124.

Ishii, S., & Tani, E.   Electron microscopic study of the blood-
    brain barrier in brain swelling.   *Acta Neuropathologica,*
    1962, *1,* 474-488.

Jeppsson, P. G.   Studies on the blood-brain barrier in hypo-
    termia.   *Acta Neurologica Scandinavica* (Suppl.), 1962,
    38, 160-229.

Johansson, B., Li, Ch.-L., Olsson, Y., & Klatzo, I.   The effect
    of acute arterial hypertension on the blood-brain barrier
    to protein tracers.   *Acta Neuropathologica,* 1970, *16,*
    117-124.

Jouvet, M.   Biogenic amines and the states of sleep.   *Science,*
    1969, *163,* 32-41.

Jouvet, M.   The role of monoamines and acetylcholine-containing
    neurons.   *Reviews in Physiology: Biochemistry and
    Experimental Pharmacology,* 1972, *64,* 166-333.

Karnovsky, M. J.   The ultrastructural basis of capillary
    permeability studied with peroxidase as a tracer.
    Journal of Cell Biology, 1967, *35,* 213-236.

Karnovsky, M. J.   The ultrastructural basis of transcapillary
    exchanges. *Journal of General Physiology*, 1968, *52*,
    64s-95s.

King, C. D.   The pharmacology of rapid eye movement sleep.
    Advances in Pharmacology and Chemotherapy, 1971, *9*, 1-91.

Landis, E. M., & Pappenheimer, J. R.   Exchange of substances
    through the capillary walls. In W. F. Hamilton and
    P. Dow (Eds.), *Handbook of Physiology, Section 2: Circu-
    lation* (Vol. 2). Washington, D. C.: American Physio-
    logical Society, 1963.

Legendre, R., & Piéron, H.   Le probleme des facteurs du
    sommeil. Résultats d'injections vasculaires et intra-
    cérébrales des liquides insomniques. *Comptes Rendus des
    Seances de la Societe de Biologie* (Paris), 1910, *68*,
    1077-1079.

Légendre, R., & Piéron, H.   Du développement, au cours de
    l'insomnie expérimental, des propriétes hypnotoxiques
    des humeurs en relation avec le besoin crissant de
    sommeil. *Comptes Rendus des Seances de la Societe de
    Biologie* (Paris), 1911, *70*, 190-192.

Légendre, R., & Piéron, H.   De la propiété hypnotoxique des
    humeurs développée en cours d'une veille prolongée.
    Comptes Rendus des Seances de la Societe de Biologie
    (Paris), 1912, *72*, 210-212.

Mayerson, H. S., Wolfram, C. G., Shirley, H. H., Jr., &
    Wasserman, K.   Regional differences in capillary permea-
    bility. *American Journal of Physiology*, 1960, *198*, 155-160.

McGaugh, J. L.   Drug facilitation of learning and memory.
    Annual Review of Pharmacology, 1973, *13*, 229-241.

McGaugh, J. L., & Gold, P. E.   The effects of drugs and
    electrical stimulation of the brain on memory storage
    processes. In R. D. Myers and R. R. Drucker-Colín (Eds.),
    Neurohumoral Coding of Brain Function. New York:
    Plenum, 1974.

Monnier, M., & Hatt, A. M.   Humoral transmission of sleep, V.
    New evidence from production of pure sleep hemodialysate.
    Pflüegers Archiv Fuer Physiology, 1971, *329*, 231-243.

Monnier, M., & Hösli, L.   Dialysis of sleep and waking factors in blood of the rabbit.   *Science,* 1964, *146,* 796-797.

Monnier, M., & Schoenenberger, G. A.   Neurohumoral coding of sleep by the physiological sleep factor Delta.   In R. D. Myers and R. R. Drucker-Colín (Eds.), *Neurohumoral Coding of Brain Function.*   New York: Plenum, 1974.

Olsson, Y., & Hossmann, K. A.   Fine structural localization of exudated protein tracers in the brain.   *Acta Neuropatholica,* 1970, *16,* 103-116.

Palade, G. E., & Bruns, R. R.   Structural modulations of plasmalemmal vesicles.   *Journal of Cell Biology,* 1968, *37,* 633-649.

Pappenheimer, J. R.   Passage of molecules through capillary walls.   *Physiological Review,* 1953, *33,* 387-423.

Pappenheimer, J. R.   Cerebral HCO_3^- transport and control of breathing.   *Federation Proceedings,* 1966, *25,* 884-886.

Pappenheimer, J. R., Miller, T. B., & Goodrich, C. A.   Sleep promoting effects of cerebrospinal fluid from sleep-deprived goats.   *Proceedings of the National Academy of Sciences,* 1967, *58,* 543-547.

Prockop, L. D., Schanker, L. S., & Brodie, B. B.   Passage of lipidinsoluble substances from cerebrospinal fluid to blood.   *Journal of Pharmacology and Experimental Therapeutics,* 1962, *135,* 266-270.

Radulovacki, M.   5-hydroxyindoleacetic acid in cerebrospinal fluid during wakefulness, sleep, and after electrical stimulation of specific brain structures.   In R. D. Myers and R. R. Drucker-Colín (Eds.), *Neurohumoral Coding of Brain Function.*   New York: Plenum, 1974.

Rall, D. P.   Drug entry into brain and cerebrospinal fluid. In B. N. La Du, H. G. Mandel, and E. L. Way (Eds.), *Fundamentals of Drug Metabolism and Drug Disposition.* Baltimore: Williams & Wilkons, 1971.

Reese, T. S., & Karnovsky, M. J.   Fine structural localization of a blood-brain barrier to exogenous peroxidase. *Journal of Cell Biology,* 1967, *34,* 207-217.

Renkin, E. M.   Transport of large molecules across capillary
    walls. *Physiologist,* 1964, *7,* 13-28.

Van Breemen, V. L., & Clemente, C. D.   Silver deposition in
    the central nervous system and the hematoencephalic
    barrier studied with the electron microscope. *Journal
    of Biophysical and Biochemical Cytology,* 1955, *1,* 161-166.

Wislocki, G. B., & Leduc, E. H.   Vital staining of the hemato-
    encephalic barrier by silver nitrate and trypan blue, and
    cytological comparisons of the neurohypophysis, pineal
    body, area postrema, intercolumnar tubercle, and supra-
    optic crest. *Journal of Comparative Neurology,* 1952, *96,*
    371-413.

Yamamoto, T.   The cerebral distribution and migration of
    radioisotopes with special reference to autoradiograms.
    Journal of Neuropathology and Experimental Neurology,
    1959, *18,* 418-431.

Yudilevich, D. L., De Rose, N., & Sepulveda, F. V.   Facilitated
    transport of amino acids through the blood-brain barrier
    of the dog studied in a single capillary circulation.
    Brain Research, 1972, *44,* 569-578.

NEUROTRANSMITTERS AND PROTEIN SYNTHESIS IN THE CENTRAL NERVOUS SYSTEM

RICARDO TAPIA and MARÍA-ELENA SANDOVAL

Departamento de Biología Experimental
Instituto de Biología
Universidad Nacional Autónoma de México
México 20, D.F., México

Protein metabolism in the mammalian central nervous system (CNS) has been linked to some of the "higher functions" of the brain, such as learning, memory, sleep, and waking. Such a relationship, however, is difficult to understand unless it is considered within the framework of the structural and physiological site of communication among neurons, namely the synapse.

The transmission of nerve impulses across chemical synapses is mediated by neurotransmitter substances, which must be released from the presynaptic ending in order to act on the postsynaptic receptor. Thus, the participation of proteins in the function of the nervous system should be expected to be related to neurotransmitters. There are two immediate ways of visualizing this relationship: First, the proteins may act by modifying the metabolism and function of neurotransmitters; and second, the neurotransmitters may influence the metabolism of macromolecules. The first possibility is, of course, verified, since neurotransmitters are synthesized by enzymes which must be available in the synaptic terminals. Thus, an inhibition of protein synthesis would be expected to produce a decrease in the neurotransmitter pool, as soon as the concentration of the synthesizing enzyme falls to a certain value.

A modification of protein metabolism by neurotransmitters may affect not only enzyme proteins but also other functionally important macromolecules at other levels of synaptic function as well. An example of such a macromolecule would be the

17

postsynaptic neurotransmitter receptor. A modification of the
receptor quantity or conformation induced by the synaptic
transmitter could result in an increase or decrease in synaptic connectivity, with a consequent modification of its
function. A striking example of this kind of interaction is
the spread of acetylcholine receptors from their normal location in the neuromuscular junction to the entire surface of
the muscle after denervation (Axelsson & Thesleff, 1959;
Miledi, 1960). This receptor spreading is accompanied by an
increase in the incorporation of labeled leucine into protein.
This incorporation is more pronounced in the region of the
muscle not containing the end plate than it is in the plate
region (Kimura & Kimura, 1973).

In the central nervous system, several putative neurotransmitters have been studied with regard to their relationship to protein synthesis. The experimental approaches used
have been mainly of two types: First, the addition of the
transmitter substance to neural tissue preparations for the
purpose of studying its effect, *in vitro,* on the incorporation of labeled amino acids into protein; and second, the
modification of the transmitter concentration *in vivo* by
administering either a metabolic precursor, or by blocking
its synthesis pharmacologically. The latter approach permits
the study of protein synthesis *in vivo* after injecting
labeled amino acids. This technique seems to have an advantage over the *in vitro* studies, since the results can be
considered to be representative of a physiological action
rather than being a mere pharmacological effect.

The results of some of these *in vitro* and *in vivo* experimental approaches employing serotonin (5-HT), dopamine, and
γ-aminobutyric acid (GABA), are summarized in Tables 1 to 3.
When either serotonin or dopamine was added to synaptosomal
or mitochondrial fractions extracted from brain, protein
synthesis was inhibited. This effect is well correlated with
the results of experiments conducted *in vivo*, since an
increase in serotonin or dopamine levels produces both an
inhibition of protein synthesis and a disaggregation of polysomes in brain tissue. When metabolic precursors (5-hydroxy-
tryptophan for serotonin and L-DOPA for dopamine) were used
to increase transmitter concentration, these effects on
protein synthesis and polysome aggregation were prevented by
inhibitors of the transmitter biosynthetic reaction (decar-
boxylation of the precursor) or by blockers of the transmitter
receptor (Tables 1 and 2).

In relation to the effects of dopamine, it is interesting
to note that Tang, Cotzias, and Dunn (1974) have reported that
the behavioral responses of mice to L-DOPA are diminished by

TABLE 1

REPORTED EFFECTS OF SEROTONIN (5-HT) ON PROTEIN SYNTHESIS IN BRAIN

Experimental conditions	Observations related to protein metabolism in nervous tissue	Changes in neurotransmitter metabolism	Reference
5-HTP (500 mg/kg) injected i.p. to rats	Inhibition of protein synthesis and polysome disaggregation	Increase of 5-HT levels	Weiss *et al.* (1973; 1974b).
5-HTP (500 mg/kg) i.p. + MAO inhibitor (Pargyline)	Potentiation of the above effects	Same as above	*Ibid.*
5-HTP (500 mg/kg) i.p. + aromatic decarboxylase inhibitor (Ro 4-4602)	Prevention of the 5-HTP effects	Decrease of 5-HT levels	*Ibid.*
5-HTP (500 mg/kg) i.p. + 5-HT receptor blocker (methylsergide)	Prevention of the 5-HTP effects	Increase of 5-HT levels	*Ibid.*
Intracranial injection of 5-HT to 15, 20 and 30 day-old mice	Inhibition of protein synthesis	Increase of 5-HT levels	Essman (1973)
5-HT added to isolated brain cortex synaptosomes	Inhibition of protein synthesis	--	Goldberg (1972)
5-HT added to isolated brain cortex mitochondria	Inhibition of protein synthesis	--	*Ibid.*

Abbreviations: 5-HT, 5-hydroxytryptamine or serotonin; 5-HTP, 5-hydroxytryptophan; MAO, monoamine oxidase; i.p., intraperitoneal.

19

TABLE 2

REPORTED EFFECTS OF DOPAMINE ON PROTEIN SYNTHESIS IN BRAIN

Experimental Conditions	Observations related to protein metabolism in nervous tissue	Changes in neurotransmitter metabolism	Reference
L-DOPA (400 mg/kg) injected i.p. to rats	No effect	Not studied	Weiss *et al.* (1971; 1972; 1974a,b)
L-DOPA (100 mg/kg) i.p. + MAO inhibitor (pheniprazine)	Inhibition of protein synthesis and polysome disaggregation	Increase of dopamine levels	*Ibid.*
D-DOPA (500 mg/kg) i.p.	No effect	--	*Ibid.*
L-DOPA (500 mg/kg) i.p.	Inhibition of protein synthesis and polysome disaggregation	Increase of DOPA and dopamine levels	*Ibid.*
L-DOPA (500 mg/kg) i.p. + aromatic decarboxylase inhibitor (Ro 4-4602)	Prevention of the L-DOPA effects	Increase of DOPA levels	*Ibid.*
L-DOPA (500 mg/kg) i.p. + Dopamine receptor blocker (pimozide)	Prevention of the L-DOPA effects	Increase of dopamine levels	*Ibid.*

TABLE 2 (Continued)

Experimental conditions	Observations related to protein metabolism in nervous tissue	Changes in neurotransmitter metabolism	Reference
Stimulation of a specific neuron in an isolated ganglion from *Aplysia*	Specific inhibition of the synthesis of a protein in the neuron	Not studied (increase of dopamine at the synaptic cleft?)	Gainer and Barker (1974)
Dopamine added to the isolated *Aplysia* ganglion	Specific inhibition of the synthesis of a protein in the neuron	--	*Ibid.*
L-DOPA or dopamine added to isolated brain cortex synaptosomes	Inhibition of protein synthesis	--	Goldberg (1972)
L-DOPA or dopamine added to isolated brain cortex mitochondria	Inhibition of protein synthesis	--	*Ibid.*

Abbreviations: L-DOPA, L-dihydroxyphenylalanine; i.p., intraperitoneal.

TABLE 3

REPORTED EFFECTS OF γ-AMINOBUTYRIC ACID (GABA) ON PROTEIN SYNTHESIS IN BRAIN

Experimental conditions	Observations related to protein metabolism in nervous tissue[a]	Changes in neurotransmitter metabolism	Reference
GABA added to ribosomal preparations or isolated mitochondria from brain cortex	Increase of protein synthesis[b]	--	Campbell et al. (1966); Tewari & Baxter (1969); Baxter & Tewari (1970)
GABA added to brain cell suspensions	Increase of protein synthesis	--	Kelly & Luttges (1972)
GABA added to brain cortex slices	Increase of protein synthesis	--	Snodgrass (1973)
Injection i.p. of GAD inhibitor (pyridoxal phosphate-γ-glutamyl hydrazone) to mice	Inhibition of protein synthesis	Decrease of GABA levels and of GAD and DOPA decarboxylase activities	Tapia & Sandoval (1974)

Abbreviations: GABA, γ-aminobutyric acid; GAD, glutamate decarboxylase; i.p., intraperitoneal.

[a] Protein synthesis in liver was not affected under identical experimental conditions.

[b] Glycine produced a similar effect (Baxter and Tewari, 1970).

the inhibitors of protein synthesis chloramphenicol, cycloheximide, and puromycin. These inhibitors did not affect the
cerebral uptake of L-DOPA or its conversion to dopamine. The
effect of decreasing protein synthesis seems to involve dopamine receptors, since a diminished response to the dopaminergic drug apomorphine was observed under these experimental
conditions. Furthermore, the production of cyclic AMP stimulated by dopamine was decreased in caudate nuclei homogenates
obtained from chloramphenicol-treated mice.

In contrast to the above results, GABA stimulates protein
synthesis when added *in vitro* to brain ribosomal and mitochondrial systems, to brain cell suspensions, and also to
cortex slices (Table 3). In agreement with these results,
when the synthesis and the levels of GABA were decreased *in
vivo* (Table 3) or in brain slices (Table 4) by means of introducing inhibitors of glutamate decarboxylase (GAD) activity,
synthesis of protein was also decreased. However, the relationship between GABA concentration and protein synthesis is
not a simple one, since a decrease in protein synthesis after
inhibition of GAD activity has been observed at the moment
when GABA levels are increased by previous inhibition of
GABA aminotransferase (Table 5). From this result it has
been postulated that changes in only the newly synthesized
pool of GABA is probably involved in the regulation of
cerebral protein synthesis (Sandoval & Tapia, 1975).

The results summarized above suggest that serotonin,
dopamine, and GABA might be involved in the regulation of
protein synthesis in brain, but the physiological implications
of these findings are difficult to assess at the present time.
The existence of an interrelationship between the synaptic
transmitter role of these substances in the CNS and their
influence on protein synthesis is a very attractive hypothesis since such an interrelationship could be involved in
the functioning of synapses. That this is an actual possibility is suggested by the apparent involvement of serotonin
and dopamine receptors in the effect of these amines on
protein synthesis indicated by the experiments with receptor
blockers (Tables 1 and 2). Furthermore, in the ganglion of
Aplysia, Gainer and Barker (1974) have observed that after
stimulation of an identified neuron the synthesis of a
specific protein is inhibited. This effect was also
obtained when dopamine was added to the ganglion.

In the mammalian CNS we have recently studied whether
the inhibition of protein synthesis induced by a decrease of
GABA synthesis specifically affects the proteins of a
particular subcellular structure. As shown in Figure 1, the
in vivo incorporation of ^{14}C leucine into proteins of all

TABLE 4

EFFECT OF TWO INHIBITORS OF GLUTAMATE
DECARBOXYLASE (GAD) ACTIVITY ON PROTEIN SYNTHESIS
IN MOUSE BRAIN CORTEX SLICES[a]

| Preincubation | Percent of control[b] | |
	GAD	Protein synthesis
Aminooxyacetic acid (5 mM)	55	49 (100)[c]
Pyridoxal phosphate oxime-O-acetic acid (1 mM)	71	69 (105)

[a]Data from Sandoval and Tapia (1975).

[b]Control values were obtained from slices from the contra-lateral hemisphere of the same brain, incubated in a different flask without inhibitor, simultaneously to the experimental slices.

[c]The values in parentheses refer to the results obtained with liver slices.

TABLE 5

EFFECT OF THE ADMINISTRATION OF GLUTAMYL
HYDRAZIDE (1 g/kg) + PYRIDOXAL PHOSPHATE (50 mg/kg) ON
GABA LEVELS, GLUTAMATE DECARBOXYLASE (GAD) ACTIVITY
AND PROTEIN SYNTHESIS IN MICE BRAIN[a]

| Treatment[b] | Percent of control[c] | | |
	GABA	GAD	Protein synthesis
NaCl + Pyridoxal phosphate	74	91	94
Glutamyl + NaCl hydrazide	151	81	68
Glutamyl + Pyridoxal hydrazide phosphate	123	56	52

[a]Data from Sandoval and Tapia (1975).

[b]The drugs were administered intraperitoneally with a 60 min period between the injections. Protein synthesis was determined by measuring the incorporation of labeled leucine into protein, *in vivo*.

[c]Control animals were injected twice with NaCl.

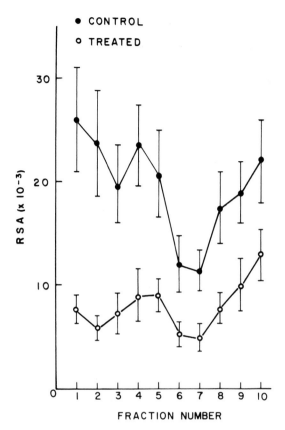

Fig. 1. *Subcellular distribution of synthesized protein in brain cortex of control mice and mice with decreased GABA synthesis. Animals (15-17 day-old) were injected with saline solution (control) or with pyridoxal phosphate-γ-glutamyl hydrazone (80 mg/kg), a drug which inhibits glutamate decarboxylase activity (Tapia & Sandoval, 1974). At 29 min after treatment ^{14}C leucine (5 μCi) was injected intraperitoneally and the mice were killed 8 min later. Cerebral cortices were homogenized in 0.32 M sucrose and the homogenates were centrifuged at 1000 g for 4 min. Aliquots of the supernatant were layered over a 0.4-1.5 M continuous sucrose gradient, and the gradients were centrifuged at 130,000 g for 2 hr. Fractions of 0.5 ml were obtained, and protein was precipitated with TCA. Protein precipitate and TCA supernatant then were separated by centrifugation and treated as previously described before radioactivity measurement (Tapia & Sandoval, 1974). Enzymatic markers and electron microscopy showed that fractions 6 and 7 were enriched in nerve endings. Fraction 1 refers to*

the top of the gradient.   RSA = cpm/mg protein/cpm in TCA-super-
natant of fraction 1.   Mean values of 5-7 experiments ± S.E.M.

subcellular fractions, including isolated nerve endings, was
inhibited in the brains of mice with decreased synthesis of
GABA. This result suggests that in central inhibitory GABA-
dependent synapses the presence of newly synthesized GABA
(Table 5) is either stimulating or maintaining a particular
rate of protein synthesis in all parts of the neurons. In
this regard it is interesting that, besides ribosomes and
mitochondria, it has been claimed by several authors that
isolated nerve endings (Gordon & Deanin, 1968; Bossman &
Hemsworth, 1970; Autilio, Appel, Pettis, & Gambetti, 1968;
Morgan & Austin, 1968; Cotman & Taylor, 1971), and also
synaptic plasma membranes are capable of synthesizing proteins
(Ramírez, Levitan, & Mushynski, 1972; Gilbert, 1972). Since
GABA is synthesized by GAD in inhibitory nerve endings
(Fonnum, 1968; Salganicoff & De Robertis, 1965; Fonnum, Storm-
Mathisen, & Walberg, 1970; Otsuka, Obata, Miyata, & Tanaka,
1971; Pérez de la Mora, Feria-Velasco, & Tapia, 1973), and
there is some evidence suggesting that the newly synthesized
GABA is immediately released into the synaptic cleft (Tapia,
1974, 1975; Tapia, Sandoval, & Contreras, 1975), it seems not
unreasonable to postulate that GABA is involved in the regulation of protein synthesis at the synaptic level, among other
possible subcellular sites.
        It is surprising that of the three putative neurotrans-
mitters possessing an action on protein synthesis, serotonin
and dopamine show an inhibitory effect while GABA seems to
increase protein synthesis (Tables 1-5). Of these transmitters, GABA is the most widely distributed in the central
nervous system, and, in contrast to serotonin and dopamine,
it possesses an inhibitory action on neuronal activity in
practically all brain regions tested (Krnjević, 1974). These
characteristics of GABA may be of importance in considering
its possible physiological role in the regulation of protein
synthesis. For example, there is evidence suggesting that
GABA-dependent inhibition at cerebral cortex synapses, and
probably also in other neuronal nuclei, is a mechanism acting
continuously to control the activity of some neurons (Pérez de
la Mora & Tapia, 1973; Crain & Bornstein, 1974; Meldrum &
Horton, 1971). Therefore, a mechanism linking the tonic
inhibitory action of GABA with its effect on protein synthesis
at the synaptic level can be hypothesized (Figure 2). GABA
may be released coupled to its synthesis (Tapia, 1974; Tapia
et al., 1975), for combination with its postsynaptic receptor.

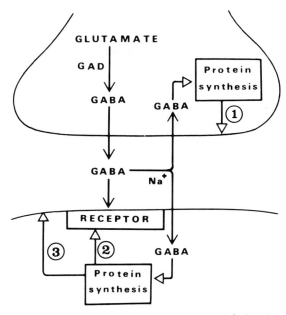

Fig. 2. *Some hypothetical ways by which the role of GABA as an inhibitory neurotransmitter might be related to its effect on protein synthesis at the synaptic level. GABA recently synthesized by glutamate decarboxylase is released from inhibitory nerve endings, combines with the receptor and is taken up by the presynaptic terminal or the postsynaptic neuron in the presence of Na+ (glial cells could also participate in this uptake). The GABA taken up by the terminal could stimulate the synthesis of membrane proteins that may be involved in release mechanisms (1). At the postsynaptic neuron GABA might stimulate the synthesis of receptor protein (2) or of other membrane proteins related to the receptor in such a way that the receptor is made conformationally more sensitive to GABA (3). See text for further discussion and justification of the assumptions implied in this figure.*

It would then be taken up by the presynaptic ending and/or by the postsynaptic neuron (glial cells could also participate in this uptake) and in one or both of these structures it maintains a given rate of protein synthesis. Among the protein molecules whose synthesis could be maintained, at least three types would be expected to be involved in the facilitation or stabilization of GABA-dependent synaptic function: 1) Proteins of the presynaptic membrane participating in the mechanism of GABA release, including those involved in the binding and transport of Ca^{++}; 2) the receptor protein; and 3) other proteins of the postsynaptic membrane that may contribute to the maintenance of an adequate conformation of the receptor protein (Figure 2).

According to this hypothesis, the tonic inhibition exerted by GABA on certain neurons would be normally in a steady state of maximum efficiency. In contrast to this general GABA-dependent inhibitory system, the participation of dopamine and serotonin in the regulation of protein synthesis would be restricted to certain discrete areas of the brain, and with a different mechanism. When a particular dopaminergic or serotoninergic neuron is firing, the sensitivity of the synaptic system would be modulated by the inhibition of protein synthesis produced by the neurotransmitter.

SUMMARY

The idea that the facilitation of synaptic function is a crucial phenomenon occurring during the process of learning or memory consolidation has gained increasing acceptance. Understanding the molecular events of synaptic facilitation appears to be a major prerequisite before the mechanisms of such functions of the CNS can be clarified. Macromolecules (proteins and nucleic acids) may be involved in these mechanisms, and it is therefore essential that the role of macromolecules in synaptic function be understood. A promising possibility is that the rate of protein synthesis may be related to the availability of the neurotransmitter at a given synapse. The results of experiments with three putative neurotransmitters in the CNS, serotonin, dopamine, and GABA, indicate that they may be regulating the rate of protein synthesis at the synaptic level. In the case of GABA, this regulatory role seems to be accomplished by maintaining a certain rate of protein synthesis by means of its newly synthesized pool. Thus, the synthesis of certain proteins important for the functioning of a synapse may be stimulated by GABA.

REFERENCES

Autilio, L. A., Appel, S. H., Pettis, P., & Gambetti, P. L. Biochemical studies of synapses *in vitro*. I. Protein synthesis. *Biochemistry*, 1968, *7*, 2615-2622.

Axelsson, J., & Thesleff, S. A study of supersensitivity in denervated mammalian skeletal muscle. *Journal of Physiology* (Lond.), 1959, *147*, 178-193.

Baxter, C. F., & Tewari, S. Regulation by amino acids of protein synthesis in a cell-free system from immature rat brain: Stimulatory effect of γ-aminobutyric acid and glycine. In A. Lajtha (Ed.). *Protein Metabolism of the Nervous System*. New York: Plenum Press, 1970.

Bossman, H. B., & Hemsworth, B. A. Intraneural mitochondria. Incorporation of amino acids and monosaccharides into macromolecules by isolated synaptosomes and isolated mitochondria. *Journal of Biological Chemistry*, 1970, *245*, 363-371.

Campbell, M. K., Mahler, H. R., Moore, W. J., & Tewari, S. Protein synthesis systems from rat brain. *Biochemistry*, 1966, *5*, 1174-1184.

Cotman, C. W., & Taylor, D. A. Autoradiographic analysis of protein synthesis in synaptosomal fractions. *Brain Research*, 1971, *29*, 366-372.

Crain, S. M., & Bornstein, M. B. Early onset of inhibitory functions during synaptogenesis in fetal mouse brain cultures. *Brain Research*, 1974, *68*, 351-357.

Essman, W. B. Age dependent effects of 5-hydroxytryptamine upon memory consolidation and cerebral protein synthesis. *Pharmacology, Biochemistry, and Behavior*, 1973, *1*, 7-14.

Fonnum, F. The distribution of glutamate decarboxylase and asparate transaminase in subcellular fractions of rat and guinea pig brain. *Biochemical Journal*, 1968, *106*, 401-412.

Fonnum, F., Storm-Mathisen, J., & Walberg, F. Glutamate decarboxylase in inhibitory neurons. A study of the enzyme in Purkinje cell axons and boutons in the cat. *Brain Research*, 1970, *20*, 259-275.

Gainer, H., & Barker, J. L. Synaptic regulation of specific protein synthesis in an identified neuron. *Brain Research,* 1974, *78,* 314-319.

Gilbert, J. M. Evidence for protein synthesis in synaptosomal membranes. *Journal of Biological Chemistry,* 1972, *247,* 6541-6550.

Goldberg, M. A. Inhibition of synaptosomal protein synthesis by neurotransmitter substances. *Brain Research,* 1972, *39,* 171-179.

Gordon, M. W., & Deanin, G. G. Protein synthesis by isolated rat brain mitochondria and synaptosomes. *Journal of Biological Chemistry,* 1968, *243,* 4222-4226.

Kelly, P. T., & Luttges, M. W. Drug effects on developing mouse brain protein synthesis *in vitro. Neuropharmacology,* 1972, *11,* 889-893.

Kimura, M., & Kimura, I. Increase of nascent protein synthesis in neuromuscular junction of rat diaphragm induced by denervation. *Nature: New Biology,* 1973, *241,* 114-115.

Krnjević, K. Chemical nature of synaptic transmission in vertebrates. *Physiological Reviews,* 1974, *54,* 418-540.

Meldrum, B. S., & Horton, R. W. Convulsive effects of 4-deoxy-pyridoxine and of bicuculline in photosensitive baboons *(Papio papio)* and in rhesus monkeys *(Macaca mulatta). Brain Research,* 1971, *35,* 419-436.

Miledi, R. The acetylcholine sensitivity of frog muscle fibres after complete or partial denervation. *Journal of Physiology* (Lond.), 1960, *151,* 1-23.

Morgan, I. G., & Austin, L. Synaptosomal protein synthesis in a cell-free system. *Journal of Neurochemistry,* 1968, *15,* 41-51.

Otsuka, M., Obata, K., Miyata, Y., & Tanaka, Y. Measurement of γ-aminobutyric acid in isolated nerve cells of cat central nervous system. *Journal of Neurochemistry,* 1971, *18,* 287-295.

Pérez de la Mora, M., Feria-Velasco, A., & Tapia, R. Pyridoxal phosphate and glutamate decarboxylase in subcellular particles of mouse brain and their relationship to convulsions. *Journal of Neurochemistry*, 1973, *20*, 1575-1587.

Pérez de la Mora, M., & Tapia, R. Anticonvulsant effect of 5-ethyl, 5-phenyl, 2-pyrrolidinone and its possible relationship to γ-aminobutyric acid dependent-inhibitory mechanisms. *Biochemical Pharmacology*, 1973, *22*, 2635-2639.

Ramírez, G., Levitan, I. B., & Mushynski, W. E. Highly purified synaptosomal membranes from rat brain. Incorporation of amino acids into membrane proteins *in vitro*. *Journal of Biological Chemistry*, 1972, *247*, 5382-5390.

Salganicoff, L., & De Robertis, E. Subcellular distribution of the enzymes of the glutamic acid, glutamine and γ-aminobutyric acid cycles in rat brain. *Journal of Neurochemistry*, 1965, *12*, 287-309.

Sandoval, M. E., & Tapia, R. GABA metabolism and cerebral protein synthesis. *Brain Research*, 1975, *96*, 279-286.

Snodgrass, R. S. Studies on GABA and protein synthesis. *Brain Research*, 1973, *59*, 339-348.

Tang, L. C., Cotzias, G. C., & Dunn, M. Changing the actions of neuroactive drugs by changing brain protein synthesis. *Proceedings of the National Academy of Science*, 1974, *71*, 3350-3354.

Tapia, R. The role of γ-aminobutyric acid metabolism in the regulation of cerebral excitability. In R. D. Myers & R. R. Drucker-Colin (Eds.). *Neurohumoral Coding of Brain Function*. New York: Plenum Press, 1974.

Tapia, R. Biochemical pharmacology of GABA in CNS. In L. L. Iversen, S. D. Iversen, & S. H. Snyder (Eds.). *Handbook of Psychopharmacology* (Vol. 4). New York: Plenum Press, 1974.

Tapia, R., & Sandoval, M. E. Possible participation of gamma-aminobutyric acid in the regulation of protein synthesis in brain, *in vivo*. *Brain Research*, 1974, *69*, 255-263.

Tapia, R., Sandoval, M. E., & Contreras, P. Evidence for a role of glutamate decarboxylase activity as a regulatory mechanism of cerebral excitability. *Journal of Neurochemistry,* 1975, *24,* 1283-1285.

Tewari, S., & Baxter, C. F. Stimulatory effect of γ-aminobutyric acid upon amino acid incorporation into protein by a ribosomal system from immature rat brain. *Journal of Neurochemistry,* 1969, *16,* 171-180.

Weiss, B. F., Munro, H. N., Ordonez, L. A., & Wurtman, R. J. Dopamine: Mediator of brain polysome disaggregation after L-dopa. *Science,* 1972, *177,* 613-615.

Weiss, B. F., Munro, H. N., & Wurtman, R. J. L-Dopa: Disaggregation of brain polysomes and elevation of brain tryptophan. *Science,* 1971, *173,* 833-835.

Weiss, B. F., Roel, L. E., Munro, H. N., & Wurtman, R. J. L-Dopa, polysomal aggregation and cerebral synthesis of protein. In *Aromatic Amino Acids in the Brain* (CIBA Foundation Symposium 22). Amsterdam: Elsevier, 1974a.

Weiss, B. F., Roel, L. E., Munro, H. N., & Wurtman, R. J. The effect of L-DOPA on brain polysomes and protein synthesis: Probable mediation by intracellular dopamine. *Advances in Neurology,* 1974b, *5,* 87-96.

Weiss, B. F., Wurtman, R. J., & Munro, H. N. Disaggregation of brain polysomes by L-5-hydroxytryptophan: Mediation by serotonin. *Life Sciences,* 1973, *13,* 411-416.

BRAIN RNA AND PROTEIN SYNTHESIS DURING TRAINING: THE INTERPRETATION OF CHANGES OF PRECURSOR INCORPORATION

ADRIAN J. DUNN and HOWARD D. REES

Department of Neuroscience
University of Florida College of Medicine
Gainesville, Florida 32610 USA

Considerable evidence now exists to indicate that changes of brain metabolism occur as a result of training in rodents and chicks (Glassman, 1969; Horn, Rose, & Bateson, 1973; Uphouse, MacInnes, & Schlesinger, 1974; Entingh, Dunn, Wilson, Glassman, Hogan, & Damstra-Entingh, 1975; Dunn, 1976b). The problem is to correctly interpret the data. Clearly the important task is to determine the specific relationships between the molecular changes and the behavior. However, the physiological significance of the precursor incorporation data must also be evaluated. In this paper we wish to discuss two aspects of these problems: the biochemical interpretation of the RNA-labelling data; and some insights that recent protein-labelling data have indicated to us.

THE INTERPRETATION OF BRAIN RNA LABELLING STUDIES

Table 1 shows the distribution of RNA following subcellular fractionation of a homogenate of mouse brain. Most of the RNA is found in the microsomal and mitochondrial fractions with only 20 percent or less recovered in the nuclear fraction (see also Adams, 1965; Balázs & Cocks, 1967). Polyacrylamide gel electrophoresis of purified brain RNA

33

TABLE 1

SUBCELLULAR DISTRIBUTION OF MOUSE BRAIN RNA

Subcellular fraction	RNA content (µg/g brain)	% of total homogenate
Homogenate	2525	[100]
Crude nuclear	936	37.0
Purified nuclear	484	19.2
Mitochondrial	531	21.0
Microsomal	861	34.1
Soluble	230	9.1

RNA was determined by the method of Fleck and Munro (1962). Nuclei were purified by treatment with 0.1% Triton X-100 (McEwen and Zigmond, 1972). Data reproduced from Dunn (1976a).

(Figure 1) shows that the major species of RNA in brain, as in other tissues, are the 18S and 28S ribosomal RNAs, which are structural components of the ribosomes. A more detailed analysis suggests that much of the RNA recovered in the mitochondrial fraction and some of that in the nuclear fraction is ribosomal, so that it is estimated that approximately 70 percent of brain RNA is of the ribosomal type (Adams, 1965).

The time course of the appearance of label in RNA of mouse brain subcellular fractions following subcutaneous injection of [3H]uridine is shown in Figure 2.

The results agree well with those of Balázs and Cocks (1967) from the rat. At times up to one hour after injection, 90 percent or so of the label was associated with the nuclear fraction. Purification of the nuclei with Triton X-100 decreased the RNA content by approximately 50 percent (Table 1) but only about 20 percent of the radioactivity was lost. The RNA in the microsomal fraction became labelled very slowly (except for a consistent very rapid appearance of a small amount of label). Even after three days the radioactivity in the microsomal fraction was only approximately equal to that in the nuclear fraction, so that the specific radioactivity of the microsomal RNA (dpm/mg) was still lower than that of the nuclear RNA. These data suggest that brain ribosomes are relatively stable, being degraded and synthesized rather infrequently, which is consistent with other estimates of their half-life obtained by measuring the loss of radioactive RNA from the ribosomes (Bondy, 1966;

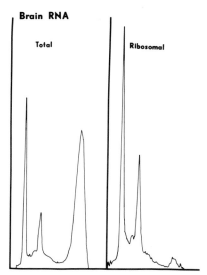

Brain RNA

Total

Ribosomal

Fig. 1.   Gel Electrophoresis of Brain RNA.   RNA was pu-
rified with phenol from a total brain homogenate or a puri-
fied ribosomal fraction.   It was electrophoresed on 2.5%
polyacrylamide gels and the presence of RNA detected by scan-
ning at 260 mμ in a Gilford spectrophotometer.   Electropho-
resis direction left to right.   The two major peaks on the
RNA extracted from ribosomes (right figure) are 28S and 18S
ribosomal RNA respectively; the third peak contains transfer
RNA, 5S RNA and small oligonucleotides.   The left hand peaks
on the "total" sample are 28S and 18S ribosomal RNA and the
major peak is probably mainly transfer RNA, nuclear RNA and
degradation products of all species of RNA.   From Dunn
(1976a).

Von Hungen, Mahler, & Moore, 1968).   Thus ribosomal RNA,
which constitutes the bulk of brain RNA, is stable and labels
very slowly.   It follows that changes in the amount of RNA of
this type are not to be expected in the brain as short-term
responses to environmental experiences.   The type of brain
RNA labelled by pulses of less than several hours is a minor
component of total brain RNA and is found in the nuclear fraction.   This RNA appears very heterogeneous by analysis on
sucrose gradients and polyacrylamide gel electrophoresis and
has been called heterogeneous nuclear RNA (hnRNA).   The data
in Figure 2 indicate that labelled RNA appears in the cyto-

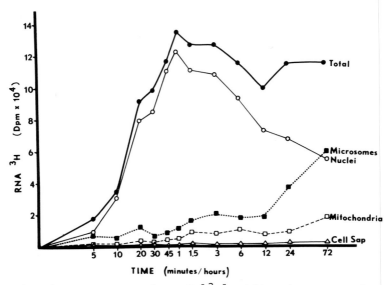

Fig. 2.   Incorporation of $[^3H]$ *uridine into RNA of Brain Subcellular Fractions.   100 μci* $[5-^3H]$ *uridine was injected subcutaneously into C57Bl/6J male mice 6 weeks old.   At various times mice were sacrificed and the brain homogenate separated into subcellular fractions.   RNA was precipitated by cetyl trimethylammonium bromide (CTAB) and the radioactivity determined (Dunn, 1971).   Note the logarithmic time scale. From Dunn (1976a).*

plasm at a small fraction of the rate at which it is synthesized in the nucleus. Thus much hnRNA never enters the cytoplasm. In fact, at times after one hour, there was a net loss of labelled RNA from the brain, probably all from the nuclear fraction.

    To examine this more closely we can calculate the relative specific radioactivity of the nuclear RNA fifteen minutes after a pulse of $[5-^3H]$ uridine. At this time the ratio of the radioactivity in nuclear RNA to that in uridine nucleotides was measured as 0.32. The base composition of brain nuclear RNA is 21.5 percent uracil by weight (Balázs & Cocks, 1967), thus the uridine in brain nuclear RNA amounts to 321 nanomoles per gram brain. The free uridine nucleotide content of brain is about 352 nanomoles per gram brain (Mandel & Harth, 1961). Assuming that all the radioactivity in the RNA was in uridine (which was very nearly true at this time after injection) and that the specific radioactivity of the free uridine nucleotides was uniform throughout the cell, the relative specific radioactivity of the uridine in brain nuclear RNA at fifteen minutes was 0.35 (= 0.32 x 352 ÷ 321). This suggests that 35 percent of the nuclear RNA was synthesized during the fifteen-minute pulse assuming that the uridine nucleotides were of the same specific radioactivity throughout the pulse. In fact, of course, the initial specific radioactivity was zero, so we are grossly underestimating the proportion of nuclear RNA synthesized during the fifteen minutes, which is probably more like 70 percent (since if the uptake increases linearly, the mean precursor specific radioactivity would be half that measured at the end of the pulse). This result is not unique for uridine, and similar values were obtained using other nucleoside precursors. If the radioactivity in the free nucleotide pools throughout the cell were not homogenous it would not substantially alter this result unless the pool of nuclear nucleotides was very much more radioactive than the mean. If the free nucleotide pools throughout the different cells of brain were not homogeneously labelled (which is probably the case) the result would not be affected provided that the rate of synthesis of nuclear RNA were similar for all the cells. Regions with high uridine nucleotide labelling would make highly labelled RNA, but the averaging of both RNA and nucleotides throughout the brain would compensate for this. We must conclude that at least a substantial part of brain nuclear RNA is being synthesized very rapidly and, since it does not appear in any other fraction, must also be rapidly degraded.

The conclusion that at least a part of nuclear RNA turns over very rapidly is not unique to the brain. On the basis of actinomycin D experiments and labelling studies, Harris (1963) concluded that nuclear RNA in liver cells turned over very rapidly. He even suggested that hnRNA *never* entered the cytoplasm. While this is probably not true, it is now generally accepted that hnRNA turns over very rapidly and that only a small fraction of it enters the cytoplasm, the rest being degraded in the nucleus (Soiero, Vaughan, Warner, & Darnell, 1968). Presumably some of it is a precursor to messenger RNA, but the function of the remainder is unknown. Thus, brain RNA labelled with short pulses of radioactive precursors is quantitatively a small class of total brain RNA which is poorly characterized and whose function is largely unknown.

Furthermore, with such a high turnover rate, the life expectancy of the hnRNA molecules is too short to be measured with pulses of radioactivity of longer than a few minutes. However, the kinetics of uptake of the precursors in the first few minutes are so complex that it is doubtful whether the synthesis rate can be estimated with such short pulses. It is thus impossible to accurately estimate the rate of synthesis of brain RNA using this technique. And, as a corollary, the rate of incorporation of tracer precursors into total brain RNA cannot be used as a meaningful index of the rate of RNA synthesis. It follows that changes in the labelling of RNA relative to that of precursors is as likely to be due to changes in precursor metabolism as to changes in RNA metabolism.

With this in mind, we re-examined the study of Zemp et al. (1966) (see also Glassman and Wilson, 1970). In their experiments [3H]- or [14C]uridine was injected intracranially, and the RNA isolated from various subcellular fractions of the brain. To control for the potential variability of the injection and the uptake of uridine into the tissue, the radioactivity in uridine monophosphate (UMP) was also measured. (UMP rather than UTP was used since the techniques for subcellular fractionation permitted the degradation of UTP, the direct RNA precursor, to UMP; other uridine nucleotides such as UDP and the UDP sugars were probably also degraded to UMP.) The double isotope design was used since neither the recovery of RNA nor that of UMP was quantitative. Thus by homogenizing the brains of two mice together, losses for both should have been equivalent, and the ratio of the RNA/UMP values for the pair of mice took account of this. Inherent in this design is the impossibility of distinguishing whether an increase in the ratio of RNA to UMP is due to an increase in RNA radioactivity or to a decrease in UMP radioactivity or a combination of both. The time parameters used in the experiments are important. The treatments for both trained and yoked animals were similar for the first 30 minutes of uridine incorporation, and were different only for the final 15 minutes. Thus a 25 percent increase in RNA:UMP in a trained animal would indicate a 75 percent increase in RNA labelling in the last 15 minutes, assuming linear incorporation throughout the 45 minute pulse. Since the incorporation was not linear (Figure 2) the increase would be even greater, perhaps 100 percent. Such a large average change throughout the brain seems unreasonable, and it is more likely that there was a decrease in UMP labelling, possibly in addition to an increased RNA labelling.

To resolve these problems quantitative methods for the determination of radioactivity in RNA and UMP were devised (Dunn, 1971; Entingh, Damstra-Entingh, Dunn, Wilson, & Glassman, 1974). We also chose to use peripheral injections since intracranial injections and the ether anesthesia used for

them impaired the behavior and intracranial injections severely inhibited brain protein synthesis (Dunn, unpublished
observations). Moreover, the distribution of radioactivity
was uneven and concentrated in periventricular structures
(see also Kottler, Bowman, & Haasch, 1971; Crockett & Quinton,
1973). Subcutaneous injections of [5-^{3}H]uridine gave higher
incorporations of radioactivity into the brain than intraperitoneal ones with greater reproducibility, and the results
were consistent enough that a double isotope procedure was
unnecessary. Using these techniques a number of experiments
were performed independently by Entingh, Damstra-Entingh and
Dunn. The results of a typical experiment are presented in
Table 2 (see also Entingh et al., 1974). There was no change

TABLE 2

INCORPORATION OF [5-^{3}H]URIDINE INTO MOUSE BRAIN
DURING JUMPBOX TRAINING

Treatment	Total incorporated dpm (mean + s.e.m.)	RNA dpm (mean + s.e.m.)	RNA/soluble (mean + s.e.m.)
Quiet	12,600 + 890	2170 + 170	0.209 + .005
Trained	12,700 + 830	2180 + 120	0.203 + .008

Six C57B1/6J mice (8 week ♂) were injected subcutaneously with 100 μCi
[5-^{3}H]uridine and trained in the jumpbox as described by Zemp *et al.*
(1966). Six quiet mice were similarly injected. Incorporation of ^{3}H
into RNA determined as described by Dunn (1971). Data reproduced from
Dunn (1975a).

in the incorporation of subcutaneously injected [^{3}H]uridine
into RNA following avoidance training under the conditions
used by Zemp et al. (1966) in the same apparatus and laboratory. Subsequently, Entingh et al. (1974) showed that there
were changes in the radioactivity of UMP in trained but not
in yoked animals and that these could account for the changes
previously observed. However, this change in UMP labelling
did not appear to account quantitatively for the changes observed by Adair, Wilson, and Glassman (1968) (or by Uphouse,
MacInnes, & Schlesinger, 1972) in the labelling of polyribosomes (Entingh et al., 1974). These results do not exclude
the possibility that changes in the labelling of particular
RNA species occur during training, but only indicate that the
major change occurs in UMP labelling. It is also possible
that the changes in UMP might be a consequence of altered RNA
metabolism.

There is other evidence that alterations of precursor nucleotide metabolism may explain changes in the labelling of RNA in nervous tissue. Shashoua (1970) reported changes in the relative incorporation of [^{3}H]orotic acid into uridine and cytidine of goldfish brain RNA during training, but changes in the incorporation of [^{3}H]orotic acid into free uridine and cytidine nucleotides have been observed when the aquarium water was poorly aerated (Baskin, Masiarz, & Agranoff, 1972). The increased incorporation of [^{3}H]uridine into RNA observed when R2 neurons of *Aplysia* abdominal ganglia were electrically stimulated has been suggested to be dependent on the uridine concentration in the incubation medium (Wilson & Berry, 1972). Also, Harris, Harris, and Dunn (1975) have recently reported that a decrease in the incorporation of [^{3}H]uridine into mouse brain RNA following morphine treatment could be totally accounted for by a decreased labelling of precursor nucleotides, due to an apparent increase in pyrimidine catabolism. It is very likely that other studies that have employed radioactive precursors to estimate RNA synthesis may have similar problems.

THE STIMULATION-INDUCED INCREASE IN THE INCORPORATION OF AMINO ACIDS INTO BRAIN PROTEIN

We recently reported that following training of mice in the conditioned avoidance task described by Zemp et al. (1966) there was an increase in the incorporation of [$4,5$-^{3}H]-lysine into brain and liver proteins when the amino acid was injected after training was completed (Rees, Brogan, Entingh, Dunn, Shinkman, Damstra-Entingh, Wilson, & Glassman, 1974). Similar incorporation increases were observed using [$4,5$-^{3}H]-leucine and [1-^{14}C]leucine as precursors (Brogan, unpublished observations). The lysine incorporation changes were also observed in the brains and livers of footshocked rats. The increase in lysine incorporation was seen rather generally over all regions of brain with the largest increases in the basal ganglia, hippocampus, cerebellum plus brain stem, and ventral cortex and essentially no change in dorsal cortex. The response was apparently not specific to training and was also observed when the mice were "yoked" to the training experience or subjected to a series of footshocks or loud buzzer soundings in the same apparatus (Table 3). When the behavioral treatment was repeated on consecutive days, the biochemical response in both the brain and the liver was diminished on the fourth and eighth days, suggesting habituation (Table 4).

TABLE 3

INCORPORATION OF $[4,5-{}^{3}H]LYSINE$ INTO MOUSE BRAIN AND LIVER PROTEIN

Treat- ment	n	Brain RR Mean $\pm$ s.e.m.	% increase over quiet	Liver RR Mean $\pm$ s.e.m.	% increase over quiet
Quiet	48	0.127 $\pm$ 0.002	[0]	0.431 $\pm$ 0.013	[0]
Trained	14	0.149 $\pm$ 0.004	+17***	0.700 $\pm$ 0.032	+62***
Yoked	4	0.144 $\pm$ 0.008	+13*	0.607 $\pm$ 0.039	+41**
Buzzers	11	0.148 $\pm$ 0.005	+16***	0.639 $\pm$ 0.023	+48***
Shocks	11	0.143 $\pm$ 0.005	+12**	0.696 $\pm$ 0.046	+61***
Lights	6	0.132 $\pm$ 0.004	+4	0.570 $\pm$ 0.039	+32**

*p < 0.05
**p < 0.01
***p < 0.001 (Student's t-test, 2-tailed)

Male C57Bl/6J mice (6-8 weeks old) were subjected to the behavioral treatment for 15 minutes. Twenty minutes later they were injected subcutaneously with 30 μCi of $[4,5-{}^{3}H]$lysine. After ten minutes incorporation, the mice were killed and the radioactivity incorporated into brain and liver free lysine and protein determined. The quiet mice were not disturbed before the injection of $[{}^{3}H]$lysine. RR (Relative Radioactivity) = radioactivity in protein/radioactivity in free lysine. For full details see Rees *et al.* (1974) from which these data are produced.

These results could clearly have been due to the stress of the experience, and indeed the plasma corticosterone concentration of shocked mice was elevated over quiet controls. To test whether the biochemical changes could have been due to the corticosterone secreted, the experiments were repeated using adrenalectomized mice. The results in Table 5 indicate that the changes observed in both brain and liver also occurred in adrenalectomized animals in which plasma corticosterone was essentially zero. Thus the increased lysine incorporation cannot have been due to plasma corticosterone but could have been due to adrenocorticotrophic hormone (ACTH). In fact the greater incorporation increase in footshocked mice would be consistent with the hypersecretion of ACTH in response to stress in adrenalectomized animals. Preliminary data showed that ACTH injected into intact animals produced responses in the lysine incorporation into brain and liver, similar to those observed with training (Table 6).

The association of increases of the incorporation of precursor amino acids into brain protein with stress is consistent with previously published data. Beach, Emmens, Kimble, and Lickey (1969) observed an increased $[{}^{3}H]$leucine incorpo-

TABLE 4

EFFECTS OF BEHAVIORAL TREATMENTS ON RELATIVE RADIOACTIVITY
OF BRAIN PROTEIN IN NAIVE AND EXPERIENCED MICE

Group	n	Brain RR (Mean $\pm$ s.e.m.)	% increase over quiet	Liver RR (Mean $\pm$ s.e.m.)	% increase over quiet
Quiet	48	.127 $\pm$ .002	[0]	.431 $\pm$ .013	[0]
Trained					
Day 1	14	.149 $\pm$ .004	+17.3**	.700 $\pm$ .031	+62**
Day 4	8	.134 $\pm$ .006	+ 5.5	.537 $\pm$ .030	+24**
30 Buzzers					
Day 1	11	.148 $\pm$ .005	+16.5**	.639 $\pm$ .023	+48**
Day 4	8	.140 $\pm$ .007	+10.2*	.438 $\pm$ .023	+ 2
Day 8	6	.132 $\pm$ .005	+ 3.9	.475 $\pm$ .022	+10

*p < .05
**p < .005 (Student's t-test, 2-tailed)

Mice were given avoidance training or exposed to 30 buzzer soundings
during a fifteen-minute session. For some mice these treatments were
administered daily for four or eight consecutive days. Twenty minutes
after the session on either day 1,4, or 8, mice received an injection
of [^{3}H]lysine and were sacrified ten minutes later. Biochemistry and
presentation of data as in Table 3. Adapted from Rees *et al.* (1974).

ration into protein of rat hippocampus during conditioned
avoidance training involving electric footshock. Altman and
Das (1966) showed an increased incorporation of [^{3}H]leucine
into brain protein of rats running in an exercise wheel which
disappeared as the rats habituated to the task. On the first
exposure of rats to light, Rose (1967) showed an increased
[^{3}H]lysine incorporation into visual cortex proteins that
subsequently decreased. Appel, Davis, and Scott (1967)
showed that on re-exposure to light, rats that were housed in
the dark for three days exhibited increased incorporation of
[^{3}H]leucine into visual cortex protein both *in vivo* and *in
vitro*. An increased aggregation of ribosomes into polyribosomes *in vivo,* indicative of an increased protein synthetic
activity, was also observed. These changes were not specific
for visual cortex but were also observed in motor cortex.

Other workers have shown that ACTH increases the incorporation of amino acids into brain protein. Semiginovsky and
Jakoubek (1971) showed that high doses of ACTH increased the
incorporation of [U-^{14}C]leucine into protein of mouse cerebral hemispheres but not spinal cord. Curiously, brain

TABLE 5

EFFECTS OF BEHAVIORAL TREATMENTS ON RELATIVE RADIOACTIVITY
OF BRAIN AND LIVER PROTEIN IN ADRENALECTOMIZED MICE

Group	n	Brain Mean $\pm$ s.e.m.	% increase over quiet	Liver Mean $\pm$ s.e.m.	% increase over quiet
Quiet	10	.131 $\pm$ .006	[0]	.552 $\pm$ .064	[0]
20 shocks	9	.161 $\pm$ .005	+23**	1.025 $\pm$ .104	+86***
30 buzzers	9	.154 $\pm$ .006	+18*	.788 $\pm$ .058	+43*

*p < .05
**p < .005
***p < .001 (Student's t-test, 2-tailed)

Adrenalectomized mice were treated as described in Table 3. The mean
plasma corticosterone was 1.5 μg per 100 ml ($\pm$ 2.3, s.e.m.) for the
adrenalectomized mice, compared with 5.2 $\pm$ 2.2 for quiet sham-operated
mice, and 15 $\pm$ 2.9 for shocked sham-operated mice. Data from Rees,
Ph.D. thesis, University of North Carolina, 1972.

slices from ACTH-treated rats incorporated less [3H]leucine
into protein *in vitro* (Jakoubek, Semiginovsky, Kraus, &
Erdossová, 1970). Rudman, Scott, Del Rio, Houser, and Sheen
(1974) have shown that ACTH or β-MSH increased the incorporation of L-[U-^{14}C]valine, L-[U-^{14}C]tyrosine, L-[U-^{14}C]leucine
and L-[U-^{14}C]lysine into mouse brain protein. In a preliminary report, Reading (1972) showed that synthetic $ACTH_{4-10}$, a
peptide fragment of ACTH that has little or no adrenocortical
activity, increased the incorporation of [^{14}C]leucine into
rat brain protein. However, with the peptide synthesized
with the phenylalanine residue at position 7 in the D (as opposed to the L) configuration, no such change was observed.
Neither Reading (1972) nor Rudman et al. (1974) observed any
changes in the liver.

Hypophysectomized rats displayed lower than normal contents of RNA and ribosomes in the brain stem plus diencephalon (Gispen, deWied, Schotman, & Jansz, 1970). The major decrease of RNA occurred in the microsomal fraction (Versteeg,
Gispen, Schotman, Witter, & de Wied, 1972). This loss of RNA
was accompanied by a decrease in the proportion of ribosomes
found aggregated into polyribosomes (Gispen & Schotman, 1970)
and a decrease in their capacity to synthesize proteins *in
vitro* (Dunn & Korner, 1966). Schotman, Gispen, Jansz, and
de Wied (1972) showed that chronic treatment of hypophysectomized rats with $ACTH_{4-10}$ stimulated the incorporation of [3H]-
leucine into brain protein. Moreover, treatment with
$ACTH_{4-10}$(D-phenylalanine) decreased the incorporation. The

TABLE 6

INCORPORATION OF [^{3}H]LYSINE INTO MOUSE BRAIN AND LIVER PROTEIN

Injection	Brain RR $\pm$ s.e.m.	% increase over saline	Liver RR $\pm$ s.e.m.	% increase over saline
Saline	0.161 $\pm$ 0.010	[0]	0.576 $\pm$ 0.046	[0]
ACTH (0.1U)	0.216 $\pm$ 0.007	+24*	0.995 $\pm$ 0.209	73*
ACTH (1U)	0.223 $\pm$ 0.010	+29*	1.081 $\pm$ 0.154	88*

*$p < 0.05$ (Student's t-test, 2-tailed)

C57B1/6J mice were injected with saline or ACTH (Park-Davis Cortico-tropin injection). Fifteen minutes later they were injected with [4,5-^{3}H]lysine for ten minutes as described in Table 3. Data reproduced from Dunn (1976a).

deficiency of protein synthesis in hypophysectomized rats was also observed with brain stem slices *in vitro,* a deficit correctable by ACTH$_{1-10}$ *in vitro* (Reith, Schotman, & Gispen, 1974). There is thus widespread support for the possibility that ACTH and similar peptides increase the incorporation of amino acids into protein without mediation by adrenocortical hormones.

In a number of studies de Wied and his co-workers have shown that ACTH can restore to normal the impaired behavior of hypophysectomized rats (de Wied, 1974). These effects are observed in adrenalectomized animals and thus are not mediated by adrenal corticosteroids. Also ACTH$_{4-10}$, which has little or no adrenocortical activity, is fully active behaviorally. Notably ACTH$_{4-10}$ retards the extinction of shuttlebox avoidance learning in normal rats, but ACTH$_{4-10}$ containing D-phenylalanine accelerates the extinction. The evidence for the extra-adrenal action of ACTH is strengthened since corticosteroids have effects on extinction opposite to those of ACTH$_{4-10}$; ACTH$_{4-10}$ is also active in these behavioral paradigms when implanted directly into the brain in the area of the parafascicular nucleus but not other areas (van Wimersma Greidanus and de Wied, 1971). This provides additional evidence for a cerebral locus of action for ACTH.

ACTH also facilitates passive avoidance performance in rats (Lissák & Bohus, 1972). Furthermore, the effects of amnestic agents may be blocked by ACTH peptides. Keyes (1974) reported that ACTH, administered four hours after training, reversed ECS-induced amnesia for passive avoidance behavior in rats. Also, Rigter, van Riezen, and de Wied (1974) observed a reversal of CO_2-induced amnesia in a simi-

lar task when ACTH was given prior to retention testing.
Moreover, in humans, Miller, Kastin, and Sandman (1974)
showed that $ACTH_{4-10}$ but not $ACTH_{1-24}$ improved visual memory
and decreased "anxiety."

Further evidence for the behavioral activity of ACTH
peptides are the studies with melanocyte-stimulating hormone
(MSH), which contains the $ACTH_{4-10}$ sequence. Kastin (this
volume) has reviewed the data indicating the stimulatory
effects of MSH in the learning of a number of different
tasks.

Other pituitary peptides may be behaviorally active.
Lysine vasopressin has been reported to retard extinction of
active and passive avoidance behavior in rats (Bohus, Ader, &
de Wied, 1972) and is active when implanted directly into the
brain in the same area where $ACTH_{4-10}$ is active (van Wimersma
Greidanus, Bohus, & de Wied, 1972). Lande, Flexner, and
Flexner, (1972) also reported that desglycinamide lysine
vasopressin, which has very little pressor activity, could
reverse puromycin-induced amnesia in mice, and probably accounts for the previously reported effect of corticotrophin
gel (Flexner & Flexner, 1971). De Wied, Sarantakis, and
Weinstein (1973) have speculated that these behavioral activities of peptides may explain the so-called transfer effects
(Ungar, 1973).

There are also electrophysiological indications that
ACTH may act directly on cells in the brain. Motta,
Fraschini, and Martini (1969) have reviewed the evidence that
elevated plasma ACTH stimulates electrical activity in areas
of the septum, somatomotor cortex, thalamus, midbrain reticular formation and amygdala, and inhibits activity in the median eminence, lateral hypothalamus and hippocampus. These
effects do not require adrenal activity since they appear in
adrenalectomized animals and corticosteroids often have opposite effects. Pfaff, Silva, and Weiss (1971) have also
shown opposing effects of ACTH and corticosterone on the firing rate of dorsal hippocampal neurons.

There is thus a body of evidence indicating that ACTH
may have direct cerebral effects in both hypophysectomized
and intact rats and mice, possibly including an increased
rate of protein synthesis. We wish to suggest that these
phenomena may play a role in learning, and that this could
explain some of the existing data on biochemical correlates
of learning.

Specifically, we propose that the novelty of the initial
training experience acts as a stressor for the animal, thus
causing the secretion of ACTH and possibly other pituitary
hormones (e.g., MSH). Aside from its action on the adrenal

cortex (and other peripheral tissues), these hormones then
directly influence cerebral metabolism, possibly manifested
in an increased rate of protein synthesis. These biochemical
responses then facilitate the adaptation of the brain to the
novel environment. This may take the form of an altered metabolic state that is conducive to the occurrence of plastic
changes (e.g., connectivity changes). The effects would be
anatomically widespread as are the observed neurochemical
changes. If the connectivity changes can only actually occur
at those precise locations where the electrophysiological
state is favorable, we can explain how a general change of
the metabolic activity can result in a small number of specifically localized changes. Moreover, if the localization
of the changes can be dictated by electrophysiological-
anatomical factors, their specificity need not be duplicated
by a chemical-behavioral specificity.

Our hypothesis essentially is that hormones secreted in
response to stress increase plasticity to facilitate adaptation to the response. This action of ACTH on the brain would
then be consistent with its direct and indirect effects on
other organs preparing the body to cope with stress. We do
not consider that ACTH is the only hormone that may have such
a role, nor that it is necessary for learning. Other hormones (e.g., lysine vasopressin or MSH) may act on different
regions, or subcellular locations or with different metabolic
responses. The hormones may be specific for certain types of
behavior, and differential secretion could account for neuronal specificity. It is interesting in this regard that
while ACTH and MSH are released in response to physical
stress, only the latter is released in response to "psychological stress" (Sandman, Kastin, Schally, Kendall, & Miller,
1973).

The rationale for a direct interaction between stress
and learning has been argued previously by Levine (1971) who
reviewed the evidence for the involvement of ACTH and adrenal
corticosteroids in the learning process. Our hypothesis in
some respects resembles that of Kety (1970) who suggested
that norepinephrine might act as a "consolidation amine." He
conceived that the "reward" associated with the arousal of
achieving a correct solution might stimulate noradrenergic
pathways in the brain, specifically the ascending tracts implicated in an arousal system. The norepinephrine released
by such stimulation could then in turn cause the adaptation
of specific synapses associated with the achievement of the
reward. He suggested that norepinephrine might act in this
way by stimulating protein synthesis which is considered to
be essential for learning. The noradrenergic system was

ideally suited since it has diffuse projections from the brain stem to almost all regions of the brain. Strong support for Kety's hypothesis is provided by the recent demonstration of a facilitation of learning by intracerebral injection of norepinephrine (Stein, Beluzzi, & Wise, 1975).

There is an interesting possibility that our hypotheses are related and that norepinephrine might be involved in ACTH action. It is significant that many of the cell bodies of origin for the ascending noradrenergic tracts lie in the locus coeruleus which is a highly vascular area of the brain stem and thus might be responsive to plasma metabolites. Furthermore, Versteeg (1973) has shown that $ACTH_{4-10}$ stimulated the turnover of norepinephrine in intact rats, a phenomenon also observed by Leonard (1974) who found that dopamine turnover was also increased. Consistent with this is the increase in norepinephrine (but not dopamine) turnover following adrenalectomy (Javoy, Glowinski, & Krodon, 1968; Fuxe, Corrodi, Hokfelt, & Jonsson, 1970), an effect partially blocked by cortisol replacement therapy (Fuxe et al., 1970).

Consistent with our hypothesis are the behavioral effects of ACTH and MSH referred to above, and the facilitation of acquisition by prior footshock (Levine, Maddey, Conner, Muskal, & Anderson, 1973; Gold, Haycock, Macri, & McGaugh, 1973). It also explains why the observed biochemical correlates of training are so general, encompassing most brain regions (Dunn, Entingh, Entingh, Gispen, Machlus, Perumal, Rees, & Brogan, 1974; Entingh et al., 1975). It should also be noted that the habituation of the lysine incorporation response to stressful stimuli indicates that learning occurred even when the mice were not "trained." Thus in this case too, ACTH might be involved in the learning.

CONCLUSIONS

1. Analysis of the biochemistry of brain RNA and in particular the kinetics of uptake of precursors suggests that it is difficult if not impossible to relate changes in the labelling of RNA to changes in RNA synthesis. A reexamination of some previously reported changes in RNA labelling during training suggests that they may be largely due to changes in the metabolism of the precursors. There are at present no data that unequivocally indicate that changes of RNA synthesis are correlated with learning.

2. A change in the incorporation of radioactive amino acids into protein that occurs after training, but which is not specific for learning aspects of the experience may be

due to a non-adrenal action of adrenocorticotrophic hormone
(ACTH). It is suggested that this phenomenon may not be un-
related to learning, since evidently learning occurs even in
stressful non-training situations. The circulating hormones
released in response to stress may increase certain anabolic
processes in the brain, facilitating the occurrence of plastic changes. The specificity of the changes finally achieved
would depend upon local electrophysiological-anatomical factors. In this way the specificity dictated by the latter
factors would not have to be duplicated by the facilitating
hormone as is required in the theory of "transfer" experiments. Evidence consistent with this idea is the documented
interaction of ACTH with cerebral tissue, the known ability
of ACTH and other peptide hormones to influence learning behavior and a similar action of mild stressful or arousing
stimuli, and the regional generalization of the neurochemical
responses observed to occur during training.

ACKNOWLEDGMENTS

Research reported here has been supported by grants from
the National Institutes of Health (MH25486, NS07457, and
MH18136), the National Science Foundation (GB 18551), and the
CIBA-Geigy Corporation. We are grateful to Drs. Edward
Glassman and John E. Wilson for the use of facilities and to
Eleanor Brown, Mark Williams, and Byron Bergert for technical
assistance. We are also indebted for many fruitful discus-
sions to Drs. Dan Entingh, Terri Damstra-Entingh, John E.
Wilson, and Edward Glassman.
Many of the data and discussions included in this paper
were previously presented at the conference on Current
Research Approaches to the Neural Mechanism of Learning and
Memory, Asilomar, California, June, 1974 and are reported in
Dunn (1976a).

REFERENCES

Adair, L. B., Wilson, J. E., & Glassman, E. Brain function
    and macromolecules, IV. Uridine incorporation during dif-
    ferent behavioral experiences. *Proceedings of the
    National Academy of Science, U.S.A.,* 1968, *61*, 917-922.

Adams, D. H. Some observations on the incorporation of pre-
    cursors into ribonucleic acid of rat brain. *Journal of
    Neurochemistry,* 1965, *12*, 783-790.

Altman, J., & Das, G. D.   Behavioral manipulations and protein metabolism of the brain: effects of motor exercise on
the utilization of leucine-H^3.   *Physiology and Behavior,*
1966 *1,* 105-108.

Appel, S. H., Davis, W., & Scott, S.   Brain polysomes: response to environmental stimulation.   *Science,* 1967, *157,*
836-838.

Balázs, R., & Cocks, W. A.   RNA metabolism in subcellular
fractions of brain tissue.   *Journal of Neurochemistry,*
1967, *14,* 1035-1055.

Baskin, F., Masiarz, F. R., & Agranoff, B. W.   Effect of various stresses on the incorporation of [^{3}H]orotic acid into
goldfish brain RNA.   *Brain Research,* 1972, *39,* 151-162.

Beach, G., Emmens, M., Kimble, D. P., & Lickey, M.   Autoradiographic demonstration of biochemical changes in the
limbic system during avoidance training.   *Proceedings of
the National Academy of Science, U.S.A.,* 1969, *62,* 692-
696.

Bohus, B., Ader, R., & Wied, D. de.   Effects of vasopressin
on active and passive avoidance behavior.   *Hormones and
Behavior,* 1972, *3,* 191-197.

Bondy, S. C.   The ribonucleic acid metabolism of brain.
Journal of Neurochemistry, 1966, *13,* 955-959.

Crockett, R. S., & Quinton, E. E.   Distribution of 5-^{3}H-
uridine incorporated into RNA of mouse brain as a function
of injection route-autoradiographic investigation.
Federation Proceedings, 1973, *32,* 597.

Dunn, A.   Use of cetyltrimethylammonium bromide for estima-.
tion of the *in vivo* incorporation of radioactive precursors into RNA.   *Analytical Biochemistry,* 1971, *41,* 460-
465.

Dunn, A. J.   Biochemical correlates of training experiences:
a discussion of the evidence.   In M. Rosenzweig and E. L.
Bennett, (Eds.), *Neural Mechanisms of Learning and Memory.*
Cambridge, Massachusetts: M.I.T. Press, 1976. (a)

Dunn, A. J.   The chemistry of learning and the formation of memory.   In W. H. Gispen (Ed.), *Chemical Neurobiology*. Amsterdam: Elsevier Publications, 1976. (b)

Dunn, A. J., & Korner, A.   Hypophysectomy and amino acid incorporation in a rat brain cell-free system. *Biochemical Journal*, 1966, 100, 76 pp.

Dunn, A., Entingh, D., Entingh, T., Gispen, W. H., Machlus, B., Perumal, R., Rees, H. D., & Brogan, L.   Biochemical correlates of brief behavioral experiences.   In F. O. Schmitt and F. G. Worden (Eds.), *The Neurosciences: Third Study Program*.   Cambridge, Massachusetts: M.I.T. Press, 1974, pp. 679-684.

Entingh, D., Damstra-Entingh, T., Dunn, A., Wilson, J. E., & Glassman, E.   Brain uridine monophosphate: reduced incorporation of uridine during avoidance learning. *Brain Research*, 1974, 70, 131-138.

Entingh, D., Dunn, A., Wilson, J. E., Glassman, E., Hogan, E., & Damstra-Entingh, T.   Biochemical approaches to the biological basis of memory.   In M. S. Gazzaniga and C. B. Blakemore, (Eds.), *Handbook of Psychobiology*.   New York: Academic Press, 1975.

Fleck, A., & Munro, H. N.   The precision of ultraviolet absorption measurements in the Schmidt-Thannhauser procedure, for nucleic acid estimation. *Biochimica et Biophysica Acta*, 1962, 55, 571-583.

Flexner, J. B., & Flexner, L. B.   Pituitary peptides and the suppression of memory by puromycin. *Proceedings of the National Academy of Science, U.S.A.*, 1971, 68, 2519-2521.

Fuxe, K., Corrodi, H., Hokfelt, T., & Jonsson, G.   Central monoamine neurons and pituitary-adrenal activity. *Progress in Brain Research*, 1970, 32, 42-56.

Gispen, W. H., & Schotman, P.   Effect of hypophysectomy and conditioned avoidance behavior on macromolecule metabolism in the brain stem of the rat. *Progress in Brain Research*, 1970, 32, 236-244.

Gispen, W. H., Wied, D. de, Schotman, P., & Jansz, H. S.   Effects of hypophysectomy on RNA metabolism in rat brain stem. *Journal of Neurochemistry*, 1970, 17, 751-761.

Glassman, E.   The biochemistry of learning: an evaluation of the role of RNA and protein. *Annual Review of Biochemistry*, 1969, *38*, 605-646.

Glassman, E., & Wilson, J. E.   The incorporation of uridine into brain RNA during short experiences. *Brain Research*, 1970, *21*, 157-168.

Gold, P. E., Haycock, J. W., Macri, J., & McGaugh, J. L. Retrograde amnesia and the "reminder effect":   An alternative interpretation. *Science*, 1973, *180*, 1199-1200.

Harris, H.   Nuclear ribonucleic acid. *Progress in Nucleic Acid Research*, 1963, *2*, 20-59.

Harris, R. A., Harris, L. S., & Dunn, A.   Effect of narcotic drugs on ribonucleic acid and nucleotide metabolism in mouse brain. *Journal of Pharmacology and Experimental Therapeutics*, 1975, *192*, 280-287.

Horn, G., Rose, S. P. R., & Bateson, P. P. G.   Experience and plasticity in the central nervous system.   Is the nervous system modified by experience?   Are such modifications involved in learning? *Science*, 1973, *181*, 506-514.

Jakoubek, B., Semiginovsky, B., Kraus, M., & Erdossová, R. The alteration of protein metabolism of the brain cortex induced by anticipation stress and ACTH. *Life Sciences*, Part I, 1970, *9*, 1169-1179.

Javoy, F., Glowinski, J., & Krodon, C.   Effects of adrenalectomy on the turnover of norepinephrine in the rat brain. *European Journal of Pharmacology*, 1968, *4*, 103-104.

Kety, S. S.   The biogenic amines in the central nervous system: their possible roles in arousal, emotion and learning.   In F. O. Schmitt (Ed.), *The Neurosciences, Second Study Program*.   New York: Rockefeller University Press, 1970, pp. 324-336.

Keyes, J. B.   Effect of ACTH on ECS-produced amnesia of a passive avoidance task. *Physiological Psychology*, 1974, *2*, 307-309.

Kottler, P. D., Bowman, R. E., & Haasch, W. D.   RNA metabolism in the rat brain during learning following intravenous and intraventricular injections of ^{3}H-cytidine. *Physiology and Behavior*, 1972, *8*, 291-297.

Lande, S., Flexner, J. B., & Flexner, L. B.   Effect of corticotropin and desglycinamide[9]-lysine vasopressin on suppression of memory by puromycin. *Proceedings of the National Academy of Science, U.S.A.*, 1972, *69*, 558-560.

Leonard, B. E.   The effect of two synthetic ACTH analogues on the metabolism of biogenic amines in the rat brain. *Archives International of Pharmacology and Therapeutics*, 1974, *207*, 242-253.

Levine, S.   Stress and behavior. *Scientific American*, 1971, *224*, 26-31.

Levine, S., Maddey, J., Conner, R. L., Muskal, J. R., & Anderson, D. C.   Physiological and behavioral effects of prior aversive stimulation (preshock) in the rat. *Physiology and Behavior*, 1973, *10*, 467-471.

Lissák, K., & Bohus, B.   Pituitary hormones and avoidance behavior of the rat. *International Journal of Psychobiology*, 1972, *3*, 103-115.

Mandel, P., & Harth, S.   Free nucleotides of the brain in various mammals. *Journal of Neurochemistry*, 1961, *8*, 116-125.

McEwen, B. S., & Zigmond, R. E.   Isolation of brain cell nuclei. In N. Marks & R. Rodnight (Eds.), *Research Methods in Neurochemistry, Vol. 1.* New York: Plenum Press, 1972, pp. 139-161.

Miller, L., Kastin, A., Sandman, C., Fink, M., & Veen, W. van.   Polypeptide influence on attention, memory and anxiety in man. *Pharmacology Biochemistry and Behavior*, 1974, *2*, 663-668.

Motta, M., Fraschini, F., & Martini, L.   "Short" feedback mechanisms in the control of anterior pituitary function. In W. F. Ganong & L. Martini (Eds.), *Frontiers in Neuroendocrinology, 1969.* New York: Oxford University Press, 1969.

Pfaff, D. W., Silva, M. T. A., & Weiss, J. M.   Telemetered recording of hormone effects on hippocampal neurons. *Science*, 1971, *172*, 394-395.

Reading, H. W.   Effects of some adrenocorticotrophin analogues on protein synthesis in brain. *Biochemical Journal*, 1972, *127*, 7P.

Rees, H. D., Brogan, L. L., Entingh, D. J., Dunn, A., Shinkman, P. G., Damstra-Entingh, T., Wilson, J. E., & Glassman, E.   Effect of sensory stimulation on the uptake and incorporation of radioactive lysine into protein of mouse brain and liver. *Brain Research*, 1974, *68*, 143-156.

Reith, M. E. A., Schotman, P., & Gispen, W. H.   Hypophysectomy, $ACTH_{1-10}$ and *in vitro* protein synthesis in rat brain stem slices. *Brain Research*, 1974, *81*, 571-575.

Rigter, R., Riezen, H. van, & Wied, D. de.   The effects of ACTH and vasopressin analogues in CO_2-induced retrograde amnesia in rats. *Physiology and Behavior*, 1974, *13*, 381-388.

Rose, S. P. R.   Changes in visual cortex on first exposure of rats to light. *Nature, London*, 1967, *215*, 253-255.

Rudman, D., Scott, J. W., Del Rio, A. E., Houser, D. H., & Sheen, S.   Effect of melanotrophic peptides on protein synthesis in mouse brain. *American Journal of Physiology*, 1974, *226*, 687-692.

Sandman, C. A., Kastin, A. J., Schally, A. V., Kendall, J. W., & Miller, L. H.   Neuroendocrine responses to physical and psychological stress. *Journal of Comparative and Physiological Psychology*, 1973, *84*, 386-390.

Schotman, P., Gispen, W. H., Jansz, H. S., & Wied, D. de.   Effects of ACTH analogues on macromolecule metabolism in the brain stem of hypophysectomized rats. *Brain Research*, 1972, *46*, 347-362.

Semiginovsky, B., & Jakoubek, B.   Effects of ACTH on the incorporation of L-[U-^{14}C]leucine into the brain and spinal cord in mice. *Brain Research*, 1971, *35*, 319-323.

Shashoua, V. E.   RNA metabolism in goldfish brain during acquisition of new behavioral patterns. *Proceedings of the National Academy of Science, U.S.A.,* 1970, *65,* 160-167.

Soiero, R., Vaughan, M. H., Warner, J. R., & Darnell, J. E. The turnover of nuclear DNA-like RNA in HeLa cells. *Journal of Cell Biology,* 1968, *39,* 112-117.

Stein, L., Beluzzi, J. D., & Wise, C. D.   Memory enhancement by central administration of norepinephrine. *Brain Research,* 1975, *84,* 329-335.

Ungar, G.   Evidence for molecular coding of neural information. In H. P. Zippel (Ed.), *Memory and Transfer of Information.* New York: Plenum Press, 1973, pp. 317-341.

Uphouse, L. L., MacInnes, J. W., & Schlesinger, K.   Effects of conditioned avoidance training on polyribosomes of mouse brain. *Physiology and Behavior,* 1972, *8,* 1013-1018.

Uphouse, L. L., MacInnes, J. W., & Schlesinger, K.   Role of RNA and protein in memory storage: A review. *Behavior Genetics,* 1974, *4,* 29-81.

Versteeg, D. H.   Effect of two ACTH analogs on noradrenaline metabolism in rat brain. *Brain Research,* 1973, *49,* 483-485.

Versteeg, D. H. G., Gispen, W. H., Schotman, P., Witter, A., & Wied, D. de.   Hypophysectomy and rat brain metabolism: effects of synthetic ACTH analogs. *Advances in Biochemical Psychopharmacology,* 1972, *6,* 219-239.

Von Hungen, K., Mahler, H. R., & Moore, P. B.   Turnover of protein and ribonucleic acid in synaptic subcellular fractions from rat brain. *Journal of Biological Chemistry,* 1968, *243,* 1415-1423.

Wied, D. de.   Pituitary-adrenal system hormones and behavior. In F. O. Schmitt & F. G. Worden (Eds.), *The Neurosciences: Third Study Program.* Cambridge, Massachusetts: M.I.T. Press, 1974, pp. 653-666.

Wied, D. de, Sarantakis, D., & Weinstein, B.   Behavioral evaluation of peptides related to scotophobin. *Neuropharmacology,* 1973, *12,* 1109-1115.

Wilson, D. L., & Berry, R. W. The effect of synaptic stimulation on RNA and protein metabolism in the R2 soma of Aplysia. *Journal of Neurobiology*, 1972, *3*, 369-379.

Wimersma Greidanus, Tj. B. van, & Wied, D. de. Effects of systemic and intracerebral administration of two opposite acting ACTH-related peptides on extinction of conditioned avoidance behavior. *Neuroendocrinology*, 1971, *7*, 291-301.

Wimersma Greidanus, Tj. B. van, Bohus, B., & Wied, D. de. Effects of peptide hormones on behavior. *Proceedings of the 4th International Congress on Endocrinology*, 1972, 197-201.

Zemp, J. W., Wilson, J. E., Schlesinger, K., Boggan, W. O., Glassman, E. Incorporation of uridine into RNA of mouse brain during short-term training experience. *Proceedings of the National Academy of Science, U.S.A.*, 1966, *55*, 1423-1431.

PHYLOGENETIC CORRELATIONS BETWEEN SLEEP AND MEMORY

J. A. ROJAS-RAMÍREZ and R. R. DRUCKER-COLÍN

*Departamento de Farmacología, Facultad de Medicina;
and Departamento de Biología Experimental,
Instituto de Biología;
Universidad National Autónoma de México
México 20, D. F., México*

Activity and inactivity, two easily observable behavioral
patterns, characterize animal existence. Generally speaking,
in vertebrates these two states correspond to wakefulness
and sleep respectively. Recent electrophysiological studies
have afforded precise methods for identifying waking and sleep
states, and have further allowed us to distinguish distinct
phases of sleep in many species.

Undoubtedly, the features of mammalian vigilance levels
have been the model for study in lower animals. Such
features have been established as follows: the awake animal
shows spontaneous motor activity, wide variations of amplitude
in the electrical activity of the neck muscles (EMG), fast
and low voltage EEG, and random eye movements. Behavioral
and EEG patterns of sleep have two phases: slow wave sleep
(SWS) which consists of loss of motor activity, adoption of
a typical curled position, diminution of the EMG amplitude,
presence of EEG spindles and slow waves, and absence of
eye movements. These characteristics are soon replaced by
those identifying rapid eye movement (REM) sleep: EMG
practically isoelectric, fast and low amplitude EEG, presence
of bursts of eye movements (Kleitman, 1963), theta rhythm in
hippocampus and entorhinal cortex (Jouvet, 1967; Hernández-
Peón, O'Flaherity, & Mazzuchelli-O'Flaherity, 1967), the
appearance of the ponto-geniculo-occipital spikes (PGO)
(Jouvet, 1967) increases in the unitary activity at cortical
occipital areas (Evarts, 1962), and the mesencephalic reticular
formation (Huttenlocker, 1961). Most likely with these
characteristics in mind, a great many studies have been

conducted in animals of different species in order to elucidate
the phylogenetic origin and evolution of sleep manifestations.

Sleep in Mammals

The mammalian species so far studied are: a) the
echidna (Allison, Van Twyver, & Goff, 1972); b) the opossum
(Van Twyver, & Allison, 1970); c) the kangaroo-rat (Astic, &
Royet, 1974); d) the mole (Allison, & Van Twyver, 1970); e) the
armadillo (Van Twyver, & Allison, 1974); f) the rabbit (Weiss,
& Roldán, 1964; Hoffmeister, 1972); g) the chinchilla; h) the
squirrel; i) the hamster (Van Twyver, 1969); j) the mouse
(Weiss, & Roldán, 1964; k) the rat (Michel, Klein, Jouvet,
& Valatax, 1961; Roldán, Weiss, & Fifkova, 1963; Timo-Iaria,
Negrao, Schmidek, Hoshino, Lobato de Menezes, & Leme da Rocha,
1970; l) the cat (Sterman, Knauss, Lehmann, & Clemente, 1965;
Ursin, 1968; Lucas, & Sterman, 1974); m) the dog (Lucas,
Powell, & Murphree, 1974); n) the fox (Dallaire, & Ruckenbusch,
1974); o) several species of farm animals such as the pig,
the horse, the sheep (Ruckenbusch, 1971), the goat (Ruckenbusch,
1962), the cow (Ruckenbusch, 1974; Ruckenbusch, Dougherty,
& Cook, 1974); and p) several species of primates, among
which we have the rhesus monkey (Weitzman, Kripke, Pollak, &
Dominguez, 1965; Kripke, Reite, Pegram, Stephens, & Lewis,
1968), the chimpanzee (Bert, Kripke, & Rhopes, 1970), the
baboon (Bert, 1973), the squirrel monkey (Adams, & Barrat,
1974), and man (Webb, & Agnew, 1970). Curiously, the gray
seal, a pinniped mammal, unlike all other mammals so far
studied shows REM sleep, accompanied by increases in respiratory and cardiac rates, prior to the SWS phase (Ridgway,
Harrison, & Joyce, 1975) (see Table I).

With the exception of the echidna, *Tachyglossus aculeatus*,
a monotreme mammal which does not have REM sleep (Allison,
et al., 1972), all mammals undergo both REM and slow wave
sleep. Apparently, monotremes are the actual representatives
of a primitive stock of mammalian development, the nontherian,
different from the therian mammals (marsupials and placentals).
The common ancestors of these two lines are the therapids,
mammalian-like reptiles which were discovered in Africa,
and existed during Permian and Triassic periods (225-275 x 10^6
years ago). It has been pointed out that therians and non-
therians were contemporary lines; therefore, they evolved
independently (Hopson, 1969). Similarities between the
echidna and some other mammals (morphology, way of life, etc.)
can be explained by a parallelism in evolution. According to
Tauber(1974) and in terms of evolutionary parallelism, the

TABLE 1

COMPARATIVE PERCENTAGES OF TOTAL WAKING (W), SLOW-WAVE SLEEP (SWS)
AND RAPID EYE MOVEMENT (REM) SLEEP IN SOME MAMMALS

S T A T E S

Subject	n	Duration of experiment (hours)	W	SWS	REM sleep	Reference
Cat	8	24	42.3	42.2	15.5	Sterman et al., 1965
"	18	24	45.2	39.3	15.5	Lucas & Sterman, 1974
Fox	3	24	59.2	30.8	10.0	Dellaire & Ruckenbusch, 1974
Dog (Pointer)	3	2	66.0	30.0	3.0	Lucas et al., 1974
Seal	6	14	55.7	33.5	10.7	Ridgway et al., 1975
Rabbit	21	12	50.0	48.0	2.0	Hoffmeister, 1972
Kangaroo rat	2	24	55.7	38.5	5.8	Astic & Royet, 1974
Rat	4	12	42.9	48.2	8.6	Our data
Cow	27	24	82.6	15.8	1.6	Ruckenbusch, 1974
Opossum	5	24	19.2	76.7	23.3	Van Twyver & Allison, 1970
Armadillo	6	24	28.0	59.0	13.0	Van Twyver & Allison, 1974
Echidna	5	48-120	64.2	35.9	0	Allison et al., 1972
Squirrel monkey	3	12	17.0	59.3	22.9	Adams & Barrat, 1974
Baboon	6	12	18.0	71.3	10.5	Bert, 1973
Man	28	24	60.6– 76.3	16.6– 28.5	6.6– 10.6	Webb & Agnew, 1970

mechanisms of REM sleep absent in echidna could have been present at some point in the evolution of monotremes and disappeared, or never participated in, parallel evolution.

Sleep in Birds

Even though Klein, Michel, & Jouvet (1964) reported 0.6% of REM sleep in young chickens and 0.3% in adults, and suggested REM sleep to be "rudimentary," subsequent studies have demonstrated without a doubt the existence of both phases of sleep in birds. One should remember, however, the following outstanding characteristics of avian REM sleep: a) it is brief and its longest duration only attains the lowest figures reached by mammals (see Table II), b) the EMG of the neck muscles is different from that of mammals; there is partial loss of muscle tonus in chickens (Klein, et al., 1964; Hishikawa, Kramer, & Kuhlo, 1969) and pigeons (Van Twyver, & Allison, 1972), while hawks have complete loss of muscle tone (Rojas-Ramírez, & Tauber, 1970). However, the muscle tone in wings and lower extremities is not completely lost since the animal is capable of maintaining itself on a perch, partially accounted for by the labyrinthine reflexes which maintain posture (Tradardi, 1966), c) there are no rapid eye movements in birds which have fixed eyeballs such as owls (Karadzic, Kovacevic, & Momirov, 1973; Susic, & Kovacevic, 1973).

Actually, it is accepted that both SWS and REM sleep patterns are present in placental and marsupial mammals as well as in birds. From a phylogenetic point of view this may

TABLE 2

COMPARATIVE PERCENTAGE OF
RAPID EYE MOVEMENT (REM) SLEEP IN SOME BIRDS

Subject	n	Duration of experiment (hours)	REM sleep (% of total sleep time)	Reference
Chicks	28	24	0.3-0.6	Klein *et al.*, 1964
Chickens	2	24	7.3+1.8	Hishikawa *et al.*, 1969
Hawks	2	24	7-10	Rojas-Ramirez & Tauber, 1970
Pigeons	6	24	6.9	Van Twyver & Allison, 1972
Owls	2	24	3.34	Karadzic *et al.*, 1973

mean that the mechanisms of SWS and of REM sleep have evolved
independently in the therian mammals and in birds from their
origin in the reptilian stock around the Cretasic period
approximately 132×10^6 years ago (Bock, 1969). However, the
existence of REM sleep in mammals and birds has stimulated
sleep studies in reptiles, amphibians, and fishes.

Sleep in Reptiles

        Phylogenetically, primitive reptiles represent the common
stem from which mammals, birds, and present day reptiles
evolved (Romer, 1970). Sleep and wakefulness have been
studied in four out of five orders of reptiles: chelonians
(tortoises and turtles), crocodilians (crocodiles, alligators),
saurians (lizards) and serpents (snakes). Only rhynchocephal-
ians (tuatara) have not been studied.
        The definition of sleep patterns in reptiles has been
a difficult task, particularly if we consider that the criterion
used has been that of mammalian sleep (Tauber, 1974). The
behavioral indices of sleep of mammalian and avian species
do not appear to be the most appropriate measures of comparison.
Furthermore, the electrophysiological indices of sleep,
considered as phenomenological signs, seem to be somewhat
different in reptiles. All these studies have recognized
a state of behavioral sleep in reptiles, however, not all
studies have reported the two phases of sleep characteristic
of mammals and birds.
        Even though there is an absence of high voltage slow
waves and spindles, SWS with low voltage slow activity has
been reported in turtles, *Testudo marginata Schopfer* (Hermann,
Jouvet, & Klein, 1964) and *Emys orbicularis* (Vasilescu, 1970),
in the caiman *(Caiman latirostis)*, the lizard *(Iguana iguana)*,
the python *(Python sebae)* (Peyreton, & Dusan-Peyreton, 1969),
and in the lizards *(Chameleo Jacksoni, C. melleri,* and
Ctenosaura pectinata) (Tauber, Roffwarg, & Weitzmann, 1966;
Tauber, Rojas-Ramirez, & Hernandez-Peon, 1968). In addition,
evidence exists which points towards the presence of rapid
eye movements during behavioral sleep, thus suggesting
the existence of REM sleep in the chamelions *C. jacksoni* and
C. melleri (Tauber, et al., 1966), in the lizard *C. pectinata*
(Tauber, et al., 1968), in the caiman *C. latirostis* (Peyreton,
& Dusan-Peyreton, 1969), and in the turtle *E. orbicularis*
(Vasilescu, 1970).
        Other studies have also shown behavioral sleep with EEG
anomalies in reptiles. Flanigan's work suggests that the
waking-sleep continuum of the caiman *C. sclerops* (Flanigan,

Wilcox, & Rechtschaffen, 1973), the turtles *Geochelone carbonaria* (Flanigan, Knight, Hartse, & Rechtschaffen, 1974), and *Terrapene carolina* (Flanigan, 1974a), and of the lizards *I. iguana* and *C. pectinata* (Flanigan, 1974b) is associated with four characteristic postures: 1) head, neck, and body elevated and supported by all four limbs; eyes open and immediate response to stimulation (active waking); 2) body resting on the floor, eyes usually open and less responsive (quiet waking); 3) head resting on the floor, eyes usually closed, and one to three limbs extended backward and positioned against body/tail, and 4) eyes closed, the four limbs extended backward and positioned against body/tail, while the behavioral arousal threshold is substantially elevated, since a certain degree of handling is necessary before arousal. Cardiac and respiratory frequencies decrease progressively from posture one to posture four. According to these authors, postures three and four (stereotypic posture, immobility, increased response threshold and rapid state reversibility) denote behavioral sleep in reptiles. From posture one to four there is a slight diminution of EEG frequency and amplitude in the caiman *(C. sclerops)* and the turtles *(T. carolina* and *G. carbonaria),* while there is a remarkable decrease in amplitude in the lizard *(C. pectinata).* The presence of high voltage sharp waves and/or monophasic and polyphasic spikes is the major polygraphic change associated with sleep behavior (postures 3 and 4) in these animals. This EEG activity has been associated with PGO spikes observed in the mammalian visual system during REM sleep (Flanigan, et al., 1973). However, since atropine sulphate, a central cholinergic antagonist which induces slow waves in mammals (Bradley, 1968), also increases spikes in the turtle *G. carbonaria,* an analogy between reptilian spikes and slow wave sleep in mammals has been suggested (Hartse, & Rechtschaffen, 1974). The presence of REM sleep in reptiles as reported by Tauber et al. (1968) was not confirmed in Flanigan's studies. This author did not find a relationship between the electrographic data of eye movements and the direct observation of the eyeballs during postures 3 and 4 in the reptiles studied.

If the electrophysiological and behavioral characteristics of sleep in the present day reptiles were represented in the primitive reptiles, it is possible that in these animals primitive mechanisms for sleep were already present. In support of these considerations we might assume that SWS and REM sleep in birds and therian mammals arose later as a result of these primitive sleep mechanisms.

Sleep in Amphibians

Sleep studies in amphibians are scanty. Segura and
de Juan (1966) described an alpha-like rhythm and an increase
in amplitude and frequency during light stimulation in
toads *(Bufo arenarum)* during spring and summer. Hobson (1967)
questioned the existence of sleep in the bullfrog *(Rana
catesbiana)*. However, he identified periods of nocturnal
activity and diurnal inactivity in three species of tree frogs
of genus *Hyla* (Hobson, Gow, & Goin, 1967). During the
inactivity or torpid state they showed an increase in arousal
threshold and he suggested the presence of a sleeping state.

Ultradian activity-inactivity cycles without significant
EEG changes have been described in the tiger salamander
by Lucas, Stermann, & McGinty (1969). Moreover, these authors
suggested that these behavioral features are the precursors
of SWS in mammals. In regard to the sleep state in amphibians,
Tauber (1974) stated that "Behavioral and electrographic
criteria referable to active (paradoxical) sleep present no
challenge since both the frogs and the salamander do not
reveal it. Whether one can define a sleep state despite
the absence of slow waves (even though such electrical
patterns are not to be expected in the amphibian brain) is
an open question."

Sleep in Fishes

The physiological correlates of a possible sleep state
in fishes have been summarized by Tauber (1974). Generally
speaking, fishes adopt a quiet, or resting, posture on the
sand of the sea. Some have a tendency to hide among the
irregularities of the sea field, while others merely rotate
their eye balls hiding their pupils. It has been mentioned
that a few minutes of stimulation is required to arouse fishes.
Some species of sharks which have eyelids and sleep during
the day in rock crevices, are awakened only by vigorous
shaking of their tails by divers. Other sea species (sharks,
tunas, mackerels, arowina, swordfish, sturgeons) are perpetual
swimmers and probably swim while asleep.

It has been observed that gill movements per minutes
show a striking decrease during rest, 70-80 to 56 ± 3 in the
Sparisoma aurofrenatum (Tauber, Weitzmann, & Korey, 1969).
From the behavioral point of view, the state of inactivity
in several species of diurnal foveate reef fish of the
Bermuda Islands (Tauber, et al., 1969) is characterized by
prolonged diminution of their motor activity; decrease and

irregularity of respiratory rhythm (gill movements); increase in the arousal threshold (tolerance to handling, color change), and at least two to four rapid eye movements within each 30 sec for several hours. In tenches *(Tinca tinca)*, afoveate fishes, neither EEG changes nor eye movements were found while inactive (Peyrethon, & Dusan-Peyrethon, 1967). This data does not allow generalizations about activity-inactivity or the wake-sleep cycle in this class of vertebrates in view of the great number of species and the great variety of habits present (Schnitzlein, 1964).

In summary, two sleep states, EEG and behaviorally defined SWS and REM sleep , occur in mammals (except in the echidna which does not show REM sleep) and in birds. Apparently, reptiles present SWS, but the existence of REM sleep is still controversial. At present, we are not completely aware of the sleep features of amphibians and fishes. Complete ethological studies are necessary in order to be able to reach conclusions as to the features and the mechanisms of sleep in these later species.

During the first stages of mammal ontogenetic development, most of the time is spent in REM sleep. Later, depending on species, the adult sleep-wake cycle develops with the presence of SWS and a greater percentage of wakefulness (Jouvet-Mounier, Astic, & Lacote, 1970). Considering the doubtful presence of REM sleep in lower classes of animals like fishes and amphibians and its existence in most mammals, it is obvious that the sleep-wake cycle does not follow Heackel's hypothesis according to which ontogeny is a recapitulation of phylogeny.

In order to explain the phylogenetic differences in sleep, several theories have been put forth. A relationship has been suggested between the presence of both sleep phases and the body capacity for thermoregulation (Allison, & Van Twyver, 1970b). Another theory has suggested that the development of the two phases of sleep are related to the development of foveate vision and binocular coordinated eye movements (Tauber, 1974). A third theory has suggested a relationship in terms of whether animals are prey or predators (Allison, & Van Twyver, 1970b).

Phylogeny of Memory

Another possible way of explaining species differences in sleep may be by looking at its phylogenetic relationship with other forms of behavior. If we look at sleep and memory processes such a relationship seems to emerge. Using simple tasks and comparing retention times, Beritashvilli

(1972) has studied the phylogeny of image memory in different species. He measured the time between the presentation of a single visual perception of food and the release of the animal to search for it, and found the time interval for recall of food searching increased significantly as he went up the phylogenetic scale. For example, maximum recall time was 8-10 sec in fishes *(Carassius auratus);* 40-90 sec in amphibians (sumer frogs); 2-2.5 min in reptiles (turtles *Emys orbitalaris* and *E. caspies);* 3-5 min in birds (hens and pigeons); 20-30 min in mammals (cats and dogs), and days to months in primates *(Papio hamadryas).* In these animals, if the perception of food was aided by olfactory, gustatory, vestibular, and proprioceptive cues, retention times were longer (1-2 min for amphibians; 3-3.5 min for reptiles; 8-10 min for birds and days or months for higher mammals). By simple daily observation, it is known that man, the highest primate, has plastic retention mechanisms which overcome the temporal level of years in situations as simple as those established in the above mentioned species.

Furthermore, it is well established experimentally that higher mammals have the brain mechanisms for long term memory (John, 1967). However, it seems that fishes and amphibians have only short term memory, and it is uncertain that reptiles have long term memory since only some turtles were able to repeat a conditioned reflex after a lapse of 30-45 days (Beritashvilli, 1972).

An Attempt at Integration

The data presented on sleep and memory in different species of vertebrates is certainly far from complete. However, in an attempt at integration, an evolutionary parallelism between sleep states and plastic retention capacity seems to emerge (see Figure 1). The simultaneous existence of REM sleep and longer retention times, and thus long term memory, seems to appear first in birds.

On the other hand, fishes and amphibians, in which the presence of REM sleep has not been established, have very short retention times (in the order of seconds). As far as reptiles are concerned, they have an intermediate position regarding both sleep and memory. They do not seem to have long term memory. However, SWS remains at a level of definitive organization, and the presence of REM is controversial.

Comparative anatomy has shown a direct relationship between morphological complexity and the advances in

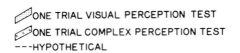

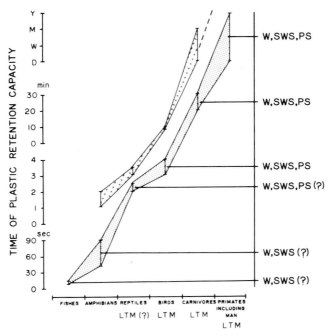

Figure 1. This graph summarizes Beritashvilli's data on retention times for various species, and attempts to correlate this with the phases of sleep. It should be noted that lower animals such as fishes and amphibians have very short retention times, thus perhaps absence of long term memory (LTM), while they also present a definite absence of REM sleep is still controversial. From birds on, LTM and REM sleep are well establihsed phenomena. The important thing to note in this graph is that the phylogenetic threshold for the appearance of LTM and REM seems to coincide in the reptiles. This coincidence may further suggest a role of REM in LTM mechanisms. W (right), waking; D, days; W (left), weeks; M, months; Y, years.

behavioral patterns throughout evolution. For example, the degree of cortical development is different from the simple vertebrates to man (Diamon, & Hall, 1969). Moreover, Broughton (1972) has suggested differences in the structures which are supposedly involved in sleep in different species of animals.

In addition, there is an increase in the number of experiments that point toward the participation of proteins in memory mechanisms (Uphouse, Macinnes, & Schlesinger, 1974) and in sleep (Pegram, Hammond, & Bridgers, 1973; Drucker-Colín, Spanis, Hunyadi, Sassin, & McGaugh, 1975). There even exists experimental evidence of a direct relationship between REM sleep and the consolidation processes (Lucero, 1970; Fishbein, Kastaniotis, & Chattman, 1974; also Bloch, this volume). The incorporation of these findings to the considerations on phylogeny of sleep and memory allows us to anticipate the following tentative interpretation: it is possible that the mechanisms of macromolecular synthesis determine, through phylogenetic evolution, a relationship between sleep and memory phenomena.

REFERENCES

Adams, P. M., & Barratt, E. S. Nocturnal sleep in squirrel monkeys. *Electroencephalography and Clinical Neurophysiology*, 1974, *36*, 201-204.

Allison, T., & Van Twyver, H. Sleep in the moles, *Scalopus aquaticus* and *Condylura cristata*. *Experimental Neurology*, 1970a, *27*, 564-578.

Allison, T., & Van Twyver, H. Evolution of sleep. *Natural History*, 1970b, *79*, 56-65.

Allison, T., Van Twyver, H., & Goff, W. R. Electrophysiological studies of the echidna *Tachyglossus aculeatus*. I. Waking and sleep. *Archives Italiennes de Biologie*, 1972, *110*, 145-184.

Astic, L., & Royet, J. P. Sommeil chez le rat-kangourou, *Potorus apicalis*. Etude chez l'adulte et chez le jeune un mois avant la sortie definitive du marsupium. Effects du sevrage. *Electroencephalography and Clinical Neurophysiology*, 1974, *37*, 483-489.

Beritashvilli, I. S.   Phylogeny of memory development in
    vertebrates. In Karczmar, A. G. & Eccles, J. E. (Eds.),
    Brain and Human Behavior. New York: Springer Verlag,
    1972.

Bert, J.   Similitudes et differences du sommeil chez deux
    babouins, *Papio hamadryas* et *Papio papio*. *Electro-
    encephalography and Clinical Neurophysiology*, 1973, *35*,
    209-212.

Bert, J., Kripke, D. F., & Rhopes, J. M.   Electroencephalo-
    gram of the mature chimpanzee: 24-hour recordings.
    Electroencephalography and Clinical Neurophysiology,
    1970, *28*, 368-373.

Bock, W. J.   The origin and radiation of birds. *Annals of
    the New York Academy of Sciences*, 1969, *167*, 147-155
    (Art. 1).

Bradley, P. B.   The effect of atropine and related drugs on
    the EEG and behavior. *Progress in Brain Research*,
    1968, *28*, 3-13.

Broughton, R.   Phylogenetic evolution of sleep studies.   In
    Chase, M. (Ed.), *The Sleeping Brain*. Los Angeles,
    California: Brain Information Service, 1972.

Dallaire, A., & Ruckenbusch, Y.   Rest-activity cycle and
    sleep patterns in captive foxes *(Vulpes vulpes)*.
    Experientia, 1974, *30*, 59-60.

Diamon, I. T., & Hall, W. C.   Evolution of neocortex. *Science*,
    1969, *164*, 251-262.

Drucker-Colin, R. R., Spanis, C. W., Hunyadi, J. F., Sassin,
    J. F., & McGaugh, J. L.   Growth hormone effects on
    sleep and wakefulness in the rat. *Neuroendocrinology*,
    1975, *18*, 1-8.

Evarts, E. V.   Activity of neurons in visual cortex of cat
    during sleep with low voltage fast activity. *Journal
    of Neurophysiology*, 1962, *25*, 812-816.

Fishbein, W., Kastaniotis, C., & Chattman, D.   Paradoxical
    sleep: prolonged augmentation following learning.
    Brain Research, 1974, *79*, 61-75.

Flanigan, W. F., Jr.   Sleep and wakefulness in chelonian
    reptiles.   II.   The red-footed tortoise, *Geochelone
    carbonaria*.   *Archives Italiennes de Biologie*, 1974a, *112*,
    253-277.

Flanigan, W. F., Jr.   Sleep and wakefulness in iguanid
    lizards, *Ctenosaura pectinata* and *Iguana iguana*.   *Brain,
    Behavior and Evolution*, 1974b, *8*, 401-436.

Flanigan, W. F., Jr., Wilcox, R. H., & Rechtschaffen, A.   The
    EEG and behavioral continuum of the crocodilian,
    Caiman sclerops.   *Electroencephalography and Clinical
    Neurophysiology*, 1973, *34*, 521-538.

Flanigan, W. F., Jr., Knight, C. P., Hartse, K. M., &
    Rechtschaffen, A.   Sleep and wakefulness in chelonian
    reptiles.   I.   The box turtle, *Terrapene carolina*.
    Archives Italiennes de Biologie, 1974, *112*, 225-252.

Hartse, K. M., & Rechtschaffen, A.   Effect of atropine
    sulfate on the sleep-related EEG spike activity of the
    tortoise, *Geochelone carbonaria*.   *Brain, Behavior and
    Evolution*, 1974, *9*, 81-94.

Hermann, H., Jouvet, M. & Klein, M.   Analyse polygraphique
    du sommeil de la tortue.   *Academie des Sciences, Paris,
    Comptes Rendus Hebdomadaires des Seances*, 1964, *258*, 2175-2178.

Hernández-Peón, R., O'Flaherty, J. J., & Mazzuchelli-
    O'Flaherty, A. L.   Sleep and other behavioral effects
    induced by acetylcholinic stimulation of basal temporal
    cortex and striate structure.   *Brain Research*, 1967, *4*,
    243-267.

Hishikawa, Y., Cramer, H., & Kuhlo, W.   Natural and melatonin-
    induced sleep in young chickens.   A behavioral and
    electrographic study.   *Experimental Brain Research*,
    1969, *7*, 84-94.

Hobson, J. A.   Electrographic correlates of behavior in the
    frog with special reference to sleep.   *Electroencephalo-
    graphy and Clinical Neurophysiology*, 1967, *22*, 113-121.

Hobson, J. A., Gow, O. B., & Goin, C. J.   Electrographic
    correlates of behavior in tree frogs.   *Nature*, 1968, *220*,
    386-387.

Hoffmeister, V. F. Elektroenzephalogramm und verhalten von
    kaninchen im physiologischen und medikamentosen schlaf.
    Arzneim-Fortschritte (Drug Research), 1972, *22*, 88–93.

Hopson, J. A. The origin and adaptive radiation of mammal-
    like reptiles and nontherian mammals. *Annals of the New
    York Academy of Science* (Art. 1), 1969, *167*, 199–216.

Huttenlocher, P. R. Evoked and spontaneous activity in
    single units of medial brain stem during natural sleep
    and waking. *Journal of Neurophysiology*, 1961, *24*,
    451–468.

John, E. R. *Mechanisms of Memory*. New York: Academic
    Press, 1967.

Jouvet, M. Neurophysiology of the states of sleep. *Physio-
    logical Review*, 1967, *47*, 117–177.

Jouvet-Mounier, D., Astic, L., & Lacote, D. Ontogenesis of
    the states of sleep in rat, cat and guinea pig during
    the first post-natal month. *Developmental Psychobiology*,
    1970, *2*, 216–239.

Karadzić, V., Kovacević, R., & Momirov, D. Sleep in the
    owl (*Strix aluco*, Strigidae). In Koella, W. P. (Ed.),
    *Sleep: Physiology, Biochemistry, Psychology, Pharma-
    cology, Clinical Implications*. Basel: Karger, 1973.

Klein, M., Michel, F., & Jouvet, M. Etude polygraphique du
    sommeil chez les oiseaux. *Comptes Rendus des Seances de
    Biologie* (Paris), 1964, *158*, 99–103.

Kleitman, N. *Sleep and Wakefulness*. Chicago and London:
    University of Chicago Press, 1963.

Kripke, D. F., Reite, M. L., Pegram, G. F., Stephens, L. M.,
    & Lewis, O. F. Nocturnal sleep in rhesus monkeys.
    Electroencephalography and Clinical Neurophysiology,
    1968, *24*, 582–586.

Lucas, E. A., Powell, E. W., & Murphree, O. D. Hippocampal
    theta in nervous pointer dogs. *Physiology and Behavior*,
    1974, *12*, 609–613.

Lucas, E. A., & Sterman, M. R.   The polycyclic sleep-wake cycle in the cat: effects produced by sensorimotor rhythm conditioning.   *Experimental Neurology*, 1974, *42*, 347-368.

Lucas, E., Sterman, M. B., & McGinty, D. J.   The salamander EEG: a model of primitive sleep and wakefulness.   *Psychophysiology*, 1969, *6*, 230.

Lucero, M.   Lengthening of REM sleep duration consecutive to learning in the rat.   *Brain Research*, 1970, *20*, 319-322.

Michel, F., Klein, M., Jouvet, D., & Valatax, J. L.   Etude polygraphique du sommeil chez le rat.   *Comptes Rendus des Seances de la Societe de Biologie (Paris)*, 1961, *155*, 2389-2392.

Pegram, V., Hammond, D., & Bridgers, W.   The effects of protein synthesis inhibition on sleep in mice.   *Behavioral Biology*, 1973, *9*, 377-382.

Peyrethon, J., & Dusan-Peyrethon, D.   Etude polygraphique du cycle veille sommeil d'un teleosteen *(Tinca tinca)*.   *Comptes Rendus des Seances de la Societe de Biologie (Paris)*, 1967, *161*, 2533-2537.

Peyrethon, J., & Dusan-Peyrethon, D.   Etude polygraphique du cycle veille sommeil chez trois genres de reptiles.   *Comptes Rendus des Seances de la Societe de Biologie (Paris)*, 1969, *163*, 181-186.

Ridgway, S. H., Harrison, R. J., & Joyce, P. L.   Sleep and cardiac rhythm in the gray seal.   *Science*, 1975, *187*, 553-555.

Rojas-Ramírez, J. A., & Tauber, E. S.   Paradoxical sleep in two species of avian predators (falconiformes).   *Science*, 1970, *167*, 1754-1755.

Roldan, E., Weiss, T., & Fifkova, E.   Excitability changes during the sleep cycle of the rat.   *Electroencephalography and Clinical Neurophysiology*, 1963, *15*, 775-785.

Romer, A. S.   *The Vertebrate Body*.   Philadelphia, Pa.:   W. B. Saunders Co., 1970.

Ruckenbusch, Y.   Activite corticale au cours du sommeil chez la chevre. *Comptes Rendus des Seances de la Societe de Biologie (Paris)*, 1962, *156*, 867-870.

Ruckenbusch, Y.   Effects de l'Autan sur les etats de veille et de sommeil chez les animaux domestiques. *Comptes Rendus du 96e Congrés National des Societes Savantes, Toulouse, 1971, Sciences*. Paris: Bibliotheque Nationale, 1974.

Ruckenbusch, Y.   Sleep deprivation in cattle. *Brain Research*, 1974, *78*, 495-499.

Ruckenbusch, Y., Dougherty, R. W., & Cook, H. M.   Jaw movements and rumen motility as criteria for measurement of deep sleep in cattle. *American Journal of Veterinary Research*, 1974, *35*, 1309-1312.

Schnitzlein, H. N.   Correlation of habit and structure in the fish brain. *American Zoologist*, 1964, *4*, 21-32.

Segura, E. T., & De Juan, A.   Electroencephalographic studies in toads. *Electroencephalography and Clinical Neurophysiology*, 1966, *21*,   373-380.

Sterman, M. B., Knauss, T., Lehmann, D., & Clemente, C. D.   Circadian sleep and waking patterns in the laboratory cat. *Electroencephalography and Clinical Neurophysiology*, 1965, *19*, 509-517.

Susic, V. T., & Kovacevic, R. M.   Sleep patterns in the owl, *Strix alauco*. *Physiology and Behavior*, 1973, *11*, 313-317.

Tauber, E. S.   Phylogeny of sleep.   In Weitzman, E. D. (Ed.), *Advances in Sleep Research, Vol. 1*.   New York: Spectrum Publications, Inc., 1974.

Tauber, E. S., Roffwarg, H. P., & Weitzman, E. D.   Eye movements and electroencephalogram activity during sleep in diurnal lizards. *Nature*, 1966, *212*, 1612-1613.

Tauber, E. S., Rojas-Ramírez, J. A., & Hernández-Peón, R.   Electrophysiological and behavioral correlates of wakefulness and sleep in the lizard, *Ctenosaura pectinata*. *Electroencephalography and Clinical Neurophysiology*, 1968, *24*, 424-443.

Tauber, E. S., Weitzman, E. D., & Korey, S. R.   Eye movements
    during behavioral inactivity in certain bermuda reef
    fish. *Communications in Behavioral Biology, Part A,*
    1969, *3,* 131-135.

Timo-Iaria, C., Negrao, N., Schmidek, W. P., Hoshino, K.,
    Lobato de Menezes, C. E., & Leme da Rocha, T.   Phases
    and states of sleep in the rat. *Physiology and Behavior,*
    1970, *5,* 1057-1062.

Tradardi, V.   Sleep in the pigeon. *Archives Italiennes de
    Biologie,* 1966, *104,* 516-521.

Uphouse, L. L., Macinnes, J. W., & Schlesinger, K.   Role of
    RNA and protein in memory storage: a review. *Behavior
    Genetics,* 1974, *4,* 29-81.

Ursin, R.   The two stages of slow wave sleep in the cat and
    their relation to REM sleep. *Brain Research,* 1968, *11,*
    347-356.

Van Twyver, H.   Sleep patterns of five rodent species.
    Physiology and Behavior, 1969, *4,* 901-906.

Van Twyver, H., & Allison, T.   Sleep in the opossum, *Didelphis
    marsupialis*. *Electroencephalography and Clinical
    Neurophysiology,* 1970, *29,* 181-189.

Van Twyver, H., & Allison, T.   A polygraphic and behavioral
    study of sleep in the pigeon, *Columbia livia*. *Experi-
    mental Neurology,* 1972, *35,* 138-153.

Van Twyver, H., & Allison, T.   Sleep in the armadillo,
    Dasypus novemcinctus at moderate and low ambient
    temperatures. *Brain, Behavior and Evolution,* 1974,
    9, 107-120.

Vasilescu, E.   Sleep and wakefulness in the tortoise, *Emys
    orbicularis*. *Revue Roubaine de Biologie Serie des
    Zoologie,* 1970, *15,* 177-179.

Webb, W. B., & Agnew, H. W., Jr.   Sleep stage characteristics
    of long and short sleepers. *Science,* 1970, *168,* 146-147.

Weiss, T., & Roldan, E.   Comparative study of sleep cycles
    in rodents. *Experientia,* 1964, *20,* 280-281.

Weitzman, E. D., Kripke, D. F., Pollak, C., & Dominguez, J.
    Cyclic activity in sleep of *Macaca mulatta*. *Archives
    of Neurology (Clinical)*, 1965, *12*, 463-467.

THE ACTIVITY OF NEURONAL NETWORKS
IN MEMORY CONSOLIDATION

MARCEL VERZEANO

*Department of Psychobiology
University of California
Irvine, California 92717 USA*

The concept that "reverberating circuits" may be implicated in the consolidation phase of learning was proposed,
some years ago, by Hilgard and Marquis (1940) and by Hebb
(1949) who suggested that the neural representation of the
events to be memorized may be maintained, by reverberation,
in the appropriate neural networks, until a permanent trace
has been established. This concept remained purely theoretical for many years since the anatomical and physiological
evidence for the existence of such reverberating circuits
remained in doubt and since no mechanism could be found which
might carry the information to be stored around the proposed
loops.

The experimental demonstration that neuronal impulses
actually circulate in the networks of the cortex and of the
thalamus was not made until the mid-fifties when it was shown
that impulses do not, simply, "reverberate" along circular
loops but that they form complex matrices, moving in a highly
organized fashion, in complicated, multi-lane, thalamic and
cortical pathways. Further work indicated that the circulating activity is modified by incoming sensory information.
This led to the suggestion, by this writer, that the circulating matrices may serve as carriers which, "modulated" by
incoming information, could transport the neural representation of the events to be stored, over the networks in which
it would ultimately be retained (Verzeano, Laufer, Spear,
& McDonald, 1970).

THE BASIC EXPERIMENTAL FINDINGS

The experimental findings which led to the development of the present theory are the circulation of neuronal activity and its modification by incoming sensory information. The evidence which indicates that neuronal activity circulates through thalamic and cortical networks has accumulated, from several sources, during the last two decades (Verzeano & Calma, 1954; Verzeano, 1956, 1963, 1972, 1973; Verzeano & Negishi, 1960, 1961; Verzeano, Laufer, Spear, & McDonald, 1965; Verzeano et al., 1970; Mescherskii, 1961; Andersen, Andersson, & Lømo, 1966; Andersen & Andersson, 1968; Petsche & Sterc, 1968; Petsche & Rappelsberger, 1970). The pertinent facts will be briefly mentioned here.

Distribution and Conditions of Occurrence

The circulation of activity can be recorded by means of arrays of microelectrodes, from all the regions of the cerebral cortex and from all the thalamic nuclei, in the states of relaxed wakefulness and "slow-wave" sleep. It is closely associated, in time and in phase, with the trains of rhythmic waves known to electroencephalographers as "spindles" (Figures 1 & 2). The activity circulates at velocities varying from 0.5 to 9 mm/sec, along a series of loops of diameters of 0.1 to 0.2 mm whose "locus" shifts continually, through the neuronal network (Verzeano & Nigishi, 1959, 1961).

Interactions with Incoming Sensory Information

The pathways of circulation and the territorial distribution of excitation and inhibition through the network are greatly modified by incoming sensory information (Verzeano & Negishi, 1960; Negishi & Verzeano, 1961; Dill, Vallecalle, & Verzeano, 1968; Verzeano, 1970). Specific changes in the characteristics of the sensory stimuli (such as frequency or intensity) cause specific changes in the patterns of circulating activity (Figure 3).

The existence of these processes is well established but the fundamental mechanisms on which they are based are not entirely known and, therefore, will be discussed with the theoretical considerations.

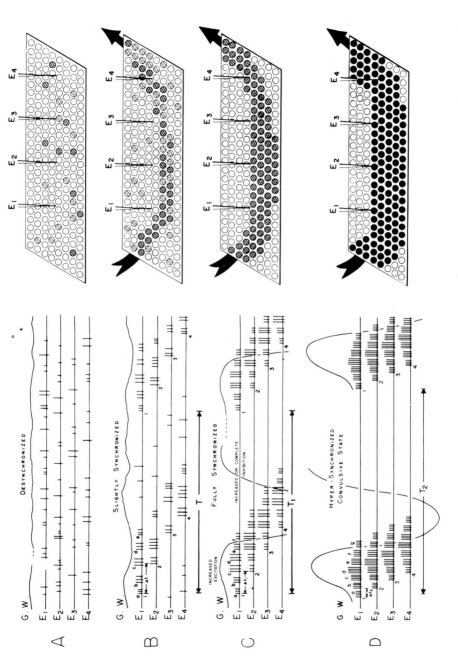

Fig. 1

Fig. 1.   Relations between neuronal discharge, circulation of neuronal activity, and synchronization of the gross waves, as they appear when recorded simultaneously by four microelectrodes with tips separated by 100 to 150 μ.   Left: Diagrammatic representation of oscilloscope tracings, showing the progressive changes which take place from the desynchronized to the hypersynchronized state.   Right: Diagrammatic two-dimensional representation of neuronal networks, showing the neuronal activity corresponding to each successive state. E_1, E_2, E_3, E_4 represent the microelectrodes through which oscilloscope tracing E_1, E_2, E_3, E_4 (at left) would be obtained, the circles represent neurons in the territory surveyed by the microelectrodes; the degree of darkness in each circle represents the degree of excitation of that particular neuron; the arrow represents the direction of the circulation of the neuronal activity.   A: Oscilloscope: infrequent clustering of spikes, no circulation of neuronal activity, no synchronization of gross waves.   Neuronal network: scattered, sporadic neuronal activity, at low level of excitation; no circulation of neuronal activity.   B: Oscilloscope: increased clustering of spikes; occurrence of neuronal activity in regular succession at each one of the tips of the microelectrodes, indicating circulation through the neuronal network; decreased activity in the interval between successive passages of circulating activity through the network; gross waves slightly synchronized.   Neuronal network: neuronal activity at higher level of excitation, concentrated mostly in the pathway of circulation (arrow); decreased activity outside this pathway.   C: Oscilloscope: high degree of clustering of spikes; increase in the velocity of circulating activity ($\Delta t_1 < \Delta t$); activity abolished in an increased interval between successive passages of circulating activity through the network; gross waves fully synchronized.   Neuronal network: neuronal activity at high level of excitation in the pathway of circulation; no activity outside the pathway.   D: Oscilloscope: extreme degree of clustering spikes; high velocity of circulation ($\Delta t_2 < \Delta t_1$); further increase in the interval between successive passages of circulating activity through the network; neuronal activity in this interval abolished; hypersynchronized gross waves of high amplitude.   Neuronal network: neuronal activity at very high level of excitation concentrated exclusively in an enlarged, multilane pathway of circulation; completely outside this pathway.

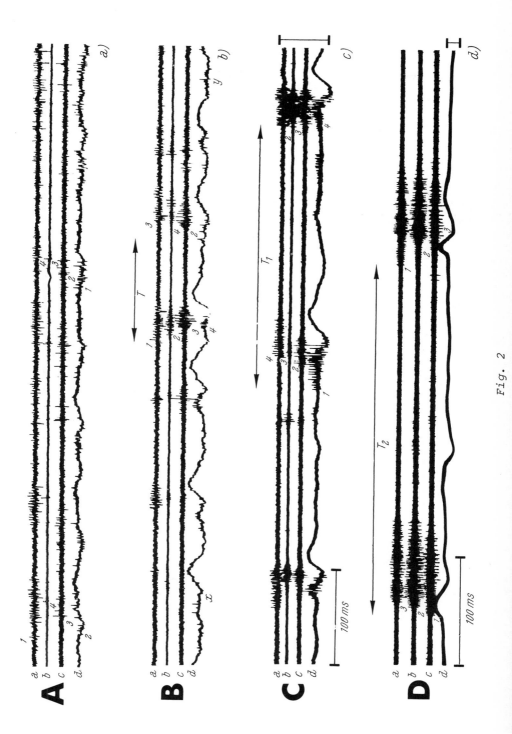

Fig. 2

79

Fig. 2. Actual experimental findings corresponding to the diagrammatic representation of Figure 1. Relations between neuronal discharge, circulation of neuronal activity, and synchronization of gross waves, in thalamic neuronal networks, shown by recordings obtained, simultaneously, with four microelectrodes (a,b,c,d). Channels a, b, and c show neuronal action potentials; channel d shows action potentials as well as gross waves.

A) Recordings obtained from n. ventralis medialis of the waking cat under gallamine. B) Another section of the same recording as in A, in which some "synchronization" of the gross waves occurs in wakefulness (x to y) and in which clustering of neuronal action potentials and circulation of neuronal activity can be seen (at 1-2-3-4), in association with the gross waves. C) Recordings obtained from the same animal in the same experiment, with the same array of micro-electrodes at the same thalamic location, in sleep induced by sodium pentobarbital; the increase in the synchronization of the gross waves is accompanied by an increase in the clus-tering of neuronal action potentials, an increase in the regularity of the circulation of neuronal activity (at 1-2-3-4), an increase in the number of neurons involved, and an increase in the duration of the period of silence (T$_1$) between successive passages of circulating activity through the network. D) Recordings obtained, in the "hypersynchro-nized" preconvulsive state, from another animal, under gallamine, 15 minutes after the administration of 0.9 mg/kg of picrotoxin. The clustering of neuronal action potentials is very marked, the circulation of neuronal activity is highly regular (1-2-3), a large number of neurons is involved in it, and the period of silence between successive passages of activity (T$_2$) through the network is much longer. These changes correspond to a great increase in the amplitude of the gross waves. The time line and amplitude calibration (0.5 mV) under C apply to A, B and C; the time line and amplitude calibration (0.5 mV) under D apply only to D. Distances between the microelectrodes: In A), B), and C): ab = 120μ; bc = 100μ; cd = 155μ; in D) ab = 50μ; bc = 80μ; cd = 90μ; microelectrode d in D) shows only gross waves. Negative up in all tracings.

Note the frequent reversals in the direction of circula-tion (at 1-2-3-4); in B) (from a-b-c-d to d-c-b-a); in C) and D) (from d-c-b-a to a-b-c-d). (From Verzeano, 1972).

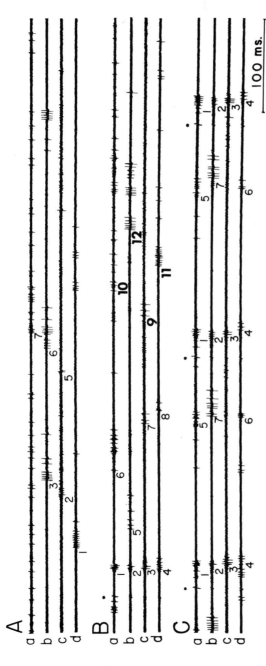

Fig. 3. Interactions between spontaneous circulating activity and incoming sensory information in the lateral geniculate body of the cat, recorded with four microelectrodes (a,b,c,d) displayed along a straight line. A: The circulating activity involves, at first, neurons at the tips of microelectrodes d, c and b (1,2,3) after which it moves to the tips of c, b and a (5,6,7). B: Visual stimulation with one brief flash of light (black dot) is followed by a volley of impulses representing the primary response (at 1,2,3,4 and 5,6,7,8), followed by a later discharge (9,10,11,12). The order in which neurons become active has been completely changed by the incoming information. C: Visual stimulation with repetitive flashes (black dots) cause a new change in the order in which neurons become active. Microelectrode diameters: a = 5μ; b = 2μ; c = 3μ; d = 4μ. Distances between tips: a to b = 156μ; b to c = 160μ; c to d = 156μ. Recordings obtained 1 hour and 20 minutes after the administration of pentobarbital, 6 mg/kg. (From Negishi & Verzeano, 1961).

THE THEORETICAL APPROACH

The theoretical structure to be developed on the basis of these findings should propose A) a mechanism by which the circulation of activity is generated; B) a mechanism by which the incoming sensory information is superimposed upon the circulating activity to form a modulated neuronal matrix; and C) a mechanism by which the modulated matrix is transported over the appropriate networks during a sufficient period for consolidation to be achieved.

Generation of Circulating Activity

Since the circulation of activity is so closely related to the development of thalamic and cortical spindles the question arises whether one and the same mechanism may be responsible for both processes. It has been proposed that the development of thalamic spindles is due to the accumulation of inhibitory postsynaptic potentials summating on the thalamic neurons by means of recurrent feedback loops (Andersen & Eccles, 1962; Andersen & Andersson, 1968) or by alternating summations of excitatory and inhibitory potentials, maintained through complex neuronal interactions (Purpura & Cohen, 1962; Purpura, 1970). While these hypotheses may explain the basic rhythmicity of the thalamic spindles, they do not fully account for all the phenomena involved in its development and in its relations with the circulating activity, such as the long periods of silence between spindles or the displacement of the circulating matrix through neuronal network (Figures 1, 2, & 6).

A more inclusive hypothesis would consider the circulation of neuronal activity and the development of thalamic rhythmicity as parts of one and the same process, whose development would include summation of postsynaptic potentials, the inhibitory action through recurrent collaterals, as well as feedback activities developing over longer intrathalamic and cortico-thalamic feedback loops (Figure 4). Similar mechanisms, based on similar feedback processes, recurrent as well as direct, may give rise to the circulating activity and the rhythmic waves in the cortex (Verzeano et al., 1965, 1970).

Modulation of the Circulating Matrix

The modulation of the circulating matrix by the incoming sensory information requires the creation of a pattern of excited and inhibited neurons corresponding to the

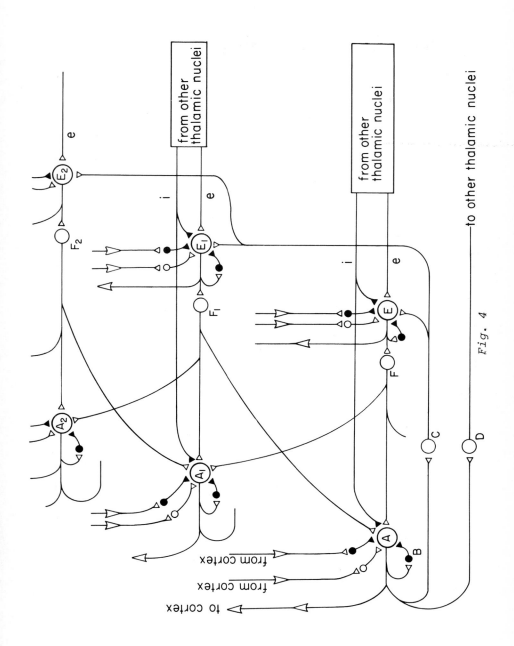

from other thalamic nuclei

from other thalamic nuclei

to other thalamic nuclei

to cortex

from cortex

from cortex

Fig. 4

Fig. 4. Proposed mechanism for the generation of circulating activity in thalamic nuclei. Large circles: principal neurons; medium and small circles; interneurons. Light circles and light triangles: excitatory neurons and excitatory synapses; black circles and black triangles: inhibitory neurons and inhibitory synapses.

Neuron A discharges, activates interneurons B, C and D and sends impulses to the cortex; interneuron B, activated by a recurrent collateral causes the early inhibition of neuron A; interneuron C activates neurons E, E_1, E_2 each of which, via interneurons such as F, F_1, and F_2, activates several neurons such as A_1, A_2, etc., thereby accelerating the circulation process. After discharging and activating neurons A_1, A_2, etc., neurons E, E_1, E_2 are inhibited via their recurrent collaterals; interneuron D, transmits the activity to another thalamic nucleus where similar processes take place. From other thalamic nuclei as well as from the cortex, excitatory and inhibitory fibers (e,i) carry inhibitory and excitatory impulses responsible for the late and prolonged inhibitory phases and for the reactivation of the process.

characteristics of the sensory stimulus. The operations required for the development of such a pattern would occur at the level of the sensory receiving network, as illustrated in Figure 5.

Transport of the Modulated Matrix

The transport of the modulated matrix to other sections of the network would be achieved under the direction of a scanning and control mechanism possibly located in the non-specific nuclei of the thalamus, as illustrated in Figure 5.

CORROBORATIVE DATA

In addition to the basic experimental findings which led, initially, to the development of the theory, other experimental data give support to some of its aspects.

A. Each "sweep" of circulating activity through the network involves several types of neurons (Figure 6). These may represent the different types of primary neurons and interneurons required for the transfer of patterns of sensory information from the receiving network to other sets of neurons in the control network and the circulating matrix.

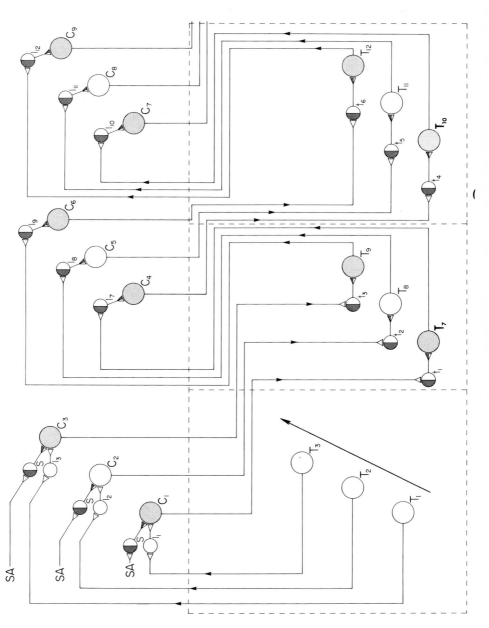

Fig. 5

85

Fig. 5. Proposed mechanism for the formation of a modulated circulating matrix. The upper part of the picture (above the horizontal dotted line) represents cortical sensory receiving and other networks. The lower part represents thalamic networks. Large circles represent principal neurons, small circles represent interneurons.

Impulses arriving through the sensory pathways over specific afferents (SA) activate specific interneurons (S), which can be excitatory or inhibitory (as shown by the light/ dark circles and light/dark synaptic terminals). These inter- neurons impose a pattern of activity on the principal neurons, which corresponds to the characteristics of the sensory stimulus. In this highly simplified diagram, this pattern is represented by the levels of activity in neurons C_1, C_2, C_3.

Neurons T_1, T_2 and T_3 belong to a thalamic network which generates circulating impulses (arrow), as indicated in Figure 4. These impulses, transmitted to the cortex, activate non-specific interneurons I_1, I_2, I_3 whose output sweeps over neurons C_1, C_2, C_3 and "scans" their state (the pattern of activity which corresponds to the peripheral stimulus) causing them to discharge at a rate related to their level of excita- tion, and to activate, via interneurons t_1, t_2, t_3, thalamic neurons T_7, T_8, T_9. These thalamic neurons, in turn, activate, via interneurons I_7, I_8, I_9, another group of cortical neurons, C_4, C_5, C_6, and reproduce, in this cortical network, their own pattern of activity. Thus the original pattern of activity C_1, C_2, C_3, engendered by the sensory stimulus, has been transported, under thalamic control and by means of circulating matrices, from one group of cortical neurons to another. By a similar mechanism, involving thalamic neurons T_{10}, T_{11}, T_{12}, the pattern of activity is further transported to cortical network C_7, C_8, C_9 and to other cortical networks over which the activity may have to circulate during the process of consolidation.

B.   While the control of the rhythmic cortical activity by the thalamus is well established, the concept that infor- mation may be fed back from the cortex to the thalamus via cortico-thalamic pathways has generated a great deal of con- troversy for over three decades. The reason for the contro- versy is that some investigators (Adrian, 1941; Morison & Basset, 1945) have shown that thalamic activity is not modi- fied by removal of the cortex, while others have shown that it is (Verzeano, Lindsley, & Magoun, 1953; Velasco & Lindsley, 1965; Velasco, Skinner, Asaro, & Lindsley, 1968). At the present time, however, anatomical and physiological evidence

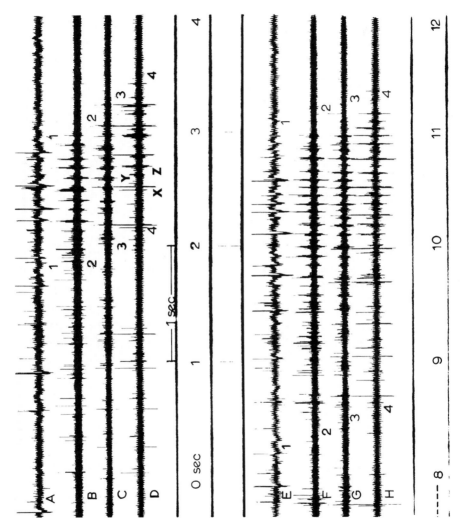

Fig. 6

87

*Fig. 6.   Circulation of activity in the nucleus
ventralis anterior of the squirrel monkey in light natural
sleep. Recordings obtained, simultaneously, with four microelectrodes (A,B,C,D), with tips displayed along a straight
line. Microelectrode A recorded neuronal action potentials
as well as slow waves; microelectrodes B, C and D recorded
only action potentials. The first part of the recording
(between time 0 and time 3.5 seconds) represents the development of one spindle (which can be seen on channel A); after a
period of complete silence (between time 3.5 and time 8
seconds) another spindle develops (between time 8 and time
11.5 seconds). During the passage of activity through the
network (1,2,3,4), different groups of neurons are sequentially
activated (such as X,Y,Z). Distance between the tips of the
microelectrodes: 170μ.*

is accumulating which indicates that feedback from the cortex
to the thalamus does, definitely, occur and that it may be an
important mechanism in the regulation of thalamocortical
rhythmicity (Scheibel & Scheibel, 1967; Kalil & Chase, 1970;
Frigyesi, 1972; Kusske, 1976). Thus, the pathways and
processes required for the transmission of information from
the receiving networks in the cortex to the control network
in the thalamus seem to be available.

     C. The interaction between thalamic nuclei in the
process of triggering the cortical activity has also been
clearly demonstrated (Verzeano et al., 1965, 1970). This
interaction could be involved in the transfer of patterns of
neuronal activity representing sensory information from one
cortical network to another, by receiving this pattern from
the cortex, moving it to another thalamic location and trans-
mitting it back to the next cortical area to be occupied by
the circulating matrix.

     D. Incoming sensory information modifies the circulating
activity according to the characteristics of the stimulus; the
modification thus imposed upon the pattern of circulation
remains the same as long as the stimulus remains unchanged
(Figure 7). Such consistency in the relation between the
stimulus and the changes which it imposes upon the circulating
matrix, is required if the process is going to carry information, unaltered, over the various neuronal networks.

     The extent to which patterns of neuronal response
engendered by incoming sensory information may be carried,
unaltered, from one network to another and the extent to
which this process is related to learning, has been shown by
John and Morgades who have found that, in animals trained to

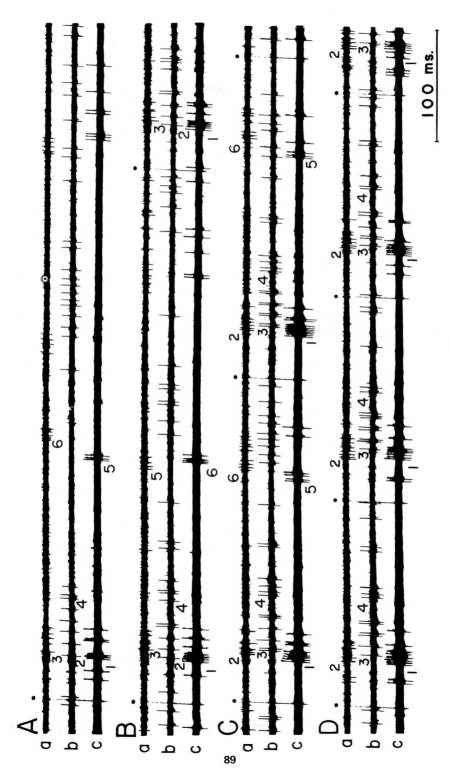

Fig. 7

Fig. 7. Circulation of activity modified by the frequency of the sensory stimulus (black dot). Recordings obtained with three microelectrodes (a,b,c) from single neurons in the visual cortex of the waking cat, under Gallamine. The order (1,2,3, etc.) in which neurons become active, their frequency of discharge, the periods of excitation and inhibition, vary with the frequency of stimulation. A specific pattern of circulation of activity corresponds to a specific frequency of stimulation and once this pattern is established it remains the same as long as the frequency of stimulation remains the same (From Negishi & Verzeano, 1961).

discriminate between light flashes of different frequencies the correct responses were associated with neuronal discharge of great similarity in the lateral geniculate body and the dorsal hippocampus (Figure 8).

E. It is well known that the administration of Metrazol enhances consolidation (Krivanek & McGaugh, 1968). It should be expected that it should also enhance the circulation of activity. Experiments in which the circulation of activity is recorded before and after the administration of Metrazol indicate that this is actually the case (Figure 9).

Several questions arise when behavioral data are taken into account. When does consolidation take place? In wakefulness? In "slow-wave" sleep? In "paradoxical" sleep? Does the circulation of activity occur during states in which consolidation also occurs? Does it last long enough for consolidation to take place? Does the circulation of activity, with its carrier matrices, develop in regions of the brain implicated in the consolidation process?

On the basis of present day knowledge, the answers to these questions give considerable support to the view that the circulation of activity may, indeed, constitute the basis of the consolidation process:

1) Consolidation does occur during wakefulness. So does the circulation of activity.

2) Consolidation requires from several seconds to several minutes or more to be completed. The circulation of activity goes on indefinitely as long as the animal remains in a state of relaxed wakefulness. This would provide sufficient time for the appropriate patterns of neuronal activity to be transported repeatedly over the appropriate networks.

3) During the state of wakefulness, the circulation of activity occurs in the sensory regions of the cortex and the sensory relay nuclei, where sensory information is

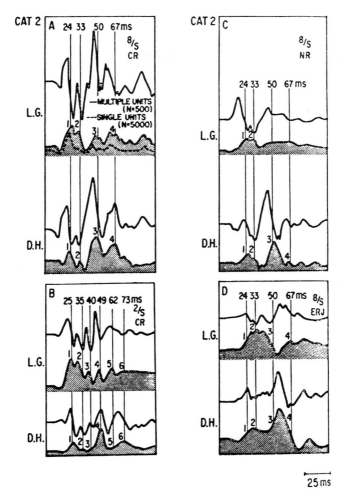

Fig. 8. (A) Average evoked responses (solid curves) and post-stimulus histograms (shaded areas) simultaneously recorded from microelectrodes in the lateral geniculate body on the left side (L.G.) and the dorsal hippocampus on the right side (D.H.) during correct performance (CR) to a 8-cps CS by Cat II. Numbered vertical lines indicate components considered to correspond with respect to relative latency. These and all other responses illustrated in this figure computed from 500 stimulus presentations, except for the post-stimulus histogram derived from a single unit in LG, shown as a dotted line (N-5000). (Note the correspondence between the curve describing the probability of firing of this single neuron observed over a long period of time and the

*post-stimulus histogram for the neural ensemble observed for
one-tenth that time.) B) Average evoked responses and post-
stimulus histograms simultaneously recorded from LG and DH
during correct performance (CR) to a differential 2-cps CS.
C) Average evoked responses and post-stimulus histograms
simultaneously recorded from LG and DH during presentation of
the 8-cps CS which resulted in no behavioral performance (NR).
D) Average evoked responses and post-stimulus histograms
simultaneously recorded from LG and DH during presentation of
a novel stimulus illuminated by the 8-cps flicker (ERJ).
(From John & Morgades, 1969).*

received over the sensory pathways, as well as in the "non-
specific" nuclei of the thalamus, where the principal control
of thalamo-cortical rhythmicity may reside (Verzeano &
Negishi, 1961; Verzeano et al., 1965, 1970).

   According to recent findings (see Bloch, this volume),
consolidation does not occur during slow wave sleep but during
"paradoxical" sleep. It is believed that during paradoxical
sleep, the cortical and thalamic activities are "desynchronized" and that circulation of activity does not occur in those
regions. How can consolidation develop during paradoxical
sleep if the circulating matrices do not develop during that
phase? The answer may be that, during paradoxical sleep, the
circulation of activity may occur in other regions of the
brain involved in the process of consolidation during that
state. It is well known that the hippocampus is involved in
memory processes (Adey, Dunlap, & Hendrix, 1960; Olds &
Hirano, 1969; Landfield, 1976; Thompson, 1976) and recent
findings suggest that events which occur during the development of the theta rhythm may be particularly important in this
respect (Landfield, 1976a,b). Investigations recently conducted
in this laboratory have shown that circulation of neuronal
activity may occur in the hippocampus and that it may be
related to the development of the theta rhythm. It is,
therefore, possible that, during paradoxical sleep, the circulation of activity associated with the theta rhythm may play
a role in the consolidation process, similar to that played
by the circulation of activity in the cortex and in the
thalamus during wakefulness.

   Similar mechanisms have been, recently, proposed by other
authors, as a possible basis for short term memory; some of
them implicate both action potentials and gross waves, with
the formation of holographic or interference patterns
(Pribram, 1974; Landfield, 1976). Other theories are based
on the phase shifting of the activities of the elements of

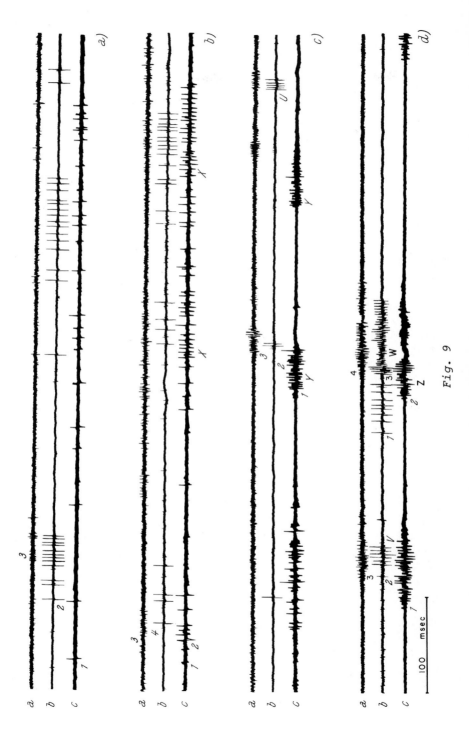

Fig. 9

100 msec

93

Fig. 9. The action of metrazol on patterns of neuronal discharge and of circulation of neuronal activity in the thalamus. Recording obtained from the n. centralis lateralis of the cat, with three microelectrodes (a = 2μ; b = 3μ; c = 4μ) displayed along a straight line. Distances between tips: a to b = 120μ; b to c = 130μ; a) control record before the administration of metrazol; b) after metrazol 4 mg/kg; c) and d) after additional doses of 8 mg/kg. Increased rates of neuronal discharge can be seen at u,v,w,x,y, and z; increased rate at which neurons are activated can be seen at v,w,y, and z; increased regularity in circulation of neuronal activity can be seen (at 1-2-3) in c) and d). (From Negishi, Bravo, & Verzeano, 1963).

neuronal networks with respect to each other (Schneider, 1975). All these models require the existence of a means for transporting the information to be stored from one region of a network to another, or from one network to another. The only physiological mechanism which may function in this capacity and whose existence and interaction with incoming information have been experimentally verified is the circulation of neuronal activity. It is, therefore, important that this mechanism be further investigated, more particularly in relation to the storage of information.

REFERENCES

Adey, W. R., Dunlop, C. W., & Hendrix, C. E. Hippocampal slow waves. Distribution and phase relationships in the course of approach learning. *Archives Neurology,* 1960, *3,* 74-90.

Adrian, E. D. Afferent discharges to the cerebral cortex from peripheral sense organs. *Journal of Physiology (London),* 1941, *100,* 159-191.

Andersen, P., & Andersson, S. A. *Physiological Basis of the Alpha Rhythm.* New York: Appleton, 1968.

Andersen, P., Andersson, S. A., & Lømo, T. Patterns of spontaneous rhythmic activity within various thalamic nuclei. *Nature,* 1966, *211,* 888-889.

Andersen, P., & Eccles, J. C. Inhibitory phasing of neuronal discharge. *Nautre* (London), 1962, *196,* 645-647.

Dill, R. C., Vallecalle, E., & Verzeano, M.   Evoked potentials, neuronal activity and stimulus intensity in the visual system. *Physiology and Behavior,* 1968, *3,* 797-801.

Frigyesi, T. L.   Intracellular recordings from neurons in dorsolateral thalamic reticular nucleus during capsular, basal ganglia and midline thalamic stimulation. *Brain Research,* 1972, *48,* 157-172.

Hebb, D. O.   *The Organization of Behavior.* New York: Wiley, 1949.

Hilgard, E. R., & Marquis, D. G.   *Conditioning and Learning.* New York: Appleton, 1940.

John, E. R., & Morgades, P. P.   The pattern and distributions of evoked potentials and multiple unit activity elicited by conditioned stimuli in trained cats. *Communications in Behavioral Biology* (Part A), 1969, *3,* 181-207.

Kalil, R., & Chase, R.   Corticofugal influence on activity of lateral geniculate neurons in the cat. *Journal of Neurophysiology,* 1970, *33,* 459-474.

Krivanek, J., & McGaugh, J. L.   Effects of pentylenetetrazol on memory storage in mice. *Psychopharmacologia,* 1968, *12,* 303-321.

Kusske, J. A.   Interactions between thalamus and cortex in experimental epilepsy in the cat. *Experimental Neurology,* 1976, *50,* 568-578.

Landfield, P. W.   Synchronous EEG rhythms: Their nature and their possible functions in memory, information transmission and behavior.   In W. H. Gispen (Ed.), *Molecular and Functional Neurobiology.* Amsterdam: Elsevier, 1976a.

Landfield, P. W.   Different effects of posttrial driving or blocking of the theta rhythm on avoidance learning in rats.   In press, 1976b.

Mescherskii, R. M.   The vectorgraphical characteristics of spontaneous rabbit brain cortex activity. *Sechenov Physiological Journal of the USSR* (English translation), 1961, *47,* 419-526.

Verzeano, M.   Activity of cerebral neurons in the transition from wakefulness to sleep. *Science,* 1956, *124,* 366-367.

Verzeano, M.   The synchronization of brain waves. *Acta Neurologica Latinoamericana,* 1963, *9,* 297-307.

Verzeano, M.   Pacemakers, synchronization, and epilepsy.   In H. Petsche & M. Brazier (Eds.), *Synchronization of EEG Activity in Epilepsies.* Vienna: Springer, 1972.

Verzeano, M.   The study of neuronal networks in the mammalian brain.   In R. F. Thompson & M. Patterson, (Eds.), *Bioelectric Recording Techniques* (Part A). New York: Academic Press, 1973.

Verzeano, M., & Calma, I.   Unit activity in spindle bursts. *Journal of Neurophysiology,* 1954, *17,* 417-428.

Verzeano, M., Laufer, M., Spear, P., & McDonald, S.   The activity of neural networks in the thalamus of the monkey. *Actualites Neurophysiologiques,* 1965, *6,* 223-252.

Verzeano, M., Laufer, M., Spear, P., & McDonald, S.   The activity of neuronal networks in the thalamus of the monkey.   In K. H. Pribram & D. E. Broadbent (Eds.), *Biology of Memory.* New York: Academic Press, 1970.

Verzeano, M., Lindsley, D. B., & Magoun, H. W.   Nature of recruiting response. *Journal of Neurophysiology,* 1953, *16,* 183-195.

Verzeano, M., & Negishi, K.   Neuronal activity and state of consciousness. *Proceedings of International Congress of Physiology* (August, 1959, Buenos Aires).   1959.

Verzeano, M., & Negishi, K.   Neuronal activity in cortical and thalamic networks. A study with multiple micro-electrodes. *Journal of General Physiology* (supplement), 1960, *43,* 177-195.

Verzeano, M., & Negishi, K.   Neuronal activity in wakefulness and in sleep.   In G. E. W. Wolstenholme & M. O'Connor (Eds.), *The Nature of Sleep* (Ciba Symposium).   London: Churchill, 1961.

Morison, R. S., & Basset, D. L.   Electrical activity of the
    thalamus and basal ganglia in decorticate cats. *Journal
    of Neurophysiology,* 1945, *8,* 309-314.

Negishi, K., & Verzeano, M.   Recordings with multiple micro-
    electrodes from the lateral geniculate body and the visual
    cortex of the cat.   In R. Jung & H. Kornhuber (Eds.),
    The Visual System: Neurophysiology and Psychophysics.
    Berlin: Springer, 1961.

Olds, J., & Hirano, T.   Conditioned responses of hippocampal
    and other neurons. *Electroencephalography and clinical
    Neurophysiology,* 1969, *26,* 159-166.

Petsche, J., & Rappelsberger, P.   Influence of cortical
    incisions upon synchronization pattern and travelling
    waves. *Electroencephalography and clinical Neuro-
    physiology,* 1970, *28,* 592-600.

Petsche, H., & Serc. J.   The significance of the cortex for
    the travelling phenomenon of brain waves. *Electro-
    encephalography and clinical Neurophysiology,* 1968,
    25, 11-22.

Pribram, K. H.   *Languages of the Brain.*   Englewood, N.J.:
    Prentice-Hall, 1974.

Purpura, D. P.   Intracellular studies of synaptic organization
    in the mammalian brain.   In G. D. Pappas & D. P. Purpura
    (Eds.), *Structure and Function of Synapses.*   New York:
    Raven Press, 1972.

Purpura, D. P., & Cohen, B.   Intracellular recording from
    thalamic neurons during recruiting responses. *Journal
    of Neurophysiology,* 1962, *25,* 621-635.

Schiebel, M. E., & Schiebel, A. B.   Structural organization
    of nonspecific thalamic nuclei and their projection
    toward cortex. *Brain Research,* 1967, *6,* 60-94.

Thompson, R. F.   Neural substrate of classical conditioning
    in the hippocampus. *Science,* 1976, *192,* 483-485.

Velasco, M., & Lindsley, D. B.   Role of orbital cortex in
    regulation of thalamocortical electrical activity.
    Science, 1965, *145,* 1375-1377.

THE INVESTIGATION OF THE ROLE OF SEROTONIN IN MAMMALIAN BEHAVIOR

BARRY L. JACOBS, SARAH S. MOSKO and MICHAEL E. TRULSON

Department of Psychology
Princeton University
Princeton, New Jersey 08540 USA

Experiments in the mid-1950's revealed that relatively
large quantities of serotonin (5-hydroxytryptamine) are
localized within the mammalian central nervous system (CNS)
(e.g., Twarog, & Page, 1953). In the twenty years since
that time an impressive body of evidence has been accumulated
to indicate that serotonin is utilized as a neurotransmitter
in the CNS. Following the seminal research of the Swedish
group in the 1960's, in which serotonin was found to be
localized almost exclusively within neurons of the brainstem
raphe nuclei and their axon terminals (Dahlstrom, & Fuxe,
1964; Fuxe, 1965), there has been an explosion in research
on the role of serotonin in the CNS.

Although serotonin has been implicated in a wide variety
of behavioral and physiological processes, our understanding
of many basic aspects of the functional characteristics of
this transmitter system can at best be described as primitive,
with many glaring gaps in our knowledge. To cite a few prime
examples: we know nothing about the afferents to the various
raphe nuclei, and little about the efferents from the specific
nuclei which comprise the raphe complex; it is not clear
whether the entire raphe-serotonin system works in concert,
or whether the component nuclei subserve separate functions;
we know little about the endogenous and exogenous factors
which regulate the activity of raphe neurons (except for the
contribution made by Aghajanian and his colleagues concerning
the effects of serotonin precursors and agonists on these
cells); unlike the catecholamines, we do not have a model
system which allows us to study the functional activity of

serotonin-mediated synapses. Because these and many other
issues concerning the dynamics of brain serotonin remain
unanswered, we feel that it may be somewhat premature to
speculate on the role of serotonin in complex behavioral
processes such as sleep and memory. This is especially
true when we consider that the behavior under study in most
experiments is treated as a unidimensional phenomenon, i.e.,
only the "amount" of the behavior manifested is examined.
One only has to look at the abundance of studies which
measure increases or decreases in sexual behavior, aggression,
sleep, etc., following manipulations of CNS serotonin. It
is almost tautological that every CNS neurotransmitter plays
some essential physiological or behavioral role, and it is,
therefore, not surprising that any drastic perturbation of a
transmitter results in a dramatic shift along the "amount of
behavior" continuum. Two basic issues, therefore, confront us:
specification of the specific aspect of the behavioral process
that is affected by the serotonin manipulation; and the
determination of whether the behavioral changes observed
following the manipulation of serotonin are primary outcomes,
or merely secondary or tertiary reflections of changes
in orthogonal behavioral or physiological processes.

    Because of these conceptual problems and the lack of
data in many of the important research areas relevant to
the raphe-serotonin system, we began a series of multidisciplinary experiments aimed at these issues. This chapter
reviews the past literature and our published and unpublished
research in the following four areas: raphe anatomy,
especially the afferent and efferent connections of the component nuclei; behavioral and regional neurochemical effects of
lesions specific to individual raphe nuclei; factors which
influence the electrophysiological (single unit) activity of
raphe neurons; and the usefulness of a model system in the
study of serotonin's synaptic activity in the CNS. Finally,
we present an integrative model which attempts to interrelate
raphe unit acitvity, the hallucinogenic properties of various
indole compounds, and the behavioral effects of serotonergic
manipulations. The biochemical, pharmacological, clinical,
and behavioral aspects of serotonin not covered here are
well reviewed in several recent publications (Barchas, &
Usdin, 1973; Chase, & Murphy, 1973; Costa, Gessa, &
Sandler, 1974a, 1974b).

*Serotonin-Containing Neurons: Localization, Efferent and
Afferent Connections*

　　Perhaps the most basic information necessary for understanding the behavioral and physiological role of CNS serotonin
is the anatomy of this neurochemical system. Fortunately,
through the application of the Falck-Hillarp technique of
fluorescence histochemistry, the basic structure of this
system has been delineated. On the basis of morphological
and topographical considerations, Dahlstrom and Fuxe (1964)
described nine serotonin-containing cell groups (B_1-B_9) in
the rat, localized exclusively within the lower brainstem,
from the medulla oblongata through the caudal mesencephalon.
The vast majority of serotonergic neurons are confined to the
nuclei of the midline raphe complex, and the total number of
serotonergic neurons in the three midbrain groups (B_7 -B_9)
exceeds those in the medulla-pons (B_1-B_6).
　　Neurons of the different raphe nuclei are morphologically
or cytoarchitectonically heterogeneous (Dahlstrom, & Fuxe, 1964;
Taber, Brodal, & Walberg, 1960), a reflection, perhaps, of
functional differentiation. It has recently been shown that
two nuclei of the raphe of the cat have a distinct organization
and vascular associations which set them apart from other raphe
nuclei (Scheibel, Tomiyasu, & Scheibel, 1975). These two
nuclei, raphe pontis and linearis rostralis, are paired and
organized along blood vessels which flank the midline. Because
their dendrites form plexes which appear intimately related to
vascular walls, it has been suggested that these neurons may
monitor blood flow or pressure, or serve chemosensory or
neurosecretory functions. In contrast to such structural
differences among subgroups of serotonin-containing neurons,
available data suggest that striking similarities exist
across species in the basic architecture of serotonergic
neurons. The distribution of serotonin-containing cell groups
in the cat and man, as revealed by fluorescence histochemistry
(Pin, Jones, & Jouvet, 1968; Olson, Boréus, & Seiger, 1973),
is similar to that in the rat. Furthermore, on the basis
of organizational similarities of the raphe complex in the
cat, rabbit and man, and the presence of raphe nuclei in
lower vertebrates, Taber et al. (1960) proposed that the raphe
nuclei have undergone "little differentiation during the
phylogenetic ascent of the vertebrates" and might be ascribed
"simple but fundamental and important tasks in the function
of the brain."
　　Relatively detailed serotonergic pathways have been traced
in the rat utilizing lesions, transections, and pharmacological

manipulations in conjunction with the fluorescence histochemical technique. Essentially all levels of the CNS are innervated by serotonergic fibers. The most caudal serotonin-containing cell groups (B_1-B_3) give rise to bulbospinal serotonergic systems which descend in the lateral and ventral funiculae, synapsing in the dorsal, intermediate and ventral horns (Dahlstrom, & Fuxe, 1965). In contrast, ascending serotonergic fibers to the di- and telencephalon originate chiefly in the most rostral cell groups (B_7-B_9) located in the caudal midbrain. Their axons sweep ventrally toward the n. interpeduncularis, bend rostrally, and run uncrossed in the median forebrain bundle (Anden, Dahlstrom, Fuxe, Larsson, Olson, & Ungerstedt, 1966b; Fuxe, 1965; Ungerstedt, 1971a). Anatomical sub-divisions of the ascending pathways have been made which describe a lateral pathway innervating primarily cortical areas and a medial sub-cortical pathway which supplies primarily the hypothalamus and preoptic area (Fuxe, & Jonsson, 1974). Recent evidence indicates that fibers from pontine cell groups (B_5-B_6) also contribute to the ascending serotonin system (Bjorklund, Nobin, & Stenevi, 1973) and travel in the more medial pathway (Fuxe, & Jonsson, 1974). Apart from these ascending and descending pathways, many structures of the lower brainstem contain serotonergic terminals, although the source nuclei of these inputs remains largely unknown.

      Little is known of the discrete localization and relative density of serotonergic innervation of various brain structures, as well as the relative contributions made by individual serotonergic cell groups to specific projection sites. However, studies based on fluorescent terminal mapping, auto-radiographic mapping and regional serotonin assay, undertaken primarily in the rat, indicate that the basal ganglia, certain regions of the amygdaloid complex, hypothalamus, septum and hippocampus, and several other structures of the midbrain and diencephalon each receive prominent serotonergic innerva-tion (Conrad, Leonard, & Pfaff, 1974; Aghajanian, Kuhar, & Roth, 1973; Dahlstrom, Haggendal, & Atack, 1973; Fuxe, 1965). The n. suprachiasmaticus, n. linearis caudalis and ventral lateral geniculate contain particularly high concentrations of serotonin terminals (Aghajanian et al., 1973), while the cerebellum is poorly innervated.

      In an attempt to differentiate the relative contributions made by the mesencephalic cell groups B_7 and B_8 (corresponding to the dorsal and median raphe nuclei) to various forebrain structures, we have compared the depletion of serotonin in four forebrain structures resulting from selective lesions of these two cell groups in the rat (Jacobs, Wise, & Taylor,

1974b). Our data indicate that lesions of dorsalis or
medianus were about equally effective in significantly
reducing cortical (30-40%) and hypothalamic levels (approximately 50%) 5 days post-lesion. Hippocampal serotonin content,
however, declined markedly (by 82%) following lesions restricted
to medianus, while lesions of dorsalis resulted in only a nonsignificant decline in hippocampal serotonin. By contrast,
dorsal raphe lesions produced a significantly greater depletion
of striatal serotonin than median lesions. These findings
have been confirmed by other investigators (Lorens, & Guldberg,
1974), and provide the first anatomical evidence for a
functional separation of these two cell groups. More recently,
this same differential pattern of dorsal and median raphe
projections has been found in the cat in studies utilizing
autoradiographic techniques (Bobillier, Petitjean, Salvert,
Ligier, & Seguin, 1975).

The greatest deficit in our current understanding of the
anatomy of the serotonin system pertains to afferents. The
early work of Brodal, Walberg, & Taber (1960) utilizing
silver stains for degeneration described projections from the
cerebral cortex, cerebellum and spinal cord to the various
raphe nuclei of the cat. They found that some of the more
caudal nuclei, in particular, received fibers from one or
more of these structures. However, since this work predated
the development of fluorescence histochemistry, it is not
clear how well the neurons in their studies correspond to
actual serotonin-containing neurons. In addition, this
study provided almost no information regarding afferents
to the more rostral raphe nuclei which are the major
source of forebrain serotonin. In the rat, catecholamine
terminals have been described in contact with several
fluorescent serotonin cell groups of the bulbar, pontine and
mesencephalic raphe nuclei (Fuxe, 1965), and evidence
suggests that at least some of these may derive from the
norepinephrine-containing neurons of the locus coeruleus
(Loizou, 1969).

This gap in our understanding of central serotonin
systems, especially as regards the more rostral cell groups,
prompted us to apply a newer method for the tracing of CNS
pathways in an effort to shed some light on the problem of
afferents. Since the enzyme horseradish peroxidase (HRP)
is taken up by axon terminals and transported in a retrograde
direction (LaVail, & LaVail, 1972), accumulation of HRP in
cell bodies distal to an injection site can provide evidence
for a projection from these cells to neurons at the site of
injection. Therefore, we injected varying amounts of HRP
(9-33% solutions in saline or phosphate buffer, pH 6.2,

0.1-0.5 µl) into the region of the dorsal raphe nucleus of
thirty adult rats (Mosko, Haubrich, & Jacobs, 1976). A small
group of cells in the dorsal aspect of the median raphe nucleus
was frequently filled with HRP-positive granules in animals
sacrificed 1-3 days later (Figure 1, left panel). In addition,
small injections placed particularly in the ventromedial
portion of the dorsal raphe consistently resulted in heavy
labelling of the cells in the more dorsal and lateral parts
of this nucleus (Figure 1, right panel). These data indicate
that cells of the dorsal raphe may receive inputs from
neighboring dorsal raphe cells as well as from cells in the
dorsal most part of the median raphe nucleus. The fact that
yellow fluorescent varicosities have been described within
the midbrain raphe (Aghajanian, & Haigler, 1973) and the
demonstration of ^{3}H-5HT uptake into nerve endings in the
midbrain central gray (Aghajanian, & Bloom, 1967) lends
support to this interpretation. Occasionally, an accumulation
of HRP-positive granules was also noted within cells of
the n. linearis caudalis and scattered regions of the
mesencephalic reticular formation. Although no other brain
areas were ever clearly labelled, it should be emphasized
that due to potential inherent weaknesses of the technique
(see Nauta, Pritz, & Lasek, 1974 for a discussion), negative
findings should not be taken as evidence against the existence
of projections to the dorsal raphe nucleus from more distal
brain sites.

Behavioral Effects of Dorsal or Median Raphe Nucleus Lesions

     As described above, virtually all CNS serotonin is
contained within neurons whose cell bodies lie within the
various raphe nuclei. From this site of origin within the
brainstem, many of these neurons send their axons out to
form synapses at sites as distant as the anterior forebrain
and lower spinal cord. The expansiveness of this system
and the diversity of its projection sites raises the interesting question of whether it functions as a unified system
working in concert, or whether its constituent nuclei subserve
distinct functions.
     Prior to the studies described in this section, no attempt
had been made to assess the separate contributions of the
raphe nuclei either to behavior or to the various forebrain
structures innervated by serotonergic neurons. Therefore,
the *de facto* notion has arisen that *whole brain* serotonin is
involved in the physiological processes in which serotonin
has been implicated. This wholistic idea is further perpetu-
ated by lesion studies which involve the destruction of more

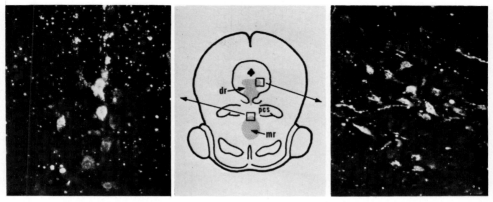

*Figure 1. Left panel: Darkfield illumination photo-
micrograph of cells in the median raphe nucleus filled with
HRP-positive granules following an HRP injection restricted
to the dorsal raphe nucleus. A few densely filled cells
are interspersed among unlabelled cells of the median nucleus
which have been counterstained with safranin-orange. Right
panel: Scattered HRP-positive cells of the dorsolateral
wing of the dorsal raphe nucleus following a localized HRP
injection into the ventromedial portion of the nucleus.
Abbreviations: dr - dorsal raphe nucleus; mr - median raphe
nucleus.*

than one specific raphe nucleus, and by pharmacological
studies in which serotonin is uniformly depleted throughout
the CNS. The present series of studies was initiated in
an attempt to differentiate the behavioral and neurochemical
effects of lesions specific to either of the two midbrain raphe
nuclei, dorsalis and medianus. These two nuclei are of
particular interest since the preponderance of forebrain
serotonin is found within the axon terminals emanating from
them.

Electrolytic lesions, confined almost exclusively to the
target nucleus, were placed in either the dorsal or median
raphe nucleus of adult male rats (Figure 2 and 3). The
differential neurochemical effects of these two lesions are
described above. In a variety of tests, the behavioral effects
of the two lesions were dramatically dichotomous.

When these lesions were placed in animals that were
chronically housed in center-balanced tilt cages, median lesions
produced an immediate 3-4 fold increase in activity which
gradually stabilized, over the next 2-3 days, at a level
approximately 100% above baseline (Figure 4) (Jacobs et al.,

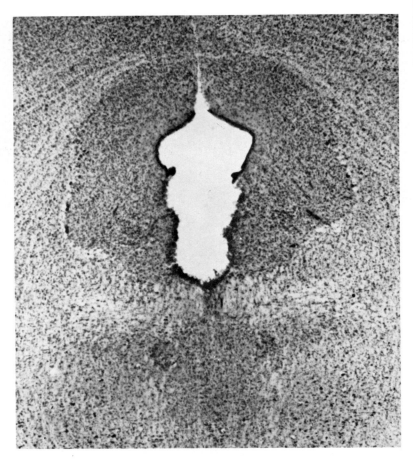

*Figure 2. Photomicrograph of a 50 µ thick cresyl violet
stained section showing an electrolytic lesion of the dorsal
raphe nucleus of the rat. The lesion is somewhat irregular
in shape due to the fact that it is the composite of three
smaller lesions (160 µA for 20 sec) in this plane. In
order to confine the lesion as much as possible to the
dorsal nucleus, six such "mini-lesions" were placed in the
nucleus by means of insulated etch-tipped microelectrodes.*

1974b). This hyperactivity persists for at least three
months. By contrast with this chronic and subtantial hyperactivity, lesions of the dorsal nucleus produced a short-
lasting depression of activity, followed by a gradual return
to baseline levels. Sham lesions of the brachium conjunctivum,
which courses between the dorsal and median nuclei, each

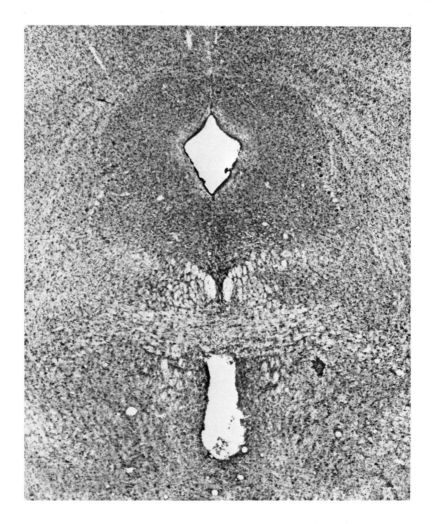

Figure 3. Photomicrograph of an electrolytic lesion of the median raphe nucleus. This lesion is a composite of four smaller lesions in this plane (see caption of Figure 2 for further details).

produced activity changes nearly identical to that following lesions of the dorsal raphe (Figure 4).

   In another series of experiments, we found that median lesions markedly potentiate the increase in tilt cage locomotor activity observed in animals administered varying doses of d-amphetamine sulfate (0.5 - 2.0 mg/kg) or scopolamine (0.125 or 0.250 mg/kg). By contrast, dorsalis

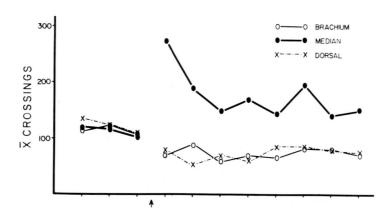

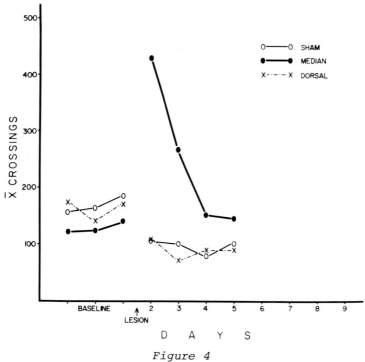

Figure 4

Figure 4. Top: Mean daily group activity for three
baseline days and eight post-lesion days (2 through 9) for
brachium conjunctivum, median, and dorsal lesioned animals.
Since some animals died as a result of the lesion, the
number of animals declined from baseline to day 9 post-lesion;
brachium (from 10 to 9); median (from 11 to 7); dorsal (from
11 to 8). Bottom: Mean daily group activity for 3 baseline
days and 4 post-lesion days (2 through 5) for sham, median
and dorsal lesioned animals. None of the animals died during
this experiment: sham (n = 4); median (n = 7); dorsal (n = 8).
Reprinted by permission of Elsevier Publishing Co., Amsterdam,
The Netherlands, from a paper by B. L. Jacobs, W. D. Wise,
and K. M. Taylor. Brain Research, 1974, 79, 353-361.

lesioned animals show no greater increase in activity in
response to these drugs than do sham lesioned control
animals (Jacobs, Wise, & Taylor, 1975b).

Since the most striking neurochemical correlate of the
median lesion was the almost total depletion of hippocampal
serotonin, we reasoned that the hyperactivity seen in these
animals might be specifically attributable to the loss of
serotonin in this structure. In an attempt to test this
hypothesis directly, we aspirated the dorsal hippocampus of
adult male rats, and following a one month recovery period
electrolytic lesions were placed in the median nucleus
(Jacobs, Trimbach, Eubanks, & Trulson), 1975a). Control
animals received either no initial lesion or aspiration of
the cortex overlying the dorsal hippocampus, followed one
month later by median raphe lesions. In unlesioned or
cortical lesioned animals, median lesions produced an
approximately four-fold increase in locomotor activity, similar to that described above. However, the median lesion was
ineffective in elevating the activity of the hippocampectomized animals. Similarly, dorsal hippocampectomy blocked the
large hyperactivity that normally follows the systemic
administration of p-chlorophenylalanine (PCPA) (400 mg/kg i.p.),
whereas the typical drug effect was observed in unlesioned or
cortical lesioned animals. Thus, both the median lesion- and
PCPA-induced hyperactivity appear to be mediated by the
depletion of hippocampal serotonin.

Examination of behavior in an open field revealed a
similar pattern of results (Jacobs, & Cohen, 1976). Following
median lesions there was a 100% increase in open filed
activity (the number of squares crossed) which was sustained
for at least three months. By contrast, dorsal and sham
lesioned animals both showed decreased post-operative activity

which gradually returned to baseline. The open field behavior
of the median animals was distinctly different from that of
either the dorsal or sham animals in several additional ways.
Median rats frequently entered non-perimeter squares of the
field whereas rats in the other two groups did so very infrequently, if ever. Median rats would "dart" from corner
to corner of the open field, running with their heads held
level, and would rear almost exclusively in corners. Animals
in the other two groups would more cautiously move from
corner to corner, sniffing and rearing on the way. Basically,
dorsal and sham animals seemed more fearful than median animals.
For example, if a loud click was presented, dorsal animals
would freeze, crouch and defecate, while median animals would
show a brief orienting response and quickly resume locomoting
through the open field.

        In the final series of experiments, we examined the
effects of the two lesions on footshock-elicited aggression
(Jacobs, & Cohen, 1976). In contrast to the obvious prediction
that the more active median animals would show a post-
operative increase in the number of "bouts" of aggression,
this was true only of the dorsal animals. Following a one-
week post-lesion recovery period, pairs of dorsal lesioned
animals showed an 83% increase, relative to the pre-operative
level, in the number of bouts occurring during a two minute
test period (2.1 ma footshocks of 0.5 sec duration were
presented every three seconds). This effect does not appear
to be due to lowered pain thresholds in these animals. By
contrast, animals in the median and sham groups displayed
approximately the same number of bouts post-operatively as
pre-operatively.

        Thus, the behavioral effects of midbrain raphe lesions
are differentiable on the basis of the specific nuclei
destroyed. In addition, the individual behavioral changes
which together comprise the complex syndromes that follow
chemically-induced depletion of CNS serotonin, e.g., following
the systemic administration of p-chlorophenylalanine, may be
separately attributable to the loss of serotonin within
specific subsets of neurons. These data challenge the
validity of the interpretation of results in experiments
which do not take the "individuality" of the raphe nuclei
into account, e.g., studies in which more than one raphe
nucleus per animal is destroyed, or studies in which
serotonin is depleted throughout the nervous system by
pharmacological means. Based on these considerations, we
have begun a series of experiments aimed at re-evaluating
the hypothesized preeminent role of the raphe nuclei and
serotonin in sleep (Jouvet, 1972).

Finally, we would like to insert a disclaimer based on the frequently abused logic of neurochemical-behavioral studies described in the general introduction to this chapter. We do not interpret these data as *necessarily* indicating the primacy of serotonin in controlling locomotion, pain-elicited aggression, emotionality, etc. The serotonin-dependent physiological factors underlying these changes may well be basic neuronal processes such as modulation of the excitability of sensory and/or motor mechanisms in the CNS. Thus, behavioral alterations that follow raphe lesions may be higher order reflections of a more basic change. Such issues can only be resolved by the application of more specific techniques such as single unit recordings.

Serotonin-Containing Neurons: Electrophysiological Studies

Considering the importance of single unit recordings in understanding the functional aspects of a neurotransmitter system, surprisingly little research has been directed toward elucidating the endogenous and exogenous factors which control the activity of serotonergic neurons. Furthermore, the studies that have been done have been confined almost exclusively to examining neuronal activity in the dorsal and median raphe nuclei of the chloral hydrate anesthetized rat. This section attempts to integrate our knowledge of raphe unit activity.

The spontaneous activity of dorsal (Figure 5) and median raphe neurons in the anesthetized rat is slow and rhythmic (Figure 6). In a sample of 46 units in these two nuclei, we found that the mean discharge rate was 1.3 spikes/sec (range 0.34 - 2.81 spikes/sec). There was no significant difference between the mean discharge rates of neurons in the two nuclei (Mosko, & Jacobs, 1974). The rhythmicity of raphe unit activity was analyzed by obtaining interspike interval (ISI) histograms with the aid of a small laboratory computer (Figure 7). The narrowness of the ISI histograms reflects the extreme regularity of discharge of these neurons, and the absence of very short ISI's indicates that they rarely, if ever, discharge in bursts. In addition to their slow, rhythmic discharge rate, raphe units display striking stability over time with discharge rates, in general, remaining stable for periods of up to two hours. A sample of neurons recorded in the more caudal nucleus raphe magnus displayed a pattern and a rate of discharge virtually identical to that of median and dorsal nucleus cells.

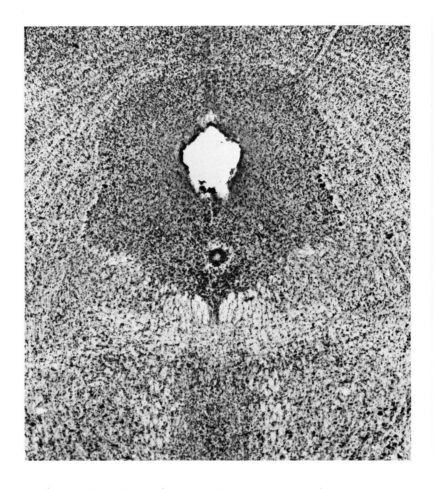

*Figure 5.   Photomicrograph of a 50 μ thick cresyl
violet stained section showing a small lesion in the dorsal
raphe nucleus made at the site of a successful raphe unit
recording by passing a small anodal current (20 μA for 20 sec)
through the tip of the microelectrode.*

In an attempt to examine the mechanism underlying the
generation of the slow rhythmic activity of midbrain raphe
neurons, we have carried out some rather extreme deafferenta-
tion experiments. Following complete transection of the
neuraxis immediately rostral to the dorsal nucleus, the
activity of raphe neurons still displays this striking
rhythmicity with perhaps some overall increase in discharge
rate (Mosko, & Jacobs, 1976a). Even more impressive is the

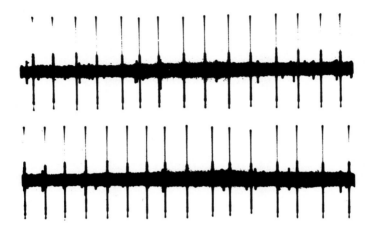

Figure 6. Oscilloscopic photograph of a recording from a typical raphe neuron in the dorsal raphe nucleus of a chloral hydrate anesthetized rat.

fact that raphe neurons maintain their stable, rhythmic discharge when their activity is recorded *in vitro* from 400 μ thick slabs of tissue containing the dorsal nucleus (Mosko, & Jacobs, 1976b). The anatomical evidence described above for the existence of intrinsic connections within the dorsal nucleus may be pertinent to a discussion of the mechanism underlying the maintenance of neuronal rhythmicity in relatively isolated nuclei recorded *in vitro*. Furthermore, the discharge rate of such units tends to be higher than the spontaneous discharge rate of units *in vivo*, indicating that there may normally be tonic inhibitory control exerted on raphe neurons. This is supported by data from our laboratory which shows that electrical stimulation of forebrain structures at low current levels, *in vivo,* produced exclusively inhibitory effects on raphe units. The inhibition has a latency of 30-60 msec, a duration of 200-400 msec, and is typically complete (Figure 8). This effect has been observed from stimulation in the hypothalamus, dorsal hippocampus, caudate, and amygdala.

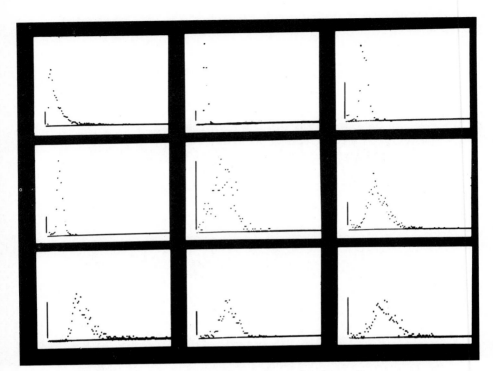

*Figure 7.   ISI histograms of typical raphe neurons.
Histograms based on 512 or 1024 spikes are arranged in order
of increasing modal ISI, ranging from 250 msec (upper left)
to 1600 msec (lower right).   Of all units studied, the
histogram with the earliest mode is shown at the top left
and the narrowest distribution is shown at the top center.
Both symmetrically and asymmetrically shaped distributions
were seen at early and late modal ISI's, suggesting that
symmetry is independent of mode.   The time-base is 50 msec/bin
and the horizontal bar in the lower right-hand corner
corresponds to 20 bins or 1000 msec.   Vertical scale bars
equal 25 counts.   Reprinted by permission of Brain Research
Publication, Inc., Fayetteville, N. Y., from a paper by
S. S. Mosko and B. L. Jacobs, Physiology and Behavior, 1974,
13, 589-593.*

Taken together, these data indicate that many brain regions
may exert an inhibitory influence on midbrain raphe neurons.
    A number of studies have shown that a reciprocal relation-
ship exists between the synaptic availability of serotonin and

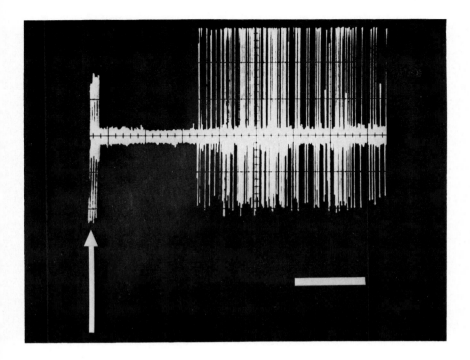

*Figure 8.   Inhibition of raphe unit activity by stimulation
to the caudate nucleus.   Stimuli were 1 msec duration square
wave pulses presented in trains of 10 msec duration at a
frequency of 300 Hz (each train contained three pulses).   The
repetition rate was 1/sec and the current level was 50 μA.
This photograph is the summed data from 128 stimulus presentations.   The arrow indicates the stimulus and the horizontal
bar indicates 200 msec.*

the discharge rate of raphe neurons. Monoamine oxidase
inhibition, which increases brain serotonin levels by
blocking the major catabolic route, depresses the activity
of raphe neurons (Aghajanian, Graham, & Sheard, 1970) with
a latency that corresponds to the time of rapid accumulation
of serotonin in the brain (Tozer, Neff, & Brodie, 1966).
Other drugs which enhance the availability of endogenous
serotonin and produce a corresponding decrease in the activity
of raphe neurons include serotonin reuptake blockers (Sheard,
Zolovick, & Aghajanian, 1970) and p-chloroamphetamine (Sheard,
1974), a potent releaser of serotonin from presynaptic stores.
Similarly, the administration of L-tryptophan (100 mg/kg, i.p.)

increases brain serotonin content (Eccleston, Ashcroft, &
Crawford, 1965) and markedly depresses raphe unit activity
(Aghajanian, 1972). However, the report that the systemic
administration of L-5-HTP, which also increases brain serotonin
levels (Bogdanski, Weissbach, & Undenfriend, 1958), was
ineffective in depressing raphe unit activity (Aghajanian,
1972), is inconsistent with this reciprocal relationship.
A systematic examination of this question in our laboratory
has revealed that L-5-HTP does inhibit raphe unit discharge
(Trulson, & Jacobs, 1975), and that the degree of inhibition
is dose-related (Trulson, & Jacobs, 1976b). A dose of
10 mg/kg i.p. produces little if any inhibition, 50 mg/kg
produces approximately 40% inhibition, and 100 mg/kg produces
maximal inhibition of approximately 80%. The depression
produced by L-tryptophan follows a similar dose-dependent
relationship.

The mechanism whereby serotonin precursors and other
agents which increase the availability of serotonin lead
to a depression of raphe activity is not known, although it
has been proposed that it involves an inhibitory neuronal
feedback loop (Aghajanian, 1972). Initial attempts to
test this hypothesis in our laboratory have failed to provide
support for such a feedback mechanism. Since the principle
efferents of the midbrain raphe are ascending (Lorens, &
Guldberg, 1974), a complete transection of the brainstem
immediately rostral to these nuclei should disrupt any
descending forebrain projections participating in a hypothetical feedback loop and thereby block the depression of
raphe units induced by the above drugs, if they act via such
a feedback mechanism. However, we have found these transections to be totally ineffective in blocking the depressant
effect of p-chloroamphetamine (1.25 - 2.5 mg/kg i.v.) or
chlorimipramine (0.15 - 0.33 mg/kg i.v.) on raphe units
(Mosko, & Jacobs, 1976a). Although these data do not rule
out the existence of a feedback loop located caudal to the
transection, they do indicate that the concept of neuronal
feedback regulation deserves further examination. Furthermore, the existence of serotonin-containing boutons over
raphe neurons (Aghajanian, & Haigler, 1973), plus the fact
that raphe neurons are depressed by iontophoretically
applied serotonin (Aghajanian, Haigler, & Bloom, 1972), suggests that drugs which increase the synaptic availability
of serotonin may exert their effects on raphe neurons via
inhibitory recurrent collaterals or intrinsic connections
between raphe neurons.

Certain compounds have also been shown to inhibit raphe
unit activity by acting directly on the cell body. D-lysergic
acid diethylamide (LSD) completely inhibits raphe unit

activity within a very short time following i.p. or i.v.
administration. To determine the mechanism of action of
LSD, Aghajanian et al. (1972) microiontophoretically applied
it directly onto dorsal raphe neuron cell bodies and observed
a powerful inhibitory effect on unit activity that was
specific to raphe cells. Another hallucinogenic compound,
N, N-dimethyltryptamine (DMT) has also been shown to act in
this manner. The hallucinogenic action of these compounds
may, therefore, be directly attributable to their potent
depressant action on raphe neurons.

Knowledge of the mechanism of action of LSD has also
been useful in elucidating the nature of the postsynaptic
effects of serotonin. Haigler and Aghajanian (1974) have
demonstrated that systemic administration of LSD results in
an increase in the activity of neurons postsynaptic to
raphe cells in the ventral lateral geniculate, superior
colliculus, and interpeduncular nucleus. This is consistent
with the fact that the effects of microiontophoretically
applied serotonin on cells with identified serotonergic
inputs is exclusively inhibitory. Thus, the increased
discharge rate of cells postsynaptic to raphe neurons following systemic administration of LSD is attributable to the
depression of a normally inhibitory serotonergic input to
these cells.

Very little is known about physiological factors which
regulate the activity of serotonergic neurons. Foote,
Lieb, Martz, and Gordon (1972) reported that intravenous
administration of hydrocortisone produces a marked inhibition
of raphe unit activity in the rat. An attempt to replicate
and extend these studies in our laboratory revealed that
neither hydrocortisone, corticosterone, nor ACTH have any
dramatic or reproducible effects on raphe unit activity in
either intact or adrenalectomized rats (Mosko, & Jacobs, 1975).
A positive correlation between body temperature and raphe
unit activity was reported by Weiss and Aghajanian (1971).
They found an average increase in unit activity of approximately 70% per C^0 rise in body temperature. Studies from our
laboratory, however, have found no evidence for a relationship
between body temperature and raphe unit activity (Trulson, &
Jacobs, unpublished). A major physiological variable which
may be related to changes in raphe unit activity is blood
pressure. We have found that changes in raphe unit activity
are often positively correlated with changes in systemic blood
pressure. It should be pointed out that it is difficult to
isolate a change in blood pressure as the causal factor since
many other physiological factors covary with it. In light
of these preliminary results relating raphe unit activity

to blood pressure, the data of Scheibel et al. (1975), described above, indicating that the dendrites of some raphe neurons make intimate contact with nearby blood vessels may be particularly relevant. Environmental lighting also appears to influence raphe units, with neuronal activity tending to be higher in the light than dark. Of 44 cells tested systematically for light-dark changes, 66% discharged at a higher rate in the light condition, and the mean rate increase was 31% (Mosko, & Jacobs, 1974).

In only two cases has the activity of raphe neurons been directly related to behavior, and in both cases these studies were carried out in freely moving, unanesthetized cats. McGinty, Fairbanks, & Harper (1973) reported that dorsal raphe neurons in the cat discharge rhythmically and at low rates in the waking state. Furthermore, this activity was very stable and markedly refractory to changes in the animal's waking behavior. When the animals entered slow wave sleep (SWS), the discharge rate showed only a slight decrease, but with the onset of rapid eye movement (REM) sleep, the activity decreased dramatically, the cells becoming virtually silent. Sheu, Nelson, & Bloom (1974), in recording from the median and magnus nuclei of cats describe results quite different from McGinty's. Cells in these nuclei had higher overall discharge rates and reached their highest rate of discharge in REM sleep and lowest rate in SWS. The discrepancy in the data from these two studies may be attributable to recording from different nuclei within the raphe complex. It is important to point out that *neither* of these studies support the notion that enhanced serotonergic activity plays an integral role in either the onset or maintenance of SWS (Jouvet, 1972).

To summarize: 1) we know a good deal about the relation of raphe unit activity to concentrations of synaptic serotonin; 2) we have strong evidence that hallucinogenic drugs may have, as their primary mode of action, a depressant effect on raphe unit activity; and, 3) we have little information relating raphe unit activity to changes in physiological or behavioral processes. It is in this latter area that we feel the major breakthrough in our understanding of the raphe-serotonin system will occur in the next few years.

A Behavioral Model for Studying the Postsynaptic Effects of Serotonin

Before we can hope to unravel the behavioral and physiological roles of serotonin, we must have information concerning the postsynaptic effects of the serotonergic manipulations used to provide the relevant data base. In the absence of such information, it is futile to attempt to interpret the behavioral effects of treatments such as tryptophan, 5-hydroxytryptophan, serotonin synthesis inhibitors, receptor blockers, etc. The advantages of such a postsynaptic model system are easily demonstrated by examining the information concerning the dopamine system that was garnered through the exploitation of the striatal rotational model (Anden, Dahlstrom, Fuxe, & Larsson, 1966a); Ungerstedt, 1971b; Ungerstedt, & Arbuthnott, 1970). Fortunately, an analogous simple behavioral model for the study of postsynaptic serotonin receptors is available. The present section describes this model system and indicates its heuristic value.

A number of pharmacological treatments which result either in increased synaptic serotonin (tryptophan administered in the presence of monoamine oxidase inhibition, nialamide, and 5-hydroxytryptophan) or in increased stimulation of post-synaptic serotonin receptors (5-methoxy-N, N-dimethyltrypt-amine) produce a complex behavioral syndrome in the rat (Figure 9) consisting most conspicuously of hyperreactivity, hyperactivity, tremor, rigidity, hindlimb abduction, lateral head weaving, reciprocal forepaw treading, and Straub tail (Hess, & Doepfner, 1961; Grahame-Smith, 1971a, 1971b; Modigh, & Svensson, 1972; Modigh, 1973). This syndrome is of special importance in that it represents, with the exception of the hyperactivity component (Green, & Grahame-Smith, 1974a), one of the few "pure" behavioral indices of central serotonergic activity. This conclusion is based on data presented below (e.g., demonstration of denervation super-sensitivity) and a variety of published evidence including: production or potentiation of the syndrome by serotonin precursors, agonists and reuptake blockers; and blockade of the syndrome-producing effects of serotonin precursors by serotonin synthesis inhibition.

Hess and Doepfner (1961) were among the first to describe this complex response in rats pretreated with a monoamine oxidase inhibitor (MAOI) and then given L-tryptophan. In recent years, Grahame-Smith and his co-workers have made important contributions in this area. In 1971, he published several papers which greatly elucidated the neurochemical mechanisms underlying this syndrome (Grahame-Smith, 1971a, 1971b). More recently, he and his colleagues have used this syndrome especially with an eye toward discovering substances which could enhance the synaptic effects of serotonin. Their objective has been to find agents which might have clinical value in the treatment of

Figure 9. Time-lapse photograph (4 sec exposure) of rat displaying the full syndrome. Note the following: forepaw treading (vertical movement of the foreground forepaw); lateral head weaving (the position of the snout and ears can be seen to change as the head moves); tremor (the fore portion of the tail is lashing, while in some other instances it is held erect); and hindlimb abduction (it is important to observe that the hindlimb does not move and, therefore, remains in focus). The rat was treated with pargyline (50 mg/kg i.p.) one hour before L-tryptophan (150 mg/kg i.p.).

neuro- or psychopathologies in which disturbances in CNS serotonin have been implicated. For example, they have shown that thyrotropin releasing hormone (used in the treatment of depression), lithium chloride (used in the treatment of mania) and diphenylhydantoin are all effective in enhancing the syndrome produced by MAOI and L-tryptophan (Green, & Grahame-Smith, 1974b; Grahame-Smith, & Green, 1974; Green, & Grahame-Smith, 1975). We have used this complex behavioral response to study various basic aspects of serotonin-mediated synapses.

Utilizing the fact that the syndrome is a reflection of the activity of postsynaptic serotonin receptors, we have provided the first behavioral evidence for the functional

interaction of two CNS neurotransmitters (Jacobs, 1974b).   If
L-DOPA (100 mg/kg) is administered to rats pretreated with
a MAOI (pargyline 50 mg/kg), one observes a syndrome with all
of the neurological signs described above.   On the basis of
the overt behavioral similarity of these two syndromes, we
hypothesized that the L-DOPA syndrome was mediated by
serotonin.   When the MAOI + L-DOPA treatment was administered
to animals pretreated with the serotonin synthesis inhibitor
p-chlorophenylalanine (PCPA; 400 mg/kg 72 hrs before), the
syndrome was either totally blocked or substantially attenuated.
However, when MAOI + L-tryptophan (150 mg/kg) is administered
to animals pretreated with the catecholamine synthesis
inhibitor, α-methyl-p-tyrosine (200 mg/kg 4 or 12 hrs before),
no change in the syndrome is seen.   In this same series of
experiments, we found that spiroperidol, a drug assumed to
be a specific dopamine receptor blocker, was also an effective
serotonin receptor blocker, since in higher doses it completely
blocked the syndrome produced by MAOI + L-tryptophan (Jacobs,
1974a; Jacobs, Eubanks, & Wise, 1974a).

    Since the syndrome is specific to serotonin, we have
utilized it in a quantitative fashion to study the development
of denervation supersensitivity in the serotonin system.
Denervation was accomplished by the intraventricular
administration of 50 μg of the relatively specific serotonin
neurotoxic agent 5,7-dihydroxytryptamine (5,7-DHT) in
combination with a catecholamine uptake blocking agent.
When the dose-response curve for the serotonin agonist
5-methoxy-N, N-dimethyltryptamine (5-M-DMT) was tested 7-21
days later, there was a significant reduction (approximately
50%) in the doses of 5-M-DMT necessary to produce the syndrome.
The same was true of the serotonin precursor 5-hydroxytrypto-
phan; the LD_{50} for this compound was sharply reduced by
5,7-DHT pretreatment, as was the ED_{50} necessary for producing
the syndrome (Trulson, Eubanks, & Jacobs, 1976).

    We have also used the syndrome for investigating the
mechanism of action of presumptive serotonergic drugs, such
as p-chloroamphetamine (PCA).   This compound has been shown
to manifest a variety of pharmacological actions including
the rapid release of endogenous stores of serotonin (see
Fuller, & Molloy, 1974, for a review).   If this latter effect
is of primary importance and of sufficient magnitude we
reasoned that: PCA should produce the syndrome after only
a short latency; and the PCA-produced syndrome should be
blocked by the depletion of the endogenous stores of serotonin
by PCPA.   Both predictions were supported by experimental
evidence.   PCA in doses of 10 mg/kg i.p. produced the syndrome
after only 3-5 minutes.   Depletion of the endogenous stores

of serotonin by PCPA pretreatment (400 mg/kg, 72 hrs before)
totally blocked any sign of the syndrome even when PCA was
administered in the suprathreshold dose of 20 mg/kg (Trulson,
& Jacobs, 1976a).

Finally, we have investigated the neuroanatomical
structures within the rat CNS which mediate the syndrome
(Jacobs, & Klemfuss, 1975). Since it is comprised of a
variety of neurological signs and simple stereotyped behaviors,
we reasoned, by analogy with the dopamine system, that the
neostriatum might be critically involved. Accordingly, we
began by aspirating the entire neostriatum and then administered a MAOI (pargyline 50 mg/kg) plus L-tryptophan (150 mg/
kg). Much to our surprise, the complete syndrome was
observed in this preparation. We then began a series of
experiments in which the neuraxis was completely transected
in the coronal plane in successively more caudal cuts until
the syndrome was abolished. Again, much to our surprise,
a cut at the caudal mesencephalic level, posterior to the
red nucleus, substantia nigra and dorsal and median raphe
nuclei, left the syndrome essentially intact (Figure 10).
We have not successfully proceeded more caudally than this
since it is difficult to maintain the viability of such
animals, and the overall neurological condition of those that
survive is so poor as to make any examination of the manifestation of the syndrome difficult. Complete cerebellectomy
also had no disruptive effect on the syndrome. In conclusion,
these data indicate that the lower brainstem and spinal cord
is sufficient for the production of this behavioral complex.
Since these caudal aspects of the neuraxis are relatively
less complexly organized than much of the forebrain, this
syndrome provides a conveniently simple preparation for
the study of the mechanism of action of serotonin in the
CNS.

We have combined our electrophysiological data and
behavioral syndrome data in an attempt to derive a model
which incorporates both the pre- and post-synaptic effects
of a variety of serotono-mimetic agents (e.g., precursors,
agonists, MAOI's, etc.). This model allows us to predict
gross behavioral effects on the basis of neuronal changes,
and reciprocally, to predict neuronal effects on the basis
of behavioral changes. There are several premises in
the model. 1) Elicitation of the syndrome by a substance is
evidence of a strong postsynaptic (postsynaptic to raphe
neurons) effect. 2) Any agent which has a strong postsynaptic effect, i.e., produces the syndrome, will also have
a presynaptic effect, i.e., depress raphe unit activity, at
a considerably lower dose. 3) Finally, tryptaminergic

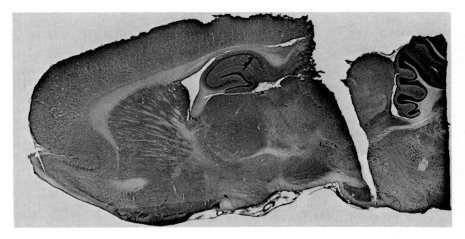

Figure 10. Photomicrograph of a 50 μ thick cresyl violet stained section showing a complete brain transection at a 0.4. On its dorsal aspect, the cut passes through the anterior portion of the inferior colliculus, and on its ventral aspect, it passes through the pons.

compounds will have hallucinogenic properties if, and only if, they totally depress the activity of raphe neurons *and* have little, or no, postsynaptic effect at the hallucinogenic dose. Various hallucinogenic compounds have a powerful depressant action on raphe unit activity, and since serotonin's postsynaptic effect is exclusively inhibitory (Haigler, & Aghajanian, 1974), this leads to a disinhibition of postsynaptic neurons. Thus, the hallucinogenic action of various tryptaminergic compounds may be directly attributable to this disinhibition. However, if a compound also affects the postsynaptic neuron independently of its action on the raphe neuron, this will prevent or suppress its hallucinogenic action because the disinhibition produced by the depression of raphe unit activity will be counterbalanced by an inhibitory effect directly on these postsynaptic neurons. Implicit in this model is the assumption that compounds that have strong postsynaptic effects on neurons in the brainstem and spinal cord (i.e., produce the syndrome), will also have such effects in the forebrain. In other words, serotonomimetic agents are thought to affect postsynaptic serotonergic receptors uniformly.

TABLE 1

HALLUCINOGEN EFFECT AND PRE- AND POST-SYNAPTIC ACTION OF VARIOUS SEROTONOMIMETIC AGENTS

Agent	Presyn. effect? (Raphe units)	Postsyn. effect? (Syndrome)	Reason	Hallucinogenic?	Reason
LSD-25	strong	none (low dose)	purely presyn. action	yes (but only in low doses)*	purely presyn.
5-M-DMT	strong	none (low dose) strong (high dose)	postsyn. action at high doses	yes (but only in low doses)*	purely presyn. in low doses
PCA	strong	strong	strong release of endog. 5-HT	no	postsyn.
Tryptophan	weak	none	lack of lge. incr. in brain 5-HT due to tryptophan hydrox.	no	weak presyn.; some postsyn.
L-5-HTP	weak	strong	produces lge. incr. in brain 5-HT	no	weak presyn.; strong postsyn.
MAOI's	weak	strong	produces lge. incr. in brain 5-HT	no	weak presyn.; strong postsyn.

*Lack of hallucinogenic action of LSD and 5-M-DMT at high doses is a prediction that derives from the model. It has not been tested.

Table I summarizes the electrophysiological (raphe unit) and behavioral (syndrome) data which generated this model and the hypotheses that derive from its application. Some of the results in Table I will be reviewed briefly here. In low doses, LSD has potent presynaptic effects and no postsynaptic activity (Haigler, & Aghajanian, 1974). It is an hallucinogen because, at low doses, it has *both* a potent presynaptic effect and *no* postsynaptic effect. These arguments with respect to LSD can also be directly applied to low doses of 5-M-DMT. Since LSD and 5-M-DMT produce the syndrome in higher doses, we make the somewhat paradoxical prediction that they would not have hallucinogenic properties at these high dose levels. Finally, L-tryptophan does not produce the syndrome because, even in very high doses, it is incapable of elevating CNS serotonin to sufficiently high levels (due to the rate-limiting action of tryptophan hydroxylase). Both its moderate postsynaptic effect and relatively weak depressant effect on raphe neurons preclude its having any hallucinogenic activity.

CONCLUSIONS

These data represent the beginning of a multidisciplinary approach to the understanding of the physiological and behavioral role(s) of CNS serotonin. Through the implementation of anatomical, neurochemical, electrophysiological, pharmacological and behavioral techniques, we see the implications of data within a broader perspective, and observe the convergence of data that otherwise might have appeared fragmentary or anomalous. We feel that it is imperative that neurochemical-behavioral studies avoid the anthropocentric trap that neurotransmitters must, of necessity, be involved in sexual behavior, sleep, aggression, etc. In the same vein, we must discard the self-fulfilling methodology which examines behavior along a single "amount" continuum following the manipulation of neurotransmitters.

ACKNOWLEDGMENTS

These studies were supported by Grant MH 23433 and a Training Grant MH 13445 from the National Institute of Mental Health, and the Spencer Foundation. We wish to thank Daniel Ruimy for his assistance in various aspects of these studies, Dr. Gary Lynch for assistance in the HRP and *in vitro* electrophysiological studies, and Dr. Charles Gross and Tom Chippendale for critical comments on the manuscript.

REFERENCES

Aghajanian, G. K.   Influence of drugs on the firing of
     serotonin-containing neurons in brain.   *Federation
     Proceedings,* 1972, *31,* 91-96.

Aghajanian, G. K., & Bloom, F. E.   Localization of tritiated
     serotonin in rat brain.   *The Journal of Pharmacology
     and Experimental Therapeutics,* 1967, *156,* 23-30.

Aghajanian, G. K., Graham, A. W., & Sheard, M. H.   Serotonin-
     containing neurons in brain: Depression of firing by
     monoamine oxidase inhibitors.   *Science,* 1970, *169,* 1100-
     1102.

Aghajanian, G. K., & Haigler, H. J.   Direct and indirect
     actions of LSD, serotonin and related compounds on
     serotonin-containing neurons.   In J. Barchas & E. Usdin
     (Eds.), *Serotonin and Behavior.*   New York: Academic
     Press, 1973.

Aghajanian, G. K., Haigler, H. J., & Bloom, F. E.   Lysergic
     acid diethylamide   and serotonin: Direct actions on
     serotonin-containing neurons in rat brain.   *Life Sciences,*
     1972, *11,* 615-622.

Aghajanian, G. K., Kuhar, M. J., & Roth, R. H.   Serotonin-
     containing neuronal perikarya and terminals: Differential
     effects of P-Chlorophenylalanine.   *Brain Research,* 1973,
     54, 85-101.

Anden, N. E., Dahlstrom, A., Fuxe, K., & Larsson, K.
     Functional role of the nigro-neostriatal dopamine
     neurons.   *Acta Pharmacologia et Toxicologica,* 1966a, *24,*
     263-274.

Anden, N. E., Dahlstrom, A., Fuxe, K., Larsson, K., Olson, L.,
     & Ungerstedt, U.   Ascending monoamine neurons to the
     telencephalon and diencephalon.   *Acta Physiologica
     Scandinavica,* 1966b, *67,* 313-326.

Barchas, J., & Usdin, E. (Eds.)   *Serotonin and Behavior.*
     New York: Academic Press, 1973.

Bjorklund, A., Nobin, A., & Stenevi, U. The use of neurotoxic dihydroxytryptamines as tools for morphological studies and localized lesioning of central indolamine neurons. *Zeitschrift für Zellforschung und Mikroscopische Anatomie*, 1973, *145*, 479-501.

Bobillier, P., Petitjean, F., Salvert, D., Ligier, M., & Seguin, S. Differential projections of the nucleus raphe dorsalis and nucleus raphe centralis as revealed by autoradiography. *Brain Research*, 1975, *85*, 205-210.

Bogdanski, D. F., Weissbach, J., & Undenfriend, S. Pharmacological studies with the serotonin precursor, 5-hydroxytryptophan. *Journal of Pharmacology and Experimental Therapeutics*, 1958, *122*, 182-191.

Brodal, A., Walberg, F., & Taber, E. The raphe nuclei of the brain stem in the cat. III. Afferent connections. *Journal of Comparative Neurology*, 1960, *114*, 261-279.

Chase, T. N., & Murphy, D. L. Serotonin and central nervous system function. *Annual Review of Pharmacology*, 1973, *18*, 181-197.

Conrad, L. C. A., Leonard, C. M., & Pfaff, D. W. Connections of the median and dorsal raphe nuclei in the rat: An autoradiographic and degeneration study. *Journal of Comparative Neurology*, 1974, *156*, 179-205.

Costa, E., Gessa, G. L., & Sandler, M. (Eds.), *Advances in Biochemical Psychopharmacology, Serotonin: New Vistas* (Vol. 10). New York: Raven Press, 1974a.

Costa, E., Gessa, G. L., & Sandler, M. (Eds.), *Advances in Biochemical Psychopharmacology, Serotonin: New Vistas* (Vol. 11). New York: Raven Press, 1974b.

Dahlstrom, A., & Fuxe, K. Evidence for the existence of monoamine-containing neurons in the central nervous system. I. Demonstration of monoamines in the cell bodies of brain stem neurons. *Acta Physiologica Scandinavica*, 1964, *62*, 1-55 (Suppl. 232).

Dahlstrom, A., & Fuxe, K. Evidence for the existence of monoamine neurons in the central nervous system. II. Experimentally induced changes in the intraneuronal amine levels of bulbo-spinal neuron systems. *Acta Physiologica Scandinavica*, 1965, *64*, 1-36 (Suppl. 247).

Dahlstrom, A., Haggendal, J., & Atack, C. Localization and
    transport of serotonin. In J. Barchas & E. Usdin (Eds.),
    Serotonin and Behavior. New York: Academic Press, 1973.

Eccleston, D., Ashcroft, G. W., & Crawford, T. B. B.   5-
    hydroxyindole metabolism in rat brain. A study of
    intermediate metabolism using the technique of tryptophan
    loading. II. Applications and drug studies. *Journal
    of Neurochemistry,* 1965, *12,* 493-503.

Foote, W. E., Lieb, J. P., Martz, R. L., & Gordon, M. W.
    Effect of hydrocortisone on single unit activity in
    midbrain raphe. *Brain Research,* 1972, *41,* 242-244.

Fuller, R. W., & Molloy, B. B.   Recent studies with 4-
    chloroamphetamine and some analogues. In E. Costa,
    G. L. Gessa, & M. Sandler (Eds.), *Advances in Biochemical
    Psychopharmacology, Serotonin: New Vistas* (Vol. 10).
    New York: Raven Press, 1974.

Fuxe, K. Evidence for the existence of monoamine neurons
    in the central nervous system. IV. The distribution
    of monoamine terminals in the central nervous system.
    Acta Physiologica Scandinavica, 1965, *64,* 41-85 (Suppl.
    247).

Fuxe, K., & Jonsson, G. Further mapping of central 5-
    hydroxytryptamine neurons: Studies with the neurotoxic
    dihydroxytryptamines. *Advances in Biochemical
    Psychopharmacology, Serotonin: New Vistas* (Vol. 10).
    New York: Raven Press, 1974.

Grahame-Smith, D. G. Inhibitory effect of chlorpromazine on
    the syndrome of hyperactivity produced by L-tryptophan
    or 5-methoxy-N. N-dimethyltryptamine in rats treated
    with a monoamine oxidase inhibitor. *British Journal of
    Pharmacology,* 1971a, *43,* 856-864.

Grahame-Smith, D. G. Studies *in vivo* on the relationship
    between brain tryptophan, brain 5-HT synthesis and
    hyperactivity in rats treated with a monoamine oxidase
    inhibitor and L-tryptophan. *Journal of Neurochemistry,*
    1971b, *18,* 1053-1066.

Grahame-Smith, D. G., & Green, A. R. The role of brain 5-
    hydroxytryptamine in the hyperactivity produced in rats
    by lithium and monoamine oxidase inhibition. *British
    Journal of Pharmacology,* 1974, *52,* 19-26.

Green, A. R., & Grahame-Smith, D. G. The role of brain dopamine in the hyperactivity syndrome produced by increased 5-hydroxytryptamine synthesis in rats. *Neuropharmacology,* 1974a, *13,* 949-959.

Green, A. R., & Grahame-Smith, D. G. TRH potentiates behavioural changes following increased brain 5-hydroxytryptamine accumulation in rats. *Nature,* 1974b, *251,* 524-526.

Green, A. R., & Grahame-Smith, D. G. The effect of diphenylhydantoin on brain 5-hydroxytryptamine metabolism and function. *Neuropharmacology,* 1975, *14,* 107-113.

Haigler, H. J., & Aghajanian, G. K. Lysergic acid diethylamide and serotonin: A comparison of effects on serotonergic neurons and neurons receiving a serotonergic input. *Journal of Pharmacology and Experimental Therapeutics,* 1974, *188,* 688-699.

Hess, S. M., & Doepfner, W. Behavioural effects and brain amine content in rats. *Archives Internationales de Pharmacodynamie et de Therapie,* 1961, *134,* 89-99.

Jacobs, B. L. Effect of two dopamine receptor blockers on a serotonin-mediated behavioral syndrome in rats. *European Journal of Pharmacology,* 1974a, *27,* 363-366.

Jacobs, B. L. Evidence for the functional interaction of two central neurotransmitters. *Psychopharmacologia,* 1974b, *39,* 81-86.

Jacobs, B. L., & Cohen, A. Differential behavioral effects of lesions of the median or dorsal raphe nuclei in rats: Open field and pain elicited aggression. *Journal of Comparative and Physiological Psychology,* 1976, *90,* 102-108.

Jacobs, B. L., Eubanks, E. E., & Wise, W. D. Effect of indolealkylamine manipulations on locomotor activity in rats. *Neuropharmacology,* 1974a, *13,* 575-583.

Jacobs, B. L., & Klemfuss, H. Brain stem and spinal cord mediation of a serotonergic behavioral syndrome. *Brain Research,* 1975, *100,* 450-457.

Jacobs, B. L., Trimbach, C., Eubanks, E. E., & Trulson, M.
    Hippocampal mediation of raphe lesion- and PCPA-
    induced hyperactivity in the rat. *Brain Research*, 1975a,
    94, 253-261.

Jacobs, B. L., Wise, W. D., & Taylor, K. M. Differential
    behavioral and neurochemical effects following lesions
    of the dorsal or median raphe nuclei in rats. *Brain
    Research*, 1974b, *79*, 353-361.

Jacobs, B. L., Wise, W. D., & Taylor, K. M. Is there a
    catecholamine-serotonin interaction in the control of
    locomotor activity? *Neuropharmacology*, 1975b, *14*, 501-
    506.

Jouvet, M. The role of the monoamines and acetylcholine-
    containing neurons in the regulation of the sleep-
    waking cycle. *Ergebnisse der Physiologie*, 1962, *64*,
    166-307.

LaVail, J. H., & LaVail, M. M. Retrograde axonal transport
    in the central nervous system. *Science*, 1972, *176*,
    1416-1417.

Loizou, L. A. Projections of the nucleus locus coeruleus in
    the albino rat. *Brain Research*, 1969, *15*, 565-566.

Lorens, S. A., & Guldberg, H. C. Regional 5-hydroxytryptamine
    following selective mid-brain raphe lesions in the rat.
    Brain Research, 1974, *78*, 45-56.

McGinty, D. J., Fairbanks, M. K., & Harper, R. M. 5-HT-
    containing neurons: Unit activity in behaving cats.
    In J. Barchas and E. Usdin (Eds.), *Serotonin and
    Behavior*. New York: Academic Press, 1973.

Modigh, K. Effects of chlorimipramine and protriptyline
    on the hyperactivity induced by 5-hydroxytryptophan
    after peripheral decarboxylase inhibition in mice.
    Journal of Neural Transmission, 1973, *34*, 101-109.

Modigh, K., & Svensson, T. H. On the role of central nervous
    system catecholamines and 5-hydroxytryptamine in the
    nialamide-induced behavioral syndrome. *British Journal
    of Pharmacology*, 1972, *46*, 32-45.

Mosko, S. S., Haubrich, D., & Jacobs, B. L.   Serotonergic afferents to the dorsal raphe nucleus: Evidence from HRP and synaptosomal uptake studies.   *Brain Research,* 1976, in press.

Mosko, S. S., & Jacobs, B. L.   Midbrain raphe neurons: Spontaneous activity and response to light.   *Physiology and Behavior,* 1974, *13,* 589-593.

Mosko, S. S., & Jacobs, B. L.   Midbrain raphe neurons: Sensitivity to glucocorticoids and ACTH in intact and adrenalectomized rats.   *Brain Research,* 1975, *89,* 368-375.

Mosko, S. S., & Jacobs, B. L.   Electrophysiological evidence against negative neuronal feedback from the forebrain controlling midbrain raphe unit activity.   *Brain Research,* 1976a, in press.

Mosko, S. S., & Jacobs, B. L.   Recording of dorsal raphe unit activity *in vitro.*   *Neuroscience Letters,* 1976b, in press.

Nauta, J. W., Pritz, M. B., & Lasek, R. J.   Afferents to the rat caudoputamen studied with horseradish peroxidase. An evaluation of a retrograde neuroanatomical research method.   *Brain Research,* 1974, *67,* 219-238.

Olson, L., Boréus, L. O., & Seiger, A.   Histochemical demonstration and mapping of 5-hydroxytryptamine- and catecholamine-containing neuron systems in the human fetal brain.   *Zeitschrift fur Anatomie und Entwicklungsgeschichte,* 1973, *139,* 259-282.

Pin, C., Jones, B., & Jouvet, M.   Topographie des neurones monoaminergiques du tronc cerebral du chat: Etude par histofluorescence.   *Comptes Rendues de la Societe de Biologie,* 1968, *162,* 2136-2141.

Scheibel, M. E., Tomiyasu, U., & Scheibel, A. B.   Do raphe nuclei of the reticular formation have a.neurosecretory or vascular sensor function?   *Experimental Neurology,* 1975, *47,* 316-329.

Sheard, M. H.   The effect of p-chloroamphetamine on single raphe neurons. In E. Costa, G. L. Gessa & M. Sandler (Eds.), *Advances in Biochemical Psychopharmacology, Serotonin: New Vistas* (Vol. 10).   New York: Raven Press, 1974.

Sheard, M. H., Zolovick, A., & Aghajanian, G. K.   Raphe neurons: Effect of tricyclic antidepressant drugs. *Brain Research,* 1970, *43,* 690-694.

Sheu, Y. S., Nelson, J. P., & Bloom, F. E.   Discharge patterns of cat raphe neurons during sleep and waking. *Brain Research,* 1974, *73,* 263-276.

Taber, E., Brodal, A., & Walberg, F.   The raphe nuclei of the brain stem in the cat.   I.   Normal topography and cytoarchitecture and general discussion. *Journal of Comparative Neurology,* 1960, *114,* 161-188.

Tozer, T. N., Neff, N. H., & Brodie, B. B.   Application of steady state kinetics to the synthesis and turnover time of serotonin in the brain of normal and reserpine-treated rats. *Journal of Pharmacology and Experimental Therapeutics,* 1966, *153,* 177-182.

Trulson, M. E., Eubanks, E. E., & Jacobs, B. L.   Behavioral evidence for supersensitivity following destruction of central serotonergic nerve terminals by 5,7-dihydroxy-tryptamine. *Journal of Pharmacology and Experimental Therapeutics,* 1976, in press.

Trulson, M. E., & Jacobs, B. L.   Raphe neurons: Depression of activity by L-5-hydroxytryptophan. *Brain Research,* 1975, *97,* 350-355.

Trulson, M. E., & Jacobs, B. L.   Behavioral evidence for the rapid release of CNS serotonin by PCA and fenfluramine. *European Journal of Pharmacology,* 1976a, *36,* 149-154.

Trulson, M. E., & Jacobs, B. L.   Dose-response relationships between systematically administered L-tryptophan or L-5-hydroxytryptophan and raphe unit activity in the rat. *Neuropharmacology,* 1976b, *15,* 339-344.

Twarog, B. M., & Page, I. H. Serotonin content of some mammalian tissues and urine and a method for its determination. *American Journal of Physiology*, 1953, *175*, 157-161.

Ungerstedt, U. Stereotaxic mapping of the monoamine pathways in the rat brain. *Acta Physiologica Scandinavica*, 1971a, 1-49 (Suppl. 367).

Ungerstedt, U. Striatal dopamine release after amphetamine or nerve degeneration revealed by rotational behaviour. *Acta Physiologica Scandinavica*, 1971b, 49-68 (Suppl. 367).

Ungerstedt, U., & Arbuthnott, G. Quantitative recording of rotational behaviour in rats after 6-hydroxy-dopamine lesions of the nigro-striatal dopamine system. *Brain Research*, 1970, *24*, 485-493.

Weiss, B. L., & Aghajanian, G. K. Activation of brain serotonin metabolism by heat: Role of midbrain raphe neurons. *Brain Research*, 1971, *26*, 37-48.

NEURONAL ACTIVITY PATTERNS DURING RAPID-EYE-MOVEMENT
SLEEP: RELATION TO WAKING PATTERNS

DENNIS J. MCGINTY and JEROME M. SIEGEL

*Neurophysiology Research
Sepulveda Veterans Administration Hospital
Sepulveda, California 91343 USA*

and

*Departments of Psychology and Anatomy
University of California
Los Angeles, California 90024 USA*

Neuronal unit spike activity as detected by extracellular
electrodes has been studied during waking, slow wave sleep
(SWS) and rapid-eye-movement sleep (REMS) in a variety of
brain sites.   A consistent finding has been that a majority
of cell types exhibit an increased neuronal discharge rate
in REMS and in waking when compared with SWS.   Indeed, REMS
rates usually equal or exceed waking rates, and REMS has been
described as a state characterized by intense excitation of
brain unit activity.   This observation, first reported by
Huttenlocher (1961) for medial midbrain cells, has been
extended to the cerebral cortex (Evarts, 1962, 1964; Noda
& Adey, 1970), thalamus (Sakakura, 1968; Mukhametov,
Rizzolotti, & Seitun, 1970; Mukhametov, Rizzolotti, & Tradardi,
1970), certain limbic sites (Noda, Manohar, & Adey, 1969;
Findlay & Hayward, 1969) and most brainstem neurons (Kasamatsu,
1970; Bizzi, Pompeiano, & Somogyi, 1964; Hobson & McCarley,
1971).   Other cell types have been found to exhibit reduced
activity in REMS compared with SWS, but a similar reduction
also occurs during waking, that is, the REMS-waking similarity
applies (Jacobs & McGinty, 1971).   Initially, these observations were interpreted as supporting concepts that SWS and REM
sleep were dissimilar states and that sleep did *not* constitute

a simple resting condition in terms of cellular discharge (Evarts, 1967). In this paper we want to emphasize another aspect of this phenomenon. Studies of the patterns of unit activity during REMS may indicate to us the nature of brain functions that are manifested during this state, assuming we can recognize the functional significance of the observed spike patterns.

Consider the amazement of the proverbial visitor from space, viewing the behavior of mammals and interpreting the significance of REM sleep. He would note that mammalian organisms periodically enter a state in which most motor neurons are paralyzed by a tonic inhibitory process (Pompeiano, 1967). Simultaneously, many other brain neurons begin to behave as if the animal were awake, exhibiting spike train patterns normally associated with waking behaviors or functions. During waking (W), cells in sensory pathways are active in a predictable fashion, exhibiting variations in activity that are determined by the changing sensory flux. It is thought that the characteristics of sensory receptors, pathways and synaptic interactions can account for these activity variations. Similarly, cells associated with motor behavior exhibit tight correlations with specific ongoing movements. But in the REMS state, these same sensory and motor cells exhibit variations in activity that seem to be grossly similar to those found in W, but the sensory flux and motor behavior that "explained" these variations no longer occur. Some examples of motor-related cellular activity in waking and REMS are shown in Figure 1. *During REMS some intrinsic brain process may be modulating cellular behavior.* From the vantage point of the cellular neurophysiologist, it seems entirely plausible that during REMS cells are involved in activities related to the regulation of behavior, possibly including learning, memory, or homeostatic functions.

However, we have speculated beyond the scope of existing data. We have suggested that neurons exhibit discharge patterns in REMS grossly similar to those in waking, but this comparison has not been given detailed consideration. We must in fact, formulate a set of basic questions. What are the similarities and differences between the behavior of cells during waking and REMS? More specifically, can unit discharge rates, interval patterns in spike trains, temporal patterns in the onset and offset of spike trains in REMS be compared with those seen during specific waking behavioral events or processes, such as certain sensory stimuli, drive states, or motor behaviors? Is it possible to recognize neuronal activity sequences in REMS that indicate that the brain is literally reconsidering recognizable unique sensory inputs or motor

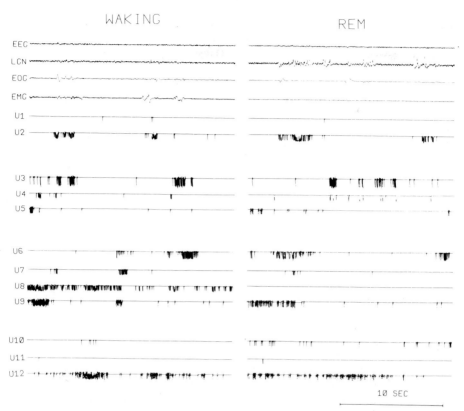

Fig. 1. Polygraph recordings from waking and REMS comparing patterns of spike activity of pontine tegmental neurons. Units (U) 2, 3, 5, 6, 7, 9, 10, and 12 exhibited bursts of spike discharge in relation to head movements in waking and during REMS, but little activity in quiet waking or SWS and were identified as FTG neurons. Note that, in these samples, bursts and pauses in spike discharge of individual FTG neurons tended to exhibit the same temporal patterns in both states.

outputs? Or do spike trains in REMS exhibit properties never seen in W, suggestive of specialized functions? Although we are far from definitive answers, these questions will be considered in the following discussion.

We will describe the results of experiments in which the behavior of single cells sampled from a specific population is recorded during certain waking behaviors and in REMS. We hope both to recognize the significance of the waking activity

of the cells and to compare its characteristics with those
observed in REMS. In attempting to design experiments which
would yield answers to our questions, we must first decide
which samples of waking should be selected for comparison with
REMS. The most common point of view is that REMS should be
compared with preceding waking, because only previously
acquired information can be processed. REMS is usually
thought of as having some recuperative or homeostatic function.
Therefore, most behavioral studies, and the unit studies
described here, relate REMS periods with previous W periods.
Logically, however, it is possible that REMS activities could
be more highly correlated with subsequent events, that REMS
has preparatory functions. We will describe data supporting
the latter point of view.

Motor "Behavior" During REMS

The medial pontine reticular formation contains a class
of scattered "giant" neurons which exhibit bursts of phasic
activity during REMS and during the pre-REM PGO waves; the
"FTG" neurons, which have been studied by Hobson and his
associates (see Hobson, this volume). These cells have been
found to have the following additional properties. During
SWS and quiet waking these cells exhibit little spontaneous
activity. During active waking these cells exhibit bursts of
activity that are correlated with specific head movements.
For example, a particular cell may exhibit a burst of spikes
during head turning in one direction, head extension, or head
lowering. Most cells discharge in relation to a single type
of movement. Movement-related cellular discharge could be
induced by either passive or active head movement and was
attenuated by head restraint.
The latter facts suggest that movement-related discharge
in FTG cells is a corollary to primary movement or movement
command, or may be related to proprioceptive or vestibular
movement correlates rather than the initiation of movement.
Nevertheless, these cells exhibited discharges which indicate
the occasion of specific movements and could be used to
compare overt waking motor behavior and covert REMS motor
"behavior." We have compared two aspects of spike train
samples from waking and REMS. First, the interval histogram
function was used to examine the internal structure of the
spike train burst. Second, the duration of bursts and inter-
burst pauses and the intra-burst spike frequency were analysed
to indicate the duration, frequency, and rate of waking and
REMS "behavior." These techniques are explained further below.

Perhaps the most thorny problem was the finding of useful criteria for choosing waking samples for comparison with REMS. Since we were aware that spike trains from waking samples reflected the specific head movements occurring during the samples, we were faced with the option of choosing samples during certain specific behaviors such as feeding, grooming, and guided head turning, or more varied behaviors such as exploration. We settled on the use of 120 second samples representing a variety of behaviors, usually the samples yielding the highest waking rate.

Burst Patterns

As shown in Figure 1, FTG neurons exhibit bursts of spikes alternating with pauses in activity. We reasoned that the duration of these bursts and pauses and the rate of spike activity within bursts were a reflection of the sequencing and rate of movements. If REMS bursts correspond to covert movement, then the duration of the burst should be similar to those during waking. Bursts were defined as any sequence of three of more spikes with no intervals exceeding 50 milliseconds. For each 120 second sample, the list of burst durations, inter-burst intervals, and average intra-burst spike frequencies were sorted to provide relative frequency distributions as illustrated for one cell in Figure 2. This figure indicates that the shapes of the three distributions were similar in waking and REMS. In order to carry out quantitative comparisons, the relative frequency distributions for each parameter and each cell were divided into portions consisting of short intervals or durations or low frequency components, intermediate components, and long intervals or durations or high frequency components. The proportions of the distribution in each component were averaged for all cells for both waking and REMS samples and were then compared statistically. The results are summarized in Table 1.

These comparisons indicate that the general pattern of motor activity, the durations of "movements," the intervals between "movements," and the rates of the "movements" (burst frequencies) are similar in waking and REMS. For example, the proportions of burst frequencies between 40 and 120 spikes per second were virtually identical in waking and REMS, and proportions of intermediate burst durations and intervals were also similar. Some differences appeared at the extremes of the distributions. A significantly larger proportion of both long duration burst (> 720 ms) and short inter-burst intervals (≤ 200 ms) were observed in REMS. These differences are

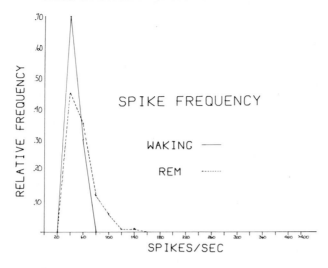

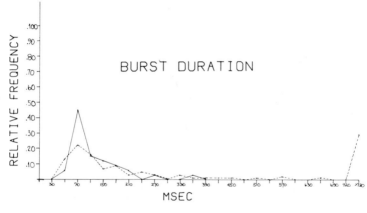

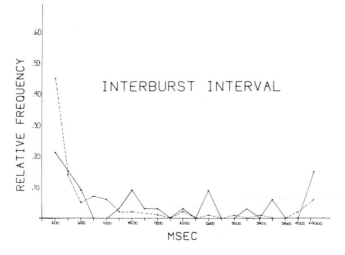

Fig. 2.   Comparison of neuronal spike burst patterns in waking and REMS.   The relative frequncy histograms of intra-burst spike frequency, burst duration, and inter-burst intervals from waking (solid line) and REMS (broken line) samples of a single FTG neuron are presented.   Note that these histograms are generally similar in both states.   The proportion of long burst durations and short inter-burst intervals were significantly elevated in REMS in our cell population.

TABLE 1

COMPARISON OF BURST PATTERNS IN WAKING AND REMS

	Intra-burst frequency		
	$\leq$ 40 s/s	41-120 s/s	> 120 s/s
Waking	.35	.63	.02
REMS	.29	.65	.04

	Burst duration		
	$\leq$ 60 ms	61-210 ms	> 720 ms
Waking	.13	.61	.02[a]
REMS	.20	.53	.09[a]

	Inter-burst interval		
	$\leq$ 200 ms	201-600 ms	> 4000 ms
Waking	.35[b]	.24	.13
REMS	.47[b]	.21	.11

[a] $p < .05$, two-tailed "t" tests

[b] $p < .02$, two-tailed "t" tests

The table compares the mean proportions of selected portions of relative frequency distributions of burst durations, inter-burst intervals, and intra-burst spike frequencies for waking and REMS.   The averages were derived from 11 cells. See text for a detailed explanation.   Intra-burst frequencies are given in spikes per second (s/s) and durations and intervals are given in milliseconds (ms).

illustrated in the example seen in Figure 2. However, they do
not represent a large proportion of the overall sample.
Tendencies for more short duration bursts in REMS and high
intra-burst frequencies were not significant.

Interval Histogram

The interval histogram provides information about the
temporal pattern within the spike train, namely, the relative
frequency of various durations of intervals between adjacent
spikes. Examples of interval histograms derived from 120
second samples obtained during REMS and from both preceding
and subsequent waking are shown in Figure 3. It is apparent
that these distributions are shifted to the left in the REMS
samples; that is, the relative proportion of short interspike
intervals is greater in REMS.
We have quantified the shape of these distributions by
calculating the interquartile points, the inter-burst intervals
delineating the shortest and longest fourths of all intervals,
plus the median interval. Table 2 compares the interquartile
points of waking and REMS samples of 12 cells. This comparison
confirms the impression given by the example; most FTG neurons
have shorter interspike intervals at their interquartile points
during REMS.

Commentary

We have examined the hypothesis that activity of FTG
neurons reflects centrally-commanded motor activity during
REMS as in waking. Since, during REMS, motor activity is
prevented by motoneuron hyperpolarization, the inference was
based on the patterns of bursts and pauses in FTG neuronal
discharge that are correlated with spontaneous waking movements. These patterns, that is, the rate, duration, and pauses
in REMS behavior, were found to be generally similar to waking
behavior. The result supports the idea that the commanded
behavior of FTG cells during REMS is qualitatively similar to
their waking behavior. Our interpretation is supported by the
data of Jouvet (1962) and Henley and Morrison (1974) who
studied cat preparations with restricted dorsolateral pontine
lesions. Such cats are thought to exhibit paradoxical sleep
episodes *without* motoneuron paralysis. During sleep they
exhibit episodes of phasic motor activity suggestive of
aggression and flight, that is, behaviors having the appearance of organized motor sequences. On the basis of these

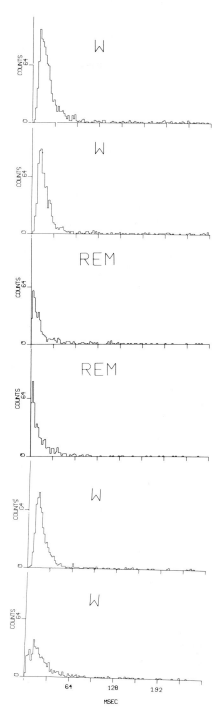

Figure 3

Fig. 3. Interval histograms of spike trains from REMS
and both preceding (upper samples) and subsequent waking (lower
samples). Analyses of two 120-second spike trains from each
of the three sample periods are shown. The interval histograms are shifted during REMS to demonstrate an increased
proportion of short interspike intervals.

TABLE 2

COMPARISON OF INTERQUARTILE POINTS OF INTERVAL
HISTOGRAMS FROM REMS AND WAKING FOR 12 FTG NEURONS

	Q1	Q2	Q3
Waking	2	3	4
REMs	10	9	8

The table shows which of the 12 samples, REMS or
waking, provided the shortest interquartile points,
indicating faster spike discharge within bursts.
Q1 and Q3 refer to the shortest and longest
quartiles, respectively, and Q2 refers to the
median point.

two kinds of results, we conclude that FTG neuronal behavior
in REMS reflects characteristics of "commanded" motor behavior.
On the other hand, we observed certain subtle differences
between REMS and waking spike trains. In most FTG neurons REMS
bursts were of longer duration, and the spike train was characterized by shorter interspike intervals. These differences
could have resulted from insufficient selection of samples from
waking, samples which neglected long and rapid spike trains.
However, since the highest rate waking samples were chosen for
analyses, this bias seems unlikely. Another possibility is
that the REMS spike trains reflect the differences between the
intensity and topography of REMS and waking motor activity,
differences which can readily be observed in the cats with
dorsolateral pontine lesions.

Motivational Influences

Basic questions affecting the understanding of unit
discharge in REMS pertain to the influence of motivational
factors. For example, we may ask if various cell types
respond to food deprivation during sleep by an altered discharge
rate as they are known to respond in waking. This question
was explored experimentally (Jacobs, Harper, & McGinty, 1970)
by measuring unit discharge rate during SWS and REMS in a

variety of midbrain and hypothalamic sites under two conditions:
(1) after 48 hour food deprivation, and (2) following satiation.
Each rate measurement was the mean of at least eight 10-second
samples. In control studies, rates were obtained from two
separate sleeping periods separated by waking time similar to
that required for "satiation," but with no food intake. Some
sample data and a summary of results are shown in Figure 4.

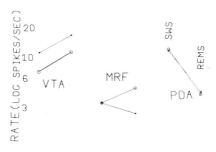

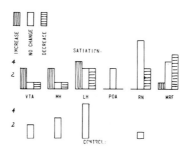

Fig. 4.   Changes in firing rate of midbrain and hypothalamic neurons during sleep before (open circles) and after
(closed circles) satiation following 48 hours food deprivation.
Upper: Examples of firing rate changes in individual neurons
from the ventral tegmental area (VTA), midbrain reticular
formation (MRF), and preoptic area (POA). The VTA unit was
changed in both SWS and REMS, the MRF cell was changed in
REMS, and the POA cell was unaffected by satiation. Lower:
Summary of number of cells exhibiting statistically significant
changes in sleep firing rate in various sites. No changes were
observed in control tests (see text for details). Other sites
included medial hypothalamus (MH), lateral hypothalamus (LH),
and red nucleus.

All 11 cells that were studied in the control condition failed to exhibit significant changes in rate, including six cells which were found to change in the experimental condition. On the other hand, 58% of our experimental cells exhibited significant rate changes in REMS following satiation. In 19 of 24 cells that showed changed discharge rates following satiation, the change was larger in REMS than in SWS. The majority of cells in regions known to be involved in motivational process, including the medial and lateral hypothalamus, midbrain reticular area and ventral tegmental area exhibited significant changes, while most cells in the red nucleus and proptic area were unaffected. The direction of change seen in the medial and lateral hypothalamus produced by satiation was consistent with earlier studies in waking or acute preparations (Oomura, Ooyama, Naka, Yamamoto, Ono, & Koyayashi, 1969). The MRF cell illustrated in Figure 4 declined in rate during REMS following satiation, possibly reflecting a reduced reticular activation. Thus, the direction of change in unit discharge in REMS produced by food deprivation appeared to be the same as in waking.

These results show that the unit discharge rate in REMS reflects a motivational condition in appropriate cells groups. This type of experience does not indicate the source of the motivational influence on rate changes or its behavioral significance. On the other hand, we can conclude that cellular interactions during REMS involving these cells groups will be influenced by these rate changes.

Relationship of REM Sleep and Food Intake

The preceding conclusions present us with a timely opportunity to digress from our emphasis on unit-recording studies, to consider the more general issue of how and when neuronal activity in REMS may influence waking behavior. The question investigated in these experiments (Siegel, 1973, 1975) was whether the amount of REM sleep that a cat had was related to the amount of food it consumed. EMG and EEG measures were recorded continuously while cats were fed *ad libitum* for periods of from five to nine days. The animals were maintained on a 12-hour light-dark cycle. They were individually caged, room temperature was kept constant and the cages were thoroughly cleaned and checked for food spillage every 10 hours. Amounts of REM sleep, SWS, waking and food intake were calculated separately for the lights-on "day" period and the lights-off "night" period.

It was found that the amount of REM sleep in a 12-hour period was significantly correlated with food intake in the *subsequent* 12-hour period (see Table 3). An example of one such relationship can be seen in Figure 5. REM sleep was never significantly correlated with food intake in the previous 12-hour period. Furthermore, no clear relationship could be seen between REM sleep and food intake which occurred within the same 12-hour period. A consistent pattern of correlations was seen in all of the cats. Either day REM or night REM, but never both, showed significant correlations with the food intake in the subsequent 12-hour interval. All but one of the significant REM sleep-subsequent food intake correlations were negative. Therefore, increased amounts of REM sleep were associated with decreased amounts of food intake in the subsequent 12-hour period.

The interval used for prediction did not overlap the subsequent predicted interval. Therefore, the observed correlations could not merely be the result of REM sleep time displacing waking time during which eating might have occurred. All of the significant correlations between REM sleep and subsequent food intake were larger in magnitude than the corresponding correlations between W, SWS, or food intake, and subsequent food intake. Similarly, all of the correlations between REM sleep and subsequent food intake were larger than the correlations between waking or SWS, and food intake when all were within the same interval. Therefore, these data show that REM sleep time is a better predictor of subsequent food intake than either previous food intake, waking or SWS, or concurrent waking or SWS.

This strong and specific relationship between REM sleep and subsequent food intake has several implications for studies relating REM sleep to behavior. These include the following: (1) REM sleep may relate more strongly to subsequent behavior than it does to previous behavior; (2) the relevant period of analysis may be the 24 hour circadian cycle and not the 30 minute REM-waking cycle; (3) REM sleep may have a relatively specific relationship to subsequent food consumption apart from any role in consolidation or other "higher" *functions*.

Commentary

The conclusions reached in this study are consistent with a variety of other experimental findings. REM deprivation has been shown to alter thresholds and rates of subsequent brain self-stimulation and food consumption (Steiner & Ellman, 1972; Dement, 1969). These results can be interpreted, in the light

TABLE 3

PERSON PRODUCT-MOMENT CORRELATIONS BETWEEN FOOD INTAKE IN ONE PERIOD
AND REM, SWS, W, AND FOOD INTAKE IN THE PRECEDING OR SAME 12-HOUR PERIOD

CAT	DAY FOOD INTAKES, PRECEDING NIGHT SLEEP MEASURES				NIGHT FOOD INTAKE, PRECEDING DAY SLEEP MEASURES				NIGHT FOOD INTAKE, CONCURRENT SLEEP MEASURES			DAY FOOD INTAKE, CONCURRENT SLEEP MEASURES			
	REM	W	SWS	FOOD	REM	W	SWS	FOOD	REM	W	SWS	REM	W	SWS	N
23	-.95[b]	+.84[a]	+.73	+.72	+.09	-.21	+.40	+.27	-.49	+.33	+.56	+.72	-.82[a]	+.75	7
24	-.34[b]	+.44	-.11	-.03	-.90[b]	+.40	+.31	-.28	+.48	-.72	+.13	+.45	+.11	-.49	8
25(1)	-.98[b]	-.09	+.38	-.65	-.19	+.36	-.38	-.67	+.64	+.81	-.95[a]	+.64	-.26	-.06	5
28(1)	-.84[a]	+.73	-.51	-.54	-.38	-.03	+.11	+.68	+.28[b]	-.14	+.04	-.52	+.04	+.04	7
25(2)	-.04	-.14	+.23	+.27	+.80[a]	-.43	-.17	-.40	-.87[b]	+.63	-.51	-.35	-.06	+.24	7
28(2)	-.74[a]	+.22	+.16	-.30	-.24	+.23	-.13	-.20	-.25	-.37	+.50	+.65	-.08	-.15	8

[a] $p < .05$, two-tailed probability value

[b] $p < .01$, two-tailed probability value

REM sleep, SWS and W are computed as a percentage of the 12-hour recording time. N is the number of observations.

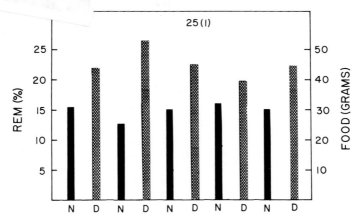

Fig. 5. Data for cat 25. Note that increased amounts of REM sleep (solid bars) are followed by decreased amount of food intake (cross-hatched bars) on the subsequent day.

of our present findings, as evidence for an alteration in motivational levels resulting from the disruption of REM sleep's regulatory influence. The unit recordings by Jacobs et al. (1970), mentioned in the previous section, provide evidence that hypothalamic neurons express their response to food deprivation most strongly during REM sleep.

The importance of circadian influences in the regulation of REM sleep has been seen in a number of recent studies. Time of day, not the amount of prior sleep, has been shown to be the most important determinant of REM sleep occurrence (Taub & Berger, 1973; Sterman, Knauss, Lehman, & Clemente, 1965; Sterman, Lucan, & MacDonald, 1972). Food intake is similarly subject to strong circadian regulation (LeMagnen & Devos, 1970). These results, in conjunction with the present findings, suggest a relationship between the amplitudes of the circadian cycles regulating REM sleep and those regulating food intake, and perhaps other motivated behavior.

The existence of a relationship between REM sleep and subsequent food intake creates problems of interpretation for studies relating REM sleep to learning, and using food as a reinforcement. Many such studies can be interpreted as reflecting postingestional consequences of food intake on REM sleep. Other studies showing changes in REM sleep preceding a change in performance (e.g., Smith, Kitahama, Valatx, & Jouvet, 1974) may, in fact, be reflecting an alteration in motivation rather than retention. A better understanding of the relationship of REM sleep to food intake and food

dependent motivation would be necessary to pr   erpret
these studies.

Serotonin-Containing Neurons

Neuron classes which are thought to be involved in the
active control of sleep have special significance for the
problem of information processing during sleep. In particular,
we have shown that a group of serotonin-containing neurons
exhibits a unique suppression of discharge during REM. Since
serotonin may play a role in regulation of biochemical
processes related to information processing as well as in
sleep (Jouvet, 1967), the unique interruption of release of
serotonin during REM is potentially significant. These results
are described below.

The recording of raphe unit discharge rate would seem to
provide the best method for obtaining a detailed description
of the time course of 5HT turnover in relation to behavioral
events (see McGinty, Harper, & Fairbanks, 1974, for a review
of this approach). Excitation of raphe neurons increases the
release and metabolism of 5HT; thus, release of 5HT, like
acetylcholine, appears to be initiated by the invasion of the
nerve terminal by an action potential. Brief and subtle
changes in 5HT release can be estimated from unit recordings.
Contemporary biochemical and histochemical methods are limited
to estimates of relatively long-term changes and are often
incompatible with the study of normal sleep states. Further
discussion of the properties of serotonin-containing neurons
is found in this volume.

We have studied the discharge patterns of 38 dorsal raphe
neurons of the type thought to contain 5HT (McGinty & Harper,
1976). These neurons exhibit a slow regular discharge rate
in waking (0.5-5 spike/second), similar to that observed in
the anesthetized rat (Aghajanian, Foote, & Sheard, 1968, 1970;
Mosko & Jacobs, 1974). Bursts of unit spikes, typical of the
pontine neurons described above, are never observed in raphe
units. Changes in discharge rate during SWS and REMS are
remarkably consistent within this cell population. The mean
discharge rate is reduced about 50% in SWS when compared with
waking. This change was statistically significant even in
most individual neurons, as well as in the group mean.

The most interesting effect was associated with REM sleep.
Raphe neurons exhibited a striking suppression of discharge
during REM when compared with SWS or waking. The mean rate
was reduced 92% compared with W. This change was significant
in most individual neurons as well as the groups. Figure 6

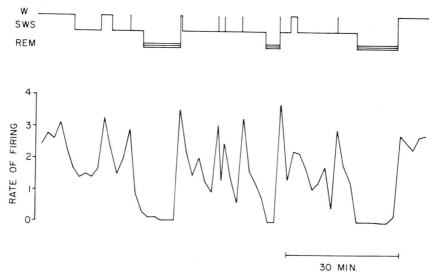

Fig. 6. Firing rate of an individual dorsal raphe neuron during an extended waking-sleep-waking cycle including three REMS episodes. Note that unit discharge was highest during waking, gradually declined during sustained periods of SWS and virtually ceased during each REMS episode.

depicts these rate changes in a typical cell, and illustrates the stability of this phenomenon during successive SWS-REM cycles.

Commentary

The depression, during REMS, of raphe unit discharge and, by implication, the release of 5HT may have special significance for theories of memory processing during REMS which include a role for protein synthesis. Essman has reported a series of findings (1) correlating retrograde amnesia phenomena, especially that induced by electroconvulsive shock (ECS), with diminished turnover of 5HT (Essman, 1974), and (2) showing that resulting high levels of 5HT are related to inhibition of protein synthesis *in vivo* and *in vitro* (Essman, 1974). Many amnesic treatments, including either anesthesia, hypothermia, hypoxia, as well as ECS, have in common a suppression of 5HT turnover (Essman, 1971). Further, ECS-induced amnesia is attenuated by treatments and methods that prevent elevation of 5HT levels that result from diminished turnover (Essman, 1968).

These findings may explain some memory changes associated with sleep. The poor memory for events occurring during short arousal from sleep, for dream content, and for material learned immediately after arousal from sleep (see the discussion by Ekstrand, this volume) may be explained by a diminished protein synthesis secondary to reduced turnover of 5HT.

In addition, diminished protein synthesis and consolidation of recent memories may be factors that will ultimately contribute to our comprehension of the functions of REMS. Perhaps the *absence* of recent memory consolidation makes possible certain types of information processing operations such as the disposal of useless information.

DISCUSSION

Sleep investigators from Aristotle to Freud, to present-day unit researchers have been attempting to explain the relationship between mental activity in sleep and waking behavior. In this quest, unit researchers have certain advantages. The foremost of these is that we are able to objectively measure brain activity during sleep and quantitatively relate it to waking activity. We do not have to rely on the subject's recollections of his dream experiences and their transformation into verbal messages during a subsequent W interval. In addition, we can, in principle, assess various elements of the cognitive and motor process, distinguishing excitatory vs. inhibitory processes, aspects of motivation, temporal order effects, and so on. We can also model the influences of drugs, neurological disturbances, and other manipulations that are not readily applied to humans. Unfortunately, the great advantage of being able to observe directly the functional "atom" of the brain is accompanied by the great disadvantage of being as yet unable to fully understand the role of these "atoms" in the complex brain "chemistry" underlying behavior. However, with the proper caution, we feel that it is possible to extract important information by careful observation of both sleep and waking unit activity.

The intriguing possibility of relating unit recording data to psychological concepts of cognitive function in sleep, such as rehearsal, hypothesis testing, integration of experience, or homeostatic adjustment, requires further comment. A primary problem is that neuronal systems are not necessarily "coded" or organized along the dimensions of psychological concepts. At best, neuronal behavior can be correlated with behavioral descriptions, as with the accuracy of a choice in a discrimination learning trial, or with the rate or intensity of a behavior. Psychological concepts such as rehearsal and consolidation which have been related to REMS must be defined in unambiguous behavioral terms. It is possible that neuro-physiological studies cannot be used at this level of analyses, that the functions of sleep can only be expressed in the complex interrelationships of groups of millions of neurons. Another possibility is that neuronal activity in sleep is exclusively reflecting intraneuronal processes during sleep, such as membrane repair, RNA and protein synthesis and energy transport. If this is the case, intracellular recording and neurochemical studies would be necessary to understand these processes. However, the parsimony of nature, and the similar-ity of sleep and waking activity in identifiable groups of cells, encourages us to hope that there are meaningful questions that can be asked of single neurons recorded extra-cellularly.

We have not succeeded in relating specific aspects of REMS "behavior" to specific samples of waking behavior. That is, we cannot yet recognize the specific type of motor behavior occurring in REMS. Our preliminary data show that REM behavior does *not* consist of simple rhythmic activities such as eating or grooming. Compared with our waking samples, REMS behavior is more variable. These observations are in agreement with analyses of dream content which usually reveal a mixture of ordinary events and unlikely times, settings, or stimuli. In current studies we are conditioning specific head movements during waking, using hypothalamic stimulation as a reward. We hope that this approach will yield patterned motor behavior which will be reflected in the REM episode. Specific patterned motor behavior will be recognized by analysis of burst structures or time series analyses. We could then assess variables which modulate the probability that a parti-cular behavior will be manifested in REMS, and the nature of modification of patterned motor behavior in REMS. This approach should be of value in interpreting the post-learning enhancement of REM as described by Bloch and his colleagues (see Bloch, this volume).

A finding that patterned motor behavior, conditioned during waking, is manifested in REM would have another benefit. It would strengthen the interpretation that the motor activity represented in FTG neurons does, indeed, reflect centrally commanded or programmed motor outflow. Our current results could be interpreted as resulting from local reflex inter-action, rather than centrally coordinated activity. It is conceivable that neurons at each level of the neuroaxis are uncoupled in REM, and operate independently. Similarly, our finding that hypothalamic and midbrain neurons are sensitive to effects of food deprivation is suggestive of interneuronal coordination, but it is possible that a variety of individual neurons can be sensitive to blood-borne or other non-specific factors associated with food ingestion. Studies of inter-action of remote neural elements will help resolve this issue.

SUMMARY

We have studied and compared the discharge patterns of single brainstem and hypothalamic neurons during wakefulness and REM sleep in the cat, in an effort to assess the functional characteristics of REMS. On the basis of these studies we have reached the following conclusions.

1. In neurons associated with motor behavior, REMS discharge patterns closely resemble those in waking, indicating an expression during REMS of normal movement patterns.

2. Neurons exhibit changed discharge rate in response to food deprivation during REMS as they do in waking, indicating a potential influence of motivational mechanisms in REMS.

3. The release of serotonin in the forebrain projection fields of dorsal raphe neurons is greatly decreased during REMS. Decreased release of 5HT has been implicated as a mechanism resulting in failure of immediate memory consolida-tion and may account for amnesia for dreams.

In addition, we have presented results of a study corre-lating the amount of REMS in a 12-hour period with food intake in the preceding, same, or subsequent 12-hour period. It was found that the amount of REMS was most highly correlated with subsequent food intake, and that this correlation was not secondary to changes in waking or SWS. This result suggests that REMS may have a stronger relationship to subsequent behavior than it does to previous behavior.

ACKNOWLEDGMENTS

This research was supported by the Veterans Administra-tion Research Project 5590-01 and National Institute of Mental Health Grant #10083. The assistance of Mary Fairbanks and Sandy Sarnoff is gratefully acknowledged.

REFERENCES

Aghajanian, G. K., Foote, W. E., & Sheard, M. H. Lysergic
acid diethylaminde: sensitive neuronal units in the
midbrain raphe. *Science,* 1968, *161,* 606-608.

Aghajanian, G. K., Foote, W. E., & Sheard, M. H. Action of
psychotogenic drugs on single midbrain raphe neurons.
Journal of Pharmacology and Experimental Therapeutics,
1970, *171,* 178-187.

Bizzi, E., Pompeiano, O., & Somogyi, I. Spontaneous activity
of single vestibular neurons of unrestrained cats during
sleep and wakefulness. *Archives Italiennes de Biologie,*
1964, *102,* 308.

Dement, W. C. The biological role of REM sleep (circa 1968).
In A. Kales (Ed.), *Sleep Physiology and Pathology.*
Philadelphia: J. B. Lippincott, 1969.

Essman, W. B. Electroshock induced retrograde amnesia and
brain serotonin metabolism: effects of several antidepressant compounds. *Psychopharmacologia,* 1968, *13,*
258-266.

Essman, W. B. Drug effects and learning and memory processes.
In S. Garattini, A. Golden, F. Hawkins, & I. J. Kopen
(Eds.), *Advances in Pharmacology and Chemotherapy.*
New York: Academic Press, 1971.

Essman, W. B. Brain 5HT and memory consolidation. In
E. Costa, G. L. Gessa, & M. Sandler (Eds.), *Serotonin--
New Vistas.* New York: Raven Press, 1974.

Evarts, E. V. Activity of neurons in visual cortex of the
cat during sleep with low voltage fast EEG activity.
Journal of Neurophysiology, 1962, *25,* 812-816.

Evarts, E. V. Temporal patterns of discharge of pyramidal
tract neurons during sleep and waking in the monkey.
Journal of Neurophysiology, 1964, *27,* 152-172.

Evarts, E. V. Activity of individual cerebral neurons during
sleep and arousal. In S. S. Kety, E. V. Evarts, &
H. L. Williams (Eds.), *Sleep and Altered States of
Consciousness* (Vol. 45). Baltimore: Williams and
Wilkins, 1967.

Findlay, A. L. R., & Hayward, J. N.   Spontaneous activity of single neurons in the hypothalamus of rabbits during sleep and waking. *Journal of Physiology* (London), *201*, 237-258.

Henley, K., & Morrison, A. R.   A re-evaluation of the effects of lesions of the pontine tegmentum and locus coeruleus on phenomena of paradoxical sleep in the cat. *Acta Neurobiologia Experimentalis*, 1974, *34*, 215-232.

Hobson, J. A., & McCarley, R. W.   Cortical unit activity in sleep and waking. *Electroencephalography and clinical Neurophysiology*, 1971, *30*, 97-112.

Huttenlocher, P. R.   Evoked and spontaneous activity in single units of medial brain stem during natural sleep and waking. *Journal of Neurophysiology*, 1961, *24*, 451-468.

Jacobs, B. L., Harper, R. M., & McGinty, D. J.   Neuronal coding of motivational level during sleep. *Physiology and Behavior*, 1970, *5*, 1139-1143.

Jacobs, B. L., & McGinty, D. J.   Amygdala unit activity during sleep and wakefulness. *Experimental Neurology*, 1971, *33*, 1-15.

Jouvet, M.   Recherches sur les structures nerveuses et les mechanismes responsables des differentes phases du sommeil physiologique. *Archives Italiennes de Biologie*, 1962, *100*, 125-206.

Jouvet, M.   Mechanisms of the states of sleep: A neuro-pharmacological approach. In S. S. Kety, E. V. Evarts, & H. L. Williams (Eds.), *Sleep and Altered States of Consciousness*. Baltimore: Williams and Wilkins, 1967.

Kasamatsu, T.   Maintained and evoked unit activity in the mesencephalic reticular formation of the freely behaving cat. *Experimental Neurology*, 1970, *28*, 450-470.

LeMagnen, J., & Devos, M.   Metabolic correlates of the meal onset in the free food intake of rats. *Physiology and Behavior*, 1970, *5*, 805-814.

McGinty, D. J., & Harper, R. M.   Dorsal raphe neurons: depression of firing during sleep in cats. *Brain Research*, 1976, *101*, 569-575.

McGinty, D. J., Harper, R. M., & Fairbanks, M. K. 5HT-containing neurons: unit activity in behaving cats. In J. Barchas & E. Usdin (Eds.), *Serotonin and Behavior.* New York: Academic Press, 1973.

McGinty, D. J., Harper, R. M., & Fairbanks, M. K. Neuronal activity and the control of sleep states. In E. D. Weitzman (Ed.), *Advances in Sleep Research* (Vol. 1). New York: Spectrum Publications, 1974.

Mosko, S., & Jacobs, B. L. Effect of peripherally administered serotonin on the neuronal activity of midbrain raphe neurons. *Brain Research,* 1974, *79,* 315-320.

Mukhametov, L. M., Rizzolotti, G., & Seitun, A. An analysis of the spontaneous activity of lateral geniculate neurons and of optic tract fibers in free moving cats. *Archives Italiennes de Biologie,* 1970, *108,* 325-347.

Mukhametov, L. M., Rizzolotti, G., & Tradardi, V. Spontaneous activity of neurones of nucleus reticularis thalami in freely moving cats. *Journal of Physiology,* 1970, *210,* 651-667.

Noda, H., & Adey, W. R. Firing variability in cat association cortex during sleep and wakefulness. *Brain Research,* 1970, *18,* 513-526.

Noda, H., Manohar, S., & Adey, W. R. Spontaneous activity of cat hippocampal neurons in sleep and wakefulness. *Experimental Neurology,* 1969, *24,* 217-231.

Oomura, Y., Ooyama, H., Naka, F., Yamamoto, T., Ono, T., & Koyayashi, N. Some stochastical patterns of single unit discharges in the cat hypothalamus under chronic conditions. *Annals of the New York Academy of Science,* 1969, *157,* 666-689.

Pompeiano, O. The neurophysiological mechanisms of the postural and motor events during desynchronized sleep. In S. S. Kety, E. V. Evarts, & H. L. Williams (Eds.), *Sleep and Altered States of Consciousness* (Vol. 45). Baltimore: Williams and Wilkins, 1967.

Sakakura, H. Spontaneous and evoked unitary activities of cat lateral geniculate neurons in sleep and wakefulness. *Japanese Journal of Physiology,* 1968, *18,* 23-42.

Siegel, J. M. Prediction of food intake from REM sleep. *Sleep Research*, 1973, *2*, 97.

Siegel, J. M. REM sleep predicts subsequent food intake. *Physiology and Behavior*, 1975, *15*, 399-403.

Smith, C., Kitahama, K., Valatx, & Jouvet, M. Increased paradoxial sleep in mice during acquisition of shock avoidance task. *Brain Research*, 1974, *77*, 221-230.

Steiner, S. S., & Ellman, S. J. Relation between REM sleep and intracranial self-stimulation. *Science*, 1972, *177*, 1122-1124.

Sterman, M. B., Knauss, T., Lehman, D., & Clemente, C. D. Circadian sleep and waking patterns in the laboratory cat. *Electroencephalography and clinical Neurophysiology*, 1965, *19*, 509-517.

Sterman, M. B., Lucas, E. A., & MacDonald, L. R. Periodicity within sleep and operant performance in the cat. *Brain Research*, 1972, *38*, 237-341.

Taub, J. M., & Berger, R. J. Sleep state patterns associated with acute shifts in the sleep-wakefulness cycle. *Electroencephalography and clinical Neurophysiology*, 1973, *35*, 613-619.

THE RECIPROCAL INTERACTION MODEL OF SLEEP CYCLE CONTROL: IMPLICATIONS FOR PGO WAVE GENERATION AND DREAM AMNESIA

J. ALLAN HOBSON

Laboratory of Neurophysiology
Department of Psychiatry
Harvard Medical School
Boston, Massachusetts 02115 USA

The setting of this meeting and the subject of my talk recall the memory of some of our predecessors whose work converges here:

Ramon y Cajal, who laid the foundation of the cellular approach to neurobiology upon which we base our investigation of synaptic transmission and its modulation in the states of sleep and waking. (Ramon y Cajal, 1909.)

Lorente de Nò, who described the vestibulo-ocular reflex arc and provided a possible neural substrate for the phasic events of the desynchronized phase of sleep. (Lorente de Nò, 1933.)

Raul Hernandez-Peon, who investigated the possibility that sleep, including its desynchronized phase, might be produced by the introduction of cholinergic substances in certain brain regions. (Hernandez-Peon, 1962.)

In this paper, a phenomenologic contrast between memory function during waking and dreaming will be emphasized. Then a cellular synaptic model of sleep cycle control will be used to explain the generation of PGO waves that are seen in the desynchronized sleep of cats. These waves may be the EEG correlates of phasic excitation of internal origin; such excitation may constitute information produced and processed by the human brain as the dream. The implications of the model for memory will then be speculated upon and it will be hypothesized that amnesia for dreams may be a consequence of the shifts in transmitter ratios inherent in the generator mechanisms of desynchronized sleep.

Since Our Dreams are Full of Memory, Why Can't We Remember Our Dreams?

Our dreams are characterized by a rich interpenetration of remote and recent memories. Yet, unless we awaken from dreaming sleep, we are almost totally amnesic for these vivid reminiscences. We are thus confronted with the paradox that though our dreams are the products of remote and recent memory, they are not, themselves, remembered.

This striking phenomenological contrast suggests a one-way street, during dreaming sleep, between memory and consciousness: memories are freely called up but the conscious experience into which they are then incorporated is not restored in memory.

Laboratory study has revealed, however, that prompt and movement-free arousal is powerfully mnemonic for dreams; this fact suggests that a state change, from dreaming sleep to waking, may be necessary to open the street to traffic in the opposite direction, allowing the dream itself to be held in memory (Aserinsky and Kleitman, 1953; Snyder, 1963; Foulkes, 1966).

Waking and dreaming sleep may thus be symmetrically contrasting states where memory is concerned:

During waking, conscious experience is entered into memory and held despite subsequent state changes; recent memory tends to predominate in waking consciousness.

During dreaming sleep, conscious experience is intense and marked by rich and abundant remote reminiscences, but these are usually not held in memory unless an immediate and unperturbed state change to waking occurs.

With the exception of some metapsychological speculations (Freud, 1938), attention to this paradox has been limited. Psychophysiologists appear to have overlooked the opportunities presented by these state-dependent variations in memory function.

For example, one possible approach to the neurophysiology of memory is to examine the physiological substrata of waking and dreaming sleep for differences that could give insight to the conditions, if not the causes, of memory construction and/or retrieval. This approach assumes that physiologic features critical to the phenomenologic contrasts experienced by humans will be observable in the sleep and waking states of the experimental animals. This assumption has a vivid precedent in the Olmec myth that postulated man's descent from the union of a woman and a jaguar. In other words, this tenet is unprovable but compelling. We cannot know if cats dream, but if they do so, it is probably during the de-

synchronized phase of sleep. And, since Nature is economical
in her means, we can assume that the mechanisms of sleep
cycle control are likely to be similar in all mammals
evincing periodic EEG desynchronization in sleep.

Using the method of chronic extracellular single unit
recording, we have recently discovered contrasting behavior
of two brain stem neuronal groups in waking and desynchronized
sleep of cats (Hobson, McCarley, & Wyzinski, 1975). The
results, interpreted in the light of recent advances in
neurotransmitter physiology, have led us to construct a
model for sleep cycle control (McCarley, & Hobson, 1975).
This model is quite general and has implications for the
mechanism of generation of phasic events in desynchronized
sleep as well as for the longer-term (tonic) fluctuations
of the sleep cycle. Since molecular as well as membrane
events are encompassed by the model, it may also be relevant
to theories of memory. In this paper I compare the model
with the data and interpretations of other workers on the
generation of pontine, geniculate, occipital (PGO) waves,
a distinctive "phasic" event stigmatic of desynchronized
sleep. I propose that PGO waves are the result of the
synchronous discharge of cholinergic, cholinoceptive giant
reticular neurons of the pontine tegmentum whose excitability
is periodically increased, during desynchronized sleep, by
the mechanisms of disinhibition and self-excitation. The
source of inhibition, which damps the excitability of the
giant cells during other phases of the sleep-waking cycle is
postulated to be the aminergic neurons of the locus coeruleus
(noradrenergic) and raphe nuclei (serotonergic); these cell
groups are postulated to be interconnected with the giant
cells in such a way that peaks of activity in one class of
cell are associated with troughs in the other and vice versa.
At peaks of giant cell activity, aminergic inhibition is
minimal and cholinergic excitation is maximal; desynchronized
sleep is the result. At peaks of aminergic neuronal activity,
the giant cells are inhibited and cholinergic influences are
minimal; waking is the result. The postsynaptic and intracellular consequences of this shift in transmitter balance
may thus be significant for dream amnesia.

Modelling the PGO Generator

Phases of EEG desynchronization occur periodically in
almost all mammals. Just prior to and during these desynchronized (D) sleep phases in the cat, single or multiple
bursts of spiking EEG waves can be observed in the pons,
lateral geniculate, and occipital cortex (PGO_D). These waves

typically consist of a large amplitude potential followed
by a smaller deflection of opposite polarity; in cerebral
cortex they may be preceded by an additional early deflection
yielding a triphasic complex. See Figure 1D for an example
of these waves in the geniculate body. Somewhat similar,
eye movement-related potentials can occasionally be observed
in waking cats (PGO$_W$), but the latter can be distinguished
from PGO$_D$ by means of amplitude, wave form, and different
responses to experimental manipulation of the visual system
(Brooks, & Gershon, 1971; Munson, 1974).

The mechanism of generation of PGO waves is a subject
of intense investigation in many research laboratories. The
problem is attractive because PGO waves provide a discrete
event susceptible to analytic neurophysiological exploration
which could reveal cellular and molecular processes essential
to REM sleep generation. PGO waves are also of psychophysiologic interest since they are contemporaneous with
other phasic events such as eye movements and these, in turn,
are correlated with the intensity of the dream experience in
man. The possibility thus arises that PGO waves may reflect
neuronal processes which underlie the generation of endogenous
information within the brain during sleep that, in man at least,
is realized as the dream. If this were true, one might gain
insight, by the study of PGO generation, to some formal aspects

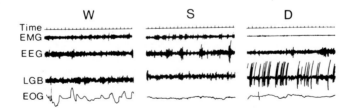

*Figure 1. PGO waves in the Lateral Geniculate Nucleus
(LGB) during desynchronized sleep (D). The figure also
serves to illustrate the other electrographic features of
D as compared with waking (W) and synchronized sleep (S):
in the electromyogram (EMG), note the absence of potentials
in D; in the electroencephalogram (EEG), note the low voltage
activity (also seen in waking) and the absence of the high-
voltage slow waves seen in S; in the electrooculogram (EOG),
note the deflections correlated with eye movements in D and
in W. Time is in seconds.*

of the dream experience such as visual imagery, emotionality, and bizarreness. The mechanism of PGO generation may also provide clues to understanding a puzzling "negative" aspect of the dream experience, namely the retrograde amnesia that makes dream recall so evanescent.

The purpose of the following selective review is to compare and contrast the experimental data and emerging models for PGO generation put forth by the following investigators and their collaborators: Jouvet (Lyon, France); Brooks (New York, U.S.A.); Pompeiano (Pisa, Italy); and Haefely (Basel, Switzerland). These models will be compared with reciprocal interaction hypothesis of McCarley and Hobson (Boston, U.S.A.).

Jouvet and Michel (1959) were the first to describe "spindle" waves associated with REM and periodic atonia in the pontine reticular formation of cats with prepontine ablations. Jouvet and his collaborators have since done recording, lesion, and drug experiments to describe and analyze these events. Although Mikiten, Niebyl, and Hendley (1961) had independently reported on these waves in the lateral geniculate body, Jouvet was the first to use the term "PGO," with its implied concepts of pontine origin(P) and rostral conduction via geniculate body (G) to occipital cortex (O). Subsequent work by the Lyon group and others has revealed that the rostral pathways are complex and diffuse (Laurent, Cespuglio, & Jouvet, 1974) but the basic idea of radiation from pontine tegmentum to forebrain has been supported and is an assumption common to all the models to be discussed in this paper. Experimental efforts by the Lyon group to determine the precise location and nature of the generator mechanism(s) have resulted in the hypothesis that both aminergic and cholinergic mechanisms may be involved; data significant for modelling are the augmentation of PGO waves by mid-line (presumably raphe) lesions (Renault, 1967) and by the amine depletor reserpine (Jouvet, 1967 a, b). The Lyon group has not yet proposed either a specific cellular or a general mathematical model for PGO generation. In a recent publication, they gave the following summary of their current hypothesis:

> We suppose that the generator corresponds to homogenous or non-homogenous group of cells in the pontine tegmentum. This cell group (which may be either) endowed with or devoid of histochemical specificity would be depolarized en masse either by a tonic disinhibition or by an automatic activation and give rise to ascending information (which would be)

TABLE 1

A COMPARISON OF CURRENT HYPOTHESES OF PGO GENERATION

Investigator	Generator Location	Generator Executive Element Cell Species	Transmitter(s)	Inhibitor Element Cell Species	Transmitter(s)	Mechanism Action	Interaction
Jouvet	pontine tegmentum	unspecified	ACh + NE	unspecified	unspecified	unspecified	unspecified
Brooks	pontine tegmentum	unspecified reticular	unspecified	Raphe	5-HT	5-HT inhibition	unspecified
Pompeiano	I-pontine tegmentum	unspecified	aminergic	unspecified	unspecified	unspecified	unspecified
	II-pontine tegmentum	reticular	ACh	unspecified	unspecified	ACh excitation	unspecified
Jalfre	pontine tegmentum	unspecified	unspecified	LC	NE	NE inhibition	unspecified
				Raphe	5-HT	5-HT inhibition	unspecified
Hobson and McCarley	pontine tegmentum	FTG	ACh	LC (esp. posteroventral portion)	NE	ACh excitation, NE inhibition	reciprocal interaction
				DRN (McGinty)	5-HT	5-HT inhibition	

transmitted to the lateral geniculate bodies and
the occipital cortex. (Laurent, et al., 1974)
The translation and parenthetical phrases are mine.

See Figure 2 for a schematic representation of the
pathway based on results of lesion experiments.

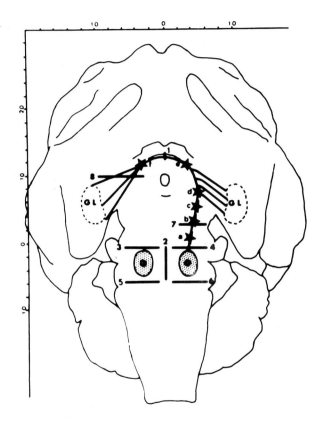

*Figure 2. Anatomical Scheme of PGO generation based on
experiments of Jouvet's Lyon group: g = generator zone in
pontine tegmentum. GL = lateral geniculate nucleus.*
*The transections are represented by numbers, and the
coagulations by letters. Transections 3 plus 4, 3 plus 7,
suppress any PGO_R activity in both lateral geniculate nuclei
and occipital cortices. 5 plus 6 do not suppress PGO_R
activity in the thalamus or cortex. 4 plus 1, 4 plus 8,
7 plus 1, suppress the PGO_R activity in the right lateral
geniculate nucleus. 3 plus 8 suppress PGO_R activity in the
left lateral geniculate nucleus. 1 plus 2 suppress the*

synchronism of PGO$_R$ waves in the two lateral geniculate nuclei. Section 1 or section 2 induce specific alterations in the bilateral synchrony of the waves. The coagulations a, b, c, d, when associated with transection 3, suppress PGO$_R$ activity in both lateral geniculate nuclei. The coagulations e and f, associated with transection 3, suppress the PGO$_R$ activity on the left lateral geniculate nucleus. Reproduced from Laurent, et al. (1974) by permission of publisher.

Brooks has used four techniques in developing his understanding of PGO generation. With Bizzi, he recorded and stimulated through macroelectrodes (1) to establish the optimal recording sites of the waves in the pontine reticular formation, oculomotor nuclei, lateral geniculate body, and cerebral cortex; and (2) to show that waves could be evoked in lateral geniculate body by pontine reticular formation stimulation (but not vice versa) in REM sleep (but not at other times) (Bizzi, & Brooks, 1963; Brooks, & Bizzi, 1963). These are crucial data supporting the hypothesis that the generator is pontine and further suggests that the excitability of the generator is a state-dependent variable. Brooks has since used lesion and pharmacological manipulations to alter the presumed generator and, in light of the results, to make assumptions about its control (Simon, Gershon, & Brooks, 1973). Since serotonin-depleting drugs (PCPA, reserpine) and paramedian brain stem cuts both produced PGO enhancement, Brooks proposed that the generator was inhibited by serotonin-containing neurons. He hypothesizes that pacemaker cells in the paramedian brain stem reticular formation constitute the generator and proposes that they are activated by dis-inhibition. See Figure 3 for a schematic representation of the Brooks PGO generator-suppressor mechanism and the caption for a summary of the Brooks hypothesis. This model does not account for sleep stage periodicity nor has it been developed mathematically.

In microelectrode studies Bizzi, Pompeiano, and Somogyi (1964) found that cells discharged at a high rate in all vestibular nuclei during desynchronized sleep. This finding weighed against vestibular disfacilitation (from Deiter's nucleus) as a possible mechanism for the atonia of desynchronized sleep and implied, by exclusion, that active inhibitory mechanisms descending from the pontine reticular formation might be involved. Cells in the medial and descending vestibular nuclei had phasic rate increases beginning 30 msec prior to the rapid eye movements of desynchronized sleep, suggesting participation of these cells in phasic activity generation.

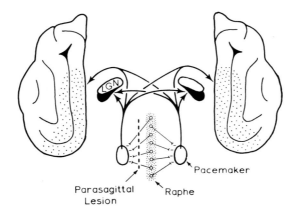

Figure 3. Brooks' Serotonin Gating Model. Schematic dorsal view of the brain, showing the raphe nuclei of the brain stem (fine stippling), the lateral geniculate nucleus (LGN) and the region of the cerebral cortex from which PGO waves may be recorded (coarse stippling). Ascending pathways from the pacemaker are indicated by arrows. According to this model, 5-HT containing neurons which have their perikarya in the nuclei of the raphe send axons laterally to terminate in that part of the pontine reticular formation which is thought to act as a pacemaker for PGO_{REM}. The tonic inhibitory influence (-) which these gating neurons exert upon the pacemaker normally diminishes only during REM sleep, permitting PGO_{REM} to appear at that time. Drugs which deplete 5-HT compromise the inhibitory role of the gating neurons and disrupt the normal regulation of PGO_{REM}. The position of the parasagittal lesions used in this study, relative to the structure of the proposed model, is shown by the dotted line. Reproduced from Simon, Gershon, and Brooks (1973) by permission of the publisher.

Lesions of these same vestibular structures were found by Pompeiano and Morrison (1965) to suppress bursts of REM and clusters of PGO waves (since called "type II" waves by Pompeiano), but not the isolated waves (type I). The conclusion was reached that type II waves were vestibular in origin and/or elaboration (Morrison, & Pompeiano, 1966). Since atonia, groups of PGO waves, and stereotyped eye movements could be induced by eserine given to decerebrate cats (Magherini, Pompeiano, & Thoden, 1971), it was reasoned

that the type II waves were produced by a cholinergic
generator; this generator was presumed to be in the pontine
reticular formation, and to deliver to the vestibular nucleus
a sinusoidal input that was then transformed into a rhythmic
output and which could, in turn, drive the bursts of eye
movement and type II PGO waves.

Pompeiano has modeled this hypothetical system with
detailed treatment of the postulated vestibular transformation
(Pompeiano, & Valentinuzzi, 1976). In this model, the
generator cells are not specifically identified but a
cholinergic reticular system (A) is postulated to produce
a tonic excitatory output, E_T; this step function is then
transformed, still outside the vestibular nuclei, into a
sinusoidal function, E_S, which then influences the ipsilateral
vestibular system, V. The latter system, owing to recurrent
inhibitory feedback, produces a rhythmic function which then
drives the eye movements and type II PGO waves. The model
is both physiological and mathematical but it is partial in
that it does not attempt to explain how the cholinergic
generator mechanism is activated or inactivated. It ascribes
the type I waves to a biogenic amine system which is not
modeled and no interactions between the type I and type II
systems are proposed. See Figure 4 for a schematic representation of the vestibular modulator mechanism proposed by
Pompeiano.

Jalfre, Ruch-Monachon, and Haefely (1974) have developed
a model based upon the results of pharmacological experiments
which suggest an inhibitory role of *both* noradrenergic and
serotonergic systems on PGO generator neurons. This
generalization was suggested earlier, but not made explicit,
by Karczmar, Longo, and Scotti de Carolis (1970) who were
perhaps the first to discuss a possible aminergic-cholinergic
interaction. The experiments of the Basel group confirmed
many previous results but added pharmacological refinements
and produced an important simplification in theory, namely
that both aminergic cell groups might be acting permissively
and concertedly in PGO generation. Continuous PGO waves
were produced by PCPA, an irreversible inhibitor of tryptophan
hydroxylase, and by the benzoquinolizine derivative RO4-1284,
an amine depletor with reserpine-like effects. Two hours
after drug administration, pontine-medullary 5-HT levels
were reduced to 50% and NE to 25% of saline controls and
remained low for 4-5 hours. The serotonin precursors 5-HTP
and L-tryptophan produced dose-related reductions and
eventual abolition of the drug-induced PGO waves and raised
brain 5-HT levels. The 5-HT blockers methiothepin and
octoclothepin markedly increased PGO density in reserpine-
treated cats (Jalfre, et al., 1974). Methiothepin also

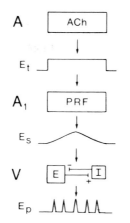

Figure 4. Pompeiano and Valentinuzzi's Vestibular Transform Model. Eserine acts on a cholinergic, self-exciting system, A, which produces a tonic excitatory output, E. This is transformed into an oscillatory signal, Es, in the dorsolateral pontine tegmentum (A₁). The vestibular nuclei, V, consisting of interconnected excitatory (E) and inhibitory (I) neurons, then produce a rhythmic phasic output, Ep, which generates the REM bursts. The Pisa group also postulate that the cholinergic system, A, excites a bulbo-spinal system (not shown here) resulting in descending inhibition of alpha motoneurons. (Figure prepared by J. A. Hobson with permission of O. Pompeiano.)

produced PGO waves in *untreated* animals and antagonized the PGO depressant effect of 5-HTP. These results supported the interpretation that reserpine-type drugs release PGOs by 5-HT depletion, and strengthen the argument that 5-HT neurons normally inhibit the neurons which generate PGO waves (Simon, et al., 1973).

In order to determine the degree of specificity of the hypothesized 5-HT inhibition of PGOs, Jalfre, et al. (1973) tested a series of imipramine-type anti-depressants which differed in their selectivity in blocking 5-HT or NE re-uptake. When a series of 15 of these agents were ranked on ability to suppress RO4-1284-induced PGO waves, several drugs which inhibit the uptake of 5-HT (chlorimipramine, imipramine, and amitriptyline) strongly reduced PGO waves, whereas agents thought to be more selective against NE uptake were much less effective in reducing the incidence of PGO waves. Jalfre et al. (1973) explored further the role of NE mechanisms in PGO control with the following results: (1) NE infused into lateral ventricles reduced the PGO waves provoked by RO4-1284 in a dose-dependent manner. (2) The alpha-adrenergic stimulator, clonidine, abolished PGO waves.   (3) The alpha-adrenergic blocker, phenoxybenzamine, increased PGO waves. (4) The NE synthesis blockers, AMPT, RO8-1981, and disulfiram, all augmented PCPA-induced PGO waves.   (5) Acute bilateral lesions of LC augmented PCPA-induced PGO waves.

   In the model based on the results of Jalfre, et al. (1973, 1974), generator cells are localized to the pontine reticular formation and their activation is hypothesized to depend upon strong excitation by "pacemaker neurons" which are spontaneously and independently active (Haefely, Jalfre, & Monachon, 1973).   The anatomical and chemical identity of generator and pacemaker elements are unspecified.   The mechanism by which tonic aminergic inhibition is withdrawn is also unspecified.   See Figure 5 for a schematic representation of the dual aminergic suppression system envisaged by the Swiss group.

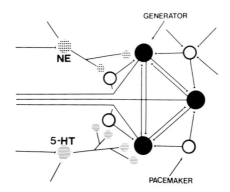

Figure 5.   Basel Group's Aminergic Gating Model.   The following description of this schema is taken from the text of the paper in which this figure appeared.

"Diffusely scattered pacemaker cells with spontaneous asynchronous activity and hypothetical excitatory inputs from different structures impinge on generator cells.

Generator cells for PGO-waves, located in the dorsal pontine reticular formation are not spontaneously active; when the input from the pacemaker cells is strong enough,

they start discharging synchronously because of reciprocal
connections.

Serotonergic raphe neurons (5-HT) tonically damp the
generator cells; the control of the former cells is unknown.

The postulated NE neurons (from the locus coeruleus)
exert an additional inhibitory effect on generator and/or
pacemaker cells." Reproduced from Haefely, Jalfre, and
Monachon (1973) by permission of the publisher.

In a series of lesion experiments (Hobson, 1965) it
was found that dorsal prepontine brain stem transection
abolished forebrain PGO activity but that pontine waves,
though seen less frequently, were still recordable in
association with eye movements. This gave further support
to Jouvet's concept that the waves were of pontine origin.
It was later found, however, that complete destruction of
both geniculate bodies did not eliminate cortical waves;
in fact wave amplitude was enhanced though the frequency of
both eye movements and PGO waves were reduced after geniculate destruction. It could, therefore, be concluded that
radiation to the cortex was not exclusively, if at all, via
the LGB (Hobson, Alexander, & Frederickson, 1969).
In direct tests of the pontine generator hypothesis our
microelectrode recordings have since shown that the giant
cells of the pontine reticular formation (FTG neurons) have
earlier, more prominent phasic rate increases prior to eye
movements and PGO waves than other brain stem neuronal groups
(Hobson, & McCarley, 1973; Hobson, McCarley, Pivak, & Freedman,
1974; Hobson, McCarley, & Pivik, 1972). The anticipatory
discharge of FTG neurons is often quite striking during the
transition from the synchronized to the desynchronized sleep
phase (Hobson, et al., 1974). At such times FTG discharge
may anticipate the PGO by several seconds (see Figure 6).
During desynchronized sleep, there is also a marked increase
in probability of FTG unit discharge that begins 70 msec
before and peaks at 10-20 msec before maximum surface
negativity of the cortical PGO wave; a more gradual rise in
the probability of discharge begins 600-800 msec before the
reference PGO spike (McCarley, Pivik, & Hobson, 1973). We
have, therefore, proposed that FTG neurons are output elements
of the generator (Hobson, 1974).
Noting reciprocal rate changes by FTG cells and cells of
the nucleus locus coeruleus (Hobson, et al., 1975) we have
proposed a reciprocal interaction model for sleep cycle
oscillation which can be applied to the PGO generator
mechanism (McCarley, & Hobson, 1975). At the physiological

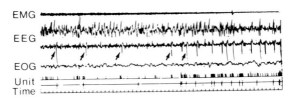

Figure 6. Anticipatory discharge by an FTG Unit prior to the isolated PGO waves (arrows) occuring during the transition from synchronized to desynchronized sleep. There is a cluster of action potentials in the 1-3 seconds prior to each of the five PGO waves shown. EMG = electromyogram; EEG = bipolar electroencephalogram of cortical surface (upper trace) and transcortical derivations (lower trace). Time is in seconds. (Modified from Hobson, McCarley, Freedman, & Pivik, 1974.)

level, the model specifies connections, transmitters, and sign of synaptic action. Figure 7 is a schematic representation of this model. The raphe nuclei are included in the model and given the same role as locus coeruleus (LC) cells, because McGinty and Harper (1972) have shown that dorsal raphe nucleus neurons, like LC neurons, decrease rate in desynchronized sleep, and in addition show phasic decreases prior to PGO waves, complementing the Brooks hypothesis of PGO inhibition by serotonin, and also producing physiological confirmation of the pharmacological model of Jalfre et al. (1973).

The mathematical model of this cellular system applies to both tonic and phasic electrical events and is applicable to both the synaptic and the molecular levels of organization (see Figure 8). It is based upon the Lotka-Volterra equations which were designed to describe the interaction of prey and predator in population biology. This model does not yet specify a time constant element but several possibilities exist to account for the long period of the sleep cycle. They include inactivation of transmitter enzyme or a decrease in enzyme synthesis during periods of cell inhibition or disfacilitation, transport times for transmitter enzymes from nucleus to terminals once synthesis has begun, and chemically determined periodicity of intra-cellular protein synthesis. All of these mechanisms are probably membrane-coupled; that is, they could be expected to be influenced by presynaptic input and in turn to influence postsynaptic neuronal populations.

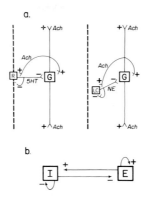

*Figure 7. Physiological Assumptions of Reciprocal
Interaction Model. In (a) the giant cells (G) are cholinergic
and cholinoceptive (ACh) and excitatory (+) to post-synaptic
elements including one another. Self-excitation is then
possible within the FTG generatory pool. FTG neurons are
reciprocally interconnected with two groups of aminergic
cells: The raphe (R) and locus coeruleus (LC) which use
norepinephrine (NE) as their transmitter. Both aminergic
groups are inhibitory (-) to self and other. At any given
time, the excitability of FTG population is thus an inverse
function of the level of activity in the aminergic populations (and vice versa). In (b) the assumptions of (a) are
shown to be reducible to reciprocally interconnected excitatory (E) and inhibiting (I) populations and this scheme is
formally identical to that shown in Figure 8.*

    In our first direct tests of our reciprocal interaction
model, we have injected small amounts of the long-acting
cholinergic agent, carbachol, into the pontine tegmentum
(Amatruda, Black, McKenna, McCarley, & Hobson, 1975; McKenna,
McCarley, Amatruda, Black, & Hobson, 1974). At FTG sites,
carbachol produced a dose-dependent increase (compared to
baseline desynchronized sleep) in atonia associated with EEG
desynchronization. This syndrome was sometimes associated
with intense and sustained PGO-like wave activity and/or
eye movements. At adjacent reticular sites, less potent
effects were observed while at LC sites, a dose-dependent
suppression of desynchronized sleep phenomena was observed.
The latter effect could not be confidently interpreted as
due to cholinergic activation of an inhibitory system because

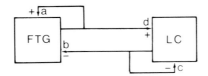

*Figure 8. Formal Properties of the Reciprocal Inter-
action Model. The four kinds of synaptic interconnections
are labelled with the symbols used in the Volterra-Lotka
equations below. The model assumes, as indicated in Figure 7,
the FTG units are self-excitatory and excitatory to the LC.
The LC population is assumed inhibitory to the FTG and to
itself. Interactions are non-linear since the effect of an
input is proportional to the current level of activity in
the affected population. If x = level of activity in LC
population and a, b, c, and d are positive constants
representing the potency of interaction, then:*

$$\frac{d\,x}{d\,t} = a\,x - b\,x\,y,\ and$$

$$\frac{d\,y}{d\,t} = -\,c\,y + d\,x\,y$$

*These equations, when solved and graphed give curves
with which the actual data can be compared. The system is
capable of generating both long term and short term oscil-
lations depending upon the time constants involved.*

the number of LC sites was small and the suppression did not
significantly exceed that produced by the CSF vehicle alone.
However, both the cholinergic potentiation of desynchronized
sleep phenomena at FTG sites and the possibly cholinergic
suppression at LC sites are as predicted by the model. We
are currently characterizing the activity of the giant
cells during the carbachol induced desynchronized sleep-like
syndrome, but the effects of presumed inhibitory transmitters
have not, as yet, been tested.

Comparison of the Models for PGO Generation

All of the models discussed place the generator in the
pontine tegmentum (see Table I). Brooks, Pompeiano,
Hobson, & MCarley see the reticular formation as probably
executive while Jouvet is equivocal on this point and Jalfre,

Ruch-Monachon, & Haefely are noncommital. Hobson and McCarley
designate the pontine reticular giant cells as essential
output elements in the generator system. With Brooks, they
see the raphe as providing tonic inhibitory control of the
generator, especially during waking and synchronized sleep.
In equating LC and DRN effects as tonically inhibitory, the
reciprocal interaction model also shares the major specific
assumption of the Jalfre, Ruch-Monachon, and Haefely model.
Thus the Brooks and Jalfre models are component parts of
the reciprocal interaction model.

     The Pompeiano (type II waves) model shares some assump-
tions about the generator itself with the reciprocal interaction model but omits the feedback control element. A short
time constant oscillatory element is placed within the
vestibular system; this feature may provide an important
complement to the reciprocal interaction model since microelectrode studies have not provided evidence for short term
rhythmicity within the pontine reticular formation itself.
However, in contrast to the predictions of the Pompeiano model,
the cellular data suggest that the FTG neurons produce
neither a square wave nor a sinusoidal output but rather a
three second triangular ramp of differential form which we
ascribe to self-excitation within the FTG neuronal pool.
This triangular ramp could enter a parallel loop in the
vestibular nuclei and be transformed into a rhythmic function
as suggested by Pompeiano. Combining these two neurophysiological models would yield one with the following features:

(1) specified generator cells (FTG) to account for
     tonic and phasic outputs.
(2) tonic, long time constant, control system (FTG-LC,
     DRN interaction) to account for state specificity
     of tonic output.
(3) phasic, short time constant modulation of
     triangular ramp from FTG (by vestibular nuclei)
     to account for rhythmicity of phasic output during
     desynchronized sleep phase of cycle.

     In the resulting hybrid model, no qualitative distinctions
need be made between type I and type II waves. Hence one
need not postulate different basic generator mechanisms for
isolated and clustered PGO waves. This distinction could
be quantitative and depend solely upon the suprathreshold
duration of the triangular ramp; when short, the vestibular
rhythmic generator is not triggered and a single spike
occurs; when long, the vestibular loop is triggered and a
cluster of spikes is generated by rhythmic EPSP-IPSP

sequences. The Pompeiano model is thus simplified (box A and A_1 being replaced by box E) while the Brooks model is incorporated within box I. All existing data are accounted for and the resulting system has two desirable features: (1) it is capable of doing all that needs to be done to generate PGO waves in desynchronized sleep; and (2) it is amenable to further experimental tests and modifications in the light of the results.

Implications of the Reciprocal Interaction Hypothesis for the Psychophysiology of Dream Amnesia

In the reciprocal interaction model, waking and de-synchronized sleep are contrasted by opposite extremes in the ratio of aminergic (a) to cholinergic (C) activity. This ratio will be referred to as the A/C ratio and it can be considered general for cells in the brain stem generator zone and in target areas of the forebrain since both sets of brain stem control neurons have extensive rostral pro-jections. How might such differences relate to the contrast-ing memory phenomena of the two states described in the introduction? The speculative explanation offered here is based upon the assumption that neurotransmitters affect not only the membrane properties of post-synaptic neurons but may also alter intracellular metabolism in such a way as to enhance or impede the processes underlying long-term memory. The general idea that the amines might act so as to enhance memory has been previously suggested (Kety, 1970). A detailed hypothesis linking specific neurotransmitters, second messengers, and intracellular processes, which has been proposed to account for the growth and differentiation of embryonic cells, is also relevant to the present argument (McMahon, 1974). That this general approach may be useful in understanding specific CNS effects is indicated by recent evidence that cyclic AMP and cyclic GMP may mediate different responses by pyramidal tract neurons of the cerebral cortex in rats (Stone, Taylor, & Bloom, 1975).

According to our cellular data, the waking state is likely to be characterized by the highest A/C ratios. Phenomenologically it is characterized by ease of retention of new conscious experience and by relative difficulty in retrieving remote memories. Our data suggest that, at the brain stem level, giant cells are strongly inhibited during waking so that only the strongest sensory stimuli elicit a response. In the forebrain, this inhibition may be relatively weak but still adequate to modulate responsiveness to exogenous excitatory inputs. In addition, aminergic inhibition may be a necessary condition for the permanent storage of the membrane effects of excitatory inputs mediated through cholinergic synapses. The suggestion is, therefore, that high A/C ratios favor the modulation and retention of the effects of excitatory inputs.

Dreaming sleep occurs when A/C ratios are lowest. At the brain stem level, this disinhibition results in selective increases in the excitability of cholinoceptive, cholinergic neurons in the reticular formation, vestibular nuclei, and oculomotor neurons. This network, first described by Lorente de Nò (1933) as the substrate for vestibular nystagmus may then come to constitute an endogenous generator in desynchronized sleep whose output the forebrain processes as dream content (see Figure 9). It would appear that the brain stem generator can be activated by local injection of cholinergic compounds; the effects are quantitatively graded and maximal for the generation of desynchronized sleep phenomena in the pontine reticular formation giving further support to the hypotheses that the generator cells are cholinoceptive and cholinergic.

In the forebrain, perhaps owing to the low A/C ratios, access to memory is free as the brain seeks "best fits" to the inputs endogenously generated by the brain stem. This process might account for some distinctive aspects of the dream experience including fusion of remote and recent memories. It should also be appreciated that the concept of endogenous information generation advanced here is not entirely devoid of specificity. For example, spatially specific information regarding the direction and velocity of eye movement could be fed forward from the brain stem generator to the forebrain in desynchronized sleep just as it may be in waking. This information might serve to set a visual frame for hallucinoid imagery. The scene shifts so typical of dreaming might thus occur as each successive burst of REMs is associated with a new set of frames fed forward from brain stem to thalamus and cortex.

Not only may access to memory be enhanced by the low A/C ratios of desynchronized sleep but the same mechanism might also account for the failure to retain dream content in memory. Only if there is an arousal, with its sudden shift to a high A/C ratio, can such experiences be remembered. How could hypothesized shifts in A/C ratios determine the correlated shifts in consolidation/retrieval? Since both A and C compounds appear to release specific second messengers, it is possible that a shift in intracellular protein metabolism could be caused by the shift in neurotransmitter ratios with consequences for memory that parallel those hypothesized to account for growth and differentiation (McMahon, 1974).

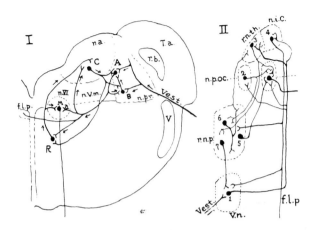

Figure 9. Two of Lorente de Nò's Drawings Depicting
the Vestibulo-Ocular Reflex Arc. On the left (I) a trans-
verse section of the brainstem at the level of the abducens
nucleus (n VI) and on the right (II) a horizontal section of
the dorsal brain stem at the level of the trochlear nucleus
(n IV). In both, note the interconnection between cells in
the reticular giant cell zone (R, r.n.p.) and the neurons in
the vestibular nuclei (V. N., n.v.m., and n.p.r.). In
Lorente de Nò's model, activation of the circuit (producing
the slow phase of nystagmus) is via the primary vestibular
afferent nerves arising in the labyrinth but the circuit would
respond similarly to endogenous excitation arising in
reticular vestibular, and/or oculomotor neurons. This
circuitry provides a substrate for linking the reciprocal
interaction model with a vestibular transform system. Not
shown in this drawing are the crossed connections essential
for sustained rhythmic aspects of nystagmus and of the REM
bursts in sleep. Reproduced from Lorente de Nò, 1933,
by permission of the publisher.

In McMahon's growth and development model, NE and 5-HT
are viewed as triggering C-AMP and, by stimulating the
assembly of microtubules, as providing a basis for cell
differentiation. ACh, on the other hand is linked to G-GMP
and, by stimulating cell division and RNA synthesis, as
providing a substrate for cell growth. It is likely that

differentiation, for the neuron, includes specific and permanent records of experience (memory) as well as genetically determined effects. Waking experience is most likely to stimulate those plastic responses of adaptive significance for the organism. These responses might be stored, over the short-term, by a mechanism involving C-AMP. Sleep, especially its desynchronized phase could then provide the basis for a shift to a consolidating mode leading to long-term memory by a shift to mechanisms mediated by GMP.

All of these speculations go far beyond the data but may be useful in that they yield specific testable hypotheses that bring the study of sleep mechanisms into contact with functional hypotheses that have lacked specification and experimental test in much recent research on sleep. At the same time, the state-dependent shifts in memory processes also present new experimental opportunities to the neurobiologist interested primarily in the physiology of memory.

ACKNOWLEDGMENT

Supported by USPHS Grant MH 13923.

REFERENCES

Amatruda, T. T., Black, D. A., McKenna, T. M., McCarley, R. W., & Hobson, J. A. Sleep cycle control and cholinergic mechanisms: Differential effects of carbachol injections at pontine brain stem sites. *Brain Research,* 1975, *98,* 501-515.

Aserinsky, E., & Kleitman, N. A motility cycle in sleeping infants as manifested by ocular and gross bodily activity. *Journal of Applied Physiology,* 1955, *8,* 11-19.

Bizzi, E., & Brooks, D. C. Functional connections between pontine reticular formation and lateral geniculate nucleus during deep sleep. *Archives Italiennes de Biologie,* 1963, *101,* 666-680.

Bizzi, E., Pompeiano, O., & Somogyi, I.   Spontaneous activity of single vestibular neurons of unrestrained cats during sleep and wakefulness.   *Archives Italiennes de Biologie,* 1964, *102,* 308-330.

Brooks, D. C., & Bizzi, E.   Brain stem electrical activity during deep sleep.   *Archives Italiennes de Biologie,* 1963, *101,* 648-665.

Brooks, D. C., & Gershon, M. D.   Eye movement potentials in the oculomotor and visual systems of the cat: A comparison of reserpine induced waves with those present during wakefulness and rapid eye movement sleep.   *Brain Research,* 1971, *27,* 223-239.

Foulkes, D.   *The Psychology of Sleep.*   New York: Scribners, 1966.

Freud, S.   The interpretation of dreams.   In *The Basic Writings of Sigmund Freud.*   New York: Random House, 1938.

Haefely, W., Jalfre, M., & Monachon, M. A.   NE-neurons and phasic sleep phenomena.   *Frontiers in Catecholamine Research,* 1973, 773-775.

Hernandez-Peon, R.   Sleep induced by localized electrical or chemical stimulation of the forebrain.   *Electroencephalography and Clinical Neurophysiology,* 1962, *14,* 423-424.

Hobson, J. A.   The effect of chronic brain stem lesions on cortical and muscular activity during sleep and waking in the cat.   *Electroencephalography and Clinical Neurophysiology,* 1965, *19,* 41-62.

Hobson, J. A.   The cellular basis of sleep cycle control.   In Weitzman, E. (Ed.), *Advances in Sleep Research.*   New York: Spectrum, 1974.

Hobson, J. A., Alexander, J., & Frederickson, C. J.   The effect of lateral geniculate lesions on phasic electrical activity of the cortex during desynchronized sleep in the cat, *Brain Research,* 1969, *14,* 607-621.

Hobson, J. A., McCarley, R. W., Freedman, R., & Pivik, R. T. Time course of discharge rate changes by cat pontine brain stem neurons during the sleep cycle. *Journal of Neurophysiology*, 1974, *37*, 1297-1309.

Hobson, J. A., McCarley, R. W., & Pivik, R. T. A comparison of phasic rate changes in brain stem and cortical neurons associated with the eye movements of desynchronized sleep. *Sleep Research*, 1972, *1*, 21.

Hobson, J. A., McCarley, R. W., Pivik, R. T., & Freedman, R. Selective firing by cat pontine brain stem neurons in desynchronized sleep. *Journal of Neurophysiology*, 1974, *37*, 497-511.

Hobson, J. A., McCarley, R. W., & Wyzinski, P. W. Sleep cycle oscillation: Reciprocal discharge by two brain stem neuronal groups. *Science*, 1975, *189*, 55-58.

Jalfre, M., Ruch-Monachon, M. A., & Haefely, W. Drugs and PGO waves in the cat. In: *Proceedings of the First Canadian International Symposium on Sleep*. Montreal: Roche Scientific Service, 1973.

Jalfre, M., Ruch-Monachon, M. A., & Haefely, W. Methods for assessing the interaction of agents with 5-hydroxy-tryptamine neurons and receptors in the brain. In Costa, E., & Greengard, P., (Eds.), *Advances in Biochemistry and Psychopharmacology* (Vol. 10). New York: Raven Press, 1974.

Jouvet, M. Mechanisms of the states of sleep: A neuropharma-cological approach. In Kety, S. S., Evarts, E. V., & Williams, H. L. (Eds.), *Sleep and Altered States of Consciousness* (Vol. XLV). Baltimore: Williams & Wilkins, 1967a.

Jouvet, M. Neurophysiology of the states of sleep. In Quarton, G. C., Melnechuk, T., & Schmitt, F. O., (Eds.), *The Neurosciences, a Study Program*. New York: Rocke-feller University Press, 1967b.

Jouvet, M., & Michel, F. Correlations électromyographiques du sommeil chez le chat décortiqué et mésencéphalique chronique. *Comptes Rendus des Seances de la Societe de Biologie (Paris)*, 1959, *153*, 422-425.

Karczmar, A. G., Longo, V. G., & Scotti de Carolis, A. A pharmacological model of the effect of paradoxical sleep: The role of cholinergic and monoamine systems. *Physiology and Behavior*, 1970, *5*, 172-182.

Kety, S. The biogenic amines in the central nervous system: Their possible roles in arousal, emotion, and learning. In Schmitt, F. O. (Ed.), *The Neurosciences, Second Study Program*. New York: Rockefeller University Press, 1970.

Laurent, J-P., Cespuglio, R., & Jouvet, M. Délimitation des voies ascendantes de l'activité ponto-géniculo-occipitale chez le chat. *Brain Research*, 1974, *65*, 29-52.

Lorente de Nò, R. Vestibulo-ocular reflex arc. *Archives of Neurology and Psychiatry*, 1933, *30*, 245-291.

Magherini, P. C., Pompeiano, O., & Thoden, U. The neurochemical basis of REM sleep: A cholinergic mechanism responsible for rhythmic activation of the vestibulo-oculomotor system. *Brain Research*, 1971, *35*, 565-569.

McCarley, R. W., & Hobson, J. A. Neuronal excitability modulation over the sleep cycle: A structural and mathematical model. *Science*, 1975, *189*, 58-60.

McCarley, R. W., Pivik, R. T., & Hobson, J. A. Relationships between discharges of neurones in the pontine reticular formation and PGO waves recorded at occipital cortex. *Sleep Research*, 1973, *2*, 31.

McGinty, D. J., & Harper, R. M. 5-HT-containing neurons: Unit activity during sleep. *Sleep Research*, 1972, *1*, 27.

McKenna, T., McCarley, R. W., Amatruda, T., Black, D., & Hobson, J. A. Effects of carbachol at pontine sites yielding long duration desynchronized sleep episodes. *Sleep Research*, 1974, *3*, 39.

McMahon, D. Chemical messengers in development: A hypothesis. *Science*, 1974, *185*, 1012-1021.

Mikiten, T. H., Niebyl, P. H., & Hendley, C. D. EEG desyn-
    chronization during behavioral sleep associated with
    spike discharges from the thalamus of the cat.
    Federation Proceedings, 1961, *20,* 327.

Morrison, A. R., & Pompeiano, O. Vestibular influences
    during sleep. II. Effects of vestibular lesions on
    the pyramidal discharge during desynchronized sleep.
    Archives Italiennes de Biologie, 1966, *104,* 214-230.

Munson, J. B. Eye movement potentials following visual
    deafferentiation. *Brain Research,* 1974, *66,* 435-442.

Pivik, R. T., Hobson, J. A., & McCarley, R. W. Eye movement
    associated rate changes in neuronal activity during
    desynchronized sleep: A comparison of brain stem regions.
    Sleep Research, 1973, *2,* 35.

Pompeiano, O., & Morrison, A. R. Vestibular influences during
    sleep. I. Abolition of the rapid eye movements of
    desynchronized sleep following vestibular lesions.
    Archives Italiennes de Biologie, 1965, *103,* 569-595.

Pompeiano, O., & Valentinuzzi, M. A mathematical model for
    the mechanism of rapid eye movements induced by an anti-
    cholinesterase in the decerebrate cat. *Archives
    Italiennes de Biologie,* 1976, *114,* 103-154.

Ramon y Cajal, S. *Histologie du système nerveux de l'home
    et les vertebrés* (Vol. 1). Paris: Maloine, 1909.

Renault, J. Monoamines et sommeils. *Role du raphé et de la
    sérotonine cérébrale dans l'endormissement.* Unpublished,
    Thèse de Médecine. Université de Lyon, France, 1967.

Simon, R. P., Gershon, M. D., & Brooks, D. C. The role of
    the raphe nuclei in the regulation of ponto-geniculo-
    occipital wave activity. *Brain Research,* 1973, *58,*
    313-330.

Snyder, F. The new biology of dreaming. *Archives of
    General Psychiatry,* 1963, *8,* 381-391.

Stone, T. W., Taylor, D. A., & Bloom, F. E. Cyclic AMP and
    cyclic GMP may mediate opposite neuronal responses in the
    rat cerebral cortex. *Science,* 1975, *187,* 845-847.

NEUROANATOMIC LOCALIZATION
AND THE NEUROBIOLOGY OF SLEEP AND MEMORY

STEVEN F. ZORNETZER, MARK S. GOLD and CARL A. BOAST

*Department of Neuroscience and
Center for Neurobiological Science,
College of Medicine,
University of Florida
Gainesville, Florida 32610 USA*

Extensive, yet independent neurobiological research has
been directed towards an understanding of memory processes
on the one hand and sleep processes on the other hand. A
much greater understanding of each of these neurobiological
phenomena has resulted from this research.

Neuroanatomic localization of brain structures participating in memory and sleep processes is an emerging area of
research. Until recently little has been known about the
degree of neuroanatomic localization attributable to either
memory or sleep. Recent research indicates, however, that
various components of both memory processes (cf. Gold,
Zornetzer, & McGaugh, 1974) and sleep processes (cf.
Jouvet, 1967, 1972) can be associated with specific brain
regions.

If the neurobiological processes underlying memory and
sleep are functionally related and interdependent, then at
least some overlap in the structural or neuroanatomic basis
for each of these complex phenomena might be expected. This
chapter describes ongoing research in our laboratory dealing
with the question of such neuroanatomic localization. The
first experiments described indicate the extent to which
such localization can occur in memory processes. These
results suggest a surprising amount of localization within
the hippocampal formation, a brain structure often associ-

ated with memory processes. Following these experiments we
describe our findings concerning the apparent overlap between sleep and memory processes in terms of a structural or
neuroanatomic coextensiveness. Our results suggest that
normal function of the locus coeruleus, a pontine brain
structure believed responsible, in part at least, for paradoxical or rapid eye movement sleep, is important for consolidation of recent memory into more permanent long-term
memory.

The study of the neuroanatomical basis of memory was
made possible by the development of techniques permitting
manipulations of discrete brain regions. Karl Lashley, a
pioneer in this field, used small lesions to investigate the
role of regions of rat cortex in associative processes. He
was singularly unsuccessful and concluded, possibly out of
frustration, that it appeared that learning was just not
possible (Lashley, 1950). An exploration of the contribution of subcortical structures to memory processes has
revealed a more promising picture. Robert Thompson, for
example, has continued in the Lashley tradition by employing
the lesion technique to study the role of many subcortical
structures in memory. He reports that different structures
are involved in different memory systems (e.g. Thompson,
1969, 1974; Spiliotis & Thompson, 1973). In addition, he
suggests that the brain regions common to all of these
systems comprise a "general memory system." This general
memory system is described as being comprised of such
structures as the posterior thalamus, posterior hypothalamus
and several brain stem regions.

Through the use of electrical stimulation of discrete
brain regions some of Thompson's findings have been confirmed
and extended. For example, it has been shown that memory
modification can occur following stimulation of the non-
specific thalamic nuclei in both animals (Mahut, 1957, 1962,
1964) and humans (Ojemann, Blick, & Ward, 1971). Stimulation of the brain stem region has sometimes resulted in
memory disruption for long-term memory (LTM) (Kesner &
Conner, 1972, 1974) as well as short-term memory (STM)
(Routtenberg & Holzman, 1973), sometimes in compensation for
a deficit due to implantation (Bloch, 1970), and sometimes
to no effect (Mahut, 1962; Hirano, 1966), depending upon the
location of the neural region being stimulated as well as
the behavioral paradigm being used. Thus, the diffuse
projection system from the brain stem and nonspecific
thalamic nuclei appears to play some role in memory
processes. It is interesting to note that these regions
are also of major importance in rhythms of sleep and

wakefulness (Jouvet, 1967, 1969; Moruzzi, 1972). While it is
not inconceivable that these brain regions are capable of
maintaining two or more independent functions simultaneously,
it also appears reasonable that the processes underlying
sleep and wakefulness may be intimately involved with, and
crucial to, memory formation (Moruzzi, 1972).

Electrical stimulation techniques have revealed other
structures that appear to play some role in memory processes.
For example, caudate nucleus stimulation has been shown to
impair inhibitory avoidance responding (Wyers, Peeke,
Williston, & Herz, 1968), maze learning (Peeke & Herz, 1971),
extinction (Herz & Peeke, 1971), habituation (Deadwyler &
Wyers, 1972) and one trial appetitive learning (Zornetzer &
Chronister, 1973). A single pulse of current delivered
bilaterally to the caudate was sufficient to cause amnesia
in all of these tasks.

The amygdala has also been implicated in memory processes. Subseizure stimulation delivered either bilaterally
or unilaterally to this group of nuclei has been shown to
result in amnesia. Several investigators have attempted to
ascertain a greater degree of localization of memory disruptive sites within the amygdala. For example, Goddard
(1964) has suggested the lateral portion of the basal nucleus
is of primary importance, while Breshnahan and Routtenberg
(1972) report the medial nucleus to be most effective in
producing amnesia. Gold, Edwards, and McGaugh (1975) have
reported that the basomedial nucleus is involved in memory
disruption to a greater extent than any of the other nuclei
of the amygdala. Thus, it would appear that there is still
some confusion as to the exact contribution of the various
amygdaloid nuclei to memory processes. Nevertheless, it
appears that a relatively high degree of localization of
function with respect to memory processes may exist.

The hippocampus has been implicated in memory processes
as a consequence of results obtained with both lesion and
stimulation techniques. The clinical observations of
Milner (1955, 1959, 1965) have suggested that the hippocampus may be important to memory formation in man. A number
of experiments using lesion techniques have implicated this
brain region in associative processes in animals (see
Isaacson, 1975 for a review). Similarly, stimulation studies
have shown that the hippocampus is involved in some way in
memory processes (Gold, et al., 1974; Kesner and Wilburn,
1974). Although anatomical and physiological studies have
revealed that the hippocampus is not a homogeneous structure,
little work has been done to assess the relative contribution
of the various hippocampal subfields to memory processes. In

order to assess the degree to which memory disruptive sites
can be localized it would be interesting to manipulate these
subfields independent of one another. One study has been
reported in which discrete hippocampal subfields of the rat
were electrically stimulated following training in a dis-
criminated avoidance task (Sideroff, Bueno, Hirsh, Weyand, &
McGaugh, 1973). Amnesia was observed following bilateral
stimulation of either CA1, CA3, or the dentate gyrus. In
contrast to this finding, work in our laboratory has revealed differential contributions of discrete hippocampal
subfields of the mouse on memory. We have examined the role
of these subfields in memory using electrolytic lesions,
electrical stimulation and simple electrode implantation.
The data to be reported below represent our efforts to
study intrahippocampal neuroanatomical organization with
regard to memory processing. Using the perspective of hind-
sight these experiments are reported in a logical rather
than a strict chronological order.

In one study (Boast, Zornetzer, & Hamrick, 1975), wire
electrodes made from Teflon-coated platinum-iridium (178 µ
in diameter) were implanted bilaterally in 53 mice, using
conventional stereotaxic techniques. Anodal lesions (0.5 µA,
15 sec) using a rectal cathode were made bilaterally in the
target structures, with electrodes in place in various
hippocampal subfields. Twenty-three mice were used as unoperated controls.

Following a 10 day recovery period, all mice were
trained in the 1-trial inhibitory avoidance task (Jarvik &
Kopp, 1967). Each mouse was placed in a small clear outer
chamber facing away from a hole leading to a larger darkened
chamber. The latency to turn and step through this hole
into the larger opaque chamber was recorded and is referred
to as the training step-through latency (STL). Upon entering the opaque chamber each mouse automatically received a
300 µA footshock and was allowed to escape to the clear
outer chamber. Either 15 min or 24 hours after training,
each mouse was again placed in the apparatus and the testing
STL was recorded. Subtraction of the training STL from the
testing STL resulted in a STL difference score. A 300 second
ceiling was imposed on this difference score. A high difference score indicates good retention of the aversive experience while a low score indicates impaired performance in the
task. On the basis of histological examination, lesioned
animals were placed into one of two groups: If both lesions
invaded any part of the dentate gyrus, regardless of additional hippocampal damage, the animal was placed in a
"bilateral dentate" group (BD); if at least one lesion did
not damage any part of the dentate gyrus, the animal was

placed in a "non-bilateral dentate" group (NBD). Animals in group NBD were derived from a number of different subgroups having either (1) unilateral dentate damage with contra-lateral extradentate damage (primarily CAl), (2) symmetrical extradentate damage, or (3) asymmetrical extradentate damage. Each of these three subgroups contained a small number of animals and were, therefore, combined to form the larger group NBD. Group BD evidenced substantial damage to both CAl and the underlying dentate gyrus. Group NBD, on the other hand, evidenced substantial lesion damage to CAl but only occasional and generally minimal damage to the dentate gyrus. Figure 1 shows examples of lesions in each of these two groups.

Groups BD, NBD, and normal mice were each further divided into two groups based upon the retention test interval of either 15 minutes or 24 hours. There were no differences among these groups in initial STL difference scores for all groups. Group BD(24 hour retention test, BD24H) was significantly impaired relative to NORM(24 hour retention test, NORM24H) $\{p < .01\}$. Group NBD(24 hour retention text, NBD24H) was not impaired relative to NORM24H $\{p > .10\}$. A comparison of group BD24H with group NBD24H revealed a significant difference $\{p < .02\}$. Group NBD(15 minute retention test, NBD15min) was impaired relative to NORM(15 minute retention test, NORM15min) $\{p < .05\}$. Group BD(15 minute retention test, BD15min) was also impaired relative to NORM15min $\{p < .02\}$. Group NBD15min was not significantly different than group BD15min $\{p = .40\}$.

As shown in Figure 2 by dot representation, individual STL difference scores in groups showing statistically significant behavioral deficits were highly variable. Thus, some mice in these groups showed no impairment, while other mice showed a moderate impairment, and still other mice were highly impaired.

One possible source of this variability might be the individual differences in the volume of tissue destruction resulting from the electrolytic lesions. Thus, we cal-culated the volume of tissue destroyed within the hippo-campus for each lesion in every animal. No significant correlations between lesion volume and STL difference scores was found in any experimental group $\{p > .10$ in all cases$\}$. These data suggest that the volume of tissue damage, within the limits of our lesion parameters, does not account for the variability in STL difference scores.

The results of the present study indicate that bi-lateral electrolytic lesions of the dentate gyrus of the mouse hippocampus result in a deficit in retention of the 1-trial inhibitory avoidance task 15 minutes and 24 hours

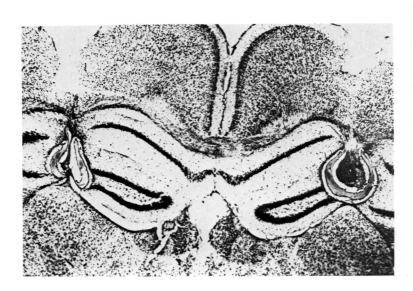

A

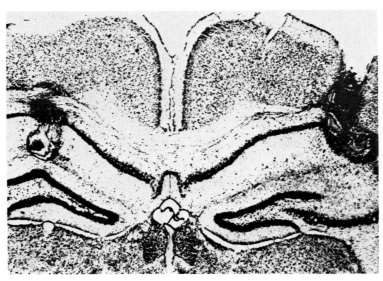

B

Fig. 1. Photomicrographs of representative electrolytic lesions in mouse hippocampal formation (cresyl violet). A. Lesions located bilaterally in the dentate gyrus (Group BD). B. Lesions located outside of the dentate gyrus (in this case CA1) and, therefore, placed in group NBD (see text).

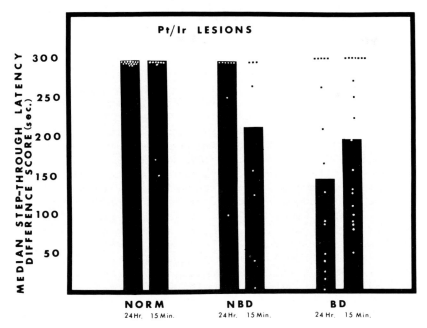

Fig. 2. *Median STL difference scores for different
groups of mice tested for retention at either 15 minutes or
24 hours after training. Normal (NORM) mice, mice with
nonbilateral dentate gyrus lesions (NBD), and mice with
bilateral dentate gyrus lesions (BD). Dots indicate individual scores within each group.*

after training. Lesions of other hippocampal subfields
(primarily CA1) result in a retention deficit in this task
15 minutes but not 24 hours after training. In order to
produce bilateral dentate gyrus lesions it was necessary to
damage the overlying CA1 region to some extent. Lesions
restricted to the CA1 region resulted in a 15 minute deficit.
Since the 15 minute deficit seen following bilateral dentate
gyrus lesions was not greater in magnitude than the 15
minute deficit seen following CA1 lesions, we suggest that
the role of bilateral dentate gyrus damage in the production
of the observed 15 minute deficit is negligible. Conversely,
CA1 damage does not contribute to 24 hour performance deficits.
Thus, the deficit seen in group BD24H appears to be the
result of damage to the dentate gyrus *per se* and not the
result of damage to overlying CA1 regions.

This conclusion should be viewed with caution since it is based on the behavioral effects of a lesion restricted to one area in relation to the effects of a lesion encroaching upon two anatomical regions. The validity of such reasoning remains to be demonstrated. The deficits observed in this experiment are probably not the result of impaired acquisition or performance (i.e., impaired response inhibition). If either acquisition or performance was impaired, deficits in both STM and LTM would be expected. The results of this experiment indicate that CA1 lesions result in STM and not LTM impairments. In addition, we have reasoned above that dentate gyrus lesions result in LTM and not STM deficits. It seems unlikely that processes subserving either acquisition or performance, common to both STM and LTM, were impaired.

These data suggest that electrolytic lesions resulting in discrete hippocampal malfunction can differentially affect STM or LTM depending upon the hippocampal subfield to which such a malfunction is localized. Behavioral (Barondes & Cohen, 1968; Geller & Jarvik, 1968; McGaugh & Landfield, 1970) as well as neuroanatomical (Kesner & Conner, 1972, 1974) evidence suggests that STM and LTM may involve separate storage and/or retrieval processes. If parallel and somewhat independent STM and LTM storage/retrieval processes exist, then it would be possible to affect STM without affecting LTM and *vice versa*. For example, an LTM storage/retrieval impairment, independent of an STM storage/retrieval impairment, would account for the observed LTM deficit following bilateral dentate gyrus lesions found in the present study. Our data are in support of a parallel multiple process theory of memory (Kesner, 1973).

As pointed out above, median STL difference scores of 150-200 seconds reflect an impairment in, but not a complete loss of, memory. These findings suggest that other brain regions, not affected by our experimental manipulation, perhaps other brain structures or remaining hippocampal tissue, might subserve a significant amount of memory processing. This conclusion is consistent with the findings of others (Gold, Macri, & McGaugh, 1973; Kesner & Conner, 1972, 1974; Wyers et al., 1968).

As pointed out earlier, electrical stimulation of localized neuroanatomic regions has also been used to assess the role of specific brain sites in memory processes. To further characterize the role of the hippocampus in memory we investigated the effects of electrical stimulation of various hippocampal subfields on longterm retention of the one-trial inhibitory avoidance response (Zornetzer, Chronister, & Ross, 1973).

Bipolar electrodes similar in construction to those used in the lesion experiment previously described were implanted bilaterally in the dorsal hippocampus of 30 mice. Fifteen animals were used as unoperated controls.

Following surgery animals were placed in individual cages and allowed one week for recovery. The mice were housed in a colony room with a 24 hour reversed light cycle (lights off at 12 o'clock noon). All electrophysiological and behavioral work with the mice was conducted between 7 PM and 11 PM. Hippocampal afterdischarge thresholds were determined for these mice. Each animal was taken from its home cage, connected to a light-weight electrically shielded cable and placed in a transparent testing chamber. Normal EEG data were recorded for approximately one minute. Immediately before the delivery of brain stimulation each S was disconnected from the polygraph and connected to the stimulator by means of a switch. Immediately following stimulation, all animals were reconnected to the polygraph for subsequent recording. For each mouse an afterdischarge threshold was determined using the method described by Racine (1972). Mice received brain stimulation once every 48 hours until a seizure threshold was determined for each S. Following seizure threshold determination the implanted mice were randomly divided into two groups.

One week after the seizure threshold determinations all animals received training in the previously described inhibitory avoidance step-through task. Immediately follow-ing the escape from footshock, each animal was removed from the apparatus attached to the shielded cable, and placed in the observation chamber. Each S in Group 1 received bilateral electrical stimulation of the hippocampus 25% above its individual predetermined seizure threshold. The current intensities ranged from 12.5-137 μA with a mean of 49 μA. Group 2 animals received sham stimulation. All animals remained in the recording chamber for one additional minute while EEG records were made. Animals were then returned to their home cages. Twenty-four hours later, the animals were tested for retention of the inhibitory avoidance response.

All animals in Group 1 developed an afterdischarge following electrical stimulation. Electrical stimulation at a current level 25% above local afterdischarge threshold typically did not result in any behavioral convulsions. Mice generally remained motionless during hippocampal seizure. In addition, hippocampal afterdischarge rarely propagated to the cortex. There was no apparent relationship between electrode location and brain seizure threshold within the hippocampus.

Analysis of the step-through latencies for Groups 1 and 2 indicated no significant difference when all stimulated animals were compared to all nonstimulated animals. Within Group 1, however, the data do indicate that those animals made amnesic for the footshock experience all had electrode placements bilaterally located in the area dentata. Figure 3A shows an example of electrode placements in an animal from group NBD while Figure 3B shows a similar example from an animal in group BD (see previous experiment for group designations).

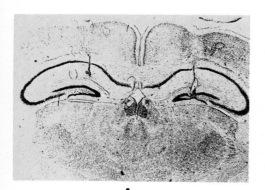 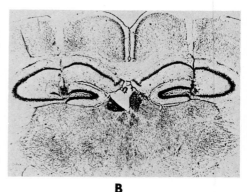

A **B**

Fig. 3. Photomicrographs of representative electrode placements in the mouse hippocampal formation (cresyl violet). A. Nonbilateral dentate gyrus placement (NBD). B. Bilateral dentate gyrus placement (BD).

As shown in Figure 4A, Group 1 animals were divided into two subgroups, BD and NBD. Stimulated mice in the BD subgroup had significantly more amnesia than NBD mice $\{p < 0.001\}$. Mice stimulated in regions other than dentate were not significantly different from implanted controls. There was no apparent relationship between electrode location and brain seizure threshold within the hippocampus.

Thus, seizure-producing stimulation of discrete hippocampal subfields of mice can result in retrograde amnesia (RA). However, the effects of hippocampal stimulation resulting in possible seizure propagation to other brain regions are difficult to interpret in relation to the contribution the stimulated region makes to the observed RA. For example, asymmetric electrode placements within the region of the

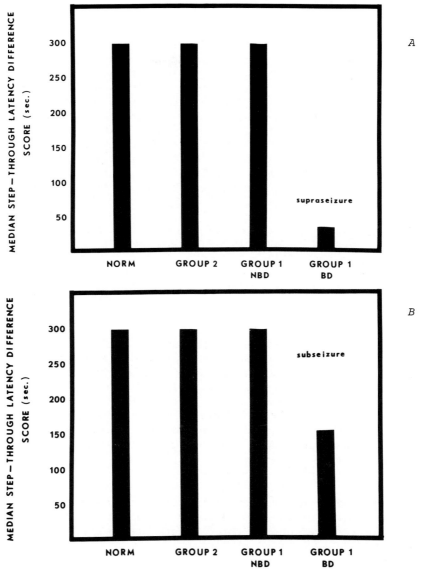

Fig. 4. Median STL difference scores for mice tested for
retention 24 hours after receiving electrical brain stimulation.
A. Mice receiving supraseizure threshold electrical stimulation immediately following training.   B. Mice receiving subseizure threshold electrical stimulation immediately following
training. Normal (NORM) mice, implanted nonstimulated control
mice (Group 2), implanted and stimulated control mice with nonbilateral dentate gyrus electrode placements (Group 1, NBD),
and implanted and stimulated mice with bilateral dentate gyrus
electrode placements (Group 1, BD).

hippocampus failed to result in amnesia in the above experiment. Anatomical evidence (Blackstad, 1956) indicates that specific areas within the hippocampal regions project via the hippocampal commissures to their contralateral homotopic loci. This finding suggests that in the case of hippocampal asymmetric electrode placements in the present study, bilateral spread of electrical stimulation-induced alterations in normal neural activity occurs. Such commissurally-mediated alterations of hippocampal function do not appear to result in memory disruption. Rather, bilateral initiation of alteration in normal neural activity appears to be an effective amnesia-producing situation. These data suggest that bilateral symmetry produced by initiation of electrical stimulation, rather than possible bilateral symmetry produced by commissural propagation, is the effective memory disruptive condition.

   Zornetzer (1972) reported a clear difference between the amnesia-producing capability of frontal cortex afterdischarge activity produced directly by frontal stimulation and that produced by propagation of afterdischarge activity to the frontal cortex from other areas of initiation. Taken together, these data suggest that a functional distinction can be made between "initiation-in" and "propagation-to" a neural structure with regard to disruption of a labile memory.

   We felt that an evaluation of the effects of subseizure stimulation of the various subfields of the hippocampus would allow more direct conclusions to be drawn concerning the role of these hippocampal subfields in memory processes. Thus, additional mice received electrodes implanted bilaterally in the dorsal hippocampus. Following recovery from surgery, hippocampal afterdischarge thresholds were determined for each mouse as previously described.

   Three days after seizure threshold determination all animals received training in the inhibitory avoidance step-through task described previously. Following footshock, animals received one of three treatments. Group 1 *Ss* were attached to a shielded cable and given bilateral brain stimulation. Each *S* received brain stimulation at a current level 25% below its individual predetermined seizure threshold. Brain stimulation was delivered from a Grass S44 stimulator through a stimulus isolation unit and a constant current unit. Brain stimulation consisted of 1.0 msec pulses delivered at 100 Hz for 1.0 seconds. The current intensities used following learning ranged from 20-175μA with a mean of 70μA. All *Ss* received brain stimulation within 15 seconds of escape; therefore, the training-brain stimulation interval was 10-15 seconds. Group 2 *Ss* were treated exactly as Group 1 animals

except no brain stimulation was delivered.   Group 3 *Ss* were
unimplanted normal controls.   Following footshock these
animals were returned to their home cages.   Twenty-four hours
after training all *Ss* were tested for retention of the footshock experience.

The distribution of electrode placements within the
hippocampus and surrounding regions did not appear different
for Group 1 and Group 2 animals.   Four of the eleven mice
(36%) in Group 1 had bilaterally symmetrical electrode placements in or near the granular layer of the area dentata of
the dorsal hippocampus (See Blackstad, 1956).   Histological
analysis of the stimulated animals not developing RA indicated that the electrode tips were asymmetrically located.
Electrophysiological analysis indicated no apparent relationship between electrode placement and brain seizure
thresholds.

The retention data shown in Figure 4B indicated a
very strong relationship between electrode position and the
development of RA.   All Group 1 mice receiving bilateral
subseizure electrical stimulation of the dentate area (BD)
developed RA $\{\rho < .01\}$.   Stimulation in any other neural
region, including nondentate placements within the hippocampi
(BD), failed to result in RA.

The results of this experiment indicate that electrical
stimulation of the dentate region of the hippocampus in mice,
25% below the afterdischarge threshold, results in RA for
an inhibitory avoidance task.   This finding supports the
conclusion that the locus of bilaterally induced neural
changes, produced by electrical stimulation, may be critical
for the development of subsequent memory disruption.
Electrode placements in the hippocampus and surrounding
tissue were not effective in producing amnesia *unless* both
electrodes were located in the area dentata.   Thus, within a
reasonably restricted region of neural tissue, i.e., the
allocortical hippocampal formation consisting of the hippocampus and the subiculum, both positive and negative amnesia-
producing sites were observed.   Such a precise localization
implies that at the time of brain stimulation (less than 15
seconds after learning), discrete regions of brain, more
specifically discrete regions of hippocampus, seem to be
involved in memory disruptive processes.

The experiments described above suggest that electrolytic
lesions, seizure-producing electrical stimulation, or subseizure stimulation of discrete hippocampal subfields result
in memory impairment.   It is tempting to speculate as to the
mechanism of this memory deficit.   One simple hypothesis that
explains the results of the lesion and stimulation experiments

is that any significant malfunction of the dentate gyrus
region of the hippocampus will interfere with some of the
normal information processing capabilities of an organism.
In order to test this hypothesis a third method of altering
normal hippocampal functioning was used (Zornetzer et al.,
1974). Thus, electrodes were implanted into various hippocampal regions and the effects of electrode-produced tissue
damage on behavior were evaluated. Previous pilot work in
our laboratory indicated that such "implanted control" mice
occasionally had memory deficits. The following experiment
explored these observations more carefully. As described in
detail below, our results indicate that vascular damage
within the hippocampal formation can result in a tissue malfunction having effects on memory.

Eighty-four mice received bipolar stainless steel
electrodes implanted bilaterally in the dorsal hippocampus.
The implantation procedures differed slightly from those
used in the previous experiments, in that each electrode
was completely embedded within the nonconductive acrylic
cement which secured the electrodes to the skull. Thus, in
this experiment no electrical connection, either for purposes
of stimulating or recording, was made to any electrode.

Following a 10 day post-operative recovery period all
mice were trained on the inhibitory avoidance step-through
task described previously. Twenty-four hours after training
each mouse was tested for retention of the footshock experience.

All mice were sacrificed within a few hours of testing.
Mice were anesthetized with ether and were perfused trans-
cardially with saline followed by 10% Formalin. Brains were
sectioned at 30 μ on a freezing microtome. Adjacent brain
sections were alternately stained with thionin or Prussian
blue at 90 μ intervals through the electrode track. Prussian
blue uses potassium ferrocyanide to stain ferric ions (Fe^{+3})
a deep blue color. Thus, this colormetric histochemical
reaction product was used in the evaluation of the presence
of metallic ions.

Two independent observers rated the brain tissue with
respect to the presence or absence of Fe^{+3}. A positive
identification of ions required that the following two criteria be met: (1) the reaction product must be visible during
initial screening at X 15 magnification on at least one
section through the electrode track and (2) the reaction
product must be detectable on at least two sections through
the electrode track when viewed at X 430 magnification.

Electrode placements were similar to those shown in
Figure 3A and B above. Upon analysis of the histological

material, operated animals were assigned to one of 3 treatment groups. Group NBD (nonbilateral dentate) mice (n = 38) did not have electrode tips bilaterally located within the dentate gyrus of the hippocampus. Included within this group are mice with (1) no Fe^{+3} (2) asymmetrical bilateral Fe^{+3} (3) unilateral Fe^{+3} (4) symmetrical extradentate Fe^{+3}. These four subgroups of Group NBD were pooled, since in some cases the number of mice in any one subgroup was too small for meaningful statistical evaluation. Group BD/Fe^{+3} (bilateral dentate with ferric ions) mice (n = 30) had electrode tips located within the dentate gyrus of each hippocampus and further, Fe^{+3} was located at each electrode tip. Finally, Group BD (bilateral dentate) mice (n = 16) had each electrode tip located within the dentate gyrus but no Fe^{+3} was detected at one or both of the electrode tips. In addition to the three groups described above, a normal unimplanted control group (n = 15) was also included in this experiment.

The STL difference scores for each group are shown in Figure 5A. Group BD/Fe^{+3} had a significantly shorter STL difference score than Group BD $\{\rho < 0.001\}$, and normal animals $\{\rho < 0.001\}$. The latter three groups had median STL difference scores of 300 seconds and were not significantly different from each other.

The results of this experiment indicate: (1) Fe^{+3} resulting from the mere presence of an electrode in brain tissue, can result in significant behavioral deficits. (2) Such behavioral deficits are not simply the result of tissue damage caused by electrode implantation *per se*, since Group BD and Group BD/Fe^{+3} shared identical electrode-produced tissue damage but had significantly different retention scores. (3) A very specific region of the hippocampal formation, the dentate gyrus, appears to be sensitive to bilateral Fe^{+3} induced behavioral deficits. This interpretation is further supported by comparison of a subgroup of Group NBD comprised of mice which had bilateral Fe^{+3} in the CA1 region (n = 8). Comparison of this subgroup with normal mice indicated no significant difference. Thus, at least when compared to the CA1 region of hippocampus the dentate gyrus appears particularly sensitive to bilateral Fe^{+3} induced behavioral deficits.

The hippocampal malfunction produced in the present study does not result from massive destruction of tissue via either electrolytic or aspirative techniques. Rather, small amounts of Fe^{+3} in the dentate gyrus appear to be capable of producing a neural malfunction similar to that produced by more traumatic methods. Other evidence from our laboratory suggests that the observed Fe^{+3} is of vascular origin (Boast et al.,

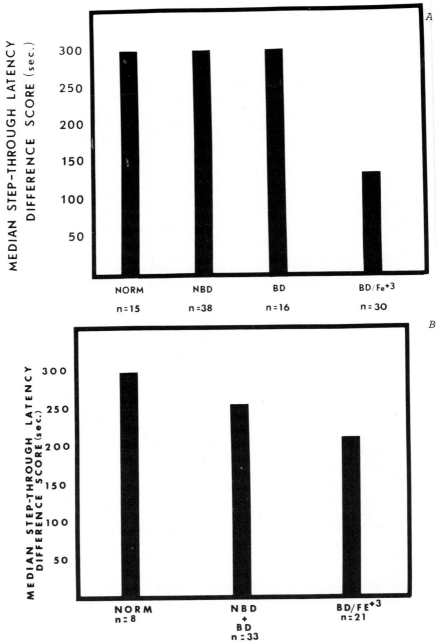

Fig. 5. Median STL difference scores for mice tested for retention either 24 hours (a) or 15 minutes (B) after training. Normal mice (NORM), mice implanted with electrodes

not located bilaterally in the dentate gyrus (NBD), mice implanted with electrodes located bilaterally in the dentate gyrus but not having Fe^{+3} located at each electrode tip (BD), mice implanted with electrodes located bilaterally in the dentate gyrus and having Fe^{+3} located at each electrode tip (BD/Fe^{+3}).

1975b). Thus, transient (or possibly permanent) ischemia and/or edema may have resulted in the malfunction of tissue subserved by the damaged blood vessels located in the hippocampal fissure overlying the dentate gyrus. Additional work is currently being carried out in our laboratory to better understand the nature of this vascular damage-induced tissue malfunction.

Our previous findings indicated that electrolytic lesions of the dentate gyrus appeared to interfere primarily with LTM whereas similar lesions of the CA1 region appeared to interfere with STM. In order to verify this finding using the present technique of electrode implantation *per se* the following experiment was performed.

Fifty-four additional mice received electrodes implanted using identical procedures to those in the experiment just described. Eight unimplanted mice served as a control group. Following a 10-day post-operative recovery period, mice were trained in the same manner as previously described.

Following training all mice were returned to their home cage. A 15 minute interval elapsed between training and STM testing. Following testing, brain tissue was histologically prepared as previously described.

Following histological analysis of brain tissue three experimental groups resulted: Group NBD (n = 28); Group BD/Fe^{+3} (n = 21); and Group BD (n = 5). Group designations were identical to those used in the previous experiments. Initial comparison between STL difference scores for Group NBD and Group BD indicated no significant difference.

Group BD is the appropriate control for Group BD/Fe^{+3} because identical electrode-produced tissue damage occurred in each group. Since a low number of mice met the criteria for inclusion in Group BD, statistical comparisons using this group were not meaningful. Therefore, Group BD was combined with the other control group, Group NBD, resulting in Group NBD+BD. Figure 5B shows the STL difference scores for the resulting groups. Subsequent statistical analyses between Group NBD+BD and normal mice indicated a significant difference $\{p < 0.001\}$. A comparison between Group NBD+BD and Group BD/Fe^{+3} indicated no significant difference $\{p > 0.29\}$.

The results of Experiment 2 indicate that Fe^{+3} in the dentate gyrus produces a STM deficit. Unlike the results of Experiment 1, however, the present results indicate that the STM deficit produced by Fe^{+3} in the dentate is no greater than the STM deficit produced by nonspecific damage to the hippocampus. Thus, it appears in the present experiment that electrode-produced damage to hippocampal tissue in general is sufficient to result in a STM deficit. As the previous experiment indicated, however, such a nonspecific hippocampal damage does not result in LTM deficits measured 24 hours later. These data suggest that different regions of the hippocampus differentially participate in both STM and LTM.

In view of the differential contributions of these dorsal hippocampal subfields, we felt it would be important to determine whether a dorsal ventral homogeneity of function existed within these subfields. Thirty-nine mice received electrodes implanted bilaterally in the region of the dentate gyrus of the ventral hippocampus according to the procedures described previously. Following a 10-day post-operative recovery period, these mice were trained as previously described, returned to their home cages and tested for retention 24 hours later. Following testing, the mouse brain tissue was histologically prepared as described above.

Following histological analysis of brain tissue, three experimental groups resulted: Group NBD (n = 18); Group BD/Fe^{+3} (n = 10); and Group BD (n = 11). An unimplanted control group (n = 15) was also used in this experiment. Group designations were identical to those used in the previous experiments. Statistical tests indicated no differences among these groups $\{p > .10\}$.

Thus, the presence of Fe^{+3} in the dentate gyrus of the *ventral* hippocampus does not result in a memory impairment. This suggests that not only can different hippocampal subfields within a given hippocampal region (dorsal hippocampus) participate differentially in memory processes, but also that a given hippocampal subfield (dentate gyrus) across different hippocampal regions (dorsal vs. ventral hippocampus) may differentially contribute to memory processes. Functional differences between dorsal and ventral hippocampus have also been observed in other contexts, for example, control of corticosteroids (Redgate, 1970; Rubin, Mandell, & Crandall, 1966).

It appears that the dentate gyrus of the dorsal hippocampus is susceptible to several types of experimental manipulations which result in local malfunctions and hence a behavioral deficit. For example, (a) electrolytic lesions

(Boast et al., 1975a) (b) electrical stimulation (Zornetzer et al., 1973) or (c) vascular damage and associated Fe^{+3} release (Boast et al., 1975b; Zornetzer et al., 1974), result in a behavioral deficit when the mouse dentate gyrus is involved bilaterally.

These experiments may provide clarification and understanding of the role of the hippocampal formation in memory as seen in the clinical situation (Milner, 1965). Human clinical data suggest that bilaterality of temporal lobe damage is an important precondition for the occurrence of a generalized memory deficit (Milner, 1959), although unilateral damage can result in specific types of memory impairment (Corkin, 1965).

Animal studies have also demonstrated the importance of bilaterality of malfunction as a precondition for affecting learning (Chow, 1961; Wyers, Deadwyler, Hirasuua, & Montgomery, 1973). These findings in conjunction with the present data support the hypothesis that bilaterally symmetrical malfunction of discrete brain regions within the hippocampal formation plays an important role in the disruption of memory storage. It remains to be determined whether or not all brain regions having the capacity to disrupt labile memory when caused to malfunction must do so by acting in bilateral concert.

Our data suggest that in addition to the role of bilateral symmetry in the disruption of memory storage processes, regional differentiation within the hippocampus is another factor in determining the effectiveness of discrete brain manipulations in producing amnesia. These data are consistent with the suggestion by Rosvold and Schwartzbart (1965) that the hippocampus is not homogeneous with regard to its functional role in learning. Such a view of functional differences within the hippocampus is consonant with classically-defined hippocampal morphology (Ramon y Cajal, 1968; Lorente de No, 1934). In addition, our data suggest that discrete regions of the hippocampal formation can differentially participate in short-term and long-term memory processes. Such differential involvement of the various hippocampal regions in memory may have been obscured in prior clinical and animal research due to the radical surgical interventions involved in hippocampectomy.

Of the various hippocampal subfields, why does the dentate gyrus appear crucial to the long-term retention of an inhibitory avoidance response? This regional specificity within the hippocampus is not surprising in view of the fact that two of the three major hippocampal afferent systems terminate upon the granule cells of the dentate gyrus. That

is, entorhinal and septal input to the hippocampus projects
independently to both the granule cells of the dentate gyrus
and the pyramidal cells of the CA regions (Blackstad, 1958).
The granule cells then relay this excitatory afferent information to the pyramidal cells of the CA3-CA4 region
(Andersen, Bliss, & Skrede, 1971), forming a neural loop
potentially capable of reinforcing extrinsic pyramidal cell
input in the "Hebbian" sense (Hebb, 1949). In addition, the
granule cells of dentate gyrus appear to be the first cells
to acquire, and to show extinction of, a conditioned response
(Segal, Disterhoft, & Olds, 1972; Segal, 1973; Segal & Olds,
1972, 1973). Because of their anatomical connections, and
because of the early response of the granule cells to
conditioning procedures, it has been suggested that the role
of the dentate gyrus in learning is to modulate or reinforce
the activity of neurons in the CA3-CA4 region (Segal, 1973).
Thus, a local malfunction of the dentate gyrus granule cells,
a nodal point within the hippocampus for convergence and
divergence of input, might result in a more widespread
impairment in normal hippocampal functioning. This more
pervasive hippocampal alteration in normal function may
underly the observed behavioral deficit.

In contrast to the dentate gyrus, the CA1 region appears
to participate in the short-term retention of an inhibitory
avoidance response. Is it possible to account for this
differential participation in short- and long-term memory
by CA1 and dentate gyrus respectively? Examination of
hippocampal efferents has recently (Andersen, Bland, &
Dudar, 1973) revealed that CA1 pyramidal cells send axons
caudally in the alveus to terminate in a localized region of
the subiculum. On the other hand, dentate gyrus granule cells
project exclusively to the CA3-CA4 pyramidal cells (Andersen
et al., 1971) which in turn send axons to other brain regions
via the fimbria and dorsal fornix (Andersen et al., 1973).
In view of these findings, Andersen et al. (1973) suggested
that the CA3 and CA1 regions may differentially modulate
hippocampal participation in behavioral situations. As
suggested by the present data, the impairment seen following
dentate gyrus malfunction may be due to alteration in
normal functioning of the CA3 region. Thus, the differential
participation of CA1 and the dentate gyrus in short- and
long-term memory is supported by anatomical evidence.

Recently Segal and Bloom (1974) demonstrated that the
locus coeruleus (LC) projects to the pyramidal cells of the
dorsal hippocampus in the rat. These projections were
found to be noradrenergic and inhibitory upon pyramidal cell
spontaneous activity. Because the LC and the DG might also

be involved in memory processes. This suggestion is compatible with other data concerned with the neurobiology and functional role of sleep. Thus, the LC appears to be strongly involved in the initiation and maintenance of rapid eye movement (REM) or paradoxical sleep (PS) (Jouvet, 1967, 1969, 1972). The LC is also a major nuclear area giving rise to norepinephrine (NE) containing cells (Ungerstedt, 1971). The projections of these cells are widespread and have recently been mapped (Dahlstrom & Fuxe, 1965; Olson & Fuxe, 1971, 1972; Jacobowitz & Palkavits, 1974a, 1974b). The LC projections to forebrain are very widespread, terminating in cerebral cortex, cerebellum, thalamus, hypothalamus, amygdala, and hippocampus.

The importance of the LC in the production of REM has generated a great deal of excitement in the area of sleep research. One fundamental question that remains to be explored, however, is "What is the functional importance of sleep, and specifically, REM sleep?" Of course, this question can be asked at many levels ranging from the cellular and general metabolic level, to the psychological/psychiatric level. One recent line of speculation concerning REM is its possible importance in information processing, specifically its role in consolidation of recent memories into permanent or long-term memory (Green, 1970; Dallett, 1973; Hennevin & Leconte, 1971). A good deal of recent evidence suggests that REM is very important for memory processes. Thus, REM deprivation by means of the pedestal method (i.e., confining an organism, usually a rodent, to a small pedestal slightly elevated above a water bath and taking advantage of the fact that during REM, loss of muscle tone occurs in antigravity muscles thus resulting in the "dunking" of the animal and its awakening from REM) has been reported to interfere with recently acquired memories (Leconte & Bloch, 1970; Leconte, Hennevin, & Bloch, 1974; Pearlman, 1971; Pearlmam & Becker, 1974; Pearlman & Greenberg, 1973). Further, following new memory formation increased REM has been reported to occur in rodents (Hennevin, Leconte, & Bloch, 1974; Leconte & Hennevin, 1971; Lucero, 1970; Smith, Kitahama, Valatx, & Jouvet, 1972). Finally, Fishbein, McGaugh, & Swarz (1971) reported that REM deprivation in the mouse led to a substantial prolongation of the period of time a recently formed memory remained susceptible to disruption by the production of retrograde amnesia by administration of electroconvulsive shock.

Since the LC has recently been found to project directly to the hippocampal formation, and is a key brain region for the initiation and maintenance of REM, and since REM appears to be important in memory processes, it seems only logical to explore the possibility that the LC is *directly* involved in memory processing. In order to test this hypothesis two experiments were done and the results of these experiments are reported below.

It is well known that newly formed memories require a period of time to become "fixed" in the brain (McGaugh, 1966). Thus, memories are susceptible to modification for some period of time after their formation. The modification of such newly made memories can take the form of either facilitation (Krivanek & McGaugh, 1969) or disruption (McGaugh, 1965). A number of experimental treatments including various pharmacological agents (cf. Hunter, Zornetzer, Jarvik, & McGaugh, 1975; McGaugh & Petrinovich, 1965), ECS (cf. McGaugh & Dawson, 1971), electrical stimulation of the brain (cf. Gold et al., 1974) have been shown to alter recently formed or labile memory. In order for the claim to be made that any of these experimental treatments are affecting memory processes *per se*, and not altering performance or learning variables in some nonspecific way, it is best to administer the treatment *after* the training experience.

Given the above considerations the following experiment was designed to determine whether discrete damage of the LC resulted in an effect on memory.

Thirty-five male Swiss mice (Flow Research Labs) were stereotaxically implanted bilaterally with teflon insulated platinum-iridium electrodes (125 μ diameter). The target structure was the LC (coordinates: anterior-posterior = -1.3 mm from lambda; medial-lateral = 0.7 mm; ventral = -3.5 mm below brain surface). Animals were anesthetized with Nembutal (50 mg/kg) during surgery. The electrodes were attached to small gold-plated contacts which were rigidly attached to the skull with dental acrylic. Following surgery all mice were returned to their home cages and allowed a seven day postoperative recovery period. At the end of the recovery period all mice were trained on the single-trial inhibitory avoidance step-through task (Jarvik & Kopp, 1967). Training and testing procedures were described previously.

Immediately following training all mice were lightly anesthetized with ether (anesthesia period = 45 seconds) and received bilateral anodal electrolytic lesions to the brain tissue underlying the implanted electrodes at the uninsulated tips. Lesions were made by passing 500 μA for 15 seconds and using a rectal cathode. Following lesioning, mice were returned to their home cages for 48 hours. Following this 48 hour interval each mouse was tested for retention of the footshock experience. Good retention was indicated by a high

STL and poor retention was indicated by a low STL. A 300 second difference limit between original STL and testing STL was imposed on each mouse. At the end of this 300 second limit, animals not stepping through the hole into the darkened chamber were removed and returned to their home cage. Shortly after retention testing all mice were sacrificed by means of decapitation. The forebrains were dissected out and immediately placed in liquid nitrogen for subsequent NE determination. Brain stems were place in 10% formalin for subsequent histological verification of electrode placement.

On the basis of histological analysis (cresyl violet staining) of electrode placements the behavioral data from the mice was separated into three groups. Group 1: Bilateral LC (n = 11). These mice were found to have lesion-produced damage to the LC bilaterally. Due to the elongated shape of the LC, however, no animals had total destruction of the LC. Rather, for animals in this group only partial damage of the LC was found. Group 2: Unilateral LC (n = 11). These mice were found to have only unilateral damage to the LC. Group 3: Bilateral lesion control (n = 13). These mice were found to have lesions in brain regions other than the LC. Thus, mice in this group did not receive any detectable damage to either LC. A representative example of each of the three patterns described above is shown in Figure 6.

Analysis of the STL difference scores using the nonparametric Mann-Whitney U-test indicated that posttrial lesions of the LC had no effect ($p > .10$) on retention of the 1-trial inhibitory avoidance response. Figure 7 shows the behavioral data obtained in this experiment. These results suggest that neither unilateral nor bilateral damage of the LC, sustained immediately after learning this very simple inhibitory response, resulted in any impairment of memory.

While these findings might seem to argue against the original hypothesis stated earlier that the LC should be involved in memory processes, it is possible that the behavioral task used in this experiment was so simple for the mouse to learn that lesion-produced alterations in LC function did not affect the memory. There is support in the literature for the idea that REM (and therefore, presumably the LC) is particularly important for the consolidation of memories associated with complex tasks but not simple ones (Pearlman & Becker, 1974). It seems that there might be a baseline or "floor effect" in terms of the direct influence of LC upon newly formed memory in such a way that non-complex memories may not require the participation of the LC in their consolidation.

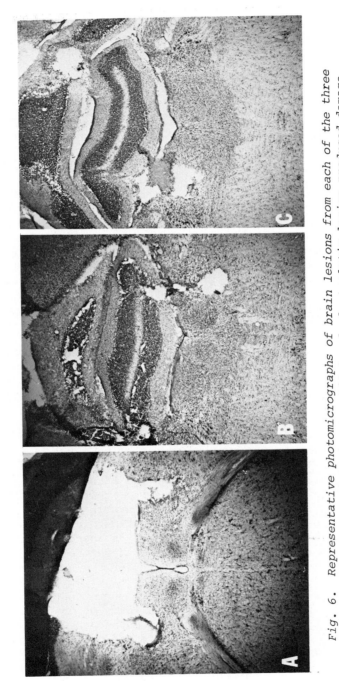

Fig. 6. Representative photomicrographs of brain lesions from each of the three treatment groups (cresyl violet). A. Bilateral electrolytic lesion-produced damage to the LC at the level of cranial nerve VII. B. Unilateral electrolytic LC damage plus a contralateral control lesion. C. Bilateral electrolytic control lesions without damage to either LC nucleus. B. and C. are both at the level of cranial nerve V.

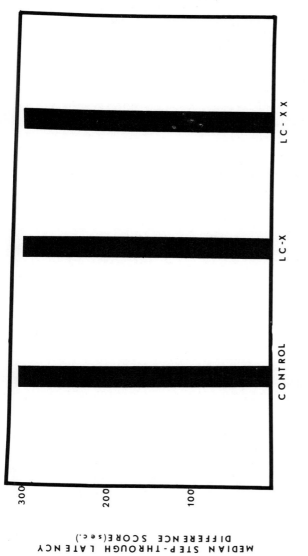

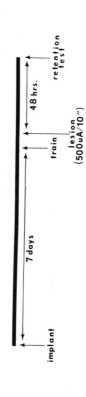

Fig. 7. Median STL difference scores for each of the three treatment groups. The schematic below the graph represents the paradigm followed in this experiment.

An alternative approach to evaluating the role of the LC in memory processes is to determine whether the structure participates in the temporal delineation of the susceptibility of a newly-formed memory to modification. Thus, even though LC damage did not appear to *directly* interfere with the retention of the step-through response, it is possible that the LC does participate in the determination of the time period new memory remains labile to modification. Such a possibility is suggested by the data of Fishbein et al. (1971) using REM deprivation and subsequent ECS-produced retrograde amnesia. In order to directly test the possibility that the LC is involved in determining the temporal lability of recent memory the following experiment was done.

Forty-seven mice of the same strain, sex and weight as used in the previous experiment were used in this experiment. Twenty-three mice were assigned to two non-implanted control groups. The remaining mice were stereotaxically implanted bilaterally using the same procedures as described above. Following surgery, mice were returned to their home cages for a seven day post-operative recovery period.

The two non-implanted control groups were trained in the step-through apparatus using the same procedures as described above. Immediately following training, one control group (Imm. ECS) received transcorneal ECS (15 μA, 200 msec). Following recovery from the tonic-clonic convulsions mice were returned to their home cages for 48 hours at which time a retention test trial was administered. Mice in the other control group were trained as above, and immediately placed back into their home cages. Following a delay of 40 hours these mice were then administered transcorneal ECS (15 μA, 200 msec) and returned to their home cages for an additional 8 hours. At the end of this 48 hour posttraining period these mice were tested for retention of the inhibitory avoidance response. The difference between these two non-implanted control groups is the time of ECS administration (either immediate or 40 hours delayed).

The animals implanted bilaterally with electrodes aimed at the LC were all trained in the step-through task after the seven day recovery period. Immediately following training all implanted mice received bilateral electrolytic lesions as described above. Following the lesions mice were returned to their home cages for 40 hours. At the end of this 40-hour period all lesioned mice were administered a trans-corneal ECS as described above. Following ECS mice were returned to their home cages for an additional 8 hours at which time they received a retention test trial. Shortly after the retention test trial mice were sacrificed and brains removed as previously described.

Figure 8 shows the results of this experiment. Non-implanted mice receiving ECS immediately after learning were amnesic as indicated by their low step-through scores on the retention trial. On the other hand, non-implanted mice receiving ECS after a 40-hour delay had normal memory when tested 8 hours later. These groups showed a significant difference in retention scores {$p < .01$}.

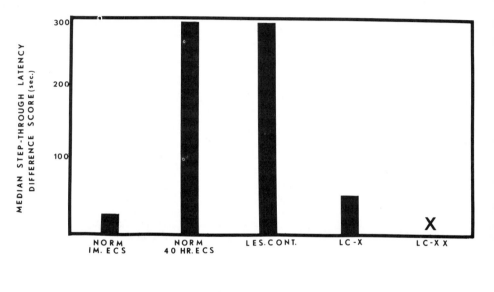

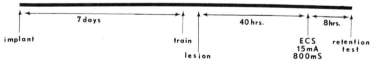

Fig. 8. *Median STL difference scores for lesioned and unlesioned mice. Normal unlesioned control mice receiving immediate ECS (NORM IM. ECS), Normal unlesioned control mice receiving 40 hour delayed ECS (NORM 40 HR. ECS), lesioned control mice with no damage to the LC (LES. CONT.), mice with unilateral LC lesion damage (LC-X), mice with bilateral LC lesion damage (LC-XX). The experimental paradigm followed for the lesioned animals in this experiment is schematized below the graph.*

On the basis of histological verification of lesion sites, implanted mice were divided into three groups as described earlier. Four lesioned mice died during the ECS-produced tonic phase of the convulsion. Each of these mice had bilateral lesion damage to the LC. No other mice were found to have bilateral LC damage. Mice with unilateral LC damage (n = 10) were impaired in their performance of the inhibitory avoidance response when compared to lesioned control mice (n = 10) having no LC damage {$p < .05$, Kolmogorov-Smirnov} and when compared to non-implanted controls receiving delayed ECS {$p < .05$}. No statistical difference was found between retention in the unilateral LC lesioned mice given 40 hour delayed ECS and non-implanted mice receiving immediate ECS. Since all bilateral LC lesioned mice died during convulsion, no retention data could be obtained from this group.

The results of this experiment suggest that damage to the LC results in profound alterations in the duration of the labile period associated with recently formed memory. Thus, while non-lesioned mice were not susceptible to ECS-produced retrograde amnesia 40 hours after memory formation, LC-lesioned mice showed a marked memory disturbance when tested eight hours later. If our interpretation is correct, that LC damage prolongs the susceptibility period of recent memory to modification, then these data suggest that the LC functions in some way to delimit this susceptibility period or promote consolidation. A survey of the experimental literature indicates that while there has been substantial controversy regarding the exact time-course of susceptibility of a newly formed memory to disruption (McGaugh & Dawson, 1971; Lewis, 1969) it is widely accepted that this susceptibility period does not extend beyond 3-6 hours in rodents. In the present study we demonstrated that LC lesions extend this period to *at least* 40 hours. Thus, fundamental neurobiological processes essential to the consolidation or fixation of new memory have been altered by LC damage.

An alternative explanation for our data is that LC damage in some way alters memory retrieval processes. The combination of posttrial LC damage coupled with 40-hour delayed ECS produced a prolonged memory retrieval deficit present 8 hours after ECS at the time of retention testing. It is clear from our control data that neither treatment alone results in a memory impairment. The cause of memory disruption, either impaired retrieval processes or prevention of long-term storage, is not understood. We are currently investigating this problem.

Damage to LC results in significant depletion of forebrain levels of NE, a putative neurotransmitter (Jones,

Bobillier, Pin, & Jouvet, 1973). One of the forebrain
neuroanatomical regions receiving substantial axonal projections from the LC is the hippocampal formation (Ungerstedt,
1971). The LC projections to the hippocampus end on pyramidal
cells throughout the specific CA subfields of the hippocampus
and are inhibitory to the spontaneous activity of hippocampal
pyramidal cells (Segal & Bloom, 1974).

The recently discovered anatomical projections of the
LC to the hippocampus, and our present findings that the LC,
when damaged, alters either the temporal aspects of the
susceptibility period of newly-formed memory to disruption
or the retrieval of such memories, suggest that the LC may
be involved in an extended neuroanatomical memory system
involving both forebrain and brainstem regions. We are
continuing to investigate this problem in the laboratory. If
the above hypothesis is correct, that LC damage results in an
extension of the susceptibility period, then it should be
posssible to demonstrate facilitation of recent memory at
extended time periods, even though such facilitation has
typically been shown to be temporally restricted to a rather
short period following the formation of a new memory (Destrade
& Cardo, 1974).

The functional relationship of REM to memory is still
poorly understood. The results of the present experiments
suggest that a brain region believed to be essential for REM
is also directly involved in certain aspects of memory
processing. Although it is possible that the LC may have
dual and independent functional roles in the initiation of REM
on the one hand, and delimiting the susceptibility period of
memory on the other hand, it seems more biologically parsimonious that these two functional roles of this brainstem
structure are interrelated and interdependent.

Clinical Correlations and Speculations

These data support the hypothesis that processes related
to REM (PS) mediated by the noradrenergic locus coeruleus (LC),
are not only important for memory consolidation, but suggest
the possibility that memories remain in a short-term labile
form without the influence of the LC. The question which
comes to mind when discussing the relevance or significance
of data derived from work with one species, is whether the
data and hypothesis can be extrapolated to other species.
Supporting extrapolation from these data is the phylogenetic
stability of the LC (Kappers, Hubber, & Crosby, 1960; Russell,
1965). The function of the LC in REM, LC neurochemistry, LC
neuroanatomy and even the total number of noradrenergic cell

bodies in each LC has been studied in many species, including
man, without conflicting reports (Chu & Bloom, 1973; Descarries
& Saucier, 1972; Hubbard & DeCarlo, 1973; Jones & Moore, 1974;
Nobin & Bjorklund, 1972; Russell, 1955; Ungerstedt, 1971).

Extrapolation to man may be justified on a phylogenetic
and a functional level, however, due to the rarity of spontaneously occurring memory disorders (DeJong, 1973) and the
relative novelty of the LC-REM-memory consolidation hypothesis,
direct confirmatory pre- or post-mortem studies are not yet
available in man. One of the most profound memory dysfunction
syndromes described in the clinical literature is the
Korsakoff syndrome. These patients are unable to form new,
permanent memories. Traditionally, it has been accepted that
the neurophathology associated with this chronic alcohol-
induced disease was restricted to forebrain structures.
Specifically, structures such as the hippocampus, fornix,
mamillary bodies, and medial dorsal nucleus of the thalamus
have been correlated with premorbid Korsakoff's memory
dysfunction (Barbizet, 1963; Delay & Brion, 1954; Lewis,
1961; Rosenbaum & Merritt, 1939; Sims, 1905; Wechsler, 1917).
Interestingly, it has recently been reported in an extensive
clinical and post-mortem neuropathological study (Victor et
al., 1971) that the LC is damaged (cell loss and depigmenta-
tion) in over two-thirds of Korsakoff patients. The incidence of LC damage was found to be considerably higher than
the incidence of hippocampal damage. This clinical finding,
in conjunction with the data reported in the present experiments suggest that the LC may play a very important role in
human memory processing. Unfortunately, the post-mortem
status of LC projections--dorsal noradrenergic bundle,
supracallosal pathway, and noradrenergic terminals in the
pyramidal region of the hippocampus (Olson & Fuxe, 1971)--
have not been studied in Korsakoff-related memory disorders.
Studies should be undertaken to document the nocturnal EEG
(percent REM) of Korsakoff's patients as well as those
which will quantify the post-mortem status of the LC's
noradrenergic cell bodies and their projections as well
as norepinephrine content. These studies could test the
predictions, from the extrapolation of the data presented
here, that the difficulty of Korsakoff's patients to form
new, permanent memory is related to interference with the
LC's function in both sleep and memory processing. With
new memories remaining in a labile form, environmental events
and stimuli could readily interfere with the Korsakoff's
patient's ability to store and retrieve new memories.

The other group of patients presenting with new long-
term memory disorders are those who have sustained vascular
insult, trauma, or surgery to their hippocampal formation

bilaterally. These "hippocampal amnesic" patients closely follow the amnesic model which we have proposed. They have profound, (new) long-term memory loss and, therefore, are unable to process and store new memories but have preserved IQ, remote memory, and other intellectual functions (Milner & Penfield, 1955; Penfield & Milner, 1958; Scoville & Milner, 1957). The possibility exists that the destruction or removal of the hippocampal formation results in the retrograde axonal degeneration of LC neurons. This could then result in loss of REM and inability to form new memories. Further neuropathological and neuropsychiatric studies are necessary to confirm this prediction from our hypothesis.

Though Dement's (1960) suggestion that the dream "most frequently elicited during REM" might be the protector of sanity is quite speculative, future investigation from the point of view of REM and information processing seem justified. Investigations in autistic children, for example, have shown that while the nocturnal EEG is grossly normal, the duration of rapid eye movement bursts is reduced (Gold & Robertson, 1975; Ornitz, Ritvo, Brown, LaFranchi, Parmelee & Walter, 1969). These data suggested to the authors that the factors sustaining REM are deficient or inhibited in these psychotic children. Further clinical and neuropathological investigations are necessary to delineate the neural basis for the cognitive and perceptual similarities between experiences in normal dreaming and schizophrenia.

General Conclusions and Speculations

The results of our research described above and of other research leads us to formulate the following hypotheses. First, we suggest that normal function of the dentate gyrus (DG) region of the anterodorsal hippocampal formation in the mouse is important for the transfer of at least some types of newly formed memories, still in a labile or susceptible state (short-term memory, STM), into a more permanent memory storage system (long-term memory, LTM). Such a hypothesis is supported by (1) the neuroanatomic organization of the intrinsic and extrinsic hippocampal projections, (2) data on the temporal aspects of single unit conditioning within the hippocampal formation, and (3) our own data described above. Second, we suggest that the locus coeruleus (LC) works in concert with the DG, through its NE-containing projections to hippocampal pyramidal cells, in terms of delimiting, in a temporal way, the susceptibility of new memory to modification. Thus, with an LC malfunction newly-formed memories remain in an extended state of vulnerability to modification. Further, even if the DG is functioning normally, and hence the transfer from STM to LTM has occurred, if the LC is not *simultaneously* functioning normally then this recently-formed long-term memory will still be susceptible to modification.

Both the DG and LC independently project to the hippo-campal pyramidal cells. The synaptic action of the former is almost exclusively excitatory while the synaptic action of the latter is inhibitory upon these pyramidal cells. We suggest, therefore, that there is a possible physiological basis (in terms of potential reciprocal action at the hippo-campal pyramidal cell level) for a DG-mediated transfer of information coupled with an LC-mediated delimitation of lability and susceptibility to modification of that newly transferred memory.

The hypotheses described above will hopefully be of heuristic value for future study of the relationships between the neurobiological processes underlying sleep and memory. We feel these hypotheses provide at least a backdrop and possible explanation for much of the recent data reporting relationships between learning and REM sleep.

REFERENCES

Andersen, P., Bland, P. H., & Dudar, S. D. Organization of the hippocampal output. *Experimental Brain Research,* 1973, *17,* 152-168.

Andersen, P., Bliss, T. V. P., & Skrede, K. K. Lamellar organization of hippocampal excitatory pathways. *Experimental Brain Research,* 1971, *13,* 222-238.

Barbizet, J. Defect of memorizing of hippocampal-mammillary origin: A review. *Journal of Neurology, Neurosurgery and Psychiatry,* 1963, *26,* 127-135.

Barondes, S. J., & Cohen, J. D. Arousal and the conversion of short-term to long-term memory. *Proceedings of the National Academy of Sciences,* 1968, *61,* 923-929.

Blackstad, J. W. Commissural connections of the hippocampal region in the rat, with special reference to their mode of termination. *Journal of Comparative Neurology,* 1956, *105,* 417-438.

Bloch, V. Facts and hypotheses concerning memory consolidation. *Brain Research,* 1970, *24,* 561-575.

Boast, C. A., Zornetzer, S. F., & Hamrick, M. R. Electrolytic lesions of various hippocampal subfields in the mouse: Differential effects on short- and long-term memory. *Behavioral Biology,* 1975a, *14,* 85-94.

Boast, C. A., Zornetzer, S. F., & Hamrick, M. R. Ferric ions located in the hippocampal subfields in the mouse: Effects on behavior. *Tower International Technomedical Journal of Life Sciences,* 1975b, *5,* 11-16.

Bresnahan, E., & Routtenberg, A. Memory disruption by unilateral low level sub-seizure stimulation of the medial amygdaloid nucleus. *Physiology and Behavior,* 1972, *9,* 513-525.

Chow, K. L. Effect of local electrographic afterdischarge on visual learning and retention in the monkey. *Journal of Neurophysiology,* 1961, *24,* 391-400.

Chu, N., & Bloom, F. E. Norepinephrine-containing neurons: Changes in spontaneous discharge patterns during sleeping and waking. *Science,* 1973, *179,* 908-910.

Corkin, S. Tactually guided maze learning in man: Effects of unilateral cortical excisions and bilateral hippocampal lesions. *Neuropsychologia,* 1965, *3,* 339-351.

Dahlstrom, A., & Fuxe, K. Evidence for the existence of monoamine-containing neurons in the central nervous system. *Acta Physiologica Scandinavica,* 1965, *232,* 1-35. *Suppl.*

Dallett, J. Theories of dream function. *Psychological Bulletin,* 1973, *79,* 408-416.

Deadwyler, S. A., & Wyers, E. J. Disruption of habituation by caudate nuclear stimulation in the rat. *Behavioral Biology,* 1972, *7,* 55-64.

DeJong, R. N. The hippocampus and its role in memory. *Journal of Neurological Science,* 1973, *19,* 73-83.

Delay, J., & Brion, S.   Syndrome de Korsakoff et corps
    mammillaires. *Encephale,* 1954, *43,* 193-200.

Dement, W. C.   The effect of dream deprivation. *Science,*
    1960, *131,* 1705-1707.

Descarries, L., & Saucier, G.   Disappearance of the locus
    coeruleus in the rat after intraventricular 6-hydroxy-
    dopamine. *Brain Research,* 1972, *37,* 310-316.

Destrade, C., & Cardo, B.   Effects of post-trial hippocampal
    stimulation on time -dependent improvement of performance
    in mice. *Brain Research,* 1974, *78,* 447-454.

Fishbein, W., McGaugh, J. L., & Swarz, J. R.   Retrograde
    amnesia: Electroconvulsive shock effects after termina-
    tion of rapid eye movement sleep deprivation. *Science,*
    1971, *172,* 80-82.

Geller, A., & Jarvik, M. E.   The time relations of ECS induced
    amnesia. *Psychonomic Science,* 1968, *12,* 169-170.

Goddard, G. V.   Amygdaloid stimulation and learning in the
    rat. *Journal of Comparative and Physiological Psychology,*
    1964, *58,* 23-30.

Gold, M. S., & Robertson, M. F.   The day/night imagery
    paradox of selected psychotic children. *Journal of
    Child Psychiatry,* 1975, *14,* 132-144.

Gold, P. E., Edwards, R. M., & McGaugh, J. L.   Amnesia produced
    by unilateral, subseizure, electrical stimulation of
    the amygdala in rats. *Behavioral Biology,* 1975, *15,*
    95-105.

Gold, P. E., Macri, J., & McGaugh J. L.   Retrograde amnesia
    produced by subseizure amygdala stimulation. *Behavioral
    Biology,* 1973, *9,* 671-680.

Gold, P. E., Zornetzer, S. F., & McGaugh, J. L.   Electrical
    stimulation of the brain: Effects on memory storage.
    In G. Newton & A. H. Riesen (Eds.), *Advance in
    Psychobiology.* New York: John Wiley & Sons, Inc., 1974.

Greenberg, R.   Dreaming and memory. *International Psychiatry
    Clinics,* 1970, *7,* (Part 2), 258-267.

Hebb, D. O. *The Organization of Behavior*. New York: John
     Wiley & Sons, Inc., 1949.

Hennevin, E., & Leconte, P.   La fonction du sommeil paradoxal:
     faits et hypotheses. *Annee Psychologie*, 1971, *71*,
     489-519.

Hennevin, E., Leconte, P., & Bloch, V.   Augmentation du
     sommeil paradoxal provoquee par l'acquisition, l'extinc-
     tion et la re'acquisition du'un apprentissage a
     renforcement positif. *Brain Research*, 1974, *70*, 43-54.

Herz, M. J., & Peeke, H. V. S.   Impairment of extinction with
     caudate nucleus stimulation. *Brain Research*, 1971, *33*,
     519-522.

Hirano, T.   Effect of hippocampal electrical stimulation on
     memory consolidation. *Psychologia*, 1966, *9*, 63-75.

Hubbard, J. E., & DiCarlo, V.   Fluorescence histochemistry of
     monoamine-containing cell bodies in the brain stem of
     the squirrel monkey. *Journal of Comparative Neurology*,
     1973, *147*, 553-565.

Hunter, B. E., Zornetzer, S., Jarvik, M. E., & McGaugh, J. L.
     Modulation of learning and memory: Effects of drugs
     influencing neurotransmitters. In L. Iverson, S.
     Iverson, & S. Snyder (Eds.), *Handbook of
     Psychopharmacology*, in press.

Isaacson, R. L.   Experimental brain lesions and memory.   In
     M. R. Rosenzweig, & E. L. Bennett (Eds.), *Neural
     Mechanisms of Learning and Memory*, Cambridge, Mass: The
     MIT Press, 1976.

Jacobowitz, D. M., & Palkovits, M.   Topographic atlas of
     catecholamine and acetylcholinesterase-containing
     neurons in the rat brain.   I.   Forebrain (Telencephalon
     and Diencephalon). *Journal of Comparative Neurology*,
     1974a, *157*, 13-28.

Jacobowitz, D. M., & Palkovits, M.   Topographic atlas of
     catecholamine and acetylcholinesterase-containing
     neurons in the rat brain.   II.   Hindbrain (Mesencephalon,
     Rhombencephalon). *Journal of Comparative Neurology*,
     1974b, *157*, 29-42.

Jarvik, M. E., & Kopp, R.   An improved 1-trial passive avoidance learning situation. *Psychological Report,* 1967, *21,* 221-224.

Jones, B. E., Bobillier, P., Pin, C., & Jouvet, M.   The effect of lesions of catecholamine-containing neurons upon monoamine content of the brain and EEG and behavioral waking in the cat. *Brain Research,* 1973, *58,* 157-177.

Jones, B. E., & Moore, R. Y.   Catecholamine-containing neurons of the nucleus locus coeruleus in the cat. *Journal of Comparative Neurology,* 1974, *157,* 43-52.

Jouvet, M.   Neurophysiology of the states of sleep. *Physiological Review,* 1967, *47,* 117-177.

Jouvet, M.   Biogenic amines and the states of sleep. *Sleep,* 1969, *163,* 32-41.

Jouvet, M.   The role of monamines and acetylcholine-containing neurons in the regulation of the sleep-waking cycle. *Ergebnisse der Physiologie,* 1972, *64,* 166-307.

Kappers, C. U. A., Hubber, G. D., & Crosby, E. C. *The Comparative Anatomy of the Nervous System of Vertebrates Including Man. Volume 1.* New York: Hafner, 1960.

Kesner, R.   A neural system analysis of memory storage and retrieval. *Psychological Bulletin,* 1973, *80,* 177-203.

Kesner, R. P., & Conner, H. S.   Independence of short- and long-term memory: A neural systems approach. *Science,* 1972, *176,* 432-434.

Kesner, R. P., & Conner, H. S.   Effects of electrical stimulation of rat limbic systems and midbrain reticular formation upon short- and long-term memory. *Physiology and Behavior,* 1974, *12,* 5-12.

Kesner, R. P., & Wilburn, M. W.   A review of electrical stimulation of the brain in the context of learning and retention. *Behavioral Biology,* 1974, *10,* 259-293.

Krivanek, J., & McGaugh, J. L.   Facilitating effects of pre- and post-trial amphetamine administration on discrimination learning in mice. *Agents and Actions,* 1969, *1,* 36-42.

Lashley, K. S.   In search of the engram.   *S. E. B. Symposium,* 1950, *4,* 454-482.

Leconte, P., & Bloch, V.   Deficit de la retention du'un conditionnement apres privation de sommeil paradoxal chez le rat.   *Comptes Rendus De L'Academie Des Science, Paris, Series D,* 1970, *271,* 226-229.

Leconte, P., & Hennevin, E.   Augmentation de la duree du sommeil paradoxal consecutive a un apprentissage chez le rat.   *Comptes Rendus De L'Academie Des Science, Paris, Series D,* 1971, *273,* 86-88.

Leconte, P., Hennevin, E., & Bloch, V.   Duration of paradoxical sleep necessary for the acquisition of conditioned avoidance in the rat.   *Physiology and Behavior,* 1974, *13,* 675-681.

Lewis, A.   Amnesic syndromes: The psychopathological aspect.   *Proceedings of the Royal Society of Medicine,* 1961, *54,* 955.

Lewis, D. J.   Sources of experimental amnesia.   *Psychological Review,* 1969, *76,* 461-472.

Lorente de No, R.   Studies on the structure of the cerebral cortex.   II.   Continuation of the study of the ammonic system.   *Journal fur Psychologie und Neurologie,* 1934, *46,* 113-177.

Lucero, M.   Lengthening of REM sleep duration consecutive to learning in the rat.   *Brain Research,* 1970, *11,* 319-322.

Mahut, H.   Effects of subcortical electrical stimulation on learning in the rat.   *American Psychologist,* 1957, *12,* 466.   (Abstract)

Mahut, H.   Effects of subcortical electrical stimulation on learning in the rat.   *Journal of Comparative and Physiological Psychology,* 1962, *55,* 472-477.

Mahut, H.   Effects of subcortical electrical stimulation on discrimination learning in cats.   *Journal of Comparative and Physiological Psychology,* 1964, *58,* 390-395.

McGaugh, J. L.   Facilitation and impairment of memory storage processes.   In D. P. Kimble (Ed.), *The Anatomy of Memory*.   Palo Alto: Science and Behavior Books, 1965.

McGaugh, J. L.   Time-dependent processes in memory storage. *Science*, 1966, *153*, 1351-1358.

McGaugh, J. L., & Dawson, R. G.   Modification of memory storage processes.   *Behavioral Science*, 1971, *16*, 45-63.

McGaugh, J. L., & Landfield, P. W.   Delayed development of amnesia following electroconvulsive shock.   *Physiology and Behavior*, 1970, *5*, 1109-1113.

McGaugh, J. L., & Petrinovich, L. F.   Effects of drugs on learning and memory.   *International Review of Neurobiology*, 1965, *8*, 139-196.

Milner, B.   The memory defect in bilateral hippocampal lesions. *Psychiatric Research Report*, 1959, *11*, 43-52.

Milner, B.   Memory disturbance after bilateral hippocampal lesions.   In P. Milner and S. Glickman (Eds.), *Cognitive Processes and the Brain*.   New York: Van Nostrand, 1965.

Milner, B., & Penfield, W.   The effect of hippocampal lesions on recent memory.   *Transactions of the American Neurological Association*, 1955, *80*, 42-48.

Moruzzi, G.   The sleep-waking cycle.   *Ergebnisse der Physiologie*, 1972, *64*, 1-165.

Nobin, A., & Bjorklund, A.   Topography of the monamine neuron systems in the human brain as revealed in fetuses.   *Acta Physiologica Scandinavica*, 1973, Supplement 388, 1-40.

Ojemann, G. A., Blick, K. I., & Ward, Jr., A. A.   Improvement and disturbance of short-term verbal memory with human ventrolateral thalamic stimulation.   *Brain*, 1971, *94*, 225-240.

Olson, L., & Fuxe, K.   On the projections from the locus coeruleus noradrenaline neurons, the cerebellar innervation.   *Brain Research*, 1971, *28*, 165-171.

Olson, L., & Fuxe, K.   Further mapping out of central
    noradrenaline neuron systems: Projections of the
    "subcoeruleus" area. *Brain Research*, 1972, *43*, 289-295.

Ornitz, E. M., Ritvo, E. R., Brown, M. D., La Franchi, S.,
    Parmelee, T., & Walter, R. D.   The EEG and rapid eye
    movements during REM sleep in normal and autistic
    children. *Electroencephalography and Clinical
    Neurophysiology*, 1969, *22*, 167-175.

Pearlman, C.   Latent learning impaired by REM sleep
    deprivation. *Psychonomic Science*, 1971, *25*, 135-136.

Pearlman, C. A., & Becker, M.   REM sleep deprivation impairs
    bar-press acquisition in rats. *Physiology and Behavior*,
    1974, *13*, 813-817.

Peeke, H. V. S., & Herz, M. J.   Caudate nucleus stimulation
    retroactively impairs complex maze learning in the rat.
    Science, 1971, *173*, 80-82.

Penfield, W., & Milner, B.   Memory deficit produced by
    bilateral lesions in the hippocampal zone. *American
    Medical Association Archives of Neurology and Psychiatry*,
    1958, *79*, 475-497.

Racine, R. J.   Modification of seizure activity by electrical
    stimulation: I. Afterdischarge threshold. *Electro-
    encephalography and clinical Neurophysiology*, 1972, *32*,
    269-279.

Ramon y Cajal, S.   *The Structure of Ammon's Horn*.   Illinois:
    Charles C. Thomas, 1968.

Redgate, E. S.   ACTH release evoked by electrical stimulation
    of brain stem and limbic system sites in the cat: The
    absence of ACTH release upon infundibular area
    stimulation. *Endocrinology*, 1970, *86*, 806-823.

Rosenbaum, M., & Merritt, H. H.   Korsakoff's syndrome.
    *American Medical Association Archives of Neurology
    and Psychiatry*, 1939, *41*, 978-983.

Rosvold, H. E., & Schwarzbart, M. K.   Neural structures
    involved in delayed response performance.   In J. M.
    Warren and K. Akert (Eds.),   *The Frontal Granular Cortex
    and Behavior.*   New York: McGraw-Hill, 1964.

Routtenberg, A., & Holzman, N.   Memory disruption by electrical
    stimulation of substantia nigra, pars compacta.   *Science,*
    1973, *181,* 83-86.

Rubin, R. T., Mandell, A. J., & Crandall, P. H.   Cortico-
    steroid responses to limbic stimulation in man:
    Localization of stimulus sites.   *Science,* 1966, *153,*
    767-768.

Russell, G. V.   The nucleus locus coeruleus (dorsolateralis
    tegmenti).   *Texas Reports of Biology and Medicine,*
    1955, *13,* 939-988.

Scoville, W. B., & Milner, B.   Loss of recent memory after
    bilateral hippocampal lesions.   *Journal of Neurology,
    Neurosurgery and Psychiatry,* 1957, *20,* 11-21.

Segal, M.   Flow of conditioned responses in limbic telen-
    cephalic system of the rat.   *Journal of Neurophysiology,*
    1973, *36,* 840-854.

Segal, M., & Bloom, F. E.   The action of norepinephrine in
    the rat hippocampus.   II.   Activation of the input
    pathway.   *Brain Research,* 1974, *72,* 99-114.

Segal, M., Disterhoft, J. F., & Olds, J.   Hippocampal unit
    activity during classical aversive and appetitive
    conditioning.   *Science,* 1972, *175,* 792-794.

Segal, M., & Olds, J.   The behavior of units in the
    hippocampal circuit of the rat during learning.   *Journal
    of Neurophysiology,* 1972, *35,* 680-690.

Segal, M., & Olds, J.   The activity units in the hippocampal
    circuit of the rat during classical conditioning.
    Journal of Comparative and Physiological Psychology,
    1973, *82,* 195-204.

Sideroff, S., Bueno, O., Hirsch, A., Weyand, T., & McGaugh,
    J. L.   Retrograde amnesia initiated by low-level
    stimulation of hippocampal cytoarchitectonic areas.
    Experimental Neurology, 1974, *43,* 285-297.

Sims, F. R. Anatomical findings in two cases of Korsakoff's symptom complex. *Journal of Nervous and Mental Disease,* 1905, *32,* 160-171.

Smith, C. F., Kitahama, K., Valatx, J. L., & Jouvet, M. Sommeil paradoxal et apprentissage chez duex souches consanguines de sovris. *Comptes Rendus De L'Academie Des Science D,* 1972, *275,* 1283-1286.

Spiliotis, P. H., & Thompson, R. The "manipulative response memory system" in the white rat. *Physiological Psychology,* 1973, *1,* 101-114.

Thompson, R. Localization of the "visual memory system" in the white rat. *Journal of Comparative and Physiological Psychology,* 1969, *69,* 1-29.

Thompson, R. Localization of the "maze memory system" in the white rat. *Physiological Psychology,* 1974, *2,* 1-17.

Ungerstedt, V. Stereotaxic mapping of the monamine pathways in the rat brain. *Acta Physiologica Scandinavica Suppl.,* 1971, *367,* 1-48.

Victor, M., Adams, R. D., & Collins, G. H. *The Wernicke-Korsakoff Syndrome.* Philadelphia: F. A. Davis, 1971.

Wechsler, D. A study of retention in Korsakoff psychosis. *Psychiatric Bulletin of New York State Hospital,* 1917, *2,* 403-451.

Wyers, E. J., Deadwyler, S. A., Hirasuua, N., & Montgomery, D. Passive avoidance retention and caudate stimulation. *Physiology and Behavior,* 1973, *11,* 809-819.

Wyers, E. J., Peeke, H. V. S., Williston, J. S., & Herz, M. J. Retroactive impairment of passive avoidance learning by stimulation of the caudate nucleus. *Experimental Neurology,* 1968, *22,* 350-366.

Zornetzer, S. F. Brain stimulation and retrograde amnesia in rats: A neuroanatomical approach. *Physiology and Behavior,* 1972, *8,* 239-244.

Zornetzer, S. F., Boast, C., & Hamrick, M.　Neuroanatomic localization and memory processing in mice:　The role of the dentate gyrus of the hippocampus.　*Physiology and Behavior*, 1974, *13*, 569–575.

Zornetzer, S. F., & Chronister, R. B.　Neuroanatomical localization of memory disruption:　Relationships between brain structure and learning task.　*Physiology and Behavior*, 1973, *10*, 747–750.

Zornetzer, S. F., Chronister, R. B., & Ross, B.　The hippocampus and retrograde amnesia:　Localization of some positive and negative memory disruptive sites.　*Behavioral Biology*, 1973, *8*, 507–518.

A NEURAL SYSTEM APPROACH TO THE STUDY OF MEMORY STORAGE AND RETRIEVAL

RAYMOND P. KESNER [*]

Department of Psychology
University of Utah
Salt Lake City, Utah 84112 USA

Current knowledge concerning the nature of memory indicates that mnemonic processing of information is based on a complex interlocking set of events. Therefore, one would not logically search for a single physiological correlate or a specific neuroanatomical locus of a memory or "engram." Instead with the use of appropriate behavioral paradigms and advanced neurobiological manipulations of the nervous system, one would attempt to delineate specific neuroanatomical and neurochemical systems that are directly or indirectly involved in the modulation of each of the multiple facets of memory. Theoreticians have envisioned memory as composed of a number of storage and retrieval systems (short term memory, STM, and long term memory, LTM) controlled by multiple processes such as decay, consolidation, higher-order organization, selective attention, arousal, rehearsal, scanning, and search.

The present paper reviews a set of electrical brain stimulation experiments aimed at demonstrating possible direct or indirect involvement of critical neuronal substrates with STM and recent vs. remote components of LTM. The findings lead to the development of a multicomponent model of memory, which in turn may provide for a theoretical framework capable of integrating some aspects of sleep with memory.

Independence of Short and Long Term Memory

Electrical stimulation of the brain represents one of a number of techniques that may be useful in examining the

227

neurobiological substrates associated with mnemonic processing of information in that a) the treatment can be applied before, during, and after a learning trial or prior to and during a retention trial and, b) the duration of action of the treatment can be quite discrete and easily reversible, especially with subseizure intensity levels of stimulation (Kesner & Wilburn, 1974).

Previous research in our laboratory and elsewhere has indicated that electrical stimulation of a number of neural structures (caudate, hippocampus, amygdala, frontal cortex, or midbrain reticular formation - MRF) applied after a learning trial results in a disruption or facilitation in long term retention of a variety of aversive and appetitive learning experiences (Bloch, 1970; McDonough & Kesner, 1971; McGaugh & Gold, 1974; Kesner & Conner, 1974; Kesner, Berman, Burton & Hankins, 1975; Wyers, Peeke, Williston, & Herz, 1968; Zornetzer & Chronister, 1973).

The standard explanation for the observed interference or facilitation of long term memory becomes one of modulation of storage or consolidation processes. However, in addition, it is also possible that changes in long term memory reflect an indirect modulation of a decay process of STM or an alteration of a rehearsal control process, which in human memory studies has been shown to delay decay of STM and affect transfer of information from STM to LTM.

In order to examine these possibilities, rats with bilateral electrodes implanted in either MRF, hippocampus, or amygdala were trained to bar press in a Skinner box for sugar water. After training, they received a 5 mA, 1 sec duration footshock (FS) contingent upon a bar press. Four seconds later they received 5 seconds of bilateral electrical stimulation applied to the MRF, hippocampus, or amygdala. Implanted and unoperated control animals received no brain stimulation. Half of the animals within each group were tested for retention of the FS experience 55 seconds after the termination of brain stimulation. The remaining half of the animals were tested 24 hours later.

On the basis of tests, the selected treatment stimulation intensities were below the intensity level required to produce a) an observable behavioral response, b) an electrographic or behavioral seizure, and c) a direct interference with an ongoing bar-pressing response.

The findings are shown in Figure 1. The control groups demonstrated a suppression of bar-pressing at both immediate (64 sec) and delayed (24 hrs) retention tests, indicating memory for the FS experience. The MRF-stimulated group failed to show suppression of barpressing at the short term retention

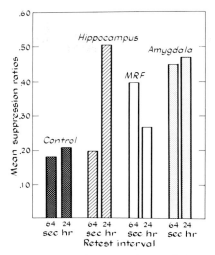

Fig. 1.   Mean suppression ratios of bar-pressing 64 seconds and 24 hours after the footshock.   Electrical stimulation
was given for 5 seconds to the hippocampus, midbrain reticular
formation, or amygdala 4 seconds after the footshock; controls
received no brain stimulation.   Suppression of bar-pressing
was used as the main indicator of retention for the FS experience.   This suppression was indexed by the ratio B/(A+B),
where A represented the total number of bar-presses during the
first 5 minutes of the session before treatment and B represented the total number of barpresses during the first 5 minutes of the session at the retest.   Thus, a ratio of .50
indicates no relative change in bar-press rate after the
treatment.   A ratio of .00 indicates complete cessation of
responding on a retest.   (From Kesner & Conner, 1974.)

test, but did show suppression of barpressing at the 24 hr
retention test. In contrast, the hippocampus-stimulated
animals showed suppression of barpressing at the 64 sec
retention test, but failed to show suppression of barpressing
at the 24 hr retention test. The amygdala-stimulated animals
failed to show suppression of barpressing at both retention
tests. A more detailed analysis of the stimulated groups
tested at the short term retest is shown in Figure 2. Both
the control and hippocampus groups maintained a high level of
suppression of barpressing throughout the 5 minutes of the
retest. In contrast, the amygdala group exhibited no
suppression of barpressing throughout the 5 minutes of the
retest. The MRF group showed the most interesting changes
across time, namely an initial suppression of barpressing

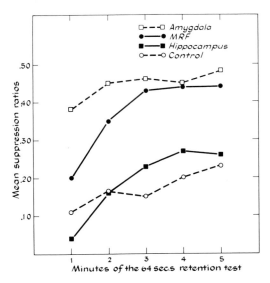

*Fig. 2. Mean suppression ratios for each minute of bar-
pressing at the 64 second retest for hippocampus, midbrain
reticular formation, amygdala, or no brain stimulation groups.
Mean suppression ratios were calculated according to the
formula described with Figure 1. In this case, A is represented by the total number of bar-presses per minute averaged
across the 10 minutes of bar-pressing before treatment, and
B is represented by the total number of bar-presses for each
of the minutes of the session at the retest. (From Kesner &
Conner, 1974.)*

at the first minute, followed by less suppression at the
second minute and no suppression at the third, fourth, and
fifth minute.

The findings that MRF stimulated animals displayed a
disruption of memory at the 64 sec, but normal memory at the
24 hr retention test, while hippocampal stimulated animals
displayed complete memory at the 64 sec but no memory at the
24 hr retention test, suggest the presence of a dual process
of memory, which might be structurally distinct with the MRF
involved in processing of aversive information in STM and the
hippocampus involved in processing of aversive information in
LTM. This interpretation is based on the assumption that for
the first 5 minutes after an FS an animal is operating primarily on an STM basis, but 24 hr after an FS an animal is operating on an LTM basis. In addition, the data suggest that STM
and LTM can operate independently. Further support for independence of STM and LTM is provided by several investigators.

Warrington and Shallice (1969) and Warrington (1971) reported that patients with lesions in the left parietal area show selective impairment of auditory verbal STM, while LTM on tasks of auditory verbal learning and recall are normal. The immediate memory span for digits and letters is accurate for only one item. On a free recall task the "recency" effect (STM component) of the serial position curve is markedly reduced, while the "primacy" effect (LTM component) is not impaired. In contrast, patients with hippocampal lesions have normal STM as illustrated by normal immediate memory span and normal decay functions for 3-digit numbers, but are deficient in the operation of the LTM system (Drachman & Arbit, 1966; Milner, 1966; Wickelgren, 1968). Furthermore, on a free recall task, the "recency" effect of the serial position curve is normal, while the "primacy" effect is markedly impaired (Baddeley & Warrington, 1970).

Kintsch and Buschke (1969) found in a probe paradigm that lists of homophones (sale-sail) disrupt STM, but have no effect upon LTM, while lists of synonyms (huge-great) produce the reverse effect, disrupting LTM without affecting STM. Finally, Kleinsmith and Kaplan (1963) and Uehling (1972) as well as others, have shown that a decreased arousal level facilitates the operation of STM while disrupting the operation of LTM, and conversely an enhanced arousal level disrupts STM while facilitating LTM.

This argument is further strengthened by Randt, Quartermain, Goldstein, & Anagnoste (1971), who demonstrated that DDC (diethyldithiocarbamate) injected prior to passive avoidance training resulted in facilitation of short term retention and complete disruption of long term retention of the aversive experience. DDC decreases biosynthesis of norepinephrine in brain and presumably decreases the level of arousal.

Short Term Memory

If it is assumed that STM is characterized by a decay process which functions as a gradual negative gradient with a progressive loss of information with time, then treatments which disrupt of facilitate STM should do so by altering either the initial level of information available in STM or by modulation of the decay process. Thus it is possible to interpret the disruptive effects of MRF stimulation upon STM as a stimulation-induced facilitation of the decay process. The data reported in the minute by minute analysis of the MRF-stimulated animals (see Figure 2) which indicated that there was an initial suppression followed by a lack of suppression provides indirect evidence that this return to bar-pressing may have been due to faster decay of the FS memory trace. One might also hypothesize that the attenuation of suppression was due to repeated barpresses which were no longer punished but in fact reinforced with sugar water. The above hypothesis, however, is not supported by (a) the observation of no reliable differences between the MRF-stimulated and control groups in the latency to onset of the first barpress, and (b) the observation that the marked increase in barpressing for the MRF-stimulated group was not paralleled at any time by the control group even though the level of barpressing for the control group during the second minute was nearly equal to that of the MRF-stimulated group during the first minute of barpressing.

In order to seek more direct evidence for the possibility that MRF stimulation disrupts STM by facilitating its decay, rats were trained in a Skinner box in a delayed alternation or a variant of a spatial matching to sample task. The box consisted of two bars and on any one trial on a random basis either the right or left bar was automatically extended into the box. After the animal had pressed the bar, it was retracted. Then at various delays both the right and left bars were extended in the box. In order to receive a sugar water reinforcement the rat had to press the opposite bar to the one that it pressed last, therefore, the rat had to remember the location of its last response. After three months of training, a day's session would consist of 50 trials (10 trials each at 0, 5, 15, 30, or 60 seconds delay randomly distributed throughout the session). After obtaining a stable STM decay function within a daily session, bilateral MRF stimulation was applied for 5 seconds immediately after the first bar press of each delay trial. No MRF stimulation was given during the zero delay trials in order to observe possible proactive effects of brain stimulation. Following each stimulation session, animals were not given brain stimulation for 1 or 2 sessions in order to ensure recovery to pre-stimulation baseline. MRF stimulation was applied for at least 5 sessions at each intensity level. Results of one animal based on 50 trials at each delay interval are shown in Figure 3. Compared to pre-stimulation baseline, MRF stimulation (40 uA, 100 Hz, .1 msec duration) produces a complete disruption of retention at all delay intervals. Hence, MRF stimulation clearly produces a facilitation in the decay of STM. It is of interest to note that 20 uA MRF stimulation had no disruptive effect, while 50 uA stimulation had aversive consequences in that the animal appeared fearful of

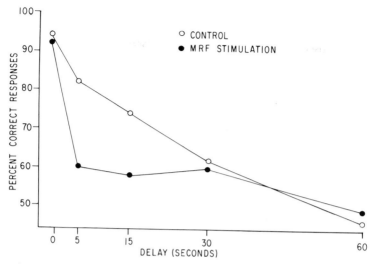

Fig. 3. *Percent correct performance as a function of the delay period and the administration of midbrain reticular formation (MRF) stimulation. (From Kesner, Bierley, & Smith, Note 1.)*

touching the bar and eventually ceased bar-pressing. The neurochemical, neuroanatomical and psychological mechanisms mediating this facilitation of STM decay are currently under investigation. For example, it is possible that MRF stimulation a) interfered with a selective attention control process with subsequent reduction in the amount of information available in STM, b) facilitated an arousal control process, which in turn may have accelerated the decay of STM, or c) was aversive and thus interfered with optimal performance. From a neurochemical and neuroanatomical perspective it is possible that MRF stimulation a) produced a local or direct disruptive effect by scrambling normal spatio-temporal firing patterns of MRF neurons, perhaps via release of an excess of neurotransmitter, b) produced indirect disruptive effects through inhibition or excitation of interconnected neuronal systems, or c) produced diffuse disruptive effects of a large number of neuroanatomical regions through modification of endogenous levels of critical neural transmitters. At present we have not been able to distinguish among these possibilities.

In summary, the data suggest that the integrity of MRF function is essential for normal and efficient processing of information in the STM system.

Long Term Memory

Given the assumption that LTM is characterized by a growth or consolidation process, the findings that post-trial subseizure hippocampal stimulation disrupts retention of an aversive experience at a 24 hrs but not 64 sec retest delay suggests that the stimulation did not alter the processes associated with STM or rehearsal but rather disrupted, blocked or altered a consolidation process leading to the formation of an incomplete memory in LTM. However, it is also possible that hippocampal stimulation destroyed the memory trace of the aversive experience, would itself have been stored as part of the memory trace, or did not disrupt the consolidation process but instead disrupted a retrieval process. With respect to neuroanatomical specificity the possible mechanisms of action that were discussed above with respect to MRF stimulation apply to hippocampal stimulation.

In order to test the possibility that the hippocampus is involved in consolidation of experiences acquired in a variety of learning situations, animals were tested in an appetitive learning task. Water deprived rats when placed in a test situation with access to an empty drinking tube will find the tube quickly, but will lick it only a few times (mean = 6 licks in a 3 min period, see Figure 4). If, on the other hand, rats are first allowed 150 licks of a drinking tube containing a sucrose solution followed at a 90 sec or a 24 hr delay with an empty drinking tube, they will lick the tube on the average 26 times within a 3 min period. Half of the animals with electrodes implanted in the hippocampus received 30 seconds of brain stimulation at 25-35 uA intensities commencing 4 seconds after completion of a 150 lick sucrose experience and retested for a 3 min period on the empty tube either 56 seconds or 24 hours after the termination of brain stimulation. The remaining half of the implanted animals underwent the same procedures but received no brain stimulation. The total number licks taken during the 3 min retest period was used as the main index of retention of the sucrose experience. Results indicated that relative to implanted and unoperated controls post-trial hippocampal stimulation produced a reliable reduction in total number of licks at the 24 hour (long-term retention) test but did not produce reliable changes at the 90 sec (short-term retention) test (see Figure 4).

Thus, the hippocampus appears to be involved with consolidation associated with both aversive and appetitive learning experiences. However, it should be stated that the hippocampus does not appear to be involved in consolidation

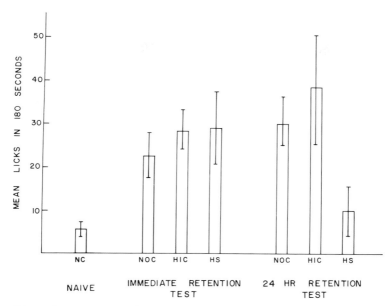

Fig. 4.   Mean number of licks (± one SE) taken in 180 sec by different groups at the 90 sec and 24 hr retention tests.   (NOC, non-operated control group; HIC, hippocampal implanted control groups; HS, hippocampal stimulated group.) Rats in group NC (naive control) were given the retention test without prior sucrose licking experience.   (From Berman & Kesner, 1976.)

processes associated with learned safety and learned aversion (Berman & Kesner, Note 2).   Hence, there are some limitations on the generality of hippocampal modulation of LTM.

REHEARSAL

In section two of this paper data was presented to indicate that post-trial amygdala stimulation is capable of completely disrupting both short and long term memory of an aversive experience (see Figure 1 and 2).   Disruption of long-term memory as a function of post-trial amygdala stimulation has also been shown in rodents and carnivores for both active and passive avoidance learning (Handwerker, Gold, & McGaugh, 1974; Gold, Macri, & McGaugh, 1973; Bresnahan & Routtenberg, 1972; McDonough & Kesner,   1971).   To account for these findings it is possible that amygdala stimulation a) disrupted

transfer operations between the STM and LTM system, especially
if one assumes that one form of the transfer process is like
rehearsal, which normally tends to delay decay of STM and
strengthens consolidation of LTM, b) disrupted the STM system
and thus indirectly the LTM, or c) disrupted both STM and LTM.
Although the author favors the first interpretation, it is
very difficult on the basis of these findings alone to differentiate between the above possibilities and assign a clear and
obvious role to the amygdala in mnemonic processing of information.   Nevertheless, additional research in our laboratory
was guided by the working hypothesis that the amygdala complex
may serve a rehearsal function triggered by the presence of a
specific class of reinforcers, such as negative reinforcers
(e.g., pain).   In the appetitive situation described above the
amygdala was stimulated for 30 sec at low subseizure intensities 4 seconds after the 150 lick sucrose experience.
Amygdala stimulation failed to disrupt either short or long
term retention of the appetitive experience (see Figure 5).
However, this negative result is not conclusive, since stimulation parameters were not varied.   It is possible that the
parameters of electrical stimulation used in the present study
produced insufficient disruption of amygdaloid function to
impair memory.   Alternatively, tests of retention may have
been insufficiently sensitive to demonstrate stimulation-
induced retention deficits.   However, the stimulation parameters which were used in the present study were similar to
those reported to produce amnesia for aversive experiences
in rats (Bresnahan & Routtenberg, 1972; Gold et al., 1973;
Kesner & Conner, 1974).   Also, the present paradigm was
sensitive enough to detect impairment following hippocampal
stimulation.   Hence, it may be that the amygdala is minimally
involved in the processing of appetitive experiences in rats.
Goddard (1964) reported that continuous amygdala stimulation
in rats impaired acquisition of an aversive shock experience
but had no effect on acquisition of an appetitive experience.
      In another experiment (Kesner et al., 1975a) rats were
either exposed to a novel flavor (learned safety paradigm) or
a novel flavor paired with an illness producing agent (apomorphine)(learned aversion paradigm).   Amygdala stimulation
applied after the novel flavor in the learned safety paradigm
had no disruptive effects upon retention of taste safety
(recovery from initial neophobia).   The same stimulation
applied after the novel flavor in the learned aversion paradigm had no disruptive effect upon retention of taste aversion, but stimulation applied after the illness produced a
time-dependent disruption of retention of taste aversion.

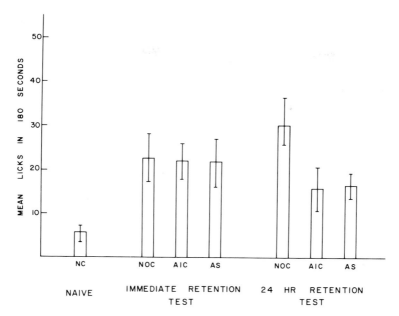

Fig. 5. Mean number of licks (± one SE) taken in 180 sec by different groups at the 90 sec and 24 hr retention tests. (AIC, amygdala implanted control; AS, amygdala stimulation group; NOC, non-operated control group; NC, naive control group tested for retention without prior sucrose licking experience.) NOC and NC scores are the same as those appearing in Figure 4. (From Berman & Kesner, 1976.)

In combination these data suggest that the amygdala is associated with negative affective reinforcement learning situations (pain in passive and active avoidance; nausea in learned aversion) but not positive reinforcement learning situations (150 lick sucrose experience and learned safety). These findings further give indirect support of amygdala function associated with rehearsal, providing one assumes that specific reinforcement contingencies trigger a rehearsal process.

Irrespective of the psychological interpretation of amygdala function, it is clear that electrical stimulation of the amygdala alters neural function in some fashion. Current work in our laboratory has focused upon possible changes in neuro-transmitter function as a function of amygdala stimulation (Todd & Kesner, 1974). Rats were given a FS experience while licking a tube in a lick box situation and tested for retention 24 hrs later. Immediately or at various delays

after the FS, cholinomimetics and cholinergic blocking agents
were injected bilaterally into the amygdala via implanted
cannulas. The injections consisted of carbachol (0.5 ug or
1.0 ug), physostigmine (5 ug or 10 ug), or atropine sulfate
(1 ug to 20 ug), dissolved in 1.0 ul isotonic saline. Unoperated controls and saline controls were also tested. Animals
that received immediate injections of 1 ug carbachol or 10 ug
physostigmine exhibited a disruption in retention (amnesia)
of the aversive experience as compared to control animals and
rats that received immediate injections of 0.5 ug carbachol
or 5 ug physostigmine into amygdala, 1 ug carbachol or 10 ug
physostigmine into ventricles, or delayed (12 hr) injection
of 10 ug physostigmine into the amygdala. Animals that
received 4 ug atropine sulfate in the amygdala demonstrated
facilitation in retention of the aversive experience; larger
doses 5-20 ug had no effect. Physostigmine injections into
structures located dorsal to the baso-cortico-medial amygdala
were ineffective. These results suggest that an increase in
release of acetylcholine within the amygdala may result in
modulation of normal neural function leading to a disruption
of long term retention. Presumably one of the mechanisms of
action of electrical stimulation of the amygdala is to produce
an increase in release of cholinergic transmitters.

Recent and Remote Components of Long Term Memory

Thus far, I have concentrated on processes associated
with storage of information, but it should also be of interest
to study processes associated with retrieval of stored or
available information. Retrieval can be studied more easily
when treatments (e.g., brain stimulation) are administered
after consolidation of information into LTM. Given that such
a treatment produces a temporary amnesic effect which cannot
be attributed to interference with some performance variable,
one can conclude that the treatment altered a retrieval
process. Furthermore, the temporary nature of such an
amnesic effect or retrieval failure would eliminate the possibility that the treatment interfered with the site of long
term memory.
In an initial attempt to study the retrieval process ECS
was used in order to test the possibility that brain stimulation treatments were capable of producing a temporary amnesic
effect. In our first experiment (Kesner & D'Andrea, 1971)
animals were trained to bar-press for sugar water on a continuous reinforcement schedule. After reaching a stable rate of
bar-pressing they received a FS contingent upon a bar-press.

After observing a marked conditioned suppression
24 hours later, an ECS was administered and the animals
retested for memory of the FS experience 3 and 24 hours after
the ECS treatment. We found a complete amnesia or retrieval
failure (complete reinstatement of bar-pressing) at the 3 hour
retest, but no amnesia (return to conditioned suppression or
bar-pressing) at the 24 hour retest. Control animals that did
not receive an ECS treatment maintained conditioned suppression at both the 3 and 24 hour retests. The retrieval failure
was temporary, occurred after consolidation of the aversive
information, and the bar-pressing behavior that occurred at
the 3 hour retest did not affect the reinstatement of conditioned suppression at the 24 hour retest. A further analysis
has shown that this temporary amnestic effect is induced by
the hypoxic consequences of ECS, since a) ECS administered in
a super-oxygenated environment does not produce a temporary
amnesia, and b) hypoxia induced by nitrogen inhalation mimics
the temporary amnesia observed with ECS (D'Andrea & Kesner,
1973).

Even though these data demonstrate that treatments (ECS
and hypoxia) administered after training can produce a temporary retrieval failure, it is possible that the observed
temporary amnesic effect reflects a performance rather than a
retrieval failure. Hence, a new experiment was designed to
test for possible performance effects by varying the age of
the memory prior to the administration of the disruptive
treatment. Given that little forgetting occurs across days
and that the treatment is dependent upon the age of memory
(e.g., produces an amnesic effect 1 day but not 7 days after
learning), one cannot only eliminate the performance problem
but one should also be able to investigate the mechanisms
mediating changes within the LTM system.

In addition, seizure stimulation of the hippocampus was
selected as the treatment since a) one of the possible consequences of hypoxia could be the production of seizure discharges in the hippocampus as well as neural damage to hippocampal pyramidal cells (Grenell, 1946; Spector, 1965),
b) Bickford, Mulder, Dodge, Svien, and Rome (1958), Brazier
(1962), and Chapman, Walter, Markham, Rand, and Crandall
(1967) demonstrated in patients that hippocampal seizures were
capable of producing a temporary global amnesic effect.
Furthermore, it appeared that the duration of the hippocampal
afterdischarge was directly related to the extension of the
retrograde amnesia or retrieval failure and time required for
recovery from this amnesia, c) the hippocampus had previously
been implicated as critical in storage of information in LTM
(Kesner, 1973). Animals were trained to barpress in a Skinner

box for sugar water. After reaching a stable level of bar
pressing the animals received a FS contingent upon bar
pressing. Each animal was given the opportunity to bar-press
for the remaining 5 min and most received a second or third
FS. Twenty-four hours later they were tested for retention of
the FS experience. After demonstrating complete suppression
of bar-pressing they received either an ECS treatment and
retested for retention of FS experience 3 hrs later or unilateral hippocampal stimulation resulting in a seizure afterdischarge with retests either 2, 15, 60, or 180 min after the
cessation of the primary after-discharge (PAD). Appropriate
operated and unoperated controls received no brain stimulation
and were tested at 2, 15, 60, and 180 min after the approximate time that experimental groups displayed the end of the
PAD. Other rats received either unilateral visual cortex
stimulation or unilateral anterior caudate stimulation
resulting in seizure after-discharges. The latter two groups
were retested 2 min after the cessation of the PAD. The
seizure after-discharges were always recorded from the contra-
lateral structure on a Beckman EEG machine. The remaining
animals were tested for retention of the FS experience 7 days
later followed by either an ECS treatment with a retest 3 hrs
later or a hippocampal seizure after-discharge with a retest
2 or 15 min later.

There were no differences among any of the groups with
respect to the mean level of suppression prior to treatment.
There were no differences among the hippocampal seizure stimulation groups with respect to mean stimulation intensity
required to produce a PAD or mean duration of PAD. The major
findings are shown in Figure 6. Hippocampal after-discharges
elicited 1 day after learning resulted in a temporary amnesic
effect (reinstatement of bar-pressing at the 2, 15, or 60 min
but not at the 180 min retest), but failed to produce an
amnesic effect when elicited 7 days after learning. Similarly
ECS produced an amnesic effect when applied 1 day but not
7 days after learning.

This age of memory dependent amnesic effect provides for
a clear elimination of the possibility that the hippocampal
seizures or ECS interfered directly with performance by way of
enhanced activity, complete disorientation or increased
hunger motivation. If the effect were due to some factor
other than a failure of memory retrieval, then hippocampal
seizures or ECS administered 7 days after training should have
resulted in an increase in barpressing. In other words with
an age of memory controlled paradigm one can potentially
separate performance from retrieval failures, given that no
marked forgetting occurs across time. One can, thus, conclude

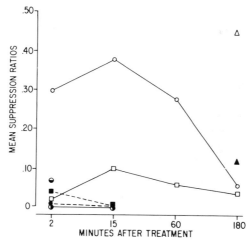

Fig. 6. *Mean suppression ratios of barpressing 2, 15, 60, or 180 min after the cessation of seizure afterdischarges induced in a number of different neural structures either 1 or 7 days after criterion learning of a passive avoidance response. Mean suppression ratios were calculated according to the formula described with Figure 1. In this case A is represented by total number of bar-presses during the 10 minutes of session prior to the footshock treatments and B is represented by the total number of bar-presses during the 10 minutes of the 2, 15, 60, or 180 min retest.*

that hippocampal seizures produce a temporary retrieval failure of a previously learned response. Additional work has demonstated that hippocampal seizures can also produce an age of memory dependent disruption in retention of an active avoidance and bar-pressing habit (Kesner et al., 1975b).

As hippocampal seizures result in a dysfunction of normal operation of hippocampal neural activity, then other treatments (KCl and protein inhibitors) that are capable of disrupting normal hippocampal functioning should also result in temporary retrieval failures of learned habits. KCl injected into the hippocampus 1 day after learning a conditional emotional response produces disruption of retention when tested 4 days but not 21 days later (Kapp & Schneider,

1971). Similar results have been obtained by Avis and
Carlton (1968). Thus KCl which produces hippocampal seizures
as well as prolonged depression of hippocampal EEG activity
produces a temporary retention deficit. Bitemporal injections
of puromycin (a protein inhibitor) which spreads throughout
the hippocampus and caudal third of cortex including entorhinal cortex will result in a disruption of retention of a
Y-maze or light-dark discrimination when administered 1 or 2
days after learning (Flexner, Flexner, & Roberts, 1967;
Rosenbaum, Cohen, & Barondes, 1968). Similarly, actinomycin-D
(a protein inhibitor) injected in the temporal region 1 day
after learning disrupted retention of a shock-escape position
discrimination (Squire & Barondes, 1970). However, acetocycloheximide (also a protein inhibitor) injected 1 day after
learning failed to produce a retention deficit in any of the
three studies mentioned above.

Since puromycin and actinomycin-D produce abnormal neural
activity in the hippocampus (Cohen, Ervin, & Barondes, 1966;
Nakajima, 1969), while acetocycloheximide does not produce
abnormal hippocampal EEG's (Cohen et al., 1966), it appears
that alteration of normal hippocampal neuronal activity is
responsible for the retrieval deficit rather than reduction
in protein synthesis.

Thus, it is clear that the hippocampus must play a
critical role in the production of temporary retrieval
failures, especially since seizures initiated in the visual
cortex or anterior caudate with probable involvement of
frontal cortex, KCl or protein inhibitors injected in neocortex (Flexner et al., 1967; Kapp & Schneider, 1971) fail to
produce temporary retrieval deficits. However, since hippocampal seizures are required to produce the retrieval deficit
(subseizure hippocampal stimulation being ineffective), it
appears that normal functioning of the hippocampus and interconnected subcortical neural structures is essential for
efficient retrieval of information.

The finding that hippocampal seizures were effective in
producing a retention deficit 1 day but not 7 days after
learning a specific response is supported by the observations
of Flexner et al. (1967) and Squire and Barondes (1970), who
reported that temporal injections of puromycin or actinomycin-D disrupted retention 1 day but not 7 days after the
learning of an appetitive or aversive task. Furthermore,
Uretsky and McCleary (1969) showed that isolation of the
hippocampus in cats 3 hrs after learning an active avoidance
task results in a retention deficit. Similar surgical
isolation 8 days after learning was ineffective.

It is possible to disrupt retention 7 days after learning but only with the use of treatments that involve in addition to the hippocampus most of the neocortex. For example, Flexner et al. (1967) showed that multiple injections of puromycin involving most of the neocortex injected 7 days after training did produce disruption of retention. Hughes (1969) reported that KCl injected into the hippocampus at doses that produced EEG alterations in the neocortex (Avis, 1969) 7 or 21 days after learning still resulted in retention deficits. Finally, Deutsch (1973) showed that 40 ul of DFP or physostigmine injected into the hippocampus with a possible spread of the drug to the neocortex because of the high dose and nature of the injection method also resulted in retention deficits. Thus, retrieval deficits observed a long time (weeks) after learning may be primarily a function of neocortical disruption or a function of hippocampus plus neocortical disruption.

The data suggest the possibility that retrieval from LTM is determined by two major components. The first component will be called "recent long term memory", which refers to memory for events during a period extending from the present to a few weeks back in time. The second component will be called "remote long term memory", which refers to memory of a more permanent kind back to childhood. As early as 1887 the basic idea of separating LTM into recent and remote retrieval components was presented by Ribot (1887). He formulated a law of regression which stated that when brain disease produces amnesic disturbances, they will extend from recent to quite remote memories, implying that disruption of brain function will affect recent memories more readily than remote memories. The terms recent and remote are envisioned to represent a continuum in depth and organization of information processing within LTM. In contrast other theoreticians have used the labels secondary and tertiary (Ervin & Anders, 1970); intermediate and long term memory (McGaugh, 1968); and long term working memory and long term store (Shiffrin & Geisler, 1973), which seem to imply discrete and separate stages of mnemonic processing of information.

The fact that hippocampal dysfunction can induce retrieval failures 1 day but not 7 days after criterion training suggests that the hippocampus plays a critical role in retrieval of information from recent long term memory, but plays a more limited role in information retrieval from remote long term memory. The development of remote LTM is assumed to develop with time when an important or critical item of information is subjected to repeated rehearsal processes in a variety of cognitive (internal and external) environments. The rehearsal process leads to either the

formation of multiple representations of or to the elaboration
of multiple interconnections with the specific item. Both
organizational principles imply distributed storage of information, suggesting the possibility that the neural representation of the specific item becomes anatomically or functionally
more diffuse as mediated by the development of multiple access
routes to the specific item or by multiple distribution of
similar but identical copies of the item. Thus, in addition
to the hippocampus, retrieval of information from remote long
term memory is assumed to be mediated by a number of independent neural systems (e.g., neocortex), which have gained
access to the memory representation of that item. This hypothesis can easily account for the failure of hippocampal
disruptive treatments to produce a retrieval deficit 7 days
after criterion learning. It can account for the findings
that with multiple neocortical injections of a protein inhibitor a memory loss is obtained even 7 days after learning
(Flexner et al., 1967) and that with sufficiently large neocortical lesions one can eventually disrupt retention of maze
learning (Lashley, 1963). Furthermore the hypothesis is
consistent with memory functions of patients with hippocampal
lesions, who are unable to consolidate or retrieve new information from recent LTM. However, except for a certain amount
of retrograde amnesia for preoperative events these patients
are capable of retrieving information from remote long term
memory stored prior to the operation (Milner, 1966). Finally,
the hypothesis is consistent with Lashley's (1963) notion of
mass action and John's (1967) holistic theory of memory.

A Model of Information Storage and Retrieval

The data presented in the previous sections suggest a
multicomponent model of memory. A schematic representation
is shown in Figure 7. I will summarize briefly some of the
major aspects of the model (a more detailed discussion of
parts of the model is presented in Kesner, 1973). I am
proposing that mnemonic information is processed in STM and
two components of LTM, namely recent and remote. The distinc-
tions between the systems were derived from both differential
neurobiological involvement and incorporation of selected
psychological characteristics associated with specific behavioral paradigms. For example, the data suggest that the MRF
constitutes one of the most important neural substrates
mediating functions of STM; the hippocampus is similarly critical for mediating functions of recent LTM and the neocortex
with the hippocampus may be maximally involved with the

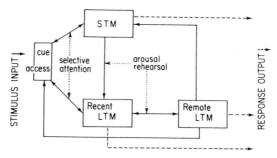

Fig. 7. A schematic representation of the proposed structural model of memory.

development of remote LTM. The data also suggest that duration of STM ranges from seconds to minutes; for recent LTM, seconds to days and for remote LTM, from minutes to a lifetime. Finally, the fundamental operating process for STM is assumed to be decay of the memory trace, but for recent LTM it is assumed to be growth or consolidation of the memory trace leading to an *increase in its strength and retrievability* and for remote LTM it is assumed to be higher-order organization via construction of multiple representations or multiple access routes to the memory trace leading to an *increase in resistance to forgetting*. I will not dwell on other possible differentiating characteristics like nature of the system, process of retrieval and nature of forgetting.

In terms of information transfer, it is assumed that once information has been encoded and attended to (processed through cue-access system), it will be transferred independently to STM and recent LTM. In addition, information in STM can be transferred to recent or remote LTM probably via rehearsal and coding types of control processes.

Information stored within the recent component of LTM can be transformed to remote LTM by a number of control processes (e.g., rehearsal, higher-order organization and perhaps dreaming). Finally, information can probably be retrieved independently from STM, recent, and remote LTM via a number of control processes (e.g., scanning, search, direct access) with subsequent activation of response. trigger and execution systems leading to a motor response.

The model outlined above represents only one of many possible directions one can take in formalizing the structure of memory. Within the framework of types of experiments conducted in the area of neurobiology and behavior, the utility of the model lies in its ability to a) integrate existing data, b) uncover the complexity of mnemonic

processing of information, c) permit correlations between
neural function and multiple facets of the memory structure,
d) suggest new behavioral paradigms in order to examine neurobiological function, and e) incorporate more readily different
phenomena that may indirectly affect memory processes (e.g.,
sleep and dreaming).

Dreaming and Memory

A number of researchers have suggested that dreaming
enhances memory by either reprogramming the brain (Dewan,
1970) through a direct involvement with memory consolidation
(Hennevin & LeConte, 1971), via an integration of recently
perceived input into existing internal structures (Breger,
1967), or by a recording of recent memories into long term
storage tapes (Greenberg & Leiderman, 1966). I would like to
combine these ideas and propose that dreaming may serve as a
process associated with the transformation of information from
recent to remote LTM. It seems reasonable to assume that
dreams can only be retrieved from LTM (both recent and remote)
implying that information associated with dreaming can only be
derived from events that indeed have been consolidated at
least into recent LTM. Thus, it is not surprising that significant events (especially emotional in nature) experienced
during the day become incorporated within the dreams of that
night (Greenberg, 1970). The argument is further strengthened
by the findings that rats and mice show marked increases in
paradoxical sleep (PS) following the acquisition of a variety
of complex tasks (Fishbein, Kastaniotis, & Chattman, 1974;
Lucero, 1970; Smith, Kitahama, Valatx, & Jouvet, 1974). This
increase in dreaming and specific incorporation of significant
events of the day may lead to the formation of multiple representations or build-up of multiple access routes leading to
greater resistance to forgetting. Hence, one would predict
that after learning dreaming should improve retention or
reduce forgetting, while dream deprivation should interfere
with retention or facilitate forgetting and patients with
presumed hippocampal damage, who are not capable of storing
or retrieving information from recent LTM, should have altered
dream patterns without incorporation of new significant experiences. In support of these predictions Jenkins and
Dallenbach (1924), van Ormer (1932), and McGaugh and Hostetter
(Note 3) have demonstrated that sleep (perhaps dreaming)
immediately after learning improved retention or reduced
forgetting. However, it is important to note that the
improvement in recall may in addition have been due to a

reduction in retroactive interference. Fishbein (1971) and Stern (1970) showed that deprivation of PS (dreaming experiences) results in deprivation effects upon recall of information acquired prior to the detrimental experience. Unfortunately the apparent retention impairments could easily reflect performance decrements induced by stress or intrusion of sleep processes. Torda (1969) and Greenberg, Pearlman, Brooks, Mayer, and Hartmann (1968) characterize the dreams of patients with either postencephalitic amnesia for recent events or Korsakoff's psychosis as short, simple with many commonplace features, stereotyped and with little affect. Presumably these patients have damage to the hippocampus and other limbic structures. Since the hippocampus has been shown to play a special role in retrieval of information from recent LTM (Kesner et al., 1975b), it is important to present additional evidence, even though indirect in support of possible hippocampal involvement with the dreaming process. First, there is the appearance of the theta rhythm recorded from the hippocampus during PS. Second, stimulation of the hippocampus facilitates the manifestation of PS (Faure, Bensch, & Vincent, 1962). Third, septal lesions which suppress the theta rhythm, also produce a reduction in both the average number and mean total duration of PS episodes (Lena & Parmeggiani, 1964). Fourth, hippocampal lesions in cats or rats reduce the occurrence and mean duration of PS episodes (Kim, Choi, Kim, Chang, Park, & Kang, 1970; Kim, Choi, Kim, Kim, Huh, & Moon, 1971). Finally, the "diencephalic" cat with neocortical, limbic (hippocampal) and striatal damage exhibits a disruption in both PS and slow wave sleep (Villablanca & Marcus, 1972). These observations suggest that the hippocampus, probably through access to information stored in recent LTM, plays a significant role in determining the nature, structure and content of dreams, which in turn may be significant for the promotion of organizational changes within remote LTM.

In summary, there appears to be behavioral and physiological evidence in support of the idea that dreaming affects memory via processes associated with continued elaboration of stored information within the existing memory structure.

ACKNOWLEDGMENT

The research reported in this chapter was supported by University of Utah Research Grant and U.S. Public Health Service Grant MH 25706-01.

REFERENCE NOTES

1. Kesner, R. P., Bierley, A. R., & Smith, C. B. Midbrain reticular formation stimulation and facilitation of decay of short term memory. In preparation, 1976.

2. Berman, R. F., & Kesner, R. P. Effects of electrical stimulation of midbrain reticular formation, hippocampus and lateral hypothalamus upon neophobia and taste aversion. In preparation, 1976.

3. McGaugh, J. L., & Hostetter, R. C. Retention as a function of the temporal position of sleep and activity following waking. Unpublished manuscript, 1961.

REFERENCES

Avis, H. H., & Carlton, P. L. Retrograde amnesia produced by hippocampal spreading depression. *Science,* 1968, *161,* 73-75.

Avis, H. H. The effects of temporary disruption of the electrical activity of the brain on retention. Doctoral dissertation, Rutgers University, 1969.

Baddeley, A. D., & Warrington, E. K. Amnesia and the distinction between long- and short-term memory. *Journal of Verbal Learning and Verbal Behavior,* 1970, *9,* 176-189.

Berman, R. F., & Kesner, R. P. Posttrial hippocampal, amygdaloid and lateral hypothalamic electrical stimulation: Effects on short- and long-term memory of an appetitive experience. *Journal of Comparative and Physiological Psychology,* 1976, *90,* 260-267.

Bickford, R. G., Mulder, D. W., Dodge, H. W., Svien, H. J., & Rome, H. P. Changes in memory function produced by electrical stimulation of the temporal lobe in man. *Research Publications Association for Research in Nervous and Mental Disease,* 1958, *36,* 227-243.

Bloch, V. Facts and hypothesis concerning memory consolidation. *Brain Research,* 1970, *24,* 561-575.

Brazier, M. A. B. Stimulation of the hippocampus in man using
    implanted electrodes. In M. A. B. Brazier (Ed.), *Brain
    Function* (Vol. 2). Berkelely: University of California
    Press, 1962.

Breger, L. Functions of dreams. *Journal of Abnormal
    Psychology* (Monograph No. 641).

Bresnahan, E., & Routtenberg, A. Memory disruption by
    unilateral low level, subseizure stimulation of the
    medial amygdaloid nucleus. *Physiology and Behavior,*
    1972, *9,* 513-525.

Chapman, L. F., Walter, R. D., Markham, C. H., Rand, R. W.,
    & Crandall, P. H. Memory changes induced by stimulation
    of hippocampus or amygdala in epilepsy patients with
    implanted electrodes. *Transactions of the American
    Neurological Association,* 1967, *92,* 50-56.

Cohen, H. D., Ervin, F., & Barondes, S. H. Puromycin and
    cycloheximide: Different effects on hippocampal
    electrical activity. *Science,* 1966, *154,* 1557-1558.

D'Andrea, J. A., & Kesner, R. P. The effects of ECS and
    hypoxia on information retrieval. *Physiology and
    Behavior,* 1973, *11,* 747-752.

Deutsch, J. A. The cholinergic synapse and the site of
    memory. In J. A. Deutsch (Ed.), *The Physiological Basis
    of Memory*. New York: Academic Press, 1973.

Dewan, E. M. The programming "P" hypothesis for REM sleep. In
    E. Hartmann (Ed.), *Sleep and Dreaming* (International Psychia-
    try Clinics Series, Vol. 7). Boston: Little, Brown, 1970.

Drachman, D. A., & Arbit, J. Memory and the hippocampal
    complex. II. Is memory a multiple process. *Archives
    of Neurology,* 1966, *15,* 52-61.

Ervin, F. R., & Anders, T. R. Normal and pathological
    memory: Data and a conceptual scheme. In F. O. Schmitt
    (Ed.), *The Neurosciences: Second Study Program*.
    New York: Rockefeller University Press, 1970.

Faure, J., Bensch, C., & Vincent, D. Role d'un systeme mesen-
    cephalolimbique dant la "phase paradoxale" du sommeil chez
    le lapin. *Comptes Rendus des Seances de la Societe de
    Biologie* (Paris), 1962, *156,* 70-74.

Fishbein, W.   Disruptive effects of rapid eye movement sleep
    deprivation on long-term memory. *Physiology and
    Behavior,* 1971, *6,* 279-282.

Fishbein, W., Kastaniotis, C., & Chattman, D.   Paradoxical
    sleep: Prolonged augmentation following learning.
    Brain Research, 1974, *79,* 61-75.

Flexner, L. B., Flexner, J. B., & Roberts, R. B.   Memory in
    mice analyzed with antibiotics. *Science,* 1967, *155,*
    1377-1383.

Goddard, G. V.   Amygdaloid stimulation and learning in the
    rat. *Journal of Comparative and Physiological Psychology,*
    1964, *58,* 23-30.

Gold, P. E., Macri, J., & McGaugh, J. L.   Retrograde amnesia
    produced by subseizure amygdala stimulation. *Behavioral
    Biology,* 1973, *9,* 671-680.

Greenberg, R.   Dreaming and memory. In E. Hartmann (Ed.),
    Sleep and Dreaming (International Psychiatry Clinics
    Series, Vol. 7). Boston: Little, Brown, 1970.

Greenberg, R., & Liederman, P. H.   Perceptions, the dream
    process and memory. *Comparative Psychiatry,* 1966, *7,* 507.

Greenberg, R., Pearlman, C., Brooks, R., Mayer, R., &
    Hartmann, E.   Dreaming and Korsakoff's psychosis.
    Archives of General Psychiatry, 1968, *18,* 203-209.

Grenell, R. G.   Central nervous system resistance. I.   The
    effects of temporary arrest of cerebral circulation for
    periods of 2 to 10 minutes. *Journal of Neuropathology
    and Experimental Neurology,* 1946, *5,* 131-154.

Handwerker, M., Gold, P. E., & McGaugh, J. L.   Effects of
    posttrial electrical stimulation of the amygdala on
    retention of an active avoidance response. *Brain
    Research,* 1974, *75,* 324-327.

Hennevin, E., & LeConte, P.   La function du sommeil paradox-
    ical: Faits et hypotheses. *L'Annee Psychologique,*
    1971, *2.*

Hughes, R. A.   Retrograde amnesia in rats produced by hippo-
    campal injections of postassium chloride: Gradient of
    effect and recovery. *Journal of Comparative and
    Physiological Psychology,* 1969, *68,* 637-644.

Jenkins, J. B., & Dallenbach, K. M.   Oblivescence during
    sleep and waking. *American Journal of Psychology,*
    1924, *35,* 605-612.

John, E. R. *Mechanisms of Memory.* New York: Academic
    Press, 1967.

Kapp, B. S., & Schneider, A. M.   Selective recovery from
    retrograde amnesia produced by hippocampal spreading
    depression. *Science,* 1971, *173,* 1149-1151.

Kesner, R. P., & D'Andrea, J.   Electroconvulsive shock
    disrupts both information storage and retrieval.
    Physiology and Behavior, 1971, *7,* 73-76.

Kesner, R.   A neural system analysis of memory storage and
    retrieval. *Psychological Bulletin,* 1973, *80,* 177-203.

Kesner, R. P., & Wilburn, M. W.   A review of electrical
    stimulation of the brain in context of learning and
    retention. *Behavioral Biology,* 1974, *10,* 259-293.

Kesner, R. P., & Conner, H. S.   Effects of electrical stimu-
    lation of limbic system and midbrain reticular formation
    upon short and long term memory. *Physiology and
    Behavior,* 1974, *12,* 5-12.

Kesner, R. P., Berman, R. G., Burton, B., & Hankins, W. G.
    Effects of electrical stimulation of amygdala upon
    neophobia and taste aversion. *Behavioral Biology,*
    1975a, *13,* 349-358.

Kesner, R. P., Dixon, D. A., Pickett, D., & Berman, R. F.
    Experimental animal model of transient global amnesia:
    Role of the hippocampus. *Neuropsychologia,* 1975b, *13,*
    465-480.

Kintsch, W., & Buschke, H.   Homophones and synonyms in
    short-term memory. *Journal of Experimental Psychology,*
    1969, *80,* 403-407.

Kim, C., Choi, M., Kim, J. K., Chang, H. K., Park, R. S., & Kang, I. Y. General behavioral activity and its component patterns in hippocampectomized rats. *Brain Research*, 1970, *19*, 379-394.

Kim, D., Choi, M., Kim, J. K., Kim, M. S., Huh, M. K., & Moon, Y. B. Sleep pattern of hippocampectomized cat. *Brain Research*, 1971, *29*, 223-236.

Kleinsmith, L. J., & Kaplan, S. Paired-associate learning as a function of arousal and interpolated interval. *Journal of Experimental Psychology*, 1963, *65*, 190-193.

Lashley, K. S. *Brain Mechanisms and Intelligence*. New York: Dover, 1963.

Lena, C., & Parmeggian, P. L. Hippocampal theta rhythm and activated sleep. *Helvetica Physiologica Acta*, 1964, *22*, 120-135.

Lucero, M. Lengthening of REM sleep duration consecutive to learning in the rat. *Brain Research*, 1970, *20*, 319-322.

McDonough, J. H., Jr., & Kesner, R. P. Amnesia produced by brief electrical stimulation of the amygdala or dorsal hippocampus in cats. *Journal of Comparative and Physiological Psychology*, 1971, *77*, 171-178.

McGaugh, J. L. A multi-trace view of memory storage. In D. Bonet, F. Bovet-Nitti, & A. Oliverio (Eds.), *Recent Advances on Learning and Retention* (Quaderno N. 109, Anno CCCLXV). Rome: Roma Academia Nazionale Dei Lincei, 1968.

McGaugh, J. L., & Gold, P. E. Conceptual and neurobiological issues in studies of treatments affecting memory storage. In G. H. Bower (Ed.), *The Psychology of Learning and Motivation* (Vol. 8). New York: Academic Press, 1974.

Milner, B. Amnesia following operation on the temporal lobes. In C. W. M. Whitty & O. L. Zangwill (Eds.), *Amnesia*. London: Butterworths, 1966.

Nakajima, S. Interference with relearning in the rat after hippocampal injection of actinomycin D. *Journal of Comparative and Physiological Psychology*, 1969, *67*, 457-461.

Randt, C. T., Quartermain, D., Goldstein, M., & Anagnoste, B.
Norepinephrine biosynthesis inhibition: Effects on
memory in mice. *Science,* 1971, *172,* 498-499.

Ribot, Th. *Disease of Memory.* New York: Appleton & Co., 1887.

Rosenbaum, M., Cohen, H. D., & Barondes, S. H. Effect of
intracerebral saline on amnesia produced by inhibitors
of cerebral protein synthesis. *Communications in
Behavioral Biology* (Part A), 1968, *2,* 47-50.

Shiffrin, R. M., & Geisler, W. S. Visual recognition in a
theory of information processing. In R. L. Solso (Ed.),
Contemporary Issues in Cognitive Psychology. New York:
Halstead Press, 1973.

Smith, C., Kitahama, K., Valatx, J., & Jouvet, M. Increased
paradoxical sleep in mice during acquisition of a shock
avoidance task. *Brain Research,* 1974, *77,* 221-230.

Stern, W. C. The relationship between REM sleep and learning:
Animal studies. In E. Hartmann (Ed.), *Sleep and
Dreaming* (International Psychiatry Clinics Series,
Vol. 7). Boston: Little, Brown, 1970.

Spector, R. G. Enzyme chemistry of anoxic brain injury. In
C. W. M. Adams (Ed.), *Neurohistochemistry.* Amsterdam:
Elsevier, 1965.

Squire, L. R., & Barondes, S. H. Actinomycin-D: Effects on
memory at different times after training. *Nature,* 1970,
225, 649-650.

Todd, J. W., & Kesner, R. P. Effects of localized cholinomimetics in the amygdala on retention of one trial
passive avoidance. *Society for Neurosciences Abstract,*
1974, 451.

Torda, C. Dreams of subjects with bilateral hippocampal
lesions. *Acta Psychiatrica Scandinavia,* 1969, *45,* 277-288.

Uehling, B. S. Arousal in verbal learning. In C. P. Duncan,
L. Sechrest, & A. W. Melton (Eds.), *Human Memory:
Festschrift for Benton J. Underwood.* New York:
Appleton-Century-Crofts, 1972.

Uretsky, E., & McCleary, R. A.   Effect of hippocampal
    isolation on retention. *Journal of Comparative and
    Physiological Psychology,* 1969, *68,* 1-8.

Van Ormer, E. B.   Retention after intervals of sleep and
    waking. *Archives of Psychology* (No. 137), 1932.

Villablanca, J., & Marcus, R.   Sleep-wakefulness, EEG and
    behavioral studies of chronic cats without neocortex and
    striatum: The "diencephalic" cat.   *Archives Italiennes
    de Biologie,* 1972, *110,* 348-382.

Warrington, E. K.   Neurological disorders of memory. *British
    Medical Bulletin,* 1971, *27,* 243-247.

Warrington, E. K., & Shallice, T.   The selective impairment of
    auditory verbal short-term memory. *Brain,* 1969, *92,*
    885-896.

Wickelgren, W. A.   Sparing of short-term memory in an amnesic
    patient: Implications for strength theory of memory.
    Neuropsychology, 1968, *6,* 235-244.

Wyers, E. J., Peeke, H. V. S., Williston, J. S., & Herz, M. J.
    Retroactive impairment of passive avoidance learning by
    stimulation of the caudate nucleus.   *Experimental
    Neurology,* 1968, *22,* 350-366.

Zornetzer, S. F., & Chronister, R. B.   Neuroanatomical
    localization of memory disruption: Relationship between
    brain structure and learning task. *Physiology and
    Behavior,* 1973, *10,* 747-750.

INTERACTION BETWEEN POST-TRIAL RETICULAR STIMULATION AND SUBSEQUENT PARADOXICAL SLEEP IN MEMORY CONSOLIDATION PROCESSES

VINCENT BLOCH, ELIZABETH HENNEVIN and PIERRE LECONTE

Université de Paris - Sud

and

Département de Psychophysiologie
Laboratoire de Physiologie Nerveuse
Centre National de la Recherche Scientifique
91190 Gif-sur-Yvette, France

A whole body of data suggests that storage of a new information depends upon some brain activation occurring at critical periods after the registration of this information (Bloch, 1970, 1973). The first critical period is known as phase of consolidation. The post-trial administration of drugs which have excitatory properties such as strychnine, picrotoxin and amphetamine has been found to enhance memory consolidation (McGaugh & Herz, 1970). Furthermore, it has been demonstrated that mild electrical stimulation of the reticular activating system increases retention when it is delivered during the first 90 sec of the consolidation period (Bloch, Denti & Schmaltz, 1966; Bloch, DeWeer & Hennevin, 1970; Denti, McGaugh, Landfield & Shinkman, 1970).

But, many data suggest that processing is not completed at the end of the consolidation phase and that the first episodes of paradoxical sleep (PS) following acquisition trials could be involved in memory processes. First, paradoxical sleep deprivation, immediately after learning, impairs the maintenance of memory (Leconte & Bloch, 1970; Pearlman & Becker, 1974a; Pearlman & Greenberg, 1973). This effect is most evident for complex tasks (Greenberg & Pearlman, 1974; Pearlman & Becker, 1973, 1974b).

Secondly, acquisition sessions are followed by an increase of time spent in PS; the evidence for this observation has come from experiments using both positive and negative reinforcement in rats (Hennevin, Leconte & Bloch, 1971, 1974; Leconte & Hennevin, 1971; Leconte, Hennevin & Bloch, 1973; Lucero, 1970), negative reinforcement in mice (Fishbein, Kastaniotis & Chattman, 1974; Smith, Kitaham, Valatx & Jouvet, 1972, 1974), positive reinforcement in cats (Lecas, 1975), and human infants (Paul & Dittrichova, 1975).

Thus, the phase of memory consolidation occurring immediately after learning and the phenomenon of PS augmentation in the subsequent period of sleep are both very susceptible to experimental perturbation, the suppression of one or the other either prevents or disturbs the fixation of information. Both are dependent upon brain arousal since the first phase can be facilitated by reticular stimulation and the second phase occurs in PS which is a state mainly characterized by reticular and cortical activation (Benoit, 1964; Evarts, 1962, 1967; Hobson & McCarley, 1971; Huttenlocher, 1961; Noda & Adey, 1970).

The following experiments have been performed to investigate the possible relationship between the mechanisms involved in these two phases of memory processing. The problem was to see whether the facilitation of the first phase would produce a modification of the second or, in the case of the experimental suppression of the latter, a compensatory effect on the memory fixation. So, first the amplitude of PS augmentation phenomenon was measured after post-trial reticular stimulation. Then the effect of 3 hour sleep deprivation on subsequent retention was studied after a post-trial reticular stimulation.

For the first two experiments, 66 male Wistar rats were used. They weighed approximately 200 g each and were maintained in individual cages. Cortical and reticular electrodes were implanted in all animals under pentobarbital anesthesia. The cortical fronto-parietal derivation at the level of the interhemispheric suture enabled us to record the hippocampal activity (Timo-Iaria, Negrao, Schmidek, Hoshino, Lobato de Menezes & Leme Da Rocha, 1970). The onset and cessation of high amplitude theta activity was used as the criterion measure of the phases of PS. In preliminary studies, we observed that this criterion was highly correlated with other measures such as cortical activity, electromyogram, and behavior. A bipolar coaxial electrode was implanted in the mesencephalic reticular formation at the following stereotaxic coordinates: anterior 1.4 mm, lateral 1.5 mm and vertical + 3 mm (Albe-Fessard, Stutinsky & Libouban, 1966).

All the electrodes were connected to the pins of a miniature socket, which was fixed to the skull with acrylic resin.

During the three weeks between the implantation and the onset of training, in both experiments several familiarization procedures were employed. They included: (1) daily handling of animals to familiarize them with the experimenters; (2) familiarization with partial food deprivation (half of usual daily ration) which did not produce any weight loss; (3) familiarization with a daily short ration of sweetened condensed milk in the goal box of the maze; (4) for each animal, determination of behavioral arousal threshold for a 2 sec, 300 Hz constant current stimulation of the reticular activating formation; (5) for experiment 1, familiarization with recording cables: connection and disconnection of cables at the hour when the recordings following each daily learning trial would be made; and (6) for experiment 2, progressive familiarization with a 3 hour total sleep deprivation. Animals were placed on pedestals surrounded by water. A 6 cm pedestal diameter did not allow any sleep. The choice of this method was based upon the results of a previous experiment (Leconte & Hennevin, 1973) in which we showed that this deprivation severely disturbs an avoidance conditioning.

Animals were also given one maze-learning trial each day. All the animals were connected to the stimulation circuitry during this trial. The maze was formed from a series of T units (Figure 1) with interchangeable doors. Sweetened condensed milk was placed in the goal box as the reward. The day before the first learning trial, a pre-learning trial was carried out: each animal was placed in the maze with all the blind alleys removed. The animals thus learned the direction of reward and its presence in the goal box. For the learning problem we chose a simple task: right-left-right-left alternation (Figure 1). Starting time, running time and the sequence of blocks crossed by the animals (this last parameter divided by the running time gives an indication of speed) were recorded for each learning trial. Upon arrival at the goal box, the door was closed and the animal could drink the sweetened condensed milk, which took about 20 seconds.

Following each learning trial, experimental animals received reticular stimulation for 90 sec in the goal box; this stimulation was divided in 10 cycles, each cycle separated by a 3 sec rest period. The intensity was fixed at a 10% level below the behavioral arousal threshold (mean value: 5 uA). Control animals did not receive this stimulation but were left in the goal box for 90 sec after drinking the sweetened condensed milk.

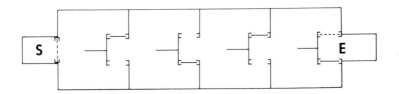

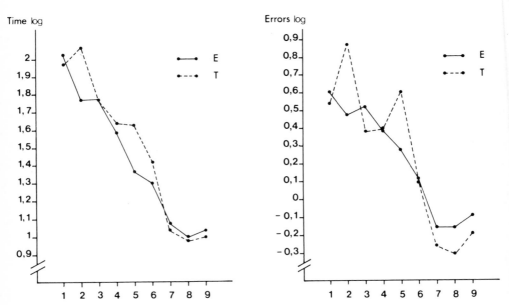

Fig. 1. Upper: plan of maze for the learning 1;
S: starting box; E: goal box. Lower: learning curves for
the two groups (E: stimulated; T: not stimulating). Left:
running time (log); right: number of errors (log); abscissa:
each daily trial of learning 1.

Nineteen rats were studied in the first experiment. They were divided into groups according to their pre-learning performance: an experimental group (group E, N = 10) received reticular stimulation after each daily trial, a control group (group T, N = 9) did not receive this stimulation.

The reference sleep duration was measured for 4 days (days 1 - 4) before the pre-learning trial. In order to control for the effect of reticular stimulation alone on subsequent sleep, reference recordings were taken with and without previous reticular stimulation.

The animals were first placed in the goal box of the maze where they drank the sweetened condensed milk. Then, on days 2 and 4, they received reticular stimulation for 90 sec and were then returned to their home cages for monitoring sleep. On days 1 and 3, the animals were placed in the home cages without previous reticular stimulation and recording was begun. The recording period of 2 hours was always at the same time of day for each rat. Thus, for both situations (with previous stimulation and without previous stimulation) we obtained the reference durations of slow wave sleep (SWSo) and paradoxical sleep (PSo). Following these reference recordings, the pre-learning trial was performed and the next day, the first learning trial took place (R.L.R.L.). Following the ninth day of learning 1, learning 2 began: the maze plan was reversed (L.R.L.R.). At that time neither group received the reticular stimulation. Following each daily trial, a 2 hour recording was taken for each animal. The slow wave sleep (SWS) and paradoxical sleep (PS) were then compared with the reference durations.

In order to determine if reticular stimulation had an effect on subsequent sleep, we compared, for all 19 animals, the duration of SWS and PS obtained during the "without previous stimulation" and the "with previous stimulation" recording periods.

We did not observe any reticular stimulation effect on the subsequent SWS and PS durations: these being respectively of 3792 sec (SWS) and 406 sec (PS) without previous stimulation, and of 3833 sec (SWS) and 429 sec (PS) after reticular stimulation.

Figure 1 shows the running time durations and the error numbers for the 2 groups and for all the trials of learning 1. For both parameters, group E performed significantly better (P < .05) than group T on the 2nd and 5th days of learning.

Tables I, II, and III show that the learning situation was not followed by significant modifications of SWS and total sleep durations. By contrast, alterations of the PS duration and PS ratio can be seen. Figure 2 shows the daily variations of PS ratio for the two groups in the first learning situation. Group T showed an increase in PS ratio on the 5th (P < .02) and 6th (P < .001) days of conditioning while group E showed only one increase of PS ratio on the 6th day (P < .05); the amplitude of that increase was significantly smaller than the increase observed the same day in group T (P < .05). In the second situation (following modification of the maze) where group E received no reticular stimulation, we observed a significant increase for the two groups (P < .02) of PS ratio following the 2nd trial of this new learning: this increase had the same amplitude for the two groups (Figure 3).

All the PS ratio increases were the results of PS duration increases, without SWS modification. As we have shown for other learning situations (Leconte et al., 1973), these increases of PS duration result from an augmentation of the number of PS phases without modification of the average duration of these phases.

In the second experiment, 47 rats were used. They were divided into three groups according to their pre-learning performance.

Group E (N = 15) received reticular stimulation after each daily trial of maze learning, then was deprived of total sleep for 3 hours (it has been shown that a 3 hour post-learning sleep deprivation prevents good performance at retention testing (Leconte & Hennevin, 1973; Pearlman & Becker, 1974a,b; Pearlman & Greenberg, 1973). Group T (N = 16) did not receive reticular stimulation, and was deprived of total sleep for 3 hours after each daily trial. Group C (N = 16) also did not receive reticular stimulation, and was allowed to sleep freely for 3 hours before 3 hours of sleep deprivation. It has been shown that a 3 hour delayed sleep deprivation is without effect on retention (Leconte, Hennevin & Bloch, 1974; Pearlman & Becker, 1974a,b; Pearlman & Greenberg, 1973).

An analysis of variance (Snedecor's "F" test) was used for the inter-group statistical comparisons and Student's "T" test for intra-group comparisons (Winer, 1962). Figure 4 shows learning performances for the three groups (running time and number of errors).

From the second trial to the sixth trial of conditioning, groups E and C were significantly different from group T for the two parameters (P < .05). On the 7th trial this difference was no longer significant.

TABLE 1

EFFECT OF MAZE LEARNING TRIALS ON SUBSEQUENT 2h OF SLEEP : GROUP T (N = 9)

	0	1	2	3	4	5	6	7	8	9
SWS (sec)	3863 (± 121)	4131 (± 158)	3804 (± 251)	3829 (± 175)	2975 (± 125)	4155 (± 101)	3427 (± 263)	4025 (± 140)	3902 (± 193)	3980 (± 136)
PS (sec)	422 (± 52)	507 (± 82)	413 (± 83)	490 (± 79)	352 (± 91)	630** (± 80)	620* (± 80)	416 (± 87)	436 (± 92)	420 (± 78)
TS (sec)	4285	4638	4217	4319	3327	4785	4047	4441	4338	4440
% PS	9.85	10.94	9.80	11.36	10.60	13.17**	15.33**	9.38	10.07	9.54
PS phases number	4.44	5.66	4.77	5.55	3.77	6.33*	6*	4.88	4.37	4.50
Average duration of each PS phases (sec)	95	90	86	88	93	100	103	85	100	93

Column 0 = reference level (mean of two records)
Columns 1 to 9 = each trial of learning

Level of significance : * between $P < .05$ and $P < .02$
                             ** between $P < .01$ and $P < .005$

In parenthesis is noted Standard Error

TABLE 2

EFFECT OF MAZE LEARNING TRIALS ON SUBSEQUENT 2h OF SLEEP : GROUP E (N = 10)

	0	1	2	3	4	5	6	7	8	9
SWS (sec)	3683 (± 252)	3962 (± 337)	3682 (± 178)	3561 (± 304)	3710 (± 112)	3670 (± 164)	3900 (± 151)	4289 (± 156)	3992 (± 144)	3738 (± 127)
PS (sec)	412 (± 50)	459 (± 70)	372 (± 32)	410 (± 71)	400 (± 43)	385 (± 45)	516* (± 44)	432 (± 58)	418 (± 64)	397 (± 35)
TS (sec)	4095 (± 277)	4421	4054	3971	4110	4056	4416	4661	4410	4135
% PS	10.06	10.38	9.17	10.32	9.75	9.50	11.68*	9.26	9.5	9.62
PS phases number	4.5	5.33	4.5	4.8	4.5	4.2	5.9*	5.2	4.8	4.5
Average duration of each PS phase (sec)	91	86	83	85	88	92	87	83	87	88

Column 0 = reference level after reticular stimulation
(mean of two records)

Columns 1 to 9 : each trial of learning

Level of significance : * between P < .05 and P < .02

In parenthesis is noted Standard Error.

TABLE 3

EFFECT OF THE SECOND MAZE LEARNING ON SUBSEQUENT 2h OF SLEEP

FOR THE GROUPS E (N = 10) and T (N = 9)

GROUP T	0	1	2	3	4
SWS (sec)	3862 ($\pm$ 121)	4031 ($\pm$ 168)	3812 ($\pm$ 174)	4087 ($\pm$ 145)	4130 ($\pm$ 159)
PS (sec)	422 ($\pm$ 52)	449 ($\pm$ 66)	583* ($\pm$ 65)	449 ($\pm$ 72)	480 ($\pm$ 67)
TS (sec)	4285	4480	4395	4536	4610
% PS	9.85	10	13.27*	9.90	10.42
PS phases number	4.44	4.88	7*	4.72	4.89
Average duration of each PS phase (sec)	95	92	83	95	98

GROUP E	0	1	2	3	4
SWS (sec)	3728 ($\pm$ 128)	4200 ($\pm$ 147)	3979 ($\pm$ 121)	4005 ($\pm$ 137)	4009 ($\pm$ 179)
PS (sec)	392 ($\pm$ 57)	427 ($\pm$ 70)	596* ($\pm$ 75)	383 ($\pm$ 60)	406 ($\pm$ 36)
TS (sec)	4120	4627	4575	4388	4415
% PS	9.51	9.23	13.04*	9.65	9.21
PS phases number	4.45	4.85	7.26*	4.30	4.95
Average duration of each PS phase (sec)	88	88	82	89	82

Column 0 = reference level (mean of two records)

Columns 1 to 4 : each trial of learning

Level of significance : *between $P < .05$ and $P < .02$

In parenthesis is noted Standard Error

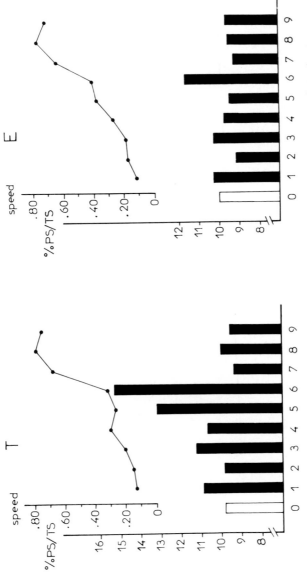

Fig. 2. PS ratio variations for the groups E (stimulated) and T (not stimulated). Column 0: reference level of PS ratio; columns 1 to 9: PS ratio following each daily trial of learning. Above the columns are shown the running speed curves (see text).

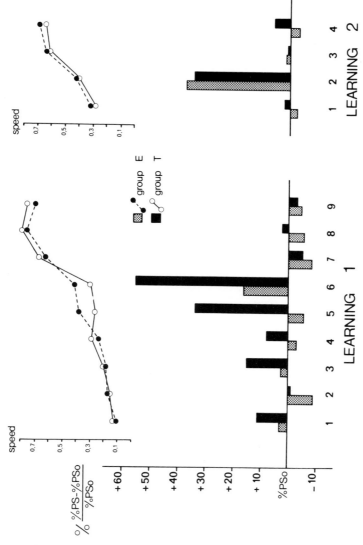

Fig. 3. Relative % PS variations (% PSo = 5 PS of reference) after each daily maze learning trial for the two groups. In the learning 1, group E receives a reticular stimulation after each trial; group T does not receive this stimulation. In the learning 2, after the modification of the maze plan, group E and T do not receive any stimulation. Above the columns is shown the running speed curve (number of blocks/second) of each group.

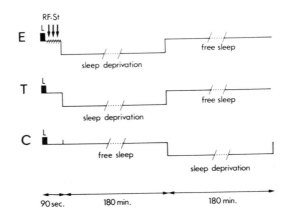

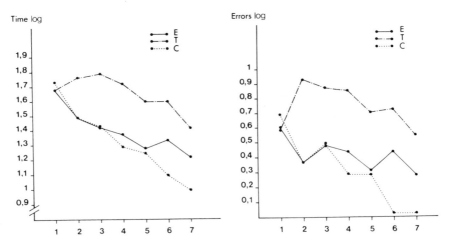

Fig. 4. Upper: experimental procedure. Group E receives a 90 sec reticular stimulation after each daily trial, then is deprived of total sleep for 3 hours; group T does not receive the stimulation but is deprived of total sleep for 3 hours; group C does not receive the stimulation, can sleep freely during 3 hours, then is deprived of total sleep during 3 hours. Lower: learning curves for the three groups. Left: running time (log); right: number of errors (log); abcissa: each daily learning trial.

Groups C and T were significantly different from 2nd to 7th trials; groups E and T differed significantly from 2nd to 5th trials; groups E and C showed no significant difference throughout the experiment.

Furthermore, the intra-group analysis revealed that group C performance improved significantly between the 1st and 4th trials, and between the 4th and 7th trials. Also group E performance improved significantly between the 1st and 4th trials but not between the 4th and 7th trials and group T performance did not improve between the 1st and 4th trials but improved significantly between the 4th and 7th trials.

These results confirm once again in a new task (linear maze) that PS augmentation occurs after acquisition (Hennevin et al., 1974). As in preceding experiments, the increase of PS during the 2 hour period of sleep following learning was related to the level of learning achieved, this increase being maximum when learning was progressing, and ceasing when the performance stabilized. It has been shown that when animals face a new situation, such a stimulus differentiation (Leconte et al., 1973) is followed by a new increase of PS. Here again, when the maze configuration was reversed, this relearning was followed by an additional increase of PS.

Sleep deprivation produces a considerable acquisition impairment only when it is imposed during the first three hours after the trial, i.e., during the period in which PS augmentation occurs in control animals. It has been previously shown that the same amount of deprivation imposed after a 3 hour delay is without any effect on retention (Leconte et al., 1974; Pearlman & Becker, 1974a,b; Pearlman & Greenberg, 1973). This finding was confirmed by the present results.

In the first experiment, there was only a slight facilitation of retention produced by reticular stimulation; this facilitation appeared only on the second and fifth days of learning in the stimulated group. At the present we cannot propose an explanation for this discrepancy with all our previous data which showed substantial facilitation in a great variety of learning tasks such as active avoidance, one trial reversal learning based on positive reinforcement, and T maze (Bloch et al., 1966, 1970; Deweer, Note 1). This is all the more puzzling because we obtained considerably greater facilitation with the same maze in another (unpublished) experiment.

The results of the first experiment showed that a weak reticular stimulation, given during the consolidation period, almost totally suppressed the post-learning PS increase. The stimulated group (group E) showed only one low PS increase at the same portion of the learning curve where the non-stimulated

group displayed two high PS increases. Moreover, in a different learning task, this same group (group E), which this time
did not receive any stimulation, displayed the typical PS
increase after the learning session.

Since we have shown that a 90 sec, 5 uA stimulation, when
delivered outside a learning situation, does not modify the
subsequent sleep, we may conclude that the post-trial stimulation acts upon the mechanisms which trigger PS post-learning
augmentation. Furthermore, results of the second experiment
show that reticular stimulation, given during the consolidation period, decreases the amnestic effect of a subsequent 3
hour sleep deprivation. Animals which received the reticular
stimulation and were then sleep deprived (group E), performed
better than animals that were sleep deprived but without
previous reticular stimulation (group T).

However, we observed that group E performances did not
improve after the 4th learning trial, unlike group C which
was not immediately sleep deprived. It was at this stage of
the learning curve in the first experiment that we observed
the largest PS increase in group T and the slight PS increase
in group E. This suggests the existence of a critical stage
in the acquisition. At this stage, consolidation processes
might continue during PS.

It seems that some need for arousal to process new information has been fulfilled by reticular stimulation immediately
after registration, and that the PS supplementary period is no
longer necessary in subsequent sleep. These data also reinforce the idea that information processing is triggered after
registration and continues during sleep in those periods when
the necessary brain activation normally occurs.

But, while we think that the information processing
hypothesis accounts for our observations, it is also possible
that PS is not directly implicated in the process of memory
storage and that its increase is a consequence of the memory
process rather than its cause. Moruzzi (1966) has suggested
that one of the functions of sleep could possibly be the
restoration of activity of neurons involved in learning. When
we consider the special case of PS, we could assume that the
high metabolic rate characteristic of this state is correlated with a high level of chemical synthesis. Therefore, as
we have discussed elsewhere (Bloch, 1973), it could be
assumed that the amount of PS increases as a function of the
neuronal substances utilized during wakefulness, in the
consolidation process.

In this line, Stern and Morgane (1974) have recently
proposed the theory that a function of PS could be to maintain
catecholamine availability in the central nervous system.

However, in the present state of our knowledge, it would be difficult to understand why a reticular stimulation, which probably activates noradrenergic ascending pathways, would suppress a restorative function of catecholamines. On the contrary, if we assume that reticular stimulation facilitates some neurophysiological events which are normally replayed during PS, we could understand that this stimulation suppresses the PS augmentation.

It has been argued, notably by John (1972), that the essential event taking place during learning is the establishment and the elaboration of spatio-temporal configurations of neuronal activity characterizing large populations of neurons ("memory read-out"). The time-factor for the occurrence of such patterns is compatible with the time-factor of a few minutes characterizing the early phase of consolidation. These dynamic patterns could possibly be reactivated by neuronal bombardment originating from the reticular formation during PS with a consequent increase in coherence.

REFERENCE NOTE

1.   Deweer, B. Selective facilitative effect of post-trial reticular stimulation in discriminative learning in the rat. Submitted for publication, 1976.

REFERENCES

Albe-Fessard, D., Stutinsky, F., & Libouban, S. *Atlas Stéréotaxique du Diencéphale du Rat Blanc*. Paris: Centre Nationale de la Recherche Scientifique, 1966.

Benoit, O. Activité unitaire du nerf optique, du corps genouillé, latéral et de la formation réticulaire durant les differénts stades du sommeil. *Journal of Physiology* (Paris), 1964, *56*, 259-262.

Bloch, V. Facts and hypotheses concerning memory consolidation processes. *Brain Research*, 1970, *24*, 561-575.

Bloch, V. L'activation cérébrale et la fixation mnésique. *Archives Italiennes de Biologie*, 1973, *3*, 577-590.

Bloch, V., Denti, A., & Schmaltz, G. Effets de la stimulation réticulaire sur la phase de consolidation de la trace mnésique. *Journal of Physiology* (Paris), 1966, *58*, 469-470.

Bloch, V., Deweer, B., & Hennevin, E. Suppression de l'amnésie
    rétrograde et consolidation d'un apprentissage à essai
    unique par stimulation réticulaire. *Physiology and
    Behavior,* 1970, *5,* 1235-1241.

Denti, A., McGaugh, J.L., Landfield, P., & Shinkman, P.
    Facilitation of learning with post-trial stimulation of
    the reticular formation. *Physiology and Behavior,* 1970,
    5, 659-662.

Evarts, E. Activity of neurons in visual cortex of the cat
    during sleep with low-voltage fast EEG activity. *Journal
    of Neurophysiology,* 1962, *25,* 812-816.

Evarts, E. Activity of individual cerebral neurons during
    sleep and arousal. In S. Kety, E. Evarts & H. Williams
    (Eds.), *Sleep and Altered States of Consciousness.*
    Baltimore: Williams and Wilkins, 1967.

Fishbein, W., Kastaniotis, C., & Chattman, D. Paradoxical
    sleep: Prolonged augmentation following learning.
    Brain Research, 1974, *79,* 61-75.

Greenberg, R., & Pearlman, C. Cutting the REM nerve: An
    approach to the adaptative role of REM sleep.
    Perspectives in Biology and Medicine, 1974, *17,* 513-521.

Hennevin, E., Leconte, P., & Bloch, V. Effet du niveau
    d'acquisition sur l'augmentation de la durée de sommeil
    paradoxal consécutive à un conditionnement d'évitement
    chez le Rat. *Comptes Rendus Hebdomadaires des seances
    des l'Academie des Sciences* (Paris), *1971, 273,* 2595-2598.

Hennevin, E., Leconte, P., & Bloch, V. Augmentation du
    sommeil paradoxal provoquée par l'acquisition,
    l'extinction et al réacquisition d'un apparentissage à
    renforcement positif. Brain Research, 1974, 70, 43-54.

Hobson, J., & McCarley, R. Cortical unit activity in sleep
    and waking. Electroencephalography and Clinical
    Neurophysiology, 1971, 30, 97-112.

Huttenlocher, P. Evoked and spontaneous activity in single
    units of medial brain stem during natural sleep and
    waking. *Journal of Neurophysiology,* 1961, *24,* 451-468.

John, E.R. Switchboard versus statistical theories of
     learning and memory. *Science,* 1972, *177,* 850-864.

Lecas, J.C. Relation entre l'activité unitaire du tegmentum
     mésencéphalique et la durée des phases de sommeil
     paradoxal chez le Chat. *Journal of Physiology* (Paris),
     1975, *71,* 338A.

Leconte, P., & Bloch, V. Déficit de la rétention d'un
     conditionnement après privation de sommeil paradoxal
     chez le Rat. *Comptes Rendus Hebdomadaires des seances
     des l'Academie des Sciences* (Paris), 1970, *271,* 226-229.

Leconte, P., & Hennevin, E. Augmentation de la durée de
     sommeil paradoxal consécutive à un apprentissage chez
     le Rat. *Comptes Rendus Hebdomadaires des seances des
     l'Academie des Sciences* (Paris), 1971, *271,* 86-88.

Leconte, P., & Hennevin, E. Caractéristiques temporelles de
     l'augmentation de sommeil paradoxal consécutif à
     l'apprentissage chez le Rat. *Physiology and Behavior,*
     1973, *11,* 677-686.

Leconte, P., Hennevin, E., & Bloch, V. Analyse des effets
     d'un apprentissage et de son niveau d'acquisition sur le
     sommeil paradoxal consécutif. *Brain Research,* 1973,
     49, 367-379.

Leconte, P., Hennevin, E., & Bloch, V. Duration of paradox-
     ical sleep necessary for the acquisition of conditioned
     avoidance in the rat. *Physiology and Behavior,* 1974, *13,*
     675-681.

Lucero, M. Lengthening of REM sleep duration consecutive to
     learning in the rat. *Brain Research,* 1970, *20,* 319-322.

McGaugh, J.L., & Herz, M. *Memory Consolidation.* San
     Francisco: Albion, 1972.

Moruzzi, G. The functional significance of sleep with
     particular regard to the brain mechanisms underlying
     consciousness. In J. Eccles (Ed.), *Brain and Conscious
     Experience.* New York: Springer-Verlag, 1966.

Noda, H., & Adey, W. Changes in neuronal activity in
     associative cortex of the cat in relation to sleep and
     wakefulness. *Brain Research,* 1970, *19,* 263-275.

Paul, K., & Dittrichova, J. Sleep patterns following learning in infants. In P. Levin & W. Koella (Eds.), *Sleep, 1974* (Proceedings of the 2nd European Congress on Sleep Research, Rome, 1974). Basel: Karger, 1975.

Pearlman, C., & Becker, M. Brief posttrial REM sleep deprivation impairs discrimination learning in rats. *Physiological Psychology*, 1973, *1*, 373-376.

Pearlman, C., & Becker, M. REM sleep deprivation impairs serial reversal and probability maximizing in rats. *Physiological Psychology*, 1974a, *2*, 509-512.

Pearlman, C., & Becker, M. REM sleep deprivation impairs bar press acquisition in rats. *Physiological Psychology*, 1974b, *13*, 813-817.

Pearlman, C., & Greenberg, R. Posttrial REM sleep: A critical period for consolidation of shuttlebox avoidance. *Animal Learning and Behavior*, 1973, *1*, 49-51.

Siegel, S. *Nonparametric Statistics for the Behavioral Sciences*. New York: McGraw-Hill, 1956.

Smith, C.F., Kitahama, K., Valatx, J.L., & Jouvet, M. Sommeil paradoxal et apprentissage chez deux souches consanguines de souris. *Comptes Rendus Hebdomadaires des seances des l'Academie des Sciences* (Paris), 1972, *275*, 1283-1286.

Smith, C., Kitahama, K., Valatx, J.L., & Jouvet, M. Increased paradoxical sleep in mice during acquisition of a shock avoidance task. *Brain Research*, 1974, *77*, 221-230.

Stern, W., & Morgane, P. Theoretical view of REM sleep function: Maintenance of catecholamine systems in the central nervous system. *Behavioral Biology*, 1974, *11*, 1-32.

Timo-Iaria, C., Negrao, N., Schmidek, W.R., Hoshino, K., Lobato de Menezes, C., & Leme Da Rocha, T. Phases and states of sleep in the rat. *Physiology and Behavior*, 1970, *5*, 1057-1062.

Winer, B. *Statistical Principles in Experimental Design*. New York: McGraw-Hill, 1962.

REMINISCENCES ELICITED BY ELECTRICAL STIMULATION OF THE TEMPORAL LOBE IN HUMANS

AUGUSTO FERNÁNDEZ-GUARDIOLA

Unidad de Investigaciones Cerebrales
Instituto Nacional de Neurología
S.S.A., México 22, D.F., México

and

Instituto de Investigaciones Biomédicas
Ciudad Universitaria
México 20, D.F., México

In this study deep chronically implanted electrodes were used in order to determine eleptogenic areas in the parenchyma and cerebral nuclei. This procedure yields more accurate localization than utilization of the surface EEG alone. It is also possible, through these electrodes, to stimulate the patient and reproduce various symptoms. This is of great importance from a diagnostic point of view.

We have been able to reproduce automatism and other components of epileptic seizures in patients suffering from temporal epilepsy by stimulating different parts of the temporal lobe. For example, we have been able to provoke memories, reminiscences, hallucinations, verbalizations, and aggressive conduct in rare occasions, and in most cases, emotional changes. These procedures seem absolutely reversible and confirm other results (Mark & Ervin, 1970; Delgado, 1966).

Our study is based upon 18 patients bilaterally implanted with 8 electrodes in the temporal lobe. Electrodes were stereotaxically directed at an angle greater than 45° (in reference to the sagittal plane) and placed along the temporal lobe from the cortex to the hippocampus, passing through the amygdala and the periamygdaloid areas. The patients were operated on by Drs. Manuel Velasco Suárez and Francisco Escobedo at the Instituto de Neurología de México. All cases were severe epileptic patients, and most were mentally retarded and suffering from some form of behavioral disturbance which required hospitalization. All of the patients had symptoms which were beyond control with medical anticonvulsive and ataraxic treatments.

The patients had leads implanted during a period varying from 5-6 days to three months. All of the patients had a pre-surgery clinical exam, as well as psychological, radiologic and electroencephalographic tests. The patients were stimulated and their EEGs were recorded twice weekly. Therefore, our data consists of separate stimulation and recording sessions in 18 different temporal epileptic patients.

Table 1 presents a summary of the results It must be kept in mind that only the temporal lobe limbic areas were stimulated, namely the hippocampal gyrus, amygdala, periamygdaloid structures, and the temporal cortex. This creates a serious limitation for the interpretation of the data since violent or agonistic reactions have been elicited in animals through stimulation of hypothalamic and rostral areas of the reticular formation. Nevertheless, amygdala activation, when strong and long-lasting, produces emotional changes and, more importantly, vivid memories or reminiscences and hallucinations.

As can be seen in Table 1, the greatest occurrence of EEG responses were paroximal (eleptiform), as was expected, due to the nature of the patient's disease. Most interestingly, stimulation of the contralateral temporal lobe opposite of epileptogenic focus) produced a great number of reminiscences. Deep sagittal stimulation produced most of the responses which were of a personal and affective type, related mainly to situations causing anger and fear. Stimulation of superficial leads led to intensely pleasant and happy experiences. Categorical memories related to learned abstract concepts were elicited extremely rarely.

Violent reactions were classified as attack behavior directed against both people and surrounding objects or against one's own body. As Table 1 shows, this type of behavior occurred on very few occasions (8.68%). An interesting fact is that all of the patients that displayed violent reactions when stimulated had a previous clinical history of repeated violent behavior. It is also interesting to point out the parallelism between the low incidence of agonistic reactions and the few subjective, categorical or abstract thought responses.

TABLE 1

LIMBIC SYSTEM ELECTRICAL STIMULATION
(Human Temporal Lobe)

Number of patients	Number of stimula- tions	EEG and clinical seizures	Arrest reactions (absences)	Reminiscences: sexual and af- fective, per- sonal, fear, anger	Reminiscences (categorially learned)	Violent reactions
18	864	320	217	240	12	75
		37.03%	25.11%	27.77%	1.38%	8.68%

275

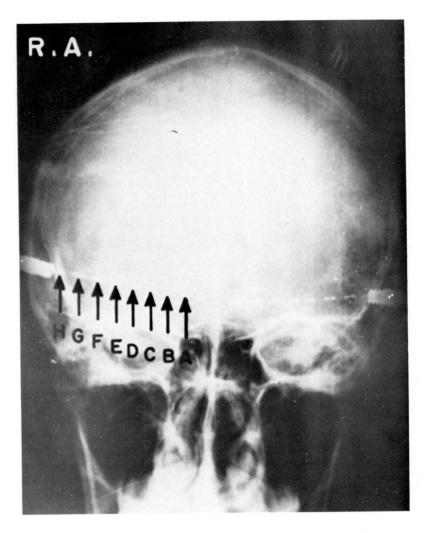

Fig. 1. *X-rays (AP) of one patient (RA) depicting 8 chronically implanted electrodes.*

Figure 1 shows the X-rays (PA) of a patient (RA) with chronically implanted multipolar electrodes. Each electrode has eight levels, which are labled A,B,C,D,E,F, and G proceeding in a rostral direction from A-G. Figures 2 and 3 show the EEG recordings taken from these electrodes, which delineate with some precision the initial eleptogenic focus of the spikes in the right temporal lobe.

DER. ROBERTO

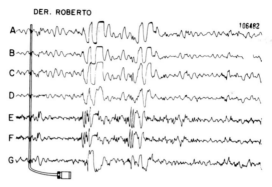

Fig. 2. Recordings from the depth (A) to the surface (G) of the temporal lobe. The epileptic discharge begins in derivations E and F (amygdalae) as polyspikes and propagates as slow waves.

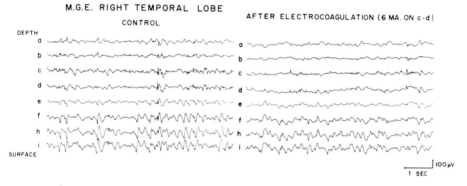

Fig. 3. Recording of the right temporal lobe in another patient. The brief spikes in C and D are coincident with periods of behavioral automatisms.

Patient RA was stimulated on April 8 and 26, 1968, with the following electrode configurations:

April 8, 1968, Right Electrode

Configuration A-B: With a minimum of stimulation, the patient's expression changed, and became sad. He began to speak and referred to the episode he was watching, a recent episode at his job, where a fellow worker lost his life. The patient asserted that the image "jumped".

Configuration B-C: Once more he referred to the death of his fellow worker and said that he saw a street (Insurgentes). When asked if it was only a remembrance, he said no, that the scene was revealed to him.

Configuration C-D: The patient's expression suddenly changed rapidly. He adopted a comfortable position and looked around the room with curiosity. He smiled and began to remember childhood episodes, trips to the country and bird-hunting. He described his grandparents with an expression of contentment.

Configuration D-E: His smile widened. He continued to refer to his infancy and episodes with his father. He moved constantly about in the bed and looked about from one to another person in the room. He put his hand on his genitals.

Configuration E-F: His satisfaction increased. He referred to a song he was hearing and felt the desire to sing. He sang and continued doing so after the stimulation ceased. He also related his first sexual experience. The patient stated that this type of memory and humor sometimes occurred before a seizure and provided him with a warning.

April 26, 1968, Right Electrode

Configuration A-B: He had a sensation of astonishment. With a somber expression he referred to different misfortunes, which included the incident where the employee died in an accident. After the stimulation ceased he continued talking and relating dramatic happenings in detail.

Configuration E-F: His features showed signs of pleasure. He smiled and remembered his little brothers.

Configuration A-B: He had a sudden change of emotion and expressed astonishment. He interrupted his conversation and related a misfortune which occurred to his sister.

Configuration E-F: The patient saw his life in the country with his grandparents, and described it in much detail.

Configuration C-D: The patient asserted that he saw Insurgentes Avenue but said that the images trembled. Additional intense stimulation of the left electrode provided only epileptic signs.

DISCUSSION

The reminiscence phenomenon produced in the cerebrum constitutes activation of past memories. This is a process that can be produced by electrical stimulation of the limbic structures. These data enable one to affirm that the reminiscence is produced concomitant to the activation of the neural circuits in which the information is presumably stored. Our experiences with human brain stimulation have provided data which seems to indicate that reminiscence activation involves very extensive areas of the brain. In our studies the following principles seemed to emerge from repeated brain stimulation: 1) It is impossible to evoke memories by applying single shocks of short duration. 2) The reminiscence phenomenon was provoked through the application of large duration pulse trains. The optimum frequencies seemed to be between 50 and 100 Hz. 3) When optimum stimulation was employed (verified through previous experiences), the memories always appeared with a long latency, between one-half and several seconds, often preceded by ipsilateral motor phenomena of much shorter latency. Our data seem to indicate the existence of a precise localized information store. In several patients, the stimulation of one particular brain area with similar stimulation parameters on successive days produced a similar reminiscence response, accompanied by the same emotional response.

One of the most important problems in the reminiscence phenomena is defining the physio-chemical nature of how information is stored. Hebb (1949) believed that this process took place in reverberating circuits. Later, Gerard (1953) and DiGiorgio (1929, 1947) demonstrated that the fixation of memories is not dependent upon EEG activity per se. That is, recent memories do need reverberating activity, but old memories remain fixed in the neural substrate.

We found that stimulation of the periamygala region always provoked very elaborate reminiscence phenomena and old memories were always related to infantile experiences. These evoked infantile memories were never of experiences earlier than 5 or 6 years of age. No patient was capable of recalling his memories during the first months or years of his life. It is evident that these data seem opposite to the Freudian hypothesis that one may have memories of fetal or perinatal life.

Despite the large number of patients, no reminiscences of recent happenings were produced. It is as though the stimulated areas were exclusively involved in old memories or that the electrical stimulations were incapable of eliciting recent memories.

It should be pointed out that this study dealt exclusively with epileptic patients capable of generalized convulsive activity at any time. The high voltage synchronized EEG activity was capable of functioning as a "memory eraser", where recent events are consolidated. This would explain why stimulation does not evoke recent reminiscences.

REFERENCES

Delgado, J. M. R.   Emotions. In J. A. Vernon (Ed.), *Introduction to Psychology.* Dubuque, Iowa: Brown, 1966.

Di Giorgio, A. M.   Persistenza, nell'animale spinale, di asimetrie posturali e motorie di origine cerebellare. II. Ricerche intorno al meccanismo funzionale di tal asimetrie. *Archives Fisiologie,* 1929, *27*, 543-557.

Di Giorgio, A. M.   Modificazione funzionali del midollo spinale per effetto di impulsi asimmetrici cerebrali o cerebellari. *Archives Fisiologie,* 1947, *47*, 254-261.

Gerard, R. W.   What is memory? *Scientific American,* 1953, *189*, 118-126.

Hebb, D. O. *Organization of Behavior.* New York: John Wiley & Sons, 1949.

Mark, V. H., & Ervin, F. R. *Violence and the Brain.* New York: Harper & Row, 1970.

PIPERIDINE: AN ENDOGENOUS HYPNOGENIC AMINE?

EZIO GIACOBINI

Laboratory of Neuropsychopharmacology
Department of Biobehavioral Sciences
University of Connecticut
Storrs, Connecticut 06268 USA

RENÉ R. DRUCKER-COLÍN

Departamento de Biologia Experimentál
Instituto de Biología
Universidad Nacional Autónoma de México
México 20, D.F., México

In 1944, von Euler (1944a,b) in the course of an investigation aimed at discovering the nature of an "active pressor amine," isolated from normal human urine "a volatile base with nicotine-like action" which he subsequently identified as piperidine (Figure 1). The pharmacological properties of piperidine had been investigated by several authors before von Euler. Moore and Row (1898) clearly showed the close resemblance between the actions of piperidine and nicotine. The nicotine-like effect of piperidine was obtained by von Euler (1945a,b) at concentrations of 1/15 - 1/20 that of nicotine.

Piperidine is a volatile amine structurally similar to pyrrolidine, proline and glutamic acid (Figure 1). Moreover, γ-aminobutyric acid (GABA) is also structurally related to piperidine and for this reason is called piperidinic acid (Figure 1). Nicotine and arecoline are also structurally similar to piperidine. Several of these substances show pronounced effects on nervous activity.

After his discovery, von Euler (1945a,b) speculated that because of its nicotinic property, piperidine might be regarded as an endogenous "synaptotropic substance."

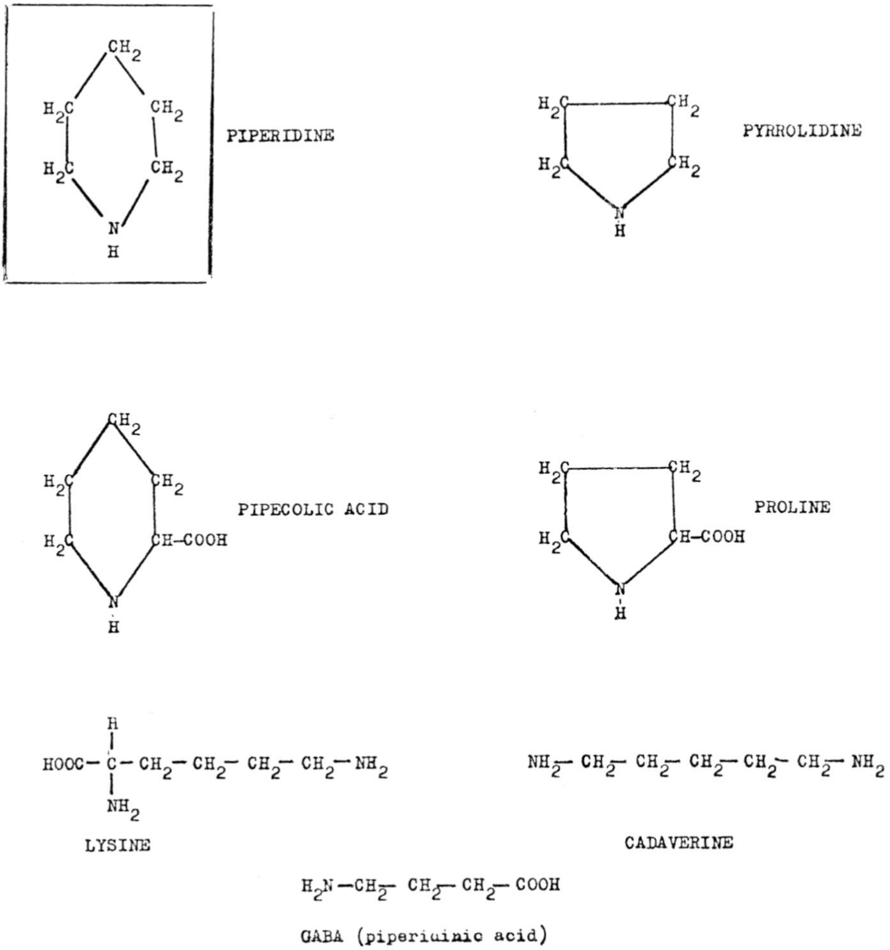

Fig. 1. Piperidine and structurally related substances.

Although piperidine was first suspected in 1960 to be present in the brain of mammals, including humans (Honegger & Honegger, 1960) it is only recently that it has been identified in our laboratory by means of mass spectrometry in the CNS of the snail (Dolezalova, Stepita-Klauco, & Fairweather, 1973) and in the brain of the mouse (Stepita-Klauco, Dolezalova, & Fairweather, 1974), rat and cat (Bohn & Giacobini, Note 1).

Table 1 reports the concentration of piperidine in different parts of the vertebrate brain. In comparing these

TABLE 1

PIPERIDINE CONCENTRATION IN VERTEBRATE BRAIN

Part	Species	Conc. pmoles/mg	Method	Ref.
Cerebellum	mouse	3.17 ± .12	DNP-piper., spectro-photometric	Nixon and Sidman, 1971
Cerebellum	mouse	3.07 ± .49	DANS – TLC – MS	Dolezalova and Stepita-Klauco, 1974
Cerebellum	dog	3.92 ± .89	DNP-piper., spectro-photometric	Nixon and Sidman, 1971
Cerebellum	dog	5.18	DNP-piper., spectro-photometric	Kataoka et al., 1970
Cerebellum	cat	0.8 ± .20	DANS – TLC – MS	Bohn and Giacobini, 1975
Cerebral hemispheres	dog	0.22	DNP-piper., spectro-photometric	Kataoka et al., 1970
Prosence-phalon	mouse	1.16 ± 0.28	DANS – TLC – MS	Dolezalova and Stepita-Klauco, 1974
Diencephalic region	dog	0.7	DNP-piper., spectro-photometric	Kataoka et al., 1970
Diencephalic region	cat	0.9 ± .17[a]	DANS – TLC – MS	Bohn and Giacobini, 1975

TABLE 1 (Continued)

Part	Species	Conc. pmoles/mg	Method	Ref.
Midbrain	dog	$(0.7)^c$	DNP-piper., spectro-photometric	Kataoka *et al.*, 1970
Midbrain	mouse	5.86 ± 2.09	DANS - TLC - MS	Dolezalova and Stepita-Klauco, 1974
Midbrain	cat	$0.9 \pm .17^b$	DANS - TLC - MS	Bohn and Giacobini, 1975
Pons	dog	$(0.9)^c$	DNP - piper., spectro-photometric	Kataoka *et al.*, 1970
Pons	cat	$0.83 \pm .14$	DANS - TLC - MS	Bohn and Giacobini, 1975
Medulla oblongata	dog	$(0.6)^c$	DNP-piper., spectro-photometric	Kataoka *et al.*, 1970
Medulla oblongata	cat	$1.23 \pm .39$	DANS - TLC - MS	Bohn and Giacobini, 1975
Spinal cord	cat	$1.03 \pm .27$	DANS - TLC - MS	Bohn and Giacobini, 1975

[a] Includes midbrain and basal ganglia

[b] Includes diencephalon and basal ganglia

[c] Lowest measureable quantity

results not only differences in species should be taken into consideration but also differences in the techniques used for the assay. In our experience (Bohn & Giacobini, Note 1) the methods involving 2,4-dinitrofluorobenzene (DNFB) piperidine, spectrophotometry or fluorimetry are significantly less reliable than the combination of dansylation, thin-layer chromatography and mass spectrometry (Schneider & Sonnenberg, 1971). In the final analysis only a mass spectrum of a substance of a chromatographically separated derivative may constitute a valid criterion for the unequivocal identification of piperidine.

Analyzing the data reported in Table 1 the following conclusions can be drawn: a) piperidine is present in measurable amounts in all parts of the brain examined of the species studies so far; b) in dog and mouse some differences in concentration are apparent between different parts; however, in the cat (Bohn & Giacobini, Note 1) no significant differences were found; c) the highest concentrations of piperidine were found by Nixon and Sidman (1971) and Kataoka, Kase, Mitaya, and Kawahito (1970) in dog cerebellum. The latter results are not supported by the data of Dolezalova and Stepita-Klauco (1974) and Bohn and Giacobini (Note 1) in the mouse and cat respectively. The discrepancy between piperidine concentrations in the brain reported in the literature should caution one from drawing any conclusion with regard to a) regional distribution of piperidine, b) changes in levels during physiological conditions (sleep included) before the validity of the methods has been clearly established. It seems likely that only an analysis of smaller and more selective parts or nuclei of the brain, performed with highly sensitive and specific methods, unfortunately not yet available, might demonstrate significant regional differences in the distribution of piperidine.

In a recent pharmacological study (Drucker-Colin & Giacobini, 1975) 16 cats were used which were stereotaxically implanted with electrodes and guides for "push-pull" cannulae with their tips lying 7 mm above the midbrain reticular formation. Ten animals were perfused through the cannula with Ringer solution and six animals with a 1 mg/ml piperidine hydrochloride solution at a speed of 20 ul/min so that over 15 min about 300 ug of piperidine passed through the brain. The latencies and the duration of the slow wave sleep (SWS) and rapid eye movement (REM) sleep was determined in each cat by visual inspection of the EEG recordings.

Table 2 summarizes our results. The animals which were locally perfused with piperidine showed a highly significant decrease (P < 0.001) in the latency to sleep from 36.5 $\pm$ 3.2

TABLE 2

LATENCIES AND DURATIONS OF SWS AND REM FOR EACH RECIPIENT CAT AFTER INTRACEREBRAL
PERFUSION OF RINGER OR PIPERIDINE

Cat. no.	Latency				Duration			
	Ringer control		Piperidine		Ringer control		Piperidine	
	SWS	REM	SWS	REM	SWS	REM	SWS	REM
1	27	48	3	9	12	2	26	18
2	46	60	8	19	9	0	17	11
3	42	60	5	12	13	0	19	8
4	31	60	7	18	22	0	21	16
5	29	43	8	14	12	6	14	21
6	33	58	10	16	20	1	22	13
7	60	60			0	0		
8	29	39			15	9		
9	37	60			23	0		
10	31	60			7	0		
Mean ± S.E.	36.5±3.2	54.8±2.5	6.8^a±1.0	14.6^a±1.5	13.7±2.0	1.6±.91	19.8±1.7	14.5^a±1.9

[a] Significantly different from control P ≤ 0.001

All values are in minutes. Note that the six piperidine subjects are independnet from the
ten Ringer controls.

to 6.8 $\pm$ 1.0 for SWS and from 54.8 $\pm$ 2.5 to 14.6 $\pm$ 1.5 for REM. Also the duration of REM sleep was significantly increased ($P < 0.001$) from 1.6 $\pm$ 91 to 14.5 $\pm$ 1.9. In another group of operated cats the same amount of piperidine was perfused through selected hippocampal regions without any effect on EEG or behavior. Although the total amount of piperidine passing through the perfusion system is small, the precise amount of the substance being locally taken up by the brain structures is not known. It can, however, be concluded that the intracerebral perfusion of piperidine in the MRF produces a selective and powerful hypnogenic effect in the cat.

Miyata, Kamata, Nishikibe, Kase, Takahama, and Okano (1974) reported that the intracerebral injection of 10-20 ug piperidine in the pontine reticular formation of the cat elicited a sleeping pattern in EEG consisting of high amplitude, irregular slow waves with spindle bursts in the cortex and caudate nucleus. According to the authors the animals "were sedated and without exception fell asleep" and piperidine induced not only SWS but also REM sleep.

Direct comparison of our results with those of Miyata et al. (1974) must be done with caution since first, the different localization in the brain stem of the chemical stimulation, and second, the smaller dose of piperidine administered with our perfusion technique. Both experiments suggest that in the reticular formation of the cat there may be piperidinoceptive structures capable of influencing sleep mechanisms, although at different levels.

These results and other reports of accumulation of piperidine (Dolezalova et al., 1973; Dolezalova, Stepita-Klauco, Fairweather, 1974; Stepita-Klauco et al., 1974) in the brain during sleep, if confirmed, becomes particularly interesting although it could be secondary to an increased cerebral metabolism of proteins or other macromolecules, occurring during sleep (Bobiller, Froment, Seguin, & Jouvet, 1973; Drucker-Colin, Spanis, Cotman, & McGaugh, 1975).

Compounds strictly related in their structure (Figure 2) to piperidine such as 2,4-Dioxo-3,3 diethyl-tetrahydro-pyridine (Persedon[R]), 2,4-Dioxo-3,3 diethyl-piperidine (Seduong[R]) and 3,3-diethyl-5-methyl-2,4 piperidione (methyprylone, Noludar[R]) have been used (Schnider, Frick, & Lutz, 1954; Lutz & Schnider, 1958) as hypnotics and sedatives for many years. Apparently the workers who introduced these drugs did not consider any relationship of these compounds to piperidine or its pharmacological action.

The present findings of a powerful and local pharmacological action of piperidine would favor the hypothesis of a

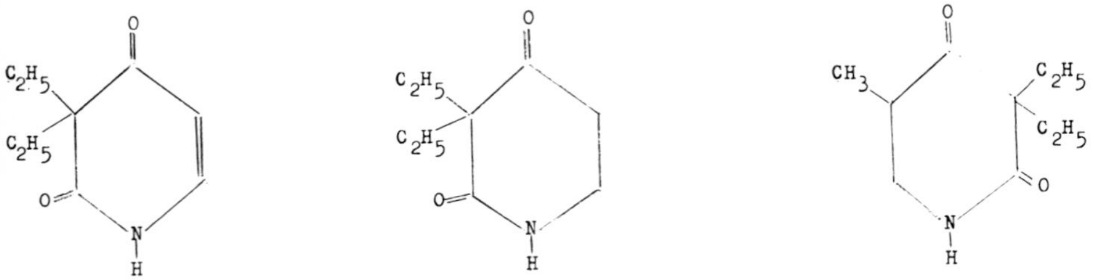

2,4 - Dioxo - 3,3 - diethyl -
tetrahydropyridine
(Persedon^R)

2,4 - Dioxo - 3,3 - diethyl -
piperidine
(Sedulon^R)

3,3 - diethyl - 5 - methyl -
2,4 - piperidione
(Noludar^R)

Fig. 2. Compounds structurally related to piperidine
used in therapy as hypnotics and sedatives.

physiological stimulation or modulation of cholinergic hypnogenic structures (Hernández-Peón, 1965; Hernández-Peón &
Drucker-Colín, 1970). These results are of particular
interest since a selective and powerful synaptic action of
piperidine has been found to occur on identified cholinoceptive neurons of the snail cerebral ganglia (Stepita-Klauco,
Dolezalova, & Giacobini, 1973). Moreover, piperidine shows
nicotine-like action in the peripheral and cerebral nervous
system of vertebrates (Kase, Miyata, & Yizono, 1967; Kase,
Miyata, Kamikawa, & Kataoka, 1969). This suggests that
piperidine would be: a) physiologically localized in nerve
cells and synapses impinging on the brain stem, and b)
released from a specific area of the brain stem during sleep,
possibly acting as a physiological "sleep modulator." This
would be consonant with reports which have shown an important
participation of descending (Hernandez-Peon, O'Flaherty, &
Mazzuchelli-O'Flaherty, 1967) and ascending (Rojas-Ramirez &
Drucker-Colín, 1973) cholinergic influences upon brain stem
"sleep pacemakers" (Jouvet, 1972). These areas are known to
show high acetylcholinesterase activity (Lewis & Schute, 1967;
Schute & Lewis, 1967).
      Presently no direct evidence for either hypothesis is
available. However, some preliminary experiments (Bohn &
Giacobini, Note 1) suggest an increased release of piperidine
in the perfusate collected from the brain stem of the cat
during 15 min periods of sleep within the same localization
where piperidine acts pharmacologically. The output of piperidine from the brain stem during two typical perfusion experiments is shown in Figure 3. Using a similar technique, Gadea-
Ciria, Stadler, Lloyd, and Bartholini (1973) investigated the
acetylcholine output from the cat striatum during SWS and REM

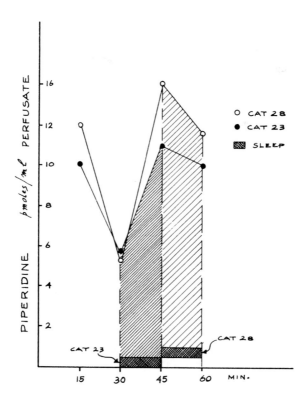

*Fig. 3. Release of piperidine from microperfusates
collected from the brain stem of 2 cats during 15 min periods
of sleep or wakefulness. The cross-hatched areas indicate
the sleeping period for each cat.*

sleep, and found an increased output of acetylcholine during
REM periods.

In summary, the first pharmacological evidence for a
direct hypnogenic effect of piperidine in the CNS seems
established, suggesting a possible involvement of piperidine
in the physiological processes of sleep and hibernation
(Giacobini, 1975). The present evidence for this hypothesis
is supported by: a) the physiological presence of piperidine
in the brain of vertebrates and invertebrates; b) its physiological accumulation in the brain of dormant invertebrates
and vertebrates; c) its topical pharmacological action
and possible release; and d) the hypnotic effect of drugs
closely related in their structure to piperidine.

ACKNOWLEDGMENT

This work was supported by grant no. 171-000-06-0220-35-029 from the University of Connecticut Research Foundation to E. G. and by Fellowship grant no. 72-552 from the Foundations Fund for Research in Psychiatry to R. R. D.-C, and a grant from the Swindells Charitable Foundation to E. G.

REFERENCE NOTE

1.   Bohn, M., & Giacobini, E.   Unpublished results, 1975.

REFERENCES

Bobiller, P., Froment, J. L., Seguin, S., & Jouvet, M. Effects de la P-chlorophenylalanine et du 5-hydroxytryptophane sur le sommeil et le metabolisme central des monoamines et des proteines chez le chat. *Biochemical Pharmacology*, 1973, *22*, 3077-3090.

Dolezalova, H., & Stepita-Klauco, M.   Piperidine concentration changes in the brain and blood of dormant mice. *Brain Research*, 1974, *74*, 182-184.

Dolezalova, H., Stepita-Klauco, M., & Giacobini, E. Variation of endogenous and exogenous piperidine in the brain of active and dormant snails. *Society for Neuroscience*, 1973, 349.   (Abstract)

Dolezalova, H., Stepita-Klauco, M., & Fairweather, R.   The accululation of piperidine in the central ganglia of dormant snails. *Brain Research*, 1974, *72*, 115-122.

Drucker-Colin, R. R., & Giacobini, E.   Sleep inducing effect of piperidine. *Brain Research*, 1975, *88*, 186-189.

Drucker-Colín, R. R., Spanis, C. W., Cotman, C. W., & McGaugh, J. L.   Changes in protein levels in perfusates of freely moving cats: Relation to behavioral state. *Science*, 1975, *187*, 963-965.

Euler, U. S. von.   Identification of a urine base with nicotine-like action. *Nature*, 1944, *154*, 17.   (a)

Euler, U. S. von. Piperidine as a normal pressor constituent of human urine. *Acta Physiologica Scandinavica,* 1944, *8,* 380-384. (b)

Euler, U. S. von. The occurrence and determination of piperidine in human and animal urine. *Acta Pharmacologica,* 1945, *1,* 29-59. (a)

Euler, U. S. von. The piperidine output in urine during muscular work. *Acta Physiologica Scandinavica,* 1945, *9,* 382-386. (b)

Gadea-Ciria, M., Stadler, H., Lloyd, K. G., & Bartholini, G. Acetylcholine release within the cat striatum during the sleep-wakefulness cycle. *Nature,* 1973, *243,* 518-519.

Giacobini, E. Seasonal and activity dependent variation of biogenic amine levels in the invertebrate CNS. In P. Levin & W. P. Koella (Eds.), *Sleep, 1974* (2nd European Congress on Sleep Research, Rome, 1974). Basel: Karger, 1975.

Hernandez-Peon, R. Central neurohumoral transmission in sleep and wakefulness. In K. Akert, C. Bally, & J. P. Schade (Eds.), *Sleep Mechanisms.* Amsterdam: Elsevier, 1965.

Hernandez-Peon, R., & Drucker-Colin, R. R. A neurographic study of corticobulbar hypnogenic pathways. *Physiology and Behavior,* 1970, *5,* 721-725.

Hernandez-Peon, R., O'Flaherty, J. J., & Mazzuchelli-O'Flaherty, A. L. Sleep and other behavioral effects induced by acetylcholinic stimulation of basal temporal cortex and striate structure. *Brain Research,* 1967, *4,* 243-267.

Honegger, C. G., & Honegger, R. Volatile amines in brain. *Nature,* 1960, *185,* 530-532.

Jouvet, M. The role of monoamines and acetylcholine containing neurons in the regulation of the sleep-waking cycle. *Reviews in Physiology: Biochemistry and Experimental Pharmacology,* 1972, *64,* 166-308.

Kasé, Y., Miyata, T., & Yuizono, T.   Pharmacological studies
on alicyclic amines. Report I: Comparison of
pharmacological activities of piperidine with those of
other amines. *Japanese Journal of Pharmacology*, 1967,
17, 475-490.

Kasé, Y., Miyata, T., Kamikawa, Y., & Kataoka, M.   Pharmacological studies on alicyclic amines. II. Central
actions of piperidine, pyrrolidine and piperazine.
Japanese Journal of Pharmacology, 1969, *19*, 300-314.

Kataoka, M., Kasé, Y., Miyata, T., & Kawahito, E.   Piperidine
in the cerebellum of the dog. *Journal of Neurochemistry*,
1970, *17*, 291-292.

Lewis, P. R., & Schute, C. C. A.   The cholinergic limbic
system: Projections to hippocampal formation, medial
cortex, nuclei of the ascending cholinergic reticular
system and the subfornical organ and supraoptic crest.
Brain, 1967, *90*, 521-543.

Lutz, A. H. von, & Schnider, O.   Schlafmittel aus der
Tetrahydro-pyridin und Piperidinreihe. *Chimia*, 1958,
12, 291-294.

Miyata, T., Kamata, K., Nishikibe, M., Kasé, Y., Takahama, K.,
& Okano, Y.   Effects of intracerebral administration of
piperidine on EEG and behavior. *Life Sciences*, 1974,
15, 1135-1152.

Moore, B., & Row, R.   A comparison of the physiological
actions and chemical constitution of piperidine, coniine
and nicotine. *Journal of Physiology (Lond.)*, 1898,
22, 273-295.

Nixon, R., & Sidman, R. I.   Alicyclic amines in mouse brain
and other tissues. *Federation Proceedings*, 1971, *30*,
190.

Rojas-Ramírez, J. A., & Drucker-Colín, R. R.   Sleep induced
by spinal cord cholinergic stimulation. *International
Journal of Neuroscience*, 1973, *5*, 215-221.

Schnider, O., Frick, H., & Lutz, A. H.   Synthese neuer
Schlafmittel der Pyridin- und Piperidinreihe.
Experientia, 1954, *10*, 135.

Schute, C. C. D., & Lewis, P. R. The ascending cholinergic reticular system: neocortical olfactory and subcortical projections. *Brain,* 1967, *90,* 497-520.

Seiler, N., Schneider, H. H., & Sonnenberg, K. D. Mass spectrometry of 1-dimethylaminonaphtalene-5-sulfonyl amino acids. *Analytical Biochemistry,* 1971, *44,* 451-457.

Stepita-Klauco, M., Dolezalova, H., & Giacobini, E. The action of piperidine on cholinoceptive neurons of the snail. *Brain Research,* 1973, *63,* 141-152.

Stepita-Klauco, M., Dolezalova, H., & Fairweather, R. Piperidine increase in the brain of dormant mice. *Science,* 1974, *183,* 536-537.

BIOSYNTHESIS OF RNA IN RABBIT CEREBRAL CORTEX DURING PERIODS OF SYNCHRONIZED SLEEP AND WAKEFULNESS

ANTONIO GIUDITTA, BRUNO RUTIGLIANO, ANNA VITALE-NEUGEBAUER, and RENATO TRAVERSO

International Institute of Genetics and Biophysics
Naples, Italy

In the general belief that sleep is a period of restoration of nervous and mental capacities and of further processing acquired information, we have considered that such events are likely to involve a coordinated pattern of change in cellular mechanisms mediating genetic expression. On that basis we have started an investigation of the biosynthesis of cortical RNA in rabbits undergoing periods of physiological sleep and wakefulness. The rabbit was selected because of the substantial amount of cortical tissue which it yields and for the readiness with which normal sleep can be induced (Sterner, 1963). As episodes of paradoxical sleep are of rather short duration in rabbits, and have never been detected in our experimental conditions, the data reported below refer to a comparison between wakefulness and synchronized or slow wave sleep.

In the first experiment, carried out some years ago (Vitale-Neugebauer, Giuditta, Vitale, & Giaquinto, 1970), rabbits were implanted under barbiturate anesthesia with four dural electrodes over the dorsal cortex. At the same time a small hole was drilled in the right frontal bone to expose the dura membrane, which was then covered with beeswax. After the operation the rabbit was left to recover in a large metal cage in the animal room. Unless otherwise noted, the rabbit was taken daily for the following 4-5 days to the experimental room where it remained undisturbed in a wooden box for 1-2 hours. The experimental room had sound-attenuated walls and was dimly lighted. This procedure was intended to accustom the animal to the experimental

environment and thereby facilitate the occurrence of sleep
(Sterner, 1963). Food pellets and water were always available ad libitum.

In the morning of the day of the experiment, electrodes
were connected to the EEG recorder and then a volume of
150 µl of neutralized ^{14}C-orotate (100 µC, 60 mC/mmole,
obtained from the Radiochemical Centre, Amersham, England)
was slowly injected under the dura membrane by means of a
hand-operated syringe with a curved needle. Recording was
continued during the period of incorporation, usually 60 or
105 min. Following this period the rabbit was disconnected
from the cable, stunned by a blow on the head and sacrificed.
The brain was quickly dissected out and placed in ice-cold
isotonic sucrose with a delay of 2-3 min from the time of
killing.

Only the dorsal cortex was taken for analysis. Before
RNA extraction it was freed from adhering membranes, large
blood vessels and clots. Total RNA was extracted by a phenol
method (Di Girolamo, Henshaw, & Hiatt, 1964) from an homogenate in 10 mM Tris-HCl buffer pH 7.4 previously treated with
RNAase-free DNAase. Purified RNA was centrifuged over a
5-20% sucrose gradient which, upon fractionation, was
analyzed for absorbance at 260 nm and for RNA radioactivity.

Two main families of newly synthesized high molecular
weight brain RNA were observed (Vesco & Giuditta, 1967). One
was characterized by a heterogeneous distribution in sucrose
gradients (heterogeneous RNA) and is presumed to be precursor
of mRNA. The other was characterized by discrete molecular
species sedimenting at 45S and lower sedimentation values
(preribosomal RNA). The distribution of radioactive RNA in
the gradient was compared in terms of the ratio of radioactivity present in the region between 28S and 50S over that
sedimenting more rapidly than 50S. The latter region
contained only heterogeneous RNA while the former consisted
of preribosomal RNA species contaminated by heterogeneous
RNA.

As shown in Figure 1, the values of this ratio of
radioactivities between the two regions varied as a function
of the percentage of EEG synchronization, decreasing with
increasing percentage of sleep. In awake animals the ratio
tended to be higher after 105 min than after 60 min. This
observation appeared to be in accord with an enhanced
synthesis of ribosomal RNA during wakefulness, although the
presence of heterogeneous RNA in the 28S-50S region did not
preclude the possibility of a shift in the relative amounts
of heterogeneous RNA present in the two regions of the
gradient. Irrespective of the molecular species involved,

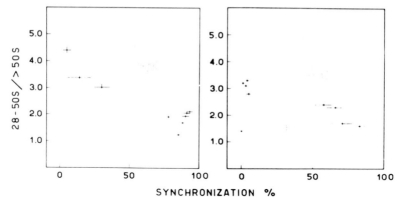

*Fig. 1.   Effect of percentage EEG synchronization on the
ratio of RNA radioactivity present in two regions of the
sedimentation gradient (28S - 50S and > 50S).   (A) Incorporation time 105 min, surgical procedures carried out shortly
before the experiment.   (B) Incorporation time 60 min, surgical procedures carried out 5 days before the experiment.
(From Vitale-Neugebauer et al., 1970.)*

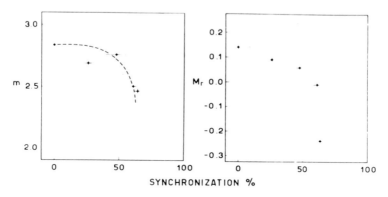

*Fig. 2.   Dependence of the median $\underline{m}$ and the moment $\underline{Mr}$
calculated with respect to the position of the 28S rRNA
component on the percentage of EEG synchronization.   (From
Vitale-Neugebauer et al., 1970.)*

the data indicated a pronounced difference in the types of RNA
synthesized during sleep and wakefulness.   This conclusion was
further confirmed by a more formal analysis of a homogeneous

group of rabbits in terms of the distribution of radioactive
RNA in the sucrose gradient. The values of the moments
calculated with respect to the position of the 28S rRNA
component and the median of the distribution showed a decrease
with increasing values of EEG synchronization (Figure 2).
Similarly, the moments $\mu2$ to $\mu10$ showed a non-random, consistent dependence on the percentage of synchronization parameter.
A reduced formation of rRNA during sleep would be consistent
with such a model.

In the effort to identify the cellular classes involved
in such a process a subsequent experiment (Giuditta, Rutigliano,
Traverso, & Vitale-Neugebauer, 1975) was designed to yield
information on the amount of radioactive RNA present in two
nuclear fractions separated by centrifugation of the cortex
homogenate over a discontinuous sucrose gradient. With this
procedure a class of large nuclei and a class of small nuclei
can rapidly and reproducibly be obtained in a state of high
purity (Giuditta, Rutigliano, Casola, & Romano, 1972). The
fraction containing large nuclei is mainly derived from large
neurons and astroglial cells while the other fraction contains
chiefly oligodendroglial nuclei. On the basis of work carried
out with rat brain it had previously been established that
following an intracerebral injection of ^{14}C-orotate large nuclei
contain progressively greater amounts of radioactive RNA than
small nuclei. The large nuclei attained within a few hours
values approximately 3 times greater than the small nuclei.
Several differences were also shown to occur in the kinetics
of formation of ribosomal RNA components in the two nuclear
fractions, indicating a more active rate of synthesis of rRNA
in the large nuclei (Giuditta et al., 1972). It should be
noted that with the short periods of incorporation used in
this study most of the newly synthesized RNA was still present
in the nuclear fraction (Balàzs & Cocks, 1967).

In the next experiment rabbits were prepared as in the
previous experiment except that a needle, bent at about 60
degrees, was implanted under the dura membrane and then fixed
to the skull with dental cement. After the operation the
rabbit was left to recover in the metal cage in the experimental room. The following morning, usually between 9 and 10
AM, while the animal was kept in a wooden box with only its
head protruding, the patency of the needle was checked and
a cannula containing 50 to 100 μl of neutralized ^{3}H-orotate
(100 μC, 600 mC/mmole, obtained from New England Nuclear,
Boston, Mass. USA) was connected to the needle. The cannula
was filled with isotonic saline which was separated from the
radioactive solution by a small air bubble. The other side
of the cannula was attached to a peristaltic pump. After

connecting the electrodes to the EEG recorder the rabbit was
returned to its cage and left undisturbed in the lighted and
silent room for several hours during which the electrical
activity of the cortex was intermittently monitored. At the
appropriate time, when the EEG record had shown the occurrence
of persistent synchronization, the solution of ^{3}H-orotate
was slowly injected by operating the peristaltic pump for a
period of 2-3 min. Incorporation was allowed to occur for
60 min. If the rabbit had to be kept awake mild acoustic
stimulation of different kinds and gentle handling were
applied whenever needed and to the minimum extent required.

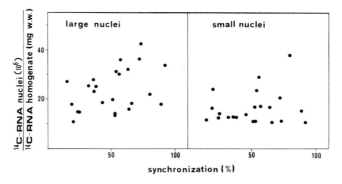

*Fig. 3. Content of radioactive RNA in the fractions of
large and small nuclei, as function of the percentage of
EEG synchronization. The values of nuclear radioactivity
(DPM per 10^6 nuclei) have been referred to the amount of
radioactive RNA present in 0.1 g tissue wet weight in order
to eliminate the variability due to the dose of ^{3}H-orotate
actually reaching neural cells.*

As shown in Figure 3, the amount of radioactive RNA per
nucleus increased markedly with increasing percentage of EEG
synchronization in the fraction containing large nuclei but
showed essentially no variation in the small nuclei. The
effect observed in the large nuclei was statistically significant ($P < 0.05$). On the average, the amount of radioactive
RNA per nucleus was more than double at 100% EEG synchronization as compared to that observed in the fully awake
condition. These results indicated that the rate of one or
more of the processes of synthesis, release or degradation of
nuclear RNA was influenced by the physiological state of the
cortex and moreover that the effect was limited to the class
of neural cells from which large nuclei were derived.

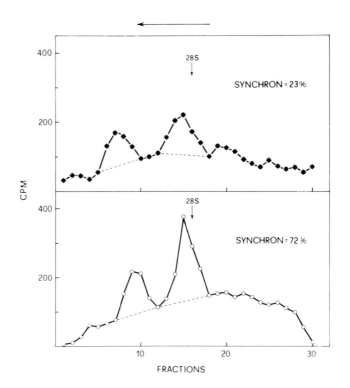

Fig. 4. Sedimentation patterns of radioactive RNA estracted from the fraction of large nuclei after a period of incorporation of one hour with ^3H-orotate. The arrow indicates the position of the 28S rRNA.

A separate experiment was performed in order to provide some understanding of the nature of the molecular species involved. In this experiment the RNA extracted from large nuclei after a period of incorporation of one hour was analyzed by centrifugation on a sucrose gradient. As shown in Figure 4, the overall pattern of distribution of radioactive RNA was similar at low and high values of EEG synchronization. These patterns show the occurrence of two main ribosomal peaks in the region of 45S and 32S superimposed on a background of heterogeneous RNAs. From the accepted model of rRNA synthesis in eukariotic cells it is known that the 45S species is the initial precursor from which the 32S component is derived. This molecule is, in turn, degraded to a mature 28S rRNA, which is eventually transported out of the nucleus to the surrounding cytoplasm (Attardi & Amaldi, 1970). In comparison with the 45S precursor molecule the relative amount of the 32S peak increased with increasing percentage of EEG synchronization (Figure 5).

The 32S peak was wider in rabbits experiencing low percentage of sleep, presumably because of the presence of a mature 28S rRNA component. The latter observation has been preliminarily confirmed by a computer analysis of nine distribution patterns of radioactive RNA. While in 3 out of 4 awake animals the 32S peak was wide enough to be fitted by two gaussian curves (one at the 28S position), in rabbits with synchronization values above 70%, only one gaussian curve could fit the experimental data.

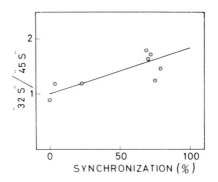

Fig. 5. Ratio of 32S to 45S radioactive peaks as function of percent of EEG synchronization.

These results suggest that, compared to wakefulness, during synchronized sleep, the process of maturation of rRNA slows down in cortical cells endowed with large nuclei. This view is in accord with the data on total RNA previously reported (Figure 1). On the other hand, the higher content of labelled 28S component present in the large nuclei during wakefulness might be explained by a reduced transfer of mature rRNA in the cytoplasm. A choice between these two alternatives should be determined by analysis of the radio-active RNA present in the cytoplasm of the same cells. Furthermore, it remains to be established whether the increase in labelled RNA detected in the large nuclei during sleep reflects solely a modification of rRNA processing or, in addition, a different turnover of heterogeneous RNA.

REFERENCES

Attardi, G., & Amaldi, F. The structure and synthesis of ribosomal RNA. *Annual Review of Biochemistry*, 1970, *39*, 183-226.

Balàzs, R., & Cocks, W. A. RNA metabolism in subcellular fractions of brain tissue. *Journal of Neurochemistry*, 1967, *14*, 1035-1055.

Di Girolamo, A., Henshaw, E. C., & Hiatt, H. H. Messenger ribonucleic acid in rat liver nuclei and cytoplasm. *Journal of Molecular Biology*, 1964, *8*, 479-488.

Giuditta, A., Rutigliano, B., Casola, L., & Romano, M. Biosynthesis of RNA in two nuclear classes separated from rat cerebral cortex. *Brain Research*, 1972, *46*, 313-328.

Giuditta, A., Rutigliano, B., Traverso, R., & Vitale-Neugebauer, A. Biosynthesis of RNA in rabbit cortex during sleep and wakefulness. In P. Levin & W. P. Koella (Eds.), *Sleep 1974*. Basel: Karger, 1975.

Sterner, N. Prövning av psykofarmaka med elektroencefalografi. 1. Studier av normala variationer i hjärnbarkens elektriska aktivitet hos vaken kanin. *Farmaceutisk Revy Sweden*, 1963, *62*, 121-132.

Vesco, C., & Giuditta, A. Pattern of RNA synthesis in rabbit brain. *Biochimica et Biophysica Acta*, 1967, *142*, 385-402.

Vitale-Neugebauer, A., Giuditta, A., Vitale, B., & Giaquinto, S. Pattern of RNA synthesis in rabbit cortex during sleep. *Journal of Neurochemistry*, 1970, *17*, 1263-1273.

INVESTIGATION OF THE ROLE OF PROTEINS IN REM SLEEP

R. R. DRUCKER-COLÍN

Departamento de Biología Experimental
Instituto de Biología
Universidad Nacional Autónoma de México
México 20, D. F., México

C. W. SPANIS

Department of Biology
University of San Diego
San Diego, California 92110 USA

J. A. ROJAS-RAMÍREZ

Departamento de Farmacología
Facultad de Medicina
Universidad Nacional Autónoma de México
México 20, D. F., México

At the turn of the century Legéndre and Pieron (1910, 1911, 1912) showed that when cerebrospinal fluid (CSF) was extracted from experimentally sleep deprived dogs, this fluid would induce drowsiness and sleep when injected into the fourth ventricle of non-sleep deprived dogs. On the basis of this work they suggested that during wakefulness there is an accumulation in the CSF of a "hypnotoxin" with sleep inducing properties.

Since then a few investigators have attempted to follow this line of work, with similar but more refined methods. Pappenheimer and his group have induced signs of sleep in cats and rats with CSF obtained from sleep deprived goats (Pappenheimer, Miller, & Goodrich, 1967). More recently, that group has reported that the sleep inducing factor is a low molecular weight (around 500) peptide (Fencl, Koski, & Pappenheimer, 1971; Pappenheimer, Fencl, Karnovsky, & Koski, 1974). Also in the last 15 years or so, Monnier and his group have extensively studied humoral transmission of sleep via the circulatory system. In these experiments the jugular of a donor rabbit is connected to the jugular vein of a recipient rabbit. Then the donor's medio-central intralaminary thalamus is stimulated at low frequencies. Such stimulation induces

synchronization of the cortical EEG or what Monnier calls
"orthodox delta sleep" in both the donor and the recipient
(Monnier, Koller, & Graber, 1963). Since the animals are
joined by the jugular vein, a sleep substance released into
the cerebral venous blood of the donor (as a result of
thalamic stimulation) is thought to penetrate the recipient's
brain over its heart, lung and carotid artery, thus showing
that sleep can be induced by blood-borne factors. Further
work showed that intravenous injections or intraventricular
infusion of dialyzates obtained from sleeping donor rabbits
induced sleep in the recipients (Monnier & Hosli, 1964, 1965;
Monnier & Hatt, 1970, 1971). More recently Monnier and
Schoenenberger (1974) have isolated from the dialyzates a low
molecular weight (around 700) polypeptide containing at least
7 amino acids, with powerful hypnogenic activity.
        We have in our laboratory taken a similar approach to the
study of the neurohumoral control of sleep. The main difference between our experiments and those of the above mentioned
authors is that we work directly within brain tissue. This
approach has been made possible by recent improvements in the
use of the "push-pull" cannula technique (Myers, 1974),
originally developed by Gaddum (1961). Since this technique
is not widely known we will make a brief description of its
major features. First of all, the "push-pull" cannula allows
one to make perfusions of specific brain areas in freely
moving conscious animals. The cannula system consists of a
17 gauge stainless steel guide tube implanted stereotaxically
in an area lying 5-7 mm above the brain area to be studied.
At this point in our preparations we also implant electrodes
which allow electrophysiological recordings of sleep and
wakefulness, i.e., cortical EEG, eye movements (EM) and
electromyogram (EMG). Following post-operative recovery, the
animals are placed in a cage where they can freely move, be
observed, and be recorded with a polygraph. At this point
the "push-pull" cannula is introduced through the guide tube
to a predetermined point corresponding to the area of desired
study, which in our case is the midbrain reticular formation
(MRF). The "push-pull" cannula consists of a 27 gauge inner
"push" stainless steel tube inserted into a 20 gauge outer
"pull" stainless steel tube. The cannula is connected through
polyethylene tubes to a pair of syringes driven by an infusion
withdrawal pump which insures equal inflow-outflow rates. The
"push" side is filled with commercial Ringer solution, and the
"pull" side collects substances presumably released into the
extracellular fluid in connection with physiological functions.
By means of this technique we have recently shown that perfusates obtained during sleep from the MRF of donor cats are

capable of inducing sleep when they are reperfused into the
homologous MRF of awake recipient cats (Drucker-Colín, Rojas-
Ramírez, Vera-Trueba, J., Monroy-Ayala, G., & Hernández-Peón,
R., 1970; Drucker-Colín, 1973; Rojas-Ramírez, 1974). These
effects are based on sleep latency decreases induced by the
sleep perfusate when compared to non-perfusions or Ringer
perfusions of the same recipient cats. From these experiments
it can be concluded that perfusates obtained from specific
brain sites appear to contain regulatory substances capable of
influencing ongoing behavior. This possibility has recently
been confirmed by Nagasaki, Iriki, Inove, and Uchizono (1974)
who have reported the existence of a sleep promoting substance
obtained from a brain stem homogenate of sleep deprived rats.

Having demonstrated that these perfusates contain sleep
modulating substances, we have made attempts to characterize
them biochemically. In an initial series of experiments we
analyzed the protein concentration of perfusates obtained from
the MRF of cats during sleep and wakefulness. It was found
that MRF perfusate contained proteins at concentrations ranging
from 23 to 206 μg/ml. Over a period of 21 hours a total of
about 2.0 mg of proteins was collected. Moreover the concentrations of proteins varied in a cyclic fashion, and as can be
seen from Figure 1, there appears to be a correlation between
the periods of peak increase of proteins and the periods of
greater time spent in REM sleep.

These cyclic changes in proteins do not appear to reflect
tissue damage or similar artifacts, since the amount of
soluble proteins in an area 4 to 5 times larger than the area
perfused was found to be less than 10% of the total proteins
obtained during the 21 hour perfusion period (Drucker-Colín,
Spanis, Cotman, & McGaugh, 1975). In view of the possibility
that the variations in levels of proteins in the perfusates
represent some active physiological process, and in view of
evidence suggesting a relationship between sleep states and
proteins, we compared the protein concentration of perfusates
obtained during wakefulness as opposed to those obtained during
REM sleep. Thus paired samples obtained from the same cat on
the same day were compared to each other. In 21 out of 23
paired samples, REM sleep was always associated with a greater
concentration of proteins in the MRF ($\bar{X}$ awake: 56. 3 μg/ml;
$\bar{X}$ REM: 124.9 μg/ml; $P < 0.001$)(Drucker-Colín & Spanis, 1975).
It must be pointed out, however, that the concentration of
proteins differed in different cats and also within the same
cat perfused on two occasions.

Polyacrylamide gel electrophoresis of the protein further
confirmed the remarkable fact that perfusates are associated
with increased levels of proteins. As can be seen from
Figure 2, it took up to 9 ml of awake perfusate to concentrate

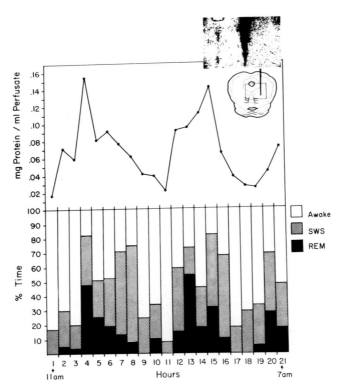

Fig. 1.   *Represents an experiment in which one cat was*
perfused during 21 continuous hours and whose sleep-wake cycle
was simultaneously monitored polygraphically.   Each point in
the upper part of the graph represents the total protein con-
tent in the perfusates within each hour.   The lower part repre-
sents the percent of time spent by the cat in wakefulness,
SWS and REM within each hour.   The diagrammatic inset of the
coronal section of the midbrain indicates the cannula place-
ment, and above the inset is a microphotograph of the area
squared off in the diagram of the midbrain.   Note the relative
correlation between increased percent time of REM sleep with
peaks of protein in perfusates.

an equivalent amount of proteins as that present in 1 ml of
REM perfusate. Although this ratio was not always so high,
the fact remains that in order to obtain similar protein
concentration as shown in REM, several mls of awake perfusate
are needed. Figure 2 further shows that there are no differences in protein bands in the gels when awake and REM perfusates are concentrated to equal protein volumes.

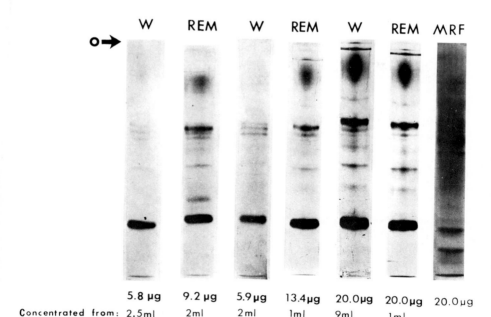

W   REM   W   REM   W   REM   MRF

5.8 µg   9.2 µg   5.9µg   13.4µg   20.0µg   20.0µg   20.0µg

Concentrated from: 2.5ml   2ml   2ml   1ml   9ml   1ml

Fig. 2. Polyacrylamide gels comparing awake perfusates (W) to REM perfusates from the Midbrain Reticular Formation (MRF). These gels show that when W and REM protein content from perfusates is brought to equal levels, no band differences can be detected. Note, however, that it takes several mls of awake perfusate to obtain the amount of protein found in 1 ml of REM. Note also differences from gel with soluble protein obtained from an MRF homogenate.

These results suggest that proteins are intimately related to the physiological processes regulating REM sleep. Furthermore, our results are in agreement with work from other laboratories which have demonstrated an important role for protein synthesis in sleep. For example, Bobillier, Sakai, Seguin, and Jouvet (1974) have reported that rats deprived of REM sleep show a decrease in protein synthesis.   In addition, it has been shown that during the recovery from inhibition of protein synthesis by cycloheximide, REM sleep is increased (Stern, Morgane, Panksepp, Zolovick, & Jalowiec, 1972).   In that paper the authors also reported that puromycin produced few changes in sleep, and as they suggested, this may be due to the fact that puromycin produces abnormal puromycin-polypeptide molecules (Nathans, 1964) which may be sensed by the brain as proteins. More recently, Pegram, Donaldson,

Hammond, Vaughan, and Bridgers (1974) and Pegram, Hamond, and
Bridgers (1973) have shown that cycloheximide in mice decreases
both the amount and the frequency of REM sleep, as well as
blocking REM rebound which normally occurs as a result of REM
sleep deprivation.

In our laboratory, we have also tested the effects of
protein synthesis inhibition on sleep (Drucker-Colín, Spanis,
Hunyadi, Sassin, & McGaugh, 1975). In these experiments we
followed for three hours the effects of anisomycin (5 mg/kg)
and growth hormone (GH)(0.1 mg/kg or 1.0 mg/kg) or a combination of both on sleep-wake patterns and whole brain proteins
in rats. As can be seen from Figure 3, anisomycin prevented
the appearance of REM sleep, while GH induced a dose-dependent
increase in REM as compared to saline controls. When GH and
anisomycin were given simultaneously, REM sleep times were
similar to controls.

When whole brain proteins were measured in animals with
similar treatments, it was found that GH alone produced a
slight but significant increase in whole brain proteins during
the second hour; anisomycin produced a decrease of proteins in
the first and second hour; while the combined treatment of GH
and anisomycin produced no changes (See Figure 4). Since GH
is an anabolic hormone which exerts important actions on
protein synthesis (Korner, 1965), our experiments may suggest
that GH increases REM sleep through its effect on proteins.
In addition, the fact that anisomycin decreased proteins as
well as REM sleep further supports this notion.

So far, we have merely described some biochemical events
related to sleep. At this point, we would like to describe
experiments which appear to relate REM sleep to processes of
neural excitability. It has recently been shown that the
administration of electroconvulsive shock (ECS) to cats (Cohen
& Dement, 1966; Kaelbling, Koski, & Hartwig, 1968) and humans
(Zarcone, Gulevich, & Dement, 1967) reduces REM sleep time.
Similar reductions in the number of sleep cycles and total
duration of REM sleep can be seen in patients with generalized
myoclonus or tonic seizures (Passouant & Cadilhac, 1970).
Conversely, rats deprived of REM sleep show a very significant
drop in ECS threshold (Cohen & Dement, 1965). REM deprivation
also increases brain excitability in epileptic patients (Pratt,
Mattson, Wikers, & Williams, 1968) and in non-epileptics
(Gunderson, Dunne, & Feher, 1973). The interaction between REM
sleep and brain excitability has further been demonstrated in
experiments which have shown that the daily administration of
ECS during sleep deprivation prevents the REM rebound which
occurs following such deprivation (Cohen, Duncan, & Dement,
1967).

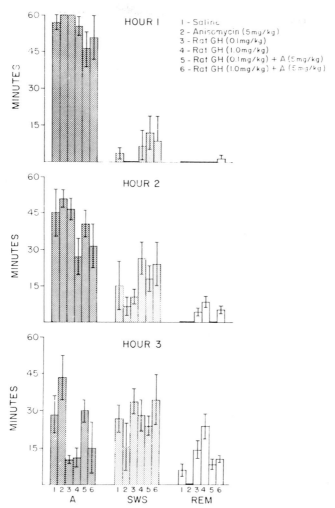

Fig. 3.   Histogram showing effects of two doses of
growth hormone (GH), one dose of anisomycin (A) or a combination of both on the sleep-wake cycle of rats during three
hours.   Note dose response increase of REM following GH
administration at hour 3, and inhibition of REM following A
throughout the three hours.   (N=4 in each group.)

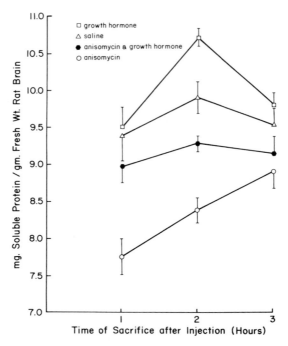

Fig. 4. Graph showing the effects of GH (1 mg/kg), anisomycin (5 mg/kg), or a combination of both, on soluble proteins of whole brain during each of three hours following their administration (N=10 at each point). The only significant differences in comparison to saline are GH at hour 2 and amysomycin at hours 1 and 2.

In related experiments, we demonstrated a number of years ago, (Satinoff, Drucker-Colín, & Hernández-Peón, 1971) that REM sleep deprivation induced changes in excitability levels of specific brain areas. In these studies, cats were implanted with bipolar electrodes in the pre-pyriform cortex and tetrapolar electrodes in the entorhinal cortex. Evoked potentials were recorded from the entorhinal cortex by applying a 1 per sec, 0.1 msec duration square wave pulse to the pre-pyriform cortex or to an area 1 mm away from the recording site. Voltage varied from cat to cat and was adjusted to the intensity which gave a stable response 100% of the time. The evoked potentials prior to sleep deprivation were then compared to those obtained during each of the 7 days of sleep deprivation and to those following one night of sleep. As can be seen in Figure 5, the amplitude of the evoked potentials increased as

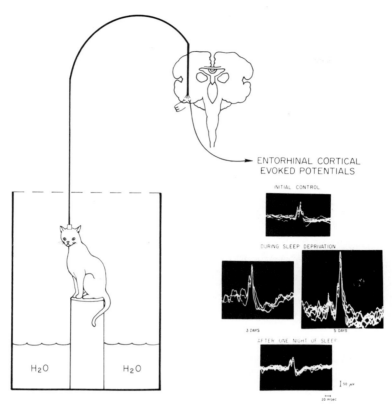

ENTORHINAL CORTICAL
EVOKED POTENTIALS

INITIAL CONTROL

DURING SLEEP DEPRIVATION

3 DAYS   5 DAYS

AFTER ONE NIGHT OF SLEEP

*Fig. 5. Illustrates the experimental arrangement whereby
a cat is deprived of sleep, and evoked potentials recorded.
Note how the amplitude of the evoked potentials increase as a
result of sleep deprivation and how they return to control
levels after 24 hours of sleep. (Modified from Satinoff,
Drucker-Colín, & Hernández-Peón, 1971.)*

REM deprivation progressed. The mean amplitude increased from
157% on the first day to 374% by the end of day seven. After
one night of sleep, amplitudes returned to control levels.
     Since the absence of REM sleep appears to increase
cerebral excitability, we carried out experiments attempting
to show the converse, namely that in the presence of REM
sleep, excitability can be decreased. Again in cats, we
implanted electrodes with a cannula adjacent to them in the
pyriform cortex. In addition, electrodes were implanted in
the bulbar reticular formation, in the neck muscles, orbit of
the eyes and Supra Sylvian cortex. Through the cannula,

microcrystals of strychnine were applied to the pyriform
cortex. The well known strychnine spikes appeared within a
few minutes and lasted at times for several hours. Throughout
the presence of strychnine spikes the animal's sleep-wake cycle
was monitored electroencephalographically. Upon the appearance of REM sleep the frequency of strychnine spikes was
remarkably reduced (Hernández-Peón & Drucker-Colín, 1970).

Since REM usually takes a good 50-60 minutes to appear in
any one cat (Drucker-Colín, 1973), it could be possible that
the decrease in spikes during REM sleep may have been the
result of a decreasing effectiveness of strychnine due merely
to time. This was discarded as a possibility since in general,
immediately upon awakening from REM, the frequency of strychnine
spikes increased. Nevertheless, in order to control for this
possibility, as well as to determine whether similar effects
could be found in another area of the brain, the hippocampus
was perfused with strychnine through a "push-pull" cannula.
A 250 µg/ml solution of strychnine was thus perfused, which
then induced very regular and continuous spikes. The regularity of spikes could be controlled by merely turning the perfusion system on or off. Figure 6 illustrates the recordings
of one cat. The upper traces show the regularity of the spikes
in the left hippocampus as a result of perfusion with strychnine. There is no effect of this procedure on the right hippocampus. The lower recording illustrates a period of time when
the cat fell into REM sleep. We can notice a dramatic fall of
both the frequency and amplitude of the spikes. Though not
shown here, the spike frequency and amplitude reverted back as
soon as the animal woke up.

These results are in agreement with clinical observations
which have described the presence or absence of REM as having
respectively inhibitory or facilitatory influences upon
seizures (Pompeiano, 1969; Daly, 1973) and furthermore points
towards the modulating influence of REM sleep upon ictal
processes. Moreover, proteins may play an important role upon
such modulation, in view of its increase during REM sleep.

Within this scheme it is conceivable to suggest a role of
REM sleep in processes of learning and memory, particularly
since Bloch and his colleagues have elegantly demonstrated a
post-learning enhancement of REM (Hennevin, Leconte, & Bloch,
1974; see also Bloch, this volume). This could perhaps be
integrated into a model as depicted in Figure 7.

In this model, in which we have borrowed from Dewan
(1970), Jouvet (1972), and Hartmann (1973), REM sleep is seen
as effecting the processes of storage of learned information
through neurotransmitters. Consolidation of short term memory,
thus leading to long term memory, is seen as being influenced

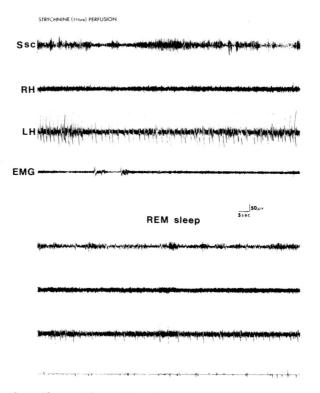

STRYCHNINE (250μg) PERFUSION

Ssc

RH

LH

EMG

REM sleep

50μv
5 sec

Fig. 6. Shows that REM sleep produces a decrease in
the frequency and amplitude of spikes produced by a 250 μg/ml
perfusion of the left hippocampus (LH). Note absence of any
effect on the right hippocampus (RH) which was simultaneously
perfused with Ringer. Ssc: Suprasylvian Cortex; EMG:
Electromyogram.

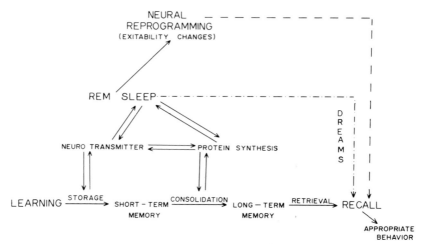

Fig. 7. *Scheme attempting to suggest a role for REM sleep in processes of learning and memory on the basis of our findings. See text for details.*

by REM sleep through its effect on protein synthesis. Simultaneously, since REM sleep appears to induce brain excitability changes, such changes may be seen as subserving neural reprogramming processes throughout the lifetime of the organism, thus permitting appropriate recall of learned material, and appropriate daily behavior. Finally, REM sleep as is well known, is accompanied by dreams. The content of dreams must in all likelihood be made up of information retrieved from long term memory. The disorganized pattern of dreams may be produced by the excitability changes in the neural circuitry during REM sleep.

ACKNOWLEDGMENT

Some of this work was carried out at the University of California, Irvine, under Fellowship Grant 72-552 from Foundation Fund for Research in Psychiatry to R. R. D.-C.

REFERENCES

Bobillier, P., Sakai, F., Seguin, S., & Jouvet, M. The effect of sleep deprivation upon *in vivo* and *in vitro* incorporation of tritiated amino acids into brain proteins in the rat at three different age levels. *Journal of Neurochemistry*, 1974, *22*, 23-31.

Cohen, H. B., & Dement, W. C. Sleep: Changes in threshold to electroconvulsive shock in rats after deprivation of paradoxical-phase. *Science*, 1965, *150*, 1318-1319.

Cohen, H. B., & Dement, W. C. Sleep: Suppression of rapid eye movement phase in the cat after electroconvulsive shock. *Science*, 1965, *154*, 1318-1319.

Cohen, H. B., Duncan, R. F., & Dement, W. C. Sleep: The effect of electroconvulsive shock in cats deprived of REM sleep. *Science*, 1966, *156*, 396-398.

Daly, D. C. Circadian cycles and seizures. In *Epilepsy: Its Phenomena in Man* (UCLA Forum in Medical Sciences, No. 17). New York: Academic Press, 1973.

Dewan, E. M. The programming "P" hypotheses for REM sleep. In F. Hartmann (Ed.), *Sleep and Dreaming* (International Psychiatry Clinics Series, Vol. 7), 1970.

Drucker-Colín, R. R. Crossed perfusion of a sleep inducing brain tissue substance in conscious cats. *Brain Research*, 1973, *56*, 123-134.

Drucker-Colín, R. R., Rojas-Ramírez, J. A., Vera-Trueba, J., Monroy-Ayala, G., & Hernández-Peón, R. Effect of crossed-perfusion of the midbrain reticular formation upon sleep. *Brain Research*, 1970, *23*, 269-273.

Drucker-Colín, R. R., & Spanis, C. W. Neurohumoral correlates of sleep: Increase of proteins during rapid eye movement sleep. *Experientia*, 1975, *31*, 551-552.

Drucker-Colín, R. R., Spanis, C. W., Cotman, C. W., & McGaugh, J. L. Changes in protein in perfusates of freely moving cats: Relation to behavioral state. *Science*, 1975, *187*, 963-965.

Drucker-Colín, R. R., Spanis, C. W., Hunyadi, J., Sassin, J. F., & McGaugh, J. L. Growth hormone effects on sleep and wakefulness in the rat. *Neuroendocrinology,* 1975, *18,* 1-8.

Fencl, V., Koski, G., & Pappenheimer, J. R. Factors in cerebrospinal fluid from goats that affect sleep and activity in rats. *Journal of Physiology,* 1971, *216,* 565-589.

Gaddum, J. H. Push-pull cannulae. *Journal of Physiology,* 1961, *155,* 1P-2P.

Gunderson, C. H., Dunne, P. B., & Feher, T. L. Sleep deprivation seizures. *Neurology,* 1973, *23,* 678-686.

Hartmann, E. *The Functions of Sleep*. New Haven: The Yale University Press, 1973.

Hennevin, E., Leconte, P., & Bloch, V. Augmentation du sommeil paradoxal provoquée par l'acquisition, l'extinction et la reacquisition d'un apprentissage a renforcement positif. *Brain Research,* 1974, *70,* 43-54.

Hernández-Peón, R., & Drucker-Colín, R. R. A neuronographic study of corticobulbar hypnogenic pathways. *Physiology and Behavior,* 1970, *5,* 721-725.

Jouvet, M. The role of monoamines and acetylcholine in the regulation of the sleep-waking cycle. *Ergebnisse der Physiologie, Biologischen Chemie, und Experimentellen Pharmakologie,* 1972, *64,* 166-307.

Kaelbling, R., Koski, E. G., & Hartwig, C. D. Reduction of rapid eye movement sleep phase in cats after electroconvulsions. *Psychophysiology,* 1968, *4,* 381.

Korner, A. Growth hormone control of biosynthesis of protein and ribonucleic acid. *Recent Progress in Hormone Research,* 1965, *21,* 205-238.

Legendre, R., & Pieron, H. Le probleme de facteurs du sommeil resultants d'injections vasculaires et intra-cerebrales des liquides insommiques. *Comptes Rendus des Seances de la Societe de Biologie* (Paris), 1910, *68,* 1077-1079.

Legendre, R., & Pieron, H. Du developpement au cours de l'insommie experimental, des proprietes hypnotoxiques des hummeurs en relation avec le besoin croissant de sommeil. *Comptes Rendus des Seances de la Societe de Biologie* (Paris), 1911, *70*, 190-192.

Legendre, R., & Pieron, H. De la propriete hypnotoxiques des hummeurs developpées au cours d'une veille prolongée. *Comptes Rendus des Seances de la Societe de Biologie* (Paris), 1912, *72*, 210-212.

Monnier, M., & Hatt, A. M. Intraventricular infusions in acute and chronic rabbits. Application of the stereo- taxic method of Monnier and Gongloff. *Pfluegers Archiv fuer Physiology*, 1970, *317*, 268-280.

Monnier, M., & Hatt, A. M. Humoral transmission of sleep. V. New evidence from productions of pure sleep hemodialysate. *Pfluegers Archiv fuer Physiology*, 1971, *329*, 231-243.

Monnier, M., & Hosli, L. Dialysis of sleep and waking factors in blood of the rabbit. *Science,* 1964, *146*, 796-798.

Monnier, M., & Hosli, L. Humoral transmission of sleep and wakefulness. II. Memodialysis of a sleep inducing humor during stimulation of the thalamic somnogenic area. *Pfluegers Archiv fuer Physiology*, 1965, *282*, 60-75.

Monnier, M., Koller, T., & Graber, S. Humoral influences of induced sleep and arousal upon electrical brain activity of animals with crossed circulation. *Experimental Neurology*, 1963, *8*, 264-277.

Monnier, M., & Schoenenberger, G. A. Neuro-humoral coding of sleep by the physiological sleep factor delta. In R. D. Myers & R. R. Drucker-Colín (Eds.), *Neurohumoral Coding of Brain Function*. New York: Plenum Press, 1974.

Myers, R. D. *Handbook of Drug and Chemical Stimulation of the Brain*. New York: Van Norstrand Reinhold, 1974.

Nagasaki, H., Iriki, M., Inove, S. & Uchizono, K. The presence of a sleep-promoting material in the brain of sleep-deprived rats. *Proceedings of the Japanese Academy*, 1974, *50*, 241-246.

Nathans, D.   Puromycin inhibition of protein synthesis: Incorporation of puromycin into peptide chains. *Proceedings of the National Academy of Science* (USA), 1964, *51*, 585-592.

Pappenheimer, J. R., Miller, J. B., & Goodrich, C. A.   Sleep-promoting effects of cerebrospinal fluid from sleep-deprived goats. *Proceedings of the National Academy of Science* (USA), 1967, *58*, 513-517.

Pappenheimer, J. R., Fencl, V., Karnovsky, M. L., & Koski, G.   Peptides in cerebrospinal fluid and their relation to sleep and activity. In F. Plum (Ed.), *Brain Dysfunction in Metabolic Disorders*. New York: Raven Press, 1974.

Passouant, P., & Cadilhac, J.   Decharges epileptiques et sommeil. In E. Nidermeyer (Ed.), *Modern Problems of Pharmacopsychiatry* (Vol. 4). Basel: Karger, 1970.

Pegram, V., Donaldson, D., Hammond, S., Vaughn, W., & Bridgers, W.   The effects of protein synthesis inhibition on REM rebound following selective sleep deprivation and drug withdrawal. *Proceedings of the Association for the Physiological Study of Sleep,* San Diego, 1974.

Pegram, V., Hamond, D., & Bridgers, W.   The effects of protein synthesis inhibition in sleep in mice. *Behavioral Biology,* 1973, *9*, 377-382.

Pompeiano, O.   Sleep mechanisms. In H. H. Jasper, A. Ward, & A. Pope (Eds.), *Basic Mechanisms of the Epilepsies*. Boston: Little, Brown, 1969.

Pratt, K. L., Mattson, R. H., Wikers, N. J., & Williams, R.   EEG activation of epileptics following sleep deprivation: A prospective study of 114 cases. *Electroencephalography and Clinical Neurophysiology,* 1968, *24*, 11-19.

Rojas-Ramírez, J. A.   Modificación de los estados de vigilia y de sueño mediante la técnica de perfusión cerebral localizada. *Resumenes del Congreso Medico* (300 Aniversario Instituto Mexicano de Seguridad Social), 1974.

Satinoff, E., Drucker-Colín, R. R., & Hernández-Peón, R.
    Paleocortical excitability and sensory filtering during
    REM sleep deprivation. *Physiology and Behavior,* 1971,
    7, 103-106.

Stern, W. C., Morgane, P. J., Panksepp, J., Zolovick, A. J.,
    & Jalowiec, J. E. Elevation of REM sleep following
    inhibition of protein synthesis. *Brain Research,* 1972,
    47, 254-258.

Zarcone, V., Gulevich, G., & Dement, W. C. Sleep and
    electroconvulsive therapy. *Archives of General Psychiatry,*
    1967, *16,* 567-577.

CHRONIC CANNULATION AND PERFUSION OF CEREBRAL VENTRICLES IN CATS: THE STUDY OF CEREBROSPINAL FLUID DURING SLEEP AND WAKEFULNESS

XAVIER LOZOYA and XAVIER VELAZQUEZ

Division of Neurophysiology
Scientific Research Department
National Medical Center
Instituto Mexicano del Seguro Social
México, D.F., México

The first attempt to implicate cerebrospinal fluid (CSF) in the regulation of sleep function was done by Legendre and Pieron (1910, 1913) at the beginning of this century. They obtained cisternal CSF from a sleep deprived dog and injected it into the ventricular system of another dog, which subsequently fell asleep. These experiments were severely criticized. With the advent of the electroencephalogram (EEG) these investigations were repeated and the classical work of Legendre and Pieron was confirmed, thus developing the theory of "hypnotoxin" (Bouckaert & Leusen, 1949; Pieron, 1913; Schnedorf & Ivy, 1939).

Recently several studies have appeared that approached the same question using different techniques developed for the study of CSF and its possible relation with sleep processes (Borton, Bligh, & Sharman, 1968; Fencl, Koski, & Pappenheimer, 1971; Levin, Nogueira, & Garcia-Argiz, 1966; Lozoya, Velasco, Estrada, & Velazquez, 1972; Marks & Rodnight, 1972; Ringle & Herndon, 1969).

Pappenheimer's group has provided new advances (Pappenheimer, Heisey, Jordan, & Downer, 1962; Pappenheimer, Miller, & Goodrich, 1967; Goodrich, Greehey, Miller, & Pappenheimer, 1969). By injecting perfusate obtained from sleep deprived goats into the cerebral ventricles of rats and found that two different substances, factor "S" and factor "E", would cause an increase in the amount of sleep

and an increase in motor activity. Feldberg, Myers, and
Veale (1970) demonstrated a method for regional perfusion of
cerebral ventricles, suggesting that some regions have
specific permeability for different substances.
     All of these findings reported above suggest the
presence of many physiologically active substances and neurotransmitters in CSF, and apparently confirm the initial
findings of Pieron (1913) and implicate the CSF in brain
function (Borton, Bligh et al., 1968; Hilton & Schain, 1961;
Knigge, 1964; Moir, Ashcroft, Crawford, Eddleston, & Guldberg,
1970; Southern & Christoff, 1962).
     A common technical difficulty has been keeping the
preparation asleep while sampling the CSF. It is also
necessary to simultaneously evaluate the EEG and the behavior
of the animal, as well as other parameters.
     In the present paper a method for chronic perfusion of
the ventricular system in cats during sleep and wakefulness
is reported. This method allows sampling of ventricular CSF,
while the animal is asleep and simultaneously provides a
quantitative evaluation of EEG activity.
     In this study, 18 male cats weighing between 2.5 - 3.0 Kg
were used. Sterile operations were performed under Nembutal
(10 mg/kg) anesthesia by cutting the scalp and retracting
the underlying muscles and tissue to expose the skull from
the frontal sinus to the first vertebral body. Trepanations
of the bone above the frontal and parietal cortex were made
in order that stainless steel screw electrodes for recording
the EEG could be implanted. A reference screw was placed
above the frontal sinus. Stainless steel cannulae (see
Figure 1) were placed into the anterior horn (A=13, L=3, H=7)
of the lateral ventricle using the stereotaxic coordinates
of Snyder and Niemer (1961). The technique reported by
Feldberg (1970) was used to test whether or not the cannula
was in the lateral ventricle. Another stainless steel
cannula was placed into the cisterna magna. In order to
place this cannula a furrow was drilled caudally from the
occipital crest through the bone and a hole was placed 3 mm
above the insertion of the occipito-atlantoid membrane. The
presence of the cannula into the cisterna magna was verified
by the extraction of CSF. Both cannulae were fixed in dental
cement to a plastic skullcap previously screwed in the bone
(Velasco, 1968). Stainless steel screws were also implanted
to record eye movements (EOG) and tungsten wire electrodes
were placed in the neck to record muscular tonus (EMG). All
the electrodes were soldered to a connector placed over the
skullcap (see Figure 2). When the connector and cannulae were
fixed, a ventriculography was performed to confirm the patency

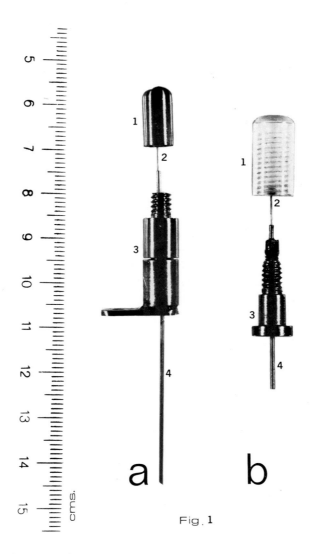

Fig. 1

Fig. 1. a) Cisternal cannula: 1 – plug; 2 – stiletto;
3 – support; 4 – needle tubing #21. b) Ventricular cannula:
1 – acrylic plug; 2 – stiletto; 3 – support; 4 – needle
tubing #23.

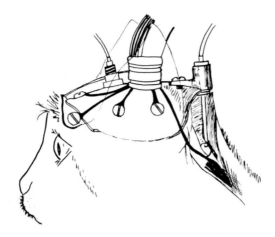

Fig. 2. Schematic representation of the complete implantation.

of the system (see Figure 3). For the next 4 days following surgery, daily extractions of CSF were performed. On the 5th day, a control EEG was recorded sometime during an 8 hour period, between 0900 - 1700 hrs. This permitted evaluation of baseline EEG characteristics and the general behavior of

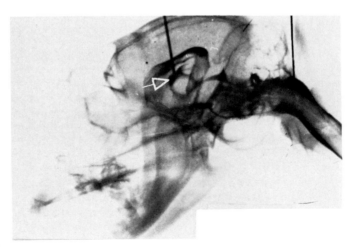

Fig. 3. Ventriculography showing the position of both cannulae and the permeability of the perfusion system.

each animal while it was in the sound attenuated cage. Rectal
electrodes permitted a continuous monitoring of the animal's
temperature.

The EEG, EOG, and EMG activity were recorded with the aid
of a polygraph (Grass Model 6). The EEG activity of frontal
derivations was recorded utilizing a frequency band analyzer
(Ahrend Van Gogh), equipped with four band-pass filters
(delta 0.8-4.0 Hz, theta 4.0-7.4 Hz, alpha 7.4-13.0 Hz, beta
13.0-26.0 Hz). The filtered signal from each band was integrated at one minute intervals in an Ahrend Van Gogh integra-
tor-plotter Model 2), which quantified and profiled the
different EEG bands during the 8 hour recording period (see
Figure 4).

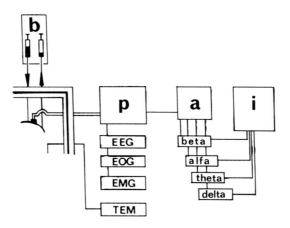

*Fig. 4. Diagram of recording procedure during ventri-
culo-cisternal perfusion. b - Infusion-withdrawal pump.
P - polygraph: 1) EEG - electroencephalogram; 2) EOG - eye
movements; 3) EMG - electromyogram; 4) TEM - rectal temperature. a - Frequency band analyzer with respective filters.
i - Integrator.*

The cats were divided into three groups, receiving (1)
artificial CSF[1], (2) 0.9% saline solution, and (3) distilled
water. The perfusion procedure utilized a Harvard infusion
pump, which connected the injection syringe to the ventricular
cannula and the withdrawal syringe to the cisternal cannula.
Perfusions were practiced by varying the pump's speed. A 10%
luxol solution was injected to check the patency of the
cannulae and to check for possible damage to the ventricular
cavities.

It was found that with the type of cannula used for this study the average time that the cannula remained patent was about 18 to 20 days. After this time, in most cases a definite obstruction of the cisternal cannulae occurred. This obstruction was due to a fibrous tissue formation at the tip of the cannula impeding the CSF outflow during perfusion. In such cases the problem was detected during the first 3 minutes of perfusion and changes in the EEG noted during these sessions were probably due to a sudden increase in intracranial pressure. Ventricular cannulae never became occluded.

Histological studies demonstrate that the perfusion fluid passed through the ventricular system toward the cisterna magna. In some cases the dye was found in the subarachnoid cortical space and part of the cervical column.

If the sound attenuation and temperature conditions remained constant and comfortable, the animals would fall asleep spontaneously. The EEG records showed clear periods of slow wave sleep (SWS) and fast wave sleep (FWS). This was clearly evident in the EEG frequency band analyses records (see Figure 5). It is interesting to note the apparent cyclicity of these EEG events, in particular, the length of the SWS periods.

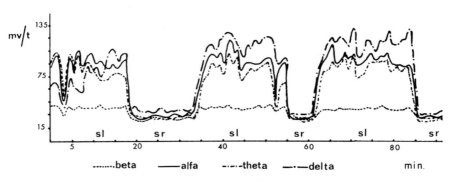

Fig. 5. *Profile of quantified EEG activity under control conditions. SL - Slow wave sleep; SR - Fast wave sleep.*

These experiments confirmed our preliminary observations (Lozoya et al., 1972) that an adequate perfusion speed was about 0.05-0.1 ml/min. At this perfusion speed a total substitution of ventricular CSF occurred during the first 15-20 minutes.

Any change in the speed of perfusion was reflected in the behavior of the animals which salivated or defecated. These are signs of increased intracranial pressure. Moreover, in such cases fast EEG activity was suddenly depressed and was followed by an increase in delta activity (see Figure 6).

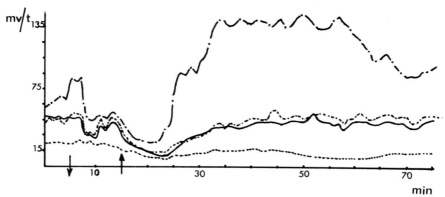

Fig. 6. EEG activity produced by blockade of perfusion system. The arrows indicate the beginning and the end of perfusion.

Perfusion with 0.9% saline solution produced an increase in body temperature followed by EEG synchrony, with the disappearance of the typical sleep pattern recorded during control situations. Although the animal seemed to be asleep, the EEG did not exactly correspond to the spontaneous sleep reported above (see Figure 7).

If distilled water was perfused through the ventricular system, it produced dramatic changes in behavior: vomiting, salivation, circling, and general excitement, followed by permanent desynchrony with a predominance of fast activity while the perfusion lasted (see Figure 8). Perfusion with distilled water produced changes in behavior which were related to the hemorrhage produced in the periventricular tissue as a result of the osmotic shock.

Perfusion with artificial CSF produced no changes in either EEG activity or behavior and a normal sleep pattern was present during and after the sampling of the ventricular fluid (see Figure 9). The artificial CSF seemed to be the best perfusion fluid, because no changes in behavior or EEG activity were detected, and the sleep pattern remained unaltered. This method is proposed as a possible technical

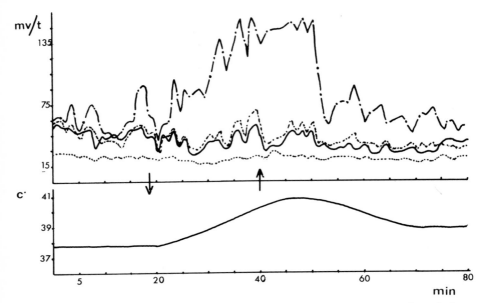

Fig. 7. EEG activity and rectal temperature produced by the perfusion of saline solution (0.9%). The arrows indicate the beginning and the end of ventriculo-cisternal perfusion.

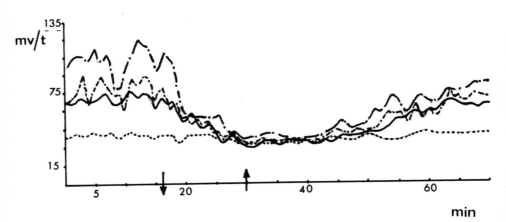

Fig. 8. EEG activity produced by perfusion of distilled water. The arrows indicate the beginning and end of ventri-culo-cisternal perfusion.

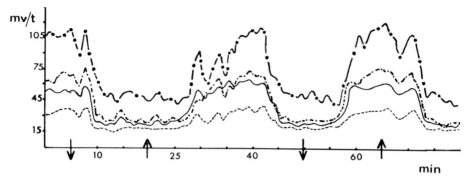

Fig. 9.   EEG activity during perfusion with artifical CSF. Sleep cycles did not suffer any alteration during perfusion time. The arrows indicate the beginning and end of perfusion.

approach to neurochemical study of the ventricular CSF during different sleep states.

Although ventriculo-cisternal perfusion is widely used in experimental physiology, a quantitative correlation of electrophysiological parameters and behavior, during perfusion of CSF had not been reported before. From the present work it is suggested that the ventriculo-cisternal perfusion is a useful technique for sampling of CSF during sleep and wakefulness. The perfusion's speed and chemical characteristics of the fluid are critical aspects of the described approach. The most important contribution lies in the quantitative evaluation of the EEG activity during this procedure, because frequently sleep effects can be attributed to abnormal situations related to increased intracranial pressure. Because a synchronized EEG pattern is observed does not mean that the animal is asleep.

Finally, the increase of body temperature produced by the perfusion of 0.9% NaCl solution has been reported before by Feldberg et al. (1970). We think that our described method could be used to further elucidate the neurohumoral mechanisms related to temperature regulation where ventricular ionic content seems to play an important role.

FOOTNOTE

[1]PO_4 Na_2 - 42.6 mg/l; $MgCl_2$ H_2O - 122.0 mg/l; NaCl
7580 mg/l; $CaCl_2$ $2H_2O$ - 161.6 mg/l; PH - 7.3 prepared by UME,
S.A. Laboratories, México.

REFERENCES

Borton, A. J., Bligh, J., & Sharman, D. F. Improved tech-
    niques for the chronic cannulation of the lateral
    cerebral ventricle and the cisterna magna of the Welsh
    Mountain Sheep. *Proceedings of the Physiological
    Society,* 1968.

Bouckaert, J. J., & Leusen, I. Technique por l'etude des
    influences directes du liquide céfalo-rachidien sur les
    centres nerveus superieure. *Experientia,* 1949, *5,*
    452-457.

Feldberg, W., Myers, R. D., & Veale, W. L. Perfusion from
    cerebral ventricles to cisterna magna in the
    unanesthetized cats. Effect of calcium on body tempera-
    ture. *Journal of Physiology,* 1970, *207,* 403-408.

Fencl, V., Koski, G., & Pappenheimer, J.R. Factors in
    cerebrospinal fluid from goats that affect sleep and
    activity in rats. *Journal of Physiology,* 1971, *26,*
    565-567.

Goodrich, C. A., Greehey, B., Miller, T. B., & Pappenheimer,
    J. R. Cerebral ventricular infusions in unrestrained
    rats. *Journal of Applied Physiology,* 1969, *26,* 137-139.

Hilton, S. M., & Schain, R. J. A search for pharmacologically
    active substances in fluid from cerebral ventricles.
    Proceedings of the Physiological Society, 1961.

Knigge, K. M. Role of the ventricular system in neuroendo-
    crine processes. In P. Seeman & G. M. Brown (Eds.),
    Frontiers in Neurology and Neuroscience Research.
    Toronto: University of Toronto Press, 1974.

Legendre, R., & Piéron, H. Des résultats histo-physiologiques
    de l'injection intra-occipito-atlantoidienne des liquides
    insomniques. *Comptes Rendus Societé Seantifique du
    Biologie,* 1910, *68,* 1108-1112.

Legendre, R., & Piéron, H. Recherches sur le besoin de sommeil consécutif a une veille prolongée. *Zeitung Allgemein Physiologie,* 1913, *14,* 235-238.

Levin, E., Nogueira, C. J., & García-Argiz, C. A. Ventriculo-cisternal perfusion of amino acids in cat brain. *Journal of Neurochemistry,* 1966, *13,* 761-764.

Lozoya, X., Velasco, M., Estrada, F., & Velázquez, X. *Mecanismos neurohumorales que regulan los estados de sincronización electrocortical. Archivos de Investigación Médica* (México), 1972, *3,* 91-96.

Marks, N., & Rodnight, R. *Research Methods in Neurochemistry.* New York: Plenum Press, 1972.

Moir, A. T. B., Ashcroft, G. W., Crawford, T. B. B., Eccleston, D., & Guldberg, H. C. Cerebral metabolites in cerebrospinal fluid as a biochemical approach to the brain. *Brain,* 1970, *93,* 357-361.

Pappenheimer, J. R., Heisey, S. R., Jordan, E. F., & Downer, J. C. Perfusion of the cerebral ventricular system in unanesthetized goats. *American Journal of Physiology,* 1962, *203,* 763-765.

Pappenheimer, J. R., Miller, T. B., & Goodrich, C. A. Sleep-promoting effects of cerebrospinal fluid from sleep-deprived goats. *Proceedings of the National Academy of Sciences,* 1967, *58,* 513-515.

Piéron, H. *Le Probleme Physiologique du Sommeil.* Paris: Masson, 1913.

Ringle, D. A., & Herndon, B. L. Effects on rats of CSF from sleep deprived rabbits. *Pfluegers Archiv Fuer Physiology,* 1969, *306,* 320-321.

Schnedorf, J. G., & Ivy, A. C. An examination of the hypno-toxin theory of sleep. *American Journal of Physiology,* 1939, *125,* 491-496.

Snider, R. S., & Niemer, W. T. *A Stereotaxic Atlas of the Cat Brain.* Chicago: The University of Chicago Press, 1961.

HYPOTHALAMO-NEUROHYPOPHYSEAL HORMONE EFFECTS ON MEMORY AND RELATED FUNCTIONS IN THE RAT

B. BOHUS, TJ. B. VAN WIMERSMA GREIDANUS,
I. URBAN, and D. DE WIED

Rudolf Magnus Institute for Pharmacology
University of Utrecht
Utrecht, The Netherlands

More than thirty years ago it was suggested that stimuli which affect emotionality provoke the release of vasopressin (antidiuretic hormone) from the posterior lobe of the pituitary gland (Rydin & Verney, 1938; O'Connor & Verney, 1945; Abrahams & Pickford, 1954). Although numerous observations demonstrated the homeostatic role of antidiuretic hormone (ADH) during behavioral adaptation (Corson & Corson, 1967; Miller, Dicara, & Wolf, 1968) the concept that the pituitary gland affects brain functions and modulates adaptive behavior through "neuropeptides" originating from this gland (de Wied, 1969) has recently become rather widely accepted.

The aim of this paper is to review some basic data on the behavioral influence of vasopressin-like neuropeptides and to describe a number of recent observations on the role of these peptides in behavioral and autonomic adaptation within the framework of the hypothesis that vasopressin and its analogues influence memory processes.

The possibility that the pituitary gland might be involved in acquisition, consolidation and maintenance of learned behavior was first suggested by observations of partially and fully hypophysectomized rats. Whereas the extirpation of the anterior pituitary or the whole gland leads to an impairment in acquisition of a shuttle box avoidance response (de Wied, 1964), the removal of the posterior pituitary does not materially affect acquisition, but interferes with the maintenance of a similar kind of conditioned response and leads to facilitation of extinction. These abnormalities could be readily reduced by treatment with various pituitary hormones such as adrenocorticotrophic hormone (ACTH), vasopressin and even with melanocyte stimulating hormone (MSH)

(de Wied), 1965). It subsequently appeared that fragments of
these peptides which are practically devoid of classical
endocrine target organ effects exhibit full or even potenti-
ated effects on avoidance behavior (de Wied, 1969; Lande,
Witter, & de Wied, 1971).

As mentioned before, administration of lysine vasopressin
(LVP) normalizes the extinction behavior of posterior lobec-
tomized rats but also improves the impaired acquisition
behavior of hypophysectomized rats (Fig. 1). It is noteworthy
that the influence of LVP on the behavioral performance of
hypophysectomized rats lasts after the discontinuation of the
treatment in contrast to ACTH analogues which have a short
term effect, disappearing after the treatment is stopped
(Bohus, Gispen, & de Wied, 1973). Accordingly, the behavioral
effect of vasopressin is of a long term nature and extends
behond the actual presence of the peptide in the body.

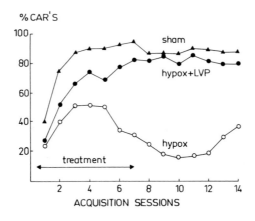

*Fig. 1. The effect of lysine vasopressin (LVP) on the
acquisition of a shuttle box avoidance response in hypophysectomized rats. LVP (1 μg/rat) was administered subcutaneously 1 hr prior to the first 7 acquisition sessions. Hypophysectomized (Hypox) and sham-operated (Sham) rats treated
with saline served as controls. 16 rats per group.*

In intact rats, vasopressin may affect acquisition of an
avoidance response, but its influence is not easily determined, probably due to the insensitivity of the measure.
Extinction of an avoidance response is, however, markedly
affected by vasopressin and vasopressin analogues. These

peptides increase resistance to extinction. As in hypophysectomized rats, vasopressin-like peptides exert a long term
effect on the maintenance of active avoidance responses.
Administration of the posterior pituitary principle,
pitressin, results in a long term maintenance of conditioned
avoidance behavior lasting for weeks after treatment with the
peptide. These observations led to the suggestion that posterior pituitary peptides may influence long term memory
processes (de Wied & Bohus, 1966). Later studies have indicated that the behaviorally active principle which elicits
this long term effect is vasopressin (de Wied, 1971). Both
LVP and desglycinamide lysine vasopressin (DG-LVP) normalized
avoidance acquisition of hypophysectomized rats (Lande,
Witter, & de Wied, 1971) and resulted in a long term resistance to extinction of an active avoidance response
(de Wied, Bohus, & van Wimersma Greidanus, 1974). DG-LVP is
an analogue of vasopressin which was isolated from hog pituitary material and is practically devoid of pressor and antidiuretic activities (de Wied, Greven, Lande, and Witter,
1972). Accordingly, the long term behavioral effect of the
peptide is independent of vasopressor or antidiuretic
functions.

Although the influence of vasopressin analogues is of a
long term nature, the behavioral effects are specific for the
response which is learned or executed under vasopressin
influence. The maximal effect on avoidance behavior was
found when the peptide was given 1 hr prior to, or immediately after, training. The peptide was much less effective when
the treatment-training or the training-treatment period
lasted longer than 3 hr (de Wied, 1971; Ader & de Wied,
1972). The specificity of the behavioral effect of vasopressin was demonstrated by experiments in which the same
rats were trained in 2 avoidance situations 6 hr apart: in a
pole jumping active avoidance test in the morning and in a
step-through passive avoidance situation in the afternoon or
vice versa (Bohus, Ader, & de Wied, 1972). Resistance to
extinction was only seen in that situation where the training
occurred in the morning, 1 hr after administration of the
peptide (Fig. 2). No evidence of generalization or transfer
of the effects of vasopressin from one behavioral situation
to the other (from active to passive avoidance or vice versa)
was obtained even though both behavioral responses were similarly motivated, presumably by the fear elicited by painful
electric shock.

Attempts to demonstrate behavioral effects of vasopressin analogues in other than fear-motivated situations were
not successful. Garrud, Gray, and de Wied (1974) failed to

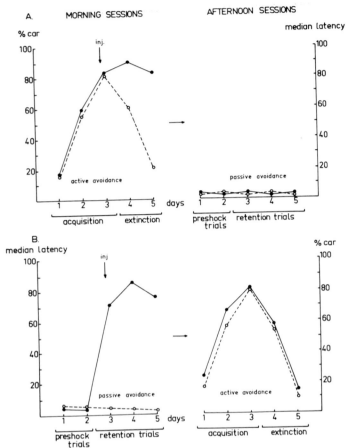

Fig. 2.   *Effects of a single injection of lysine vaso-*
pressin (LVP) on active and passive avoidance behavior. The
rats were trained in a pole jumping avoidance in the morning
session, then in a step-through passive avoidance in the
afternoon (A, upper figure), or in a passive avoidance in the
morning and an active avoidance in the afternoon (B, lower
figure). The arrows indicate the time of injection of LVP
(1 μg/rat, s.c.; solid lines) or saline (broken lines) (from
Bohus et al., 1972).

observe an effect of DG-LVP on the extinction of a straight
runway approach response in food-deprived rats. Although
DG-LVP is practically devoid of antidiuretic activity, an

interaction between the peptide, hunger drive and water
metabolism causing the failure to establish a behavioral
effect could not be excluded. Furthermore, a straight runway
might not be the proper situation to study the influence of a
substance which is supposed to affect memory processes.
Therefore, the influence of DG-LVP on a sexually motivated
approach response was investigated in a T-maze using male
rats (Bohus, 1976). A higher percentage of male rats
receiving DG-LVP immediately after each acquisition session
chose the correct arm of the T-maze in order to reach the
receptive female goal rat than did the controls. Also in
this situation DG-LVP exhibited a long term effect which
extended beyond the treatment period; DG-LVP-treated rats
displayed more correct choices than the controls after
discontinuation of the treatment (Table 1). It was also

TABLE 1

EFFECTS OF DESGLYCINAMIDE LYSINE VASOPRESSIN (DG-LVP) ON THE
SEXUALLY MOTIVATED CHOICE BEHAVIOR OF MALE RATS IN A T-MAZE[a]

Treatment	n	Acquisition		Retention	
		Total number of free trials	Total number of correct choices	Total number of free trials	Total number of correct choices
DG-LVP[b]	12	6	3.91 ± 0.28[c]	8	6.25 ± 0.39[d]
Saline	12	6	3.08 ± 0.39	8	4.58 ± 0.45

[a] The rats were trained with forced and free trials to reach a
receptive female in the goal box on the correct arm of the T-maze.
Acquisition training was followed by retention sessions with exclusively free trials. The males were allowed to ejaculate in the
goal box after each correct choice.

[b] Treatment (1 μg/rat LVP or saline, s.c.) was given immediately
after each of the 4 acquisition sessions.

[c] Mean $\pm$ S.E.

[d] $p < 0.02$

observed that DG-LVP, whether given before or immediately
after the copulatory sessions, delayed the disappearance of
intromission and ejaculatory behavior of male rats following
castration (Bohus, 1976). Accordingly, vasopressin not only
affects the maintenance of learned approach behavior but
also a genetically determined behavioral pattern such as

male sexual behavior.   Both of these effects appeared to be
of a long term nature.   Vasopressin analogues were also found
to antagonize CO_2 or ECS induced amnesia in the rat (Rigter,
van Riezen, & de Wied, 1974) and to protect against
puromycin-induced memory loss in mice (Lande, Flexner, J.B.,
& Flexner, L.B., 1972).   Accordingly, these observations, and
our data in both avoidance and approach situations, support
the notion that memory processes are affected by vasopressin-
like peptides.

 That vasopressin is physiologically involved in memory
processes has recently been demonstrated in rats with hereditary hypothalamic diabetes insipidus.   A homozygous variant
of the Brattleboro strain lacks the ability to synthetize
vasopressin (Valtin & Schroeder, 1964).   The heterozygous
littermates have a relatively normal water metabolism while
the other homozygous variant is completely normal in synthe-
tizing vasopressin.   Severe memory impairment can be observed
in rats with hereditary hypothalamic diabetes insipidus when
subjected to a step-through one-trial learning passive
avoidance test (de Wied, Bohus, & van Wimersma Greidanus,
1975).   Absence of passive avoidance 24 hr or later after the
learning trial was seen in these rats, even after receiving
a high intensity long duration punishing footshock during the
learning trial.   In contrast, heterozygous or homozygous
normal rats exhibited passive avoidance behavior after receiving much milder shock punishment.   Treatment of the
diabetes insipidus rats immediately after the shock trial
with arginine vasopressin (AVP) or DG-LVP facilitated passive
avoidance behavior.   Avoidance latencies became undis-
tinguishable from those of the heterozygous or normal homozygous rats trained under similar conditions (Table 2).   The
fact that DG-LVP, which is practically devoid of antidiuretic
effects, is as active as arginine vasopressin, which is a
principle with high antidiuretic activity, indicates that
restoration of memory was not due to normalised water metabolism.   It was further found that diabetes insipidus rats do
avoid in the absence of vasopressin if they are tested immediately after the single shock learning trial.   A slight
retention of the passive avoidance response was also seen 3
hr after the learning.   These observations indicate that
memory rather than learning processes are deficient in the
absence of vasopressin.   The fact that diabetes insipidus
rats, although slower than the heterozygous or homozygous
normal rats, do acquire a shuttle box multiple trial a-
voidance response, which they cannot maintain (Bohus, van
Wimersma Greidanus, & de Wied, 1975), corroborates this view.

 The foregoing observations indicate that vasopressin or

TABLE 2

*RETENTION OF A ONE-TRIAL STEP-THROUGH PASSIVE AVOIDANCE
RESPONSE IN RATS WITH HEREDITARY HYPOTHALAMIC DIABETES INSIP-
IDUS AND EFFECTS OF ARGININE VASOPRESSIN (AVP) AND DESGLYCIN-
AMIDE LYSINE VASOPRESSIN (DG-LVP)*

Group	n	Treatment	Retention interval[a]		
			24 hr	48 hr	120 hr
Homozygous normal	8	–	300.0[b]	300.0	300.0
Heterozygous	8	–	300.0	300.0	300.0
Homozygous diabetes insipidus	8	–	34.0[e]	42.0[e]	40.0[e]
	8	AVP[c]	300.0[d]	300.0[d]	260.0[d]
	7	DG-LVP	253.5[d]	300.0[d]	300.0[d]

[a] Time between the single shock trial (1.0 mA for 3 sec) and the retention test

[b] Median passive avoidance latency in sec

[c] A single dose of AVP or DG-LVP (1 μg/rat, s.c.) was administered immediately after the learning trial

[d] $p < 0.01$ vs. untreated homozygous diabetes insipidus rats

[e] $p < 0.01$ vs. homozygous normal rats

vasopressin-like peptides of the hypothalamo-neurohypophyseal
system participate in the consolidation and maintenance of
various adaptive behavioral responses. Morphological and
functional evidence has been obtained for the release of
posterior pituitary principles from the anterior hypothalamus
into the IIIrd ventricle, probably through the juxtaependymal
processes of neurosecretory neurons (Heller, Hasan, & Saifi,
1968; Vorherr, Bradbury, Hoghoughi, & Kleeman, 1968; Unger &
Schwarzberg, 1970; Zaidi & Heller, 1974). This route would
be an efficient way to reach the effective sites of the behavioral action of vasopressin analogues. Indeed, intraventricular administration of vasopressin analogues at much
lower doses than systemic injection induces resistance to
extinction of an avoidance response (de Wied, 1975).
Furthermore, it was found that intraventricular administration of vasopressin, but not of oxytocin antiserum, prior
to the single learning trial in a passive avoidance situation, results in a retention deficit in rats tested 4 hr or
later after the shock trial (van Wimersma Greidanus,
Dogterom, & de Wied, 1975).

The site of the behavioral action of vasopressin,

suggested by lesion- and intracerebral microinjection studies,
is in midbrain-limbic structures. Microinjection of vasopressin in the mesodiencephalic area, especially at the parafascicular thalamic level, stimulated the behavioral effect
of systemically administered peptide on active avoidance
behavior. However, bilateral lesions in this area failed to
prevent the effect of systemically injected vasopressin on
avoidance extinction. Lesions in the rostral septal area and
the dorsal hippocampus, on the other hand, abolished the consolidating effect of vasopressin on avoidance behavior (van
Wimersma Greidanus, Bohus, & de Wied, 1974, 1975). Thus, the
rostral septum, or structures with afferent and efferent connections from or to the septum, like the hippocampus, seem to
be of importance for the action of vasopressin analogues.

Studies of the physiological processes accompanying
emotional behavior indicate that vasopressin analogues modify
autonomic responses related to learning and performance.
Administration of LVP delayed extinction of a classically
conditioned cardiac response. Heart rate decrease in response to the presentation of a conditioned stimulus was
sustained for a longer period of time in rats treated with
LVP than in control rats (Bohus, 1975). This observation
indicates that vasopressin does not only affect instrumental,
but also acquired, autonomic responses.

If one considers that the conditioned cardiac response
is an autonomic correlate of classically conditioned fear,
the above observation raises the question as to whether or
not the behavioral effects of these peptides are mediated
through an influence on the classically conditioned component
of the avoidance response. In fact, King and de Wied (1974)
demonstrated that LVP can influence avoidance behavior
through classical fear conditioning. It was found that rats
which received LVP prior to classical fear conditioning,
which preceded instrumental conditioning, displayed facilitated acquisition and resistance to extinction of the conditioned avoidance response without further peptide administration. However, it was also observed that the instrumental
response was a more effective substrate for mediating long
term effects of LVP on extinction behavior than was classical
fear conditioning.

Concurrent measurement of behavioral performance and the
cardiac response in rats treated with vasopressin analogues,
or in rats of the Brattleboro strain, also favours the notion
that these peptides affect memory processes. Administration
of DG-LVP facilitated passive avoidance behavior and also the
decrease in heart rate which accompanied this behavior (Bohus,
1975). The absence of passive avoidance behavior in rats

with hereditary hypothalamic diabetes insipidus appears to be coupled with the partial absence of cardiac responses during avoidance testing. Administration of DG-LVP to diabetes insipidus rats immediately after the single learning trial restored avoidance behavior and fully normalized the cardiac response.

Although the behavioral and autonomic parameters indicate that memory processes are affected by vasopressin analogues, it is not yet clear whether consolidation, retrieval, or both processes are affected by these peptides. It has recently been shown that the dominant hippocampal theta frequency during paradoxical sleep (PS) episodes was significantly lower in rats with hereditary hypothalamic diabetes insipidus than their heterozygous littermates or normal homozygous rats. Administration of DG-LVP increased the theta frequency during PS episodes in diabetes insipidus rats up to the level of controls (Urban & de Wied, 1975). Since diabetes insipidus rats show severe memory deficits in a passive avoidance situation, and REM sleep deprivation leads to a consolidation deficit (Leconte & Bloch, 1970; Fishbein, 1971; Stern, 1971), one might speculate that impaired memory function in the absence of vasopressin is due to impaired PS mechanisms. Such a notion, however, may be premature because observations on the frequency of hippocampal theta activity during PS sleep in Brattleboro rats relative to learning performance are not yet available. In addition, the release of vasopressin during PS following learning has never been studied. Meanwhile, observations indicating that drugs which facilitate memory functions increase theta frequency in the post-learning period (Longo & Loizzo, 1973) suggest that the excitability changes in hippocampal theta system may bear important consequences for consolidation processes. Landfield, McGaugh, and Tusa (1972) suggested that theta activity in the post-learning period may be a correlate of a brain state which is optimal for memory storage. Hypophysectomized rats, which show learning and memory deficits, have shorter duration PS episodes, and the circadian rhythmicity of PS is absent (Valatx, Chouvet, & Jouvet, 1975). Therefore, it may be more than simple speculation that alterations in PS mechanisms, or PS induced septal-hippocampal excitability changes in the absence of vasopressin, are responsible for the observed memory deficit of diabetes insipidus rats.

In conclusion, the hypothalamo-neurohypophyseal system produces vasopressin and vasopressin-like peptides which exert long term effects on learned behavioral and physiological responses. It may be that the release of these peptides,

possibly in relation to PS following learning, but certainly
in response to situation-specific cues (Thompson & deWied,
1973), facilitate central nervous system processes involved
in the consolidation and retrieval of information which
enable the organism to cope adquately with environmental
changes.

REFERENCES

Abrahams, V. C., & Pickford, M. Simultaneous observations on
     the rate of urine flow and spontaneous uterine movements
     in the dog, and their relationship to posterior lobe
     activity. *Journal of Physiology,* 1954, *126,* 329-346.

Ader, R., & Wied, D. de. Effects of lysine vasopressin on
     passive avoidance learning. *Psychonomic Science,* 1972,
     29, 46-48.

Bohus, B. Pituitary peptides and adaptive autonomic
     responses. In W. H. Gispen, Tj. B. van Wimersma
     Greidanus, B. Bohus, & D. de Wied (Eds.). *Hormones,
     Homeostasis and the Brain (Progress in Brain Research,
     Vol. 42).* Amsterdam: Elsevier, 1975.

Bohus, B. Effect of desglycinamide-lysine vasopressin
     (DG-LVP) on sexually motivated T-maze behavior of the
     male rat. *Hormones and Behavior,* 1976, in press.

Bohus, B., Ader, R., & Wied, D. de. Effects of vasopressin
     on active and passive avoidance behavior. *Hormones and
     Behavior,* 1972, *3,* 191-197.

Bohus, B., Gispen, W. H., & Wied, D. de. Effect of lysine
     vasopressin and ACTH 4-10 on conditioned avoidance
     behavior of hypophysectomized rats. *Neuroendocrinology,*
     1973, *11,* 137-143.

Bohus, B., Wied, D. de, & Wimersma Greidanus, Tj. B. van.
     Behavioral and endocrine responses of rats with
     hereditary hypothalamic diabetes insipidus (Brattleboro
     strain). *Physiology and Behavior,* 1975, *14,* 609-615.

Corson, S. A., & Corson, E. O'Leary. The function of vaso-
     pressin in response to emotional stress. *Federation
     Proceedings,* 1967, *26,* 264.

Fishbein, W. Disruptive effects of rapid eye movement deprivation on long-term memory. *Physiology and Behavior,* 1971, *6,* 279-282.

Garrud, P., Gray, J. A., & Wied, D. de. Pituitary-adrenal hormones and extinction of rewarded behaviour in the rat. *Physiology and Behavior,* 1974, *12,* 109-119.

Heller, H., Hasan, S. H., & Saifi, A. Q. Antidiuretic activity in the cerebrospinal fluid. *Journal of Endocrinology,* 1968, *41,* 273-280.

King, A. R., & Wied, D. de. Localized behavioral effects of vasopressin on maintenance of an active avoidance response in rats. *Journal of Comparative and Physiological Psychology,* 1974, *86,* 1008-1018.

Lande, S., Wied, D. de, & Witter, A. Pituitary peptides. An octapeptide that stimulates conditioned avoidance acquisition in hypophysectomized rats. *Journal of Biological Chemistry,* 1971, *246,* 2058-2062.

Lande, S., Flexner, J. B., & Flexner, L. B. Effect of corticotropin and desglycinamide[9]-lysine vasopressin on suppression of memory by puromycin. *Proceedings of the National Academy of Sciences,* 1972, *69,* 558-560.

Landfield, P. W., McGaugh, J. L., & Tusa, R. J. Theta rhythm: A temporal correlate of memory storage processes in the rat. *Science,* 1972, *175,* 87-89.

Leconte, P., & Bloch, V. Déficit de la retention d'un conditionnement aprés privation de sommeil paradoxal chez le rat. *Comptes Rendus Hebdomadaires des Séances de l'Académie des Sciences,* 1970, *271,* 226-229.

Longo, V. G., & Loizzo, A. Effects of drugs on the hippocampal θ-rhythm. Possible relationships to learning and memory processes. In F. E. Bloom & G. H. Acheson (Eds.), *Pharmacology and the Future of Man (Proceedings 5th Int. Congress of Pharmacology, Vol. 4, Brain, Nerves and Synapses).* Basel: Karger, 1973.

Miller, N. E., Dicara, L. V., & Wolf, G. Homeostasis and reward: T-maze learning induced by manipulating antidiuretic hormone. *American Journal of Physiology,* 1968, *215,* 684-686.

O'Connor, W. J., & Verney, E. B.   The effect of increased activity of the sympathetic system in inhibition of water-diuresis by emotional stress. *Quarterly Journal of Experimental Physiology,* 1945, *33,* 77-90.

Rigter, H., van Riezen, H., & Wied, D. de.   The effects of ACTH and vasopressin-analogues on CO_2-induced retrograde amnesia in rats. *Physiology and Behavior,* 1974, *13,* 381-388.

Rydin, H., & Verney, E. B.   The inhibition of water diuresis by emotional stress and by muscular exercise. *Quarterly Journal of Experimental Physiology,* 1938, *27,* 343-374.

Stern, W. C.   Acquisition impairment following rapid eye movement sleep deprivation in rats. *Physiology and Behavior,* 1971, *7,* 345-352.

Thompson, E. A., & Wied, D. de.   The relationship between antidiuretic activity of rat eye plexus blood and passive avoidance behaviour. *Physiology and Behavior,* 1973, *11,* 377-380.

Unger, H., & Schwarzberg, H.   Untersuchungen über Vorkommen und Bedeutung von Vasopressin und Oxytozin in Liquor cerebrospinalis und Blut für nervöse Funktionen. *Acta Biologica Medica Germanica,* 1970, *25,* 267-280.

Urban, I., & Wied, D. de.   Inferior quality of RSA during paradoxial sleep in rats with hereditary diabetes insipidus. *Brain Research,* 1975, *97,* 362-366.

Valatx, J. L., Chouvet, G., & Jouvet, M.   The sleep-waking cycle in the hypophysectomized rat. In W. H. Gispen, Tj. B. van Wimersma Greidanus, B. Bohus, & D. de Wied (Eds.), *Hormones, Homeostasis and the Brain (Progress in Brain Research, Vol. 42).* Amsterdam: Elsevier, 1975.

Valtin, H., & Schroder, H. A.   Familial hypothalamic diabetes insipidus in rats (Brattleboro strain). *American Journal of Physiology,* 1964, *206,* 425-430.

Vorherr, H., Bradbury, M. W. B., Hoghoughi, M., & Kleeman, C. R.   Antidiuretic hormone in cerebrospinal fluid during endogenous and exogenous changes in its blood level. *Endocrinology,* 1968, *83,* 246-250.

Wied, D. de. Influence of anterior pituitary on avoidance learning and escape behavior. *American Journal of Physiology,* 1964, *207,* 255-259.

Wied, D. de. The influence of the posterior and inter-mediate lobe of the pituitary and pituitary peptides on the maintenance of a conditioned avoidance response in rats. *International Journal of Neuropharmacology,* 1965, *4,* 157-167.

Wied, D. de. Effects of peptide hormones on behavior. In W. F. Ganong & L. Martini (Eds.), *Frontiers in Neuro-endocrinology 1969.* New York: Oxford University Press, 1969.

Wied, D. de. Long term effect of vasopressin on the maintenance of a conditioned avoidance response in rats. *Nature,* 1971, *232,* 58-60.

Wied, D. de. Behavioral effects of intraventricularly administered vasopressin analogues. In H. Matthaei (Ed.), *Molecular and Cellular Analysis of Mental Disorders.* New York: Academic Press, 1975.

Wied, D. de, & Bohus, B. Long term and short term effects on retention of a conditioned avoidance response in rats by treatment with long acting pitressin and α-MSH. *Nature,* 1966, *212,* 1484-1486.

Wied, D. de, Greven, H. M., Lande, S., & Witter, A. Dissociation of the behavioural and endocrine effects of lysine vasopressin by tryptic digestion. *British Journal of Pharmacology,* 1972, *45,* 118-122.

Wied, D. de, Bohus, B., & Wimersma Greidanus, Tj. B. van. The hypothalamo-neurophypophyseal system and the preservation of conditioned avoidance behavior in rats. In D. F. Swaab & J. P. Schadé (Eds.), *The Integrative Hypothalamic Activity (Progress in Brain Research, Vol. 41).* Amsterdam: Elsevier, 1974.

Wied, D. de, Bohus, B., & Wimersma Greidanus, Tj. B. van. Memory deficit in rats with hereditary diabetes insipidus. *Brain Research,* 1975, *85,* 152-156.

Wimersma Greidanus, Tj. B. van, Bohus, B., & Wied, D. de. Differential localization of the influence of lysine vasopressin and of ACTH 4-10 on avoidance behavior: A study in rats bearing lesions in the parafascicular nuclei.   *Neuroendocrinology,* 1974, *14,* 280-288.

Wimersma Greidanus, Tj. B. van, Dogterom, J., & Wied, D. de. Intraventricular administration of anti-vasopressin serum inhibits memory in rats.   *Life Sciences,* 1975, *16,* 637-644.

Wimersma Greidanus, Tj. B. van, Bohus, B., & Wied, D. de. CNS sites of action of ACTH, MSH and vasopressin, related to avoidance behavior.   In W. E. Stumpf & L. D. Grand (Eds.), *Anatomical Neuroendocrinology. Proceedings of the Conference on Neurobiology of CNS-Hormone Interactions.   Chapel Hill, N.C., May 1974.* Basel: Karger, 1975.

Zaidi, S. M. A., & Heller, H.   Can neurohypophysial hormones cross the blood-cerebrospinal fluid barrier?   *Journal of Endocrinology,* 1974, *60,* 195-196.

PITUITARY PEPTIDE INFLUENCES ON ATTENTION AND MEMORY

CURT A. SANDMAN

Department of Psychology
Ohio State University
Columbus, Ohio 43210 USA

ABBA J. KASTIN

Veterans Administration Hospital and Department of Medicine
Tulane University School of Medicine
New Orleans, Louisiana 70112 USA

Melanocyte stimulating hormone (MSH) is known to cause pigmentary changes in the amphibian and other lower vertebrates. The adaptive significance of this phenomenon is readily apparent since it permits the animal to escape danger by changing color to blend with the environment. Pigmentary changes of mammals in response to physiological stimuli are unremarkable, if they occur at all. Therefore, the exact role of MSH in mammals has remained obscure. Several recent reviews (Brown & Barker, 1966; Lewin, 1973) have concluded that any present day effects of MSH in mammals are vestigial rather than adaptive.

A related peptide, adrenocorticotropic hormone (ACTH), which shares the first 13 amino acids with α-MSH, has been historically implicated in the stress response. Selye (1956) suggested that the pituitary-adrenal axis plays a critical role in an organism's adaptation to stress and termed this complex physiological response the General Adaptation Syndrome. Selye's forceful analysis guided the search for the behavioral consequences of alterations in ACTH levels by

347

restricting them to aversively motivated tasks.

The early research by Miller and his associates indicated that treatment of rats with ACTH significantly delayed extinction of an active avoidance response (Murphy & Miller, 1955; Miller & Ogawa, 1962). Later research by DeWied (1965, 1966) and his collaborators (DeWied & Bohus, 1966) suggested that the fractions of ACTH shared by the smaller peptide MSH, were responsible for the delayed extinction of the shock motivated avoidance response. In a series of elegant studies, Greven and DeWied (1967, 1973) discovered that the 4-10 sequence and finally that the 4-7 sequence of amino acids shared by MSH and ACTH was responsible for the behavioral actions of the peptides.

In a bold attempt to break from the historical precedent of assuming that the delayed extinction was an indication only of increased fear or stress, DeWied stated that the ACTH-MSH compounds affected "short term" memory, (DeWied & Bohus, 1966) on a "trial to trial" basis (DeWied, 1971). The effects of ACTH, MSH and their analogues were only found on active avoidance behavior in their early studies, even though a few other paradigms were studied (Bohus & DeWied, 1966). Thus, their suggestion that fractions of MSH and ACTH improved memory was based upon the exclusive use of aversive procedures and a single test of memory, namely the number of trials to extinction in the active avoidance response situation. Other explanations such as a nonadaptive perseverative tendency, or a functional overtraining effect (Spear, 1973, pp. 184-185) leading to increased cue utilization also could account for these findings.

STUDIES IN ADULT ANIMALS

Since extinction after treatment with MSH and ACTH analogues had only been investigated in aversive situations, we performed a study to assess extinction in an appetitive task (Sandman, Kastin, & Schally, 1969). Hungry animals treated with MSH or a control solution were trained to find food in one arm of a T-maze. After the response was acquired, the food was removed from the apparatus. Rats injected with MSH continued to respond in the absence of reinforcement to a significantly greater extent than control animals. These findings recently have been confirmed by others (Garrud, Gray, & DeWied, 1974) and suggest that MSH and ACTH analogues are active in appetitive as well as highly stressful or aversive situations.

The results of our passive avoidance study (Sandman,

Kastin, & Schally, 1971) tended to eliminate disinhibition or perseverative tendencies as possible explanations of MSH-related behavior. Rats were placed in one chamber of a two chamber apparatus and the time required to enter the second chamber was recorded. On the next day as the rats entered chamber two, a foot shock was delivered. The animals were rested for two days and then the procedure was repeated. Rats injected with MSH evidenced significantly greater latencies for entering chamber 2 than did controls. These results, which have been replicated (Dempsey, Kastin, & Schally, 1972; Greven & DeWied, 1973), strongly suggest that nonadaptive response perseveration does not explain behavior induced by administration of MSH.

To test a remaining major explanation of MSH related behavior--the memory hypothesis of DeWied--a visual discrimination and reversal procedure was employed. In two different studies (Sandman, Miller, Kastin, & Schally, 1972; Sandman, Alexander, & Kastin, 1973) we trained animals in a Y-maze or in a Thompson box to escape or avoid foot shock by running to a lighted or to a white door. After the animal acquired the task, the rules were reversed and the unlighted or the dark door was the correct response. We chose this task because it provided us with several kinds of information:

1. It would allow us to retest the disinhibition hypothesis since perseverating animals would continue to respond according to the first set of rules and would therefore require a greater number of trials than the control animals.

2. It would allow assessment of short term memory since (according to interference theory) improved short term memory would result in poorer reversal learning because the "memory" of the initial task would interfere with learning of the reversal task.

3. It would permit evaluation of attentional processes which, to this point, had not been related to treatment with MSH or its analogues. According to the two-stage theory of selective attention (Mackintosh, 1965; 1969), improvement in reversal learning is a result of attending to and learning the relevant dimension during initial learning. For instance, instead of just learning that the white door is correct, the highly attentional animal learns that the dimension of brightness is correct and hence its ability to shift to another value on that dimension is maximized. If the animal only learns that white is correct, then learning that black is correct during reversal has only the same response probability as learning that a value on an irrelevant dimension such as left is correct. By the same reasoning, learning the extradimensional response, e.g., left--after learning that

white is correct during initial learning, is easier for the
inattentive organism.

The animals treated with MSH performed significantly
better on the reversal task than control animals. The results argued against perseveration and, from one viewpoint,
suggested that MSH treatment disrupts short-term memory. Ad-
ditionally, MSH treatment had no effect on long term (5 day)
retention of the reversal problem. Within the context of our
previous results and those of DeWied, it seemed unlikely that
these results could be interpreted to suggest that impaired
short term memory was the result of MSH treatment. Therefore,
it appeared that the most parsimonious explanation of MSH
related behavior was that it improved selective attention.

In addition, we found that the performance of albino
rats, and rats tested in constant light, was significantly
enhanced by treatment with MSH when compared to hooded rats,
and rats tested in the dark (Sandman et al., 1973). Therefore, it seemed as if the attentional behavior of visually
deficient animals (albino, or tested in constant light) was
more profoundly affected by MSH than maximally efficient
animals (hooded, or tested in constant darkness).

We were still contending with the proposition that emotionality or generalized arousal (Stratton & Kastin, 1973)
might explain the behavior we had observed. We chose to test
this by using the same visual discrimination procedure and
injecting rats with 2 mg/kg of d-amphetamine. The results
indicated that amphetamine, putatively an arousing substance,
produced an opposite effect on reversal learning than MSH
(Beckwith, Sandman, Alexander, Gerald, & Goldman, 1974).
This admittedly inferential argument suggests that arousal
may not explain the behavior observed with injections of MSH.

It is possible, however, for an animal to become more
"motivated" by MSH without manifesting increased generalized
arousal or emotionality. Like many other conceptual words,
much depends upon the connotation. Regardless of the definition, animals receiving MSH appear more alert. This has been
shown with lizards in which tonic immobility had been induced.
MSH was found to shorten the duration of tonic immobility
(Stratton & Kastin, submitted). Although tonic immobility is
not the same as sleep, there certainly are some superficial
resemblances to sleep in the reduced responsiveness to environmental stimuli. In rats injected with MSH, an increased
latency for sleep in general, and REM sleep in particular,
was observed (Panksepp, personal communication). The increased attention manifested in all our studies by the animals receiving MSH almost could be considered as the opposite
of what occurs in the sleep state.

DEVELOPMENTAL STUDIES

All of the foregoing studies were performed with adult male animals and therefore virtually nothing is known about the developmental effects of MSH. Several developmental investigations have been conducted with the entire ACTH molecule. However, caution must be exercised in interpreting the results of these studies because the entire ACTH molecule stimulates the release of corticosterone from the rat adrenal, whereas MSH and ACTH 4-10 do not. In order to assess the developmental and the long-term effects of a naturally occurring pituitary peptide free from steroid stimulating effects, we injected infant rats from day 2 to day 7 with α-MSH in several studies. In one of these studies (Beckwith, Sandman, Hothersall, & Kastin, submitted), juvenile rats were tested at 33 days of age with a difficult operant task. On a DRL-20 schedule, food deprived rats were trained to press a lever for food pellets; however, in order to receive reinforcement they had to wait at least 20 seconds between responses. If they pressed the lever before the 20 seconds elapsed, the timer was reset and the rats had to wait another 20 seconds. An analysis of the calculated efficiency ratio indicated that the initial performance of MSH-treated rats was inferior to that of control animals. By the time the animals had achieved 70% of the practice on this schedule, however, the animals treated with MSH surpassed the control groups. This resulted in a statistically significant interaction between treatment and days of practice. One reason for the initial inferior performance of rats treated with MSH is that they made more responses during early practice sessions than did control animals.

It appears that the animals treated with MSH improved much more rapidly, after they began to demonstrate acquisition of the schedule, than control animals. Although the relationship of these data to our attentional hypothesis is not completely clear, one important aspect of attention is the implication that enhanced perceptual processing of selected stimuli is accomplished by the narrowing of the perceptual field. This enhanced selection of environmental input would, in part, be reflected by a demonstration of greater persistence and fixation upon a selected input dimension. Given that DRL performance is maintained by the development of collateral behaviors, the slump found in the performance curves for the control animals could be explained by their trying a variety of mediators before finally

adopting a particular collateral behavior which allowed efficient DRL performance. One explanation for the more consistent linear trend in the performance curves for the MSH-
treated animals is that early injections of MSH resulted in
narrowing of attention to those environmental events which
produced development of stable collateral behavior. This
speculation remains a question for further testing.

More directly related to attention, male and female rats
injected from the age of 2 to 7 days were tested as adults
with the visual discrimination procedure described earlier in
the Thompson box. MSH had no effect on the behavior of
female rats. The reasons for this are not clear but in general there is evidence in the behavioral literature for sex-
dependency of some tasks (Gray, 1971; Ray & Barrett, 1973).
Recent data from our laboratory indicate that females injected as infants with MSH evidence a greater amount of time
in contact with another female in the open than do females
treated with control solutions or do males. It is possible
that MSH influences exteroceptive processes in males and
interoceptive processes in females. The male animals treated
with MSH performed better on original learning, reversal and
extradimensional shift learning than control animals in the
Thompson box (Figure 1). Animals treated and tested as
adults demonstrated improved performance only on the reversal
shift and a subproblem of the extradimensional shift.

Thus, the effects in the groups injected as infants are
pervasive and permanent, while the effects in the animals
treated as adults are subtle and transitory. The animals injected with MSH as infants evidence increased ability both to
focus on a dimension and to switch analyzers (Mackintosh,
1965) or dimensions. Rats injected with MSH as adults appear
only to demonstrate increased dimensional attention. It is
thought that switching analyzers is relatively easier than
dimensional responding for immature subjects (Schaeffer &
Ellis, 1970). It is conceivable that early injections of MSH
maintain the switching ability and potentiate the dimensional
attention in the animal tested as an adult, whereas, only
dimensional attention can be affected in the mature nervous
system.

Our data suggested that enhancement of attention was the
most parsimonious explanation of the behavioral effects of
MSH and ACTH analogues. However, eventual alteration of our
attentional hypothesis is likely. For example, it is difficult to integrate the extinction data from the active avoidance experiments into this conception except at a superficial
level. The reversal learning paradigm suggested that if
extinction were construed as a different task than acquisi-

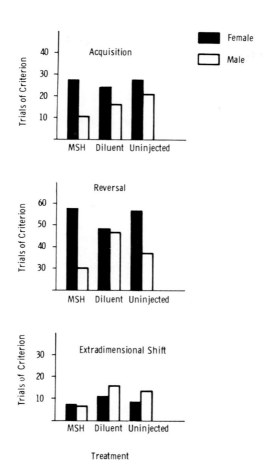

Fig. 1. Performance of original learning, reversal, and extradimensional shifts for male and female rats.

tion, facilitated extinction would be predicted as a consequence of MSH treatment. Therefore, we recently tested animals injected with MSH as infants, and other rats treated as adults, in a completely automated two-way shuttle-box. This is the first time we are reporting results obtained using the simple conditioned active avoidance response exclusively used by DeWied's group for many years. A stringent criterion of 9 out of 10 correct responses defined acquisition of the task. The rats treated with MSH and the control solution as infants acquired the avoidance response and extinguished

faster than the adult animals. Surprisingly, in view of the
results of DeWied and others, both the adult and infant rats
treated with MSH acquired and extinguished the active avoidance response faster than control animals. As predicted by
Bohus (1973, p. 416) this finding is conceptually consistent
with our previous findings but is in disagreement with the
findings of DeWied and others employing the entire ACTH
chain.

The opposite findings of investigators who used the entire ACTH chain can be dismissed because of the stimulation
of corticosterone by ACTH. However, this does not explain
the differences obtained by the investigators who used the
4-10 fraction of ACTH which does not stimulate the adrenals.
It is possible, of course, that our use of a stringent criterion and a completely automated apparatus was responsible for
the different results.

A more likely reason for the differences in some of the
results may be the different vehicle solutions employed.
DeWied (1966) stated that, "the behavioral effect of the
peptides. . .could be obtained only by the use of long acting
zinc phosphate preparations" (p. 30). The use of zinc phosphate as a vehicle solution is disconcerting since it has
been found to exert a significant effect on acquisition and
an identical effect on extinction as ACTH 4-10 (Ley & Corsen,
1970). Although DeWied has claimed that the zinc phosphate
solution does not affect behavior (DeWied & Bohus, 1966;
Bohus & DeWied, 1966), in a recent study (Garrud et al.,
1974) he implemented intricate procedures in an attempt to
guard against its possible contaminating effects.

The initial rationale for using the zinc phosphate vehicle was to insure a long acting preparation since it was
thought that the peptides caused a transitory effect which
would limit the opportunity to observe the behavioral effects.
We have consistently employed rapid stat injections in animals and found persistent behavioral effects (as reviewed
above), changes in the EEG which lasted at least an hour
(Sandman, Denman, Miller, Knott, Schally, & Kastin, 1971),
and dramatic alterations in cerebral perfusion (Goldman,
Sandman, Kastin, & Murphy, 1975). Therefore the need of long
acting preparations is uncertain, and since the behavioral
effects of the zinc solutions may be identical to those of
ACTH 4-10 (Ley & Corsen, 1970) and the interaction between
the two substances is unknown, interpretation of studies
using the zinc phosphate solutions should be restrained.

STUDIES IN MAN

We have tested our attentional hypothesis in man by
infusing 15 mg of MSH/ACTH 4-10 over 4 hours to 10 healthy
young men 21-30 years old and compared the results with those
obtained from a similar group of 10 men given diluent in a
double blind procedure (Sandman, George, Nolan, Van Riezen,
& Kastin, 1975). Behavioral tests were conducted three
times: during the first two hours of the infusion, during
the second two hours of the infusion, and during a one hour
period after the infusion was finished.

All the men were trained on a two choice discrimination
problem in which color (e.g., red) was the relevant dimension
of discrimination. Two objects of different color and different shape were put before the subject. Each time this was
done, he was instructed to choose one of the two objects and
was immediately informed whether his choice was correct.
After learning the first correct dimension, he was given
three additional series of tests. In the first, a simple
reversal problem, color remained the relevant dimension but
the reinforced cue shifted to the second color (e.g., from
red to green). In the next test, the intradimensional shift,
new stimuli were introduced but color remained the relevant
dimension. For the fourth test, the extradimensional shift,
color was no longer reinforced, but rather the shape of the
test object (e.g., square, regardless of its color). At no
time was the subject told when the "rules" had changed or
that he was receiving another of the three types of test.
He was required to realize without instruction that previously
rewarded cues were no longer being reinforced and to attempt
to determine a newly defined correct response.

In the initial testing, both groups of normal men
performed the intradimensional shift relatively rapidly and
the extradimensional shift not as fast, as expected. After
the infusion, the normal subjects not receiving the
MSH/ACTH 4-10 peptide improved on the extradimensional shift.
In contrast, the subjects receiving MSH/ACTH 4-10 did better
on the intradimensional shift and worse on the extradimensional shift, as we had found in rats tested with equivalent
problems.

These concept formation procedures involving visual discrimination are considered to be very sensitive indicators of
selective attention, as described earlier. That MSH/ACTH or
its active component affects attention in normal men was
further supported by the results from the Benton Visual
Retention Test in which a subject was instructed to reproduce

geometric forms shown briefly a few seconds previously.
After receiving MSH/ACTH 4-10, the subjects improved significantly in this test. MSH/ACTH 4-10 also resulted in better
performance in the Rod and Frame test, in which the subject
was asked to arrange a vertical pole within a square frame
which was placed in several different spatial configurations.

The improvement in the Benton Visual Retention Test in
man after MSH/ACTH 4-10 confirmed our earlier findings
(Kastin, Miller, Gonzalez-Barcena, Hawley, Dyster-Aas,
Schally, Parra, & Velasco, 1971) of improvement in this test
in normal as well as hypopituitary subjects after infusion of
α-MSH. No improvement in verbal retention as measured by the
Wechsler Memory Scale was found in that study.

The effects of MSH/ACTH 4-10 on the EEG of normal men
were examined in a study by Miller, Kastin, Sandman, Fink, and
Van Veen (1974) in which 10 mg of ACTH 4-10 was injected
rapidly IV as a bolus. The occipital EEG was analyzed in
terms of the power output from four band-pass filters. The
ten subjects who received the MSH/ACTH 4-10 exhibited a statistically significant increase in the power output of the
12+ Hz and the 7-12 Hz frequency bands as well as a small
decrease in the output of the 3-7 Hz band. All of the subjects recovered the habituated alpha blocking response; however, only the subjects treated with MSH/ACTH 4-10 showed
persistence of the response. We also found in this study
that injection of the MSH/ACTH peptide resulted in improvement in the Benton Visual Retention Test, as was observed in
our other two investigations in man. Decreased anxiety, as
measured by the State-Trait Anxiety Inventory, was found in
this study in which MSH/ACTH 4-10 was injected stat as well
as in the study in which it was infused for four hours.

In a completely cross-over designed study in man just
completed, healthy volunteers were infused for 2 hours with
15 mg of ACTH. In this sensitive design, the attentional
findings with the discrimination procedures reported earlier
(Sandman et al., 1975) after infusion of MSH/ACTH 4-10 were
partially confirmed. In addition, treatment with the MSH/
ACTH 4-10 enhanced discrimination of tachistoscopically presented stimuli but impaired detection of low contrast ta-
chistoscopic stimuli. The subjects exhibited a significantly
greater heart rate deceleration to a test stimulus within an
orienting sequence when they were infused with the peptide as
compared to the control solution. These data strongly suggest that *selective* attention and possibly stimulus processing are improved while simple stimulus intake is impaired as
a result of MSH/ACTH 4-10 infusions. This attentional-
perceptual separation is similar to the acceptance-rejection

hypothesis of the Laceys (Lacey & Lacey, 1970) as it pertains to cardiovascular-behavioral relationships and deserves further study.

CONCLUSIONS

It is apparent that MSH and its centrally active heptapeptide shared with ACTH affects several behavioral systems. The conditioned avoidance response with which DeWied's group performed many of the early studies in the field should not be discarded because of the possible inadvertent contamina - tion by a vehicle solution which may have exerted behavioral effects by itself. Certainly, this is not our reason for suggesting that memory may no longer be a viable explanation of these effects. The data we have gathered for almost ten years in rats and man strongly, but not exclusively, suggest that the predominant effect of MSH, ACTH, and their analogues is to improve selective attention and stimulus processing and that the behaviorally active chain of the MSH molecule may be uniquely coded for attentional-perceptual functioning.

REFERENCES

Beckwith, B. E., Sandman, C. A., Alexander, W. D., Gerald, M. C., & Goldman, H. d-Amphetamine effects on attention and memory in the albino and hooded rat. *Pharmacology, Biochemistry and Behavior*, 1974, *2*, 557-561.

Beckwith, B. E., Sandman, C. A., Hothersall, D., & Kastin, A. J. The effects of neonatal injections of melanocyte stimulating hormone (MSH) on the DRL performance of juvenile rats, submitted.

Bohus, B., & Wied, D. de. Inhibitory and facility effect of two related peptides on extinction of avoidance be- havior. *Science*, 1966, *153*, 318-320.

Bohus, B. Pituitary-adrenal influences on avoidance and ap- proach behavior of the rat. In E. Zimmerman, W. H. Gispen, B. H. Marks and D. de Wied (Eds.), *Progress in Brain Research*, 1973, *39*, 407-419.

Brown, J. H. U., & Barker, S. B. *Basic Endocrinology*. Philadelphia: F. A. Davis, 1966.

Dempsey, G. L., Kastin, A. J., & Schally, A. V.   The effects of MSH on a restricted passive avoidance response. *Hormones and Behavior,* 1972, *3,* 333-337.

Garrud, P., Gray, J. A., & Wied, D. de.   Pituitary-adrenal hormones and extinction of rewarded behavior in the rat. *Physiology and Behavior,* 1974, *12,* 109-119.

Goldman, H., Sandman, C. A., Kastin, A. J., & Murphy, S.   MSH affects regional perfusion of the brain. *Pharmacology, Biochemistry and Behavior,* 1975.

Gray, J. A.   *The Psychology of Fear and Stress.*   New York: McGraw-Hill, 1971.

Greven, H. M., & Wied, D. de.   The active sequence in the ACTH molecule responsible for inhibition of the extinction of conditioned avoidance behavior in rats. *European Journal of Pharmacology,* 1967, *2,* 14-16.

Greven, H. M., & Wied, D. de.   The influence of peptides derived from corticotrophin (ACTH) on performance.   Structure activity studies.   In E. Zimmerman, W. H. Gispen, B. H. Marks, & D. de Wied (Eds.), *Progress in Brain Research,* 1973, *39,* 429-441.

Kastin, A. J., Miller, L. H., Gonzalez-Barcena, D., Hawley, W. D., Dyster-Aas, K., Schally, A. V., Parra, M. L. V., & Velasco, M.   Psychophysiologic correlates of MSH activity in man. *Physiology and Behavior,* 1971, *7,* 893-896.

Lacey, J. J., & Lacey, B. C.   Some autonomic-central nervous system interrelationships.   In P. Black (Ed.), *Physiological Correlates of Emotion.*   New York: Academic Press, 1970, 205-227.

Lewin, R.   *Hormones.*   Garden City: Anchor Press, 1973.

Ley, K. F., & Corsen, J. A.   Effects of ACTH and zinc phosphate vehicle on shuttlebox CAR. *Psychonomic Science,* 1970, *20,* 307-309.

Mackintosh, N. J.   Selective attention in animal discrimination learning. *Psychological Bulletin,* 1965, *64,* 124-150.

Mackintosh, N. J.   Further analysis of the overtraining re-
    versal effect. *Journal of Comparative and Physiological
    Psychology Monograph,* 1969, *17* (2, Pt. 2).

Miller, L. H., Kastin, A. J., Sandman, C. A., Fink, M., &
    VanVeen, W. J. Polypeptide influences on attention,
    memory and anxiety in man. *Pharmacology, Biochemistry
    and Behavior,* 1974, *2,* 663-668.

Miller, R. E., & Ogawa, N.   The effect of adrenocortico-
    trophic hormone (ACTH) on avoidance conditioning in the
    andrenalectomized rat. *Journal of Comparative and
    Physiological Psychology,* 1962, *55,* 211-213.

Murphy, J. V., & Miller, R. E.   The effect of adrenocortico-
    trophic hormone (ACTH) on avoidance conditioning in the
    rat. *Journal of Comparative and Physiological Psychol-
    ogy,* 1955, *48,* 47-49.

Ray, O. S., & Barrett, R. J.   Interaction of learning and
    memory with age in the rat.   In C. Eisdorfer and W. E.
    Fann (Eds.), *Psychopharmacology and aging.* New York:
    Plenum Publishing Corporation, 1973, 17-39.

Sandman, C. A., Alexander, W. D., & Kastin, A. J.   Neuroendo-
    crine influences on visual discrimination and reversal
    learning in the albino and hooded rat. *Physiology and
    Behavior,* 1973, *11,* 613-617.

Sandman, C. A., Denman, P. M., Miller, L. H., Knott, J. R.,
    Schally, A. V., & Kastin, A. J.   Electroencephalographic
    measures of melanocyte-stimulating hormone activity.
    Journal of Comparative and Physiological Psychology,
    1971, *76,* 103-109.

Sandman, C. A., George, J., Nolan, J. D., Van Riezen, H., &
    Kastin, A. J.   Enhancement of attention in man with
    ACTH/MSH 4-10. *Physiology and Behavior,* 1975.

Sandman, C. A., Kastin, A. J., & Schally, A. V.   Melanocyte-
    stimulating hormone and learned appetitive behavior.
    Experentia, 1969, *25,* 1001-1002.

Sandman, C. A., Kastin, A. J., & Schally, A. V.   Behavioral
    inhibition as modified by melanocyte-stimulating hormone
    (MSH) and light-dark conditions. *Physiology and Be-
    havior,* 1971, *6,* 45-48.

Sandman, C. A., Miller, L. H., Kastin, A. J., & Schally, A.V. Neuroendocrine influence on attention and memory. *Journal of Comparative and Physiological Psychology,* 1972, *80,* 54-58.

Schaeffer, B., & Ellis, S.   The effects of overtraining on children's nonreversal and reversal learning using un-related stimuli. *Journal of Experimental Child Psychology,* 1970, *10,* 1-7.

Selye, H. *The stress of life.* New York: McGraw-Hill, 1956.

Spear, N. E.   Retrieval of memory in animals. *Psychological Review,* 1973, *80,* 169-194.

Stratton, L. O., & Kastin, A. J.   Melanocyte-stimulating hor-mone in learning and extinction of two problems. *Physiology and Behavior,* 1973, *10,* 689-692.

Stratton, L. O., & Kastin, A. J. α-MSH and MSH/ACTH 4-10 may disinhibit the lizard cerebrum druing tonic immobility, submitted.

Wied, D. de.   The influence of the posterior and intermediate lobe of the pituitary and pituitary peptides on the maintenance of a conditioned avoidance response in rats. *International Journal of Neuropharmacology,* 1965, *4,* 157-167.

Wied, D. de.   Inhibitory effect of ACTH and related peptides on extinction of conditioned avoidance behavior in rats. *Proceedings of the Society for Experimental Biology and Medicine,* 1966, *122,* 28-32.

Wied, D. de.   Long term effect of vasopressin on the mainte-nance of a conditioned avoidance response in rats. *Nature,* 1971, *232,* 58-60.

Wied, D. de, & Bohus, B.   Long term and short term effect on retention of a conditioned avoidance response in rats by treatment respectively with long acting pitressin or α-MSH. *Nature,* 1966, *222,* 1484-1486.

SLEEP-RELATED HORMONES

JON F. SASSIN

Departments of Medicine and Psychobiology
University of California at Irvine
Irvine, California 92717 USA

A recent development in the field of sleep research has been the demonstration that a number of polypeptide pituitary hormones are secreted in close relationship to various phases of the sleep-waking cycle. In fact, each hormone studied to date in humans has shown a distinctive relationship to the sleep-waking cycle, whether it be secretion directly dependent on sleep or in the form of a circadian rhythm. Another important finding has been the demonstration that pituitary hormones and most target organ hormones are secreted episodically or in pulses.

The descriptions of episodic release and relationships of hormone secretion to the sleep-waking cycle are based on data obtained from plasma samples. These samples are usually drawn every 20 to 30 minutes through long indwelling venous catheters extended for distances of up to ten feet and kept patent with heparinized saline. Sleep-waking cycles have usually been monitored by standard polygraphic techniques. The limitations in application of the findings of these sleep-hormone studies however, rests precisely in the fact that only limited conclusions can be drawn about activity in neuroendocrine pathways from the study of plasma hormone concentrations and polygraphic sleep data.

The present discussion will deal, for the most part, with those hormones which have been found to have major secretion dependent on sleep: human growth hormone, prolactin and luteinizing hormone in puberty.

HUMAN GROWTH HORMONE

During the first hour after the onset of sleep in normal adult human subjects there is a major release of growth hormone into the plasma (Takahashi, Kipnis, & Daughaday, 1968; Parker, Sassin, Mace, Gotlin, & Rossman, 1969). The magnitude of peak plasma concentrations reached at this time parallels that of concentrations reached by stimulation of the human growth hormone (HGH) system by more classical techniques such as hypoglycemia or amino acid infusion (Parker et al, 1969). In normal subjects, the largest release of growth hormone ordinarily occurs during the first four hours of sleep, this first peak frequently being reached sometime near the end of the first sleep cycle. One or more subsequent peaks may occur but are usually of lower magnitude than the

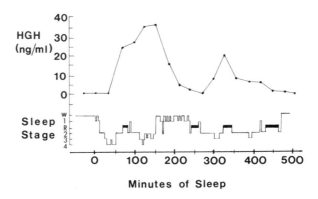

Fig. 1. *Plasma concentration of HGH in a normal young man during sleep.*

first peak. Acute sleep reversal studies reveal that this release of growth hormone is dependent on the development of sleep and not on clock time. Indeed, further analysis of the initiation of the growth hormone release in sleep indicates a relationship to the non-Rapid Eye Movement (REM) portions of the short-term sleep cycle (Sassin, Parker, Mace, Gotlin, Johnson, & Rossman, 1969), especially to stages 3 and 4 of Slow Wave Sleep. Deprivation of stages 3 and 4 sleep results in a diminished or absent sleep-related growth hormone peak (Sassin, Parker, Johnson, Rossman, Mace, & Gotlin, 1969).

While secretion does occasionally occur in REM sleep, for the most part this stage of sleep seems to be inhibitory to human growth hormone release.

When the investigation of the secretion of growth hormone was extended to 24-hour periods, it appeared that very little growth hormone is secreted when subjects are sedentary in a laboratory environment. There is at present conflicting evidence as to the comparative frequency of episodes of secretion of human growth hormone during ordinary daily activity (Plotnick, Thompson, Kowarski, DeLacerdal, Migeon, & Blizzard, 1975).

It has been demonstrated that shortened sleep periods are sufficient to initiate release of growth hormone if sleep is maintained for over 30 minutes (Weitzman, Nogeire, Perlow, Fukushima, Sassin, McGregor, Gallagher, & Hellman, 1974). In addition, there appear to be male-female differences in secretion patterns with less consistent night to night release patterns seen in menstruating women (Takahashi et al., 1968; Parker et al., 1969; Pawel, Sassin, & Weitzman, 1972). Blindness from birth does not seem to influence the sleep-related release of growth hormone in adults, indicating that the light-dark cycle itself is not a prominent controlling factor in this release (Weitzman, Perlow, Sassin, Fukushima, Burack, & Hellman, 1972).

There are definite changes in the release of growth hormone in sleep with age (Finkelstein, Roffwarg, Boyar, Kream, Hellman, 1972). Neonates, whose sleep-wake patterns have not coalesced to the adult pattern, were reported to have consistently high plasma concentrations of growth hormone (Vigneri & d'Agata, 1971). By three months of age, as sleep consolidates into adult patterns, the release of growth hormone becomes linked to the sleep period. Older children have approximately the same release pattern as adults, while adolescents are reported to have increased release of growth hormone over the 24-hour period (Finkelstein et al., 1972). Older adults have been found to release smaller quantities of growth hormone during sleep, an interesting finding in view of the diminished stage 4 sleep in the older adult.

At present the biological significance of HGH release in sleep is unknown. It is clearly not a response to "stress," a term which has little meaning in relationship to the paradigms used in these experiments. In addition, exercise, known to cause release of growth hormone in humans, seems to have no influence on the sleep-related release (Zir, Smith, & Parker, 1971).

Numerous attempts to define a substrate-oriented mechanism have been for the most part unsuccessful. Striking levels of hyperglycemia have no effect (Parker & Rossman, 1971), and the release of growth hormone does not correlate temporally with circadian changes in the amino acid pool as measured by plasma tyrosine (Zir, Parker, Smith, & Rossman, 1972). Infusions of free fatty acids can blunt or eliminate the sleep-related release of growth hormone (Lipman, Taylor, Schenk, & Mintz, 1972; Lucke & Glick, 1971b) but it is unlikely that physiological changes in fatty acids are the cause of release under normal circumstances.

Infusions of cortisol and pathological conditions in which hypercortisolemia is prominent have yielded conflicting effects on growth hormone release in sleep (Krieger & Glick, 1974).

Somatostatin, the recently discovered growth hormone inhibiting factor from the hypothalamus does eliminate the sleep-related release of growth hormone (Parker, Rossman, Siler, Rivier, Yen, & Guillemin, 1974).

A number of other hormones and drugs have been given in attempts at modulating release. To date, medroxyprogesterone (Lucke & Glick, 1971a) and clomiphene (Perlow, Sassin, Boyar, Hellman, & Weitzman, 1973) have been found to diminish the nocturnal release of growth hormone, and in a pilot study imipramine was found to have a similar effect (Takahashi et al., 1968). Drugs which have been found ineffective are Thorazine, phenobarbital and Dilantin (Takahashi et al., 1968) and propranolol and phentolamine, the adrenergic blockers (Lucke et al., 1971b).

Little work has been done in humans to delineate the importance of this release of HGH to growth. A preliminary report of the sleep patterns of psychosocial dwarfs reveals that during periods of poor growth, there are also interrupted sleep and poor sleep habits, suggesting a possible relationship between the sleep pattern, insufficient hormone release and subsequent poor growth (Wolff & Money, 1973). We are at present collaborating with Dr. E. Sachar in his study of possible growth impairment in children taking amphetamines for hyperkinetic behavior disorders, testing the hypothesis that the drug may interfere with growth hormone secretion in sleep.

An aspect of the sleep-related release of human growth hormone of interest to this Symposium is its possible importance in brain protein synthesis thought to occur during sleep. Growth hormone enhances amino acid transport into cells and also enhances both RNA and protein synthesis. While data demonstrating an effect of growth hormone on protein synthesis in the brain are still equivocal, it has been demonstrated that growth hormone administered parenterally to rats will increase the percentage of REM sleep in subsequent hours (Stern, Jalowiec, & Morgane, 1974). In addition, growth hormone has been shown to block the inhibiting effect of anisomycin on soluble brain proteins (Drucker-Colin, Spanis, Hunyadi, Sassin, & McGaugh, in press).

A number of animal species have been investigated for sleep-related HGH release in the search for models of the human pattern. While there is preliminary evidence that baboons have a sleep-related release of growth hormone (Parker, Morishima, Koerker, Gale, & Goodner, 1972), under ordinary laboratory conditions neither rhesus monkeys (Jacoby, Sassin, Greenstein, & Weitzman, 1974) nor dogs (Takahashi, K., Takahashi, Y., Takahashi, S., & Honda, 1974) have any augmentation of growth hormone secretion during sleep. Augmented release can apparently be produced in both of these animals, however, in recovery sleep after significant sleep deprivation (Jacoby, Smith, Sassin, Greenstein, & Weitzman, in press; Takahashi, K. et al., 1974). To date, the more common laboratory animals, the cat and the rat, have not demonstrated sleep-related growth hormone release.

PROLACTIN

Another polypeptide pituitary hormone found to be related to sleep in humans is prolactin. The recent development of a sensitive radioimmunoassay for prolactin (Hwang, Guyda, & Friesen, 1971) and the demonstration of its distinction, in the human, from growth hormone (Frantz & Kleinberg, 1970) have accelerated the study of this hormone. Prolactin is best known for its effects on breast growth and development and lactation, but it also has growth hormone-like properties of nitrogen retention, insulin antagonism, and lipolysis. In addition to these metabolic functions, prolactin affects maternal behavior in animals and may have some effects on salt and water metabolism in humans as well as in lower animals.

Twenty-four hour studies of plasma prolactin concentrations reveal that this hormone is released episodically with measurable concentrations in plasma present at all times (Sassin, Frantz, Weitzman, & Kapen, 1972). This is in distinction from growth hormone which is frequently undetectable in plasma. Soon after the onset of sleep, there occur a series of episodes of prolactin secretion resulting in progressively higher plasma concentrations as sleep proceeds, with highest concentrations during the early morning hours, followed by a precipitous drop in concentration after the

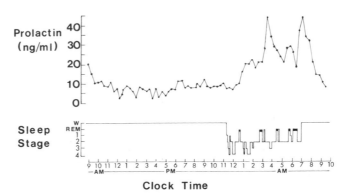

Fig. 2. Plasma concentration of Prolactin in a normal
young man over twenty-four hours.

cessation of sleep. Sleep reversal studies demonstrate this
augmentation of prolactin secretion is dependent on sleep itself and, like growth hormone, not related to clock time
(Sassin, Frantz, Kapen, & Weitzman, 1973). While there is
inconclusive evidence that the episodes of prolactin secretion are initiated during periods of rapid eye movement sleep
(Parker, Rossman, & Van der Laan, 1974), there has not yet
been demonstrated a clear-cut stage relationship as shown for
growth hormone.
     Because of the lack of good information on the biologi-
cal effects of prolactin in humans, and the only very recent
development of the radioimmunoassay, experiments have not yet
been reported that shed light on the mechanisms or biological significance of the sleep-related release of prolactin.

GONADOTROPINS

     Gonadotropin release, while episodic, does not appear to
have any direct relationship to the sleep-waking cycle in
children or in adults, with the possible exception of a diminution of release in women during the first three hours of
sleep (Kapen, Boyar, Hellman, & Weitzman, 1973). There is,
however, a striking sleep-related augmentation of luteinizing
hormone (LH) during puberty in both males and females (Boyar,
Finkelstein, Roffwarg, Kapen, Weitzman, & Hellman, 1972).
There are a series of secretory episodes occurring during

sleep raising plasma concentrations to the maxima of the 24-hour period. Augmented release will occur during sleep even after reversal of the sleep-waking cycle, but enhanced secretion also persists during the clock time of sleep before reversal (Kapen, Boyar, Finkelstein, Hellman, & Weitzman, 1974). There is evidence that the episodes of LH release occurring during sleep may be initiated in nonREM sleep (Kapen et al., 1974). Thus, LH secretion in puberty is sleep-related and perhaps stage-related. Unlike either growth hormone or prolactin, however, LH secretion continues to show augmented nocturnal secretion after sleep reversal, a pattern similar to that seen in the ACTH-cortisol system.

The gonadal steroids, estradiol and testosterone, have been studied over 24-hour periods and show episodic secretion with the peak for testosterone occurring in the morning, possibly related to REM sleep (Evans & MacLean, 1971; Alford, Baker, Burger, deDretser, Hudson, Johns, Masterton, Patel, & Rennie, 1973a).

OTHER HORMONES

TSH - Thyroxin

Thyroid-stimulating hormone (TSH) shows a circadian rhythm with a peak around 2 to 3 in the morning in an inverse relationship to cortisol (Alford, Baker, Burger, deDretser, Hudson, Johns, Masterton, Patel, & Rennie, 1973b). Thyroxin secretion is episodic and appears to be slightly increased during wakefulness (O'Connor, Wu, Gallagher, & Hellman, 1974). These hormones will be discussed further in another section, along with ACTH and cortisol.

Posterior Pituitary

A satisfactory assay for vasopressin has not been as easily developed as for the larger polypeptide hormones. Initial data appear to indicate episodic secretion for this hormone over 24 hours is without relationship to sleep stage (R. Rubin, personal communication, January 18, 1975) despite the changes in urine osmolality and volume which occur during REM sleep (Mandell, Chaffey, Brill, Mandell, M., Rodnick, Rubin, & Sheff, 1966).

SUMMARY

Growth hormone, prolactin and leutinizing hormone during puberty are each secreted during sleep in humans. Each hormone has a distinctive pattern of sleep secretion. Of these, growth hormone seems at present the best candidate for interaction between sleep and memory systems through both its general anabolic functions and, if proven, any specific effect on brain protein synthesis occurring in sleep. The effect of growth hormone on REM sleep suggests that such a relationship exists. It must be borne in mind, however, that human beings appear able to learn, remember and function quite normally without growth hormone.

REFERENCES

Alford, F. P., Baker, H. W., Burger, H. G., deDretser, D. M., Hudson, B., Johns, M. W., Masterton, J. P., Patel, Y. C., & Rennie, G. C. Temporal patterns of integrated plasma hormone levels during sleep and wakefulness. II. Follicle-stimulating hormone, luteinizing hormone, testosterone and estradiol. *Journal of Clinical Endocrinology and Metabolism*, 1973, *37*, 848. (a)

Alford, F. P., Baker, H. W., Burger, H. G., deDretser, D. M., Hudson, B., Johns, M. W., Masterton, J. P., Patel, Y. C., & Rennie, G. C. Temporal patterns of integrated plasma hormone levels during sleep and wakefulness. I. Thyroid-stimulating hormone, growth hormone and cortisol. *Journal of Clinical Endocrinology and Metabolism*, 1973, *37*, 841. (b)

Boyar, R., Finkelstein, J., Roffwarg, H., Kapen, S., Weitzman, E., & Hellman, L. Synchronization of augmented luteinizing hormone secretion with sleep during puberty. *New England Journal of Medicine*, 1972, *287*, 582.

Drucker-Colin, R., Spanis, C. W., Hunyadi, J., Sassin, J., & McGaugh, J. Growth hormone: Effects on sleep and wakefulness in the rat. *Neuroendocrinology*, in press.

Evans, J. I., & MacLean, A. M. Circulating levels of plasma testosterone during sleep. *Proceedings of the Royal Society of Medicine*, 1971, *64*, 841.

Finkelstein, J. W., Roffwarg, H. P., Boyar, R. M., Kream, J., & Hellman, L. Age related change in the 24-hour spontaneous secretion of growth hormone. *Journal of Clinical Endocrinology and Metabolism,* 1972, *35,* 665.

Frantz, A. G., & Kleinberg, D. L. Prolactin: Evidence that it is separate from growth hormone in human blood. *Science,* 1970, *170,* 745.

Hwang, P., Guyda, H., & Friesen, H. Radioimmunoassay for human prolactin. *Proceedings of the National Academy of Science United States,* 1971, *68,* 1902.

Jacoby, J., Sassin, J. F., Greenstein, M., & Weitzman, E. D. Patterns of spontaneous cortisol and growth hormone secretion in rhesus monkeys during the sleep-waking cycle. *Neuroendocrinology,* 1974, *14,* 165.

Jacoby, J., Smith, E., Sassin, J., Greenstein, M., & Weitzman, E. Altered growth hormone secretory patterns following prolonged sleep deprivation in the rhesus monkey. *Neuroendocrinology,* in press.

Kapen, S., Boyar, R., Finkelstein, J., Hellman, L., & Weitzman, E. Effect of sleep-wake cycle reversal on luteinizing hormone secretory pattern in puberty. *Journal of Clinical Endocrinology and Metabolism,* 1974, *39,* 293.

Kapen, S., Boyar, R., Hellman, L., & Weitzman, E. D. Episodic release of luteinizing hormone at mid-menstrual cycle in normal adult women. *Journal of Clinical Endocrinology and Metabolism,* 1973, *36,* 724.

Krieger, D. T., & Glick, S. M. Sleep EEG stages and plasma growth hormone concentration in states of endogenous and exogenous hypercortisolemia or ACTH elevation. *Journal of Clinical Endocrinology and Metabolism,* 1974, *39,* 986.

Lipman, R. L., Taylor, A. L., Schenk, A., & Mintz, D. H. Inhibition of sleep-related growth hormone release by elevated free fatty acids. *Journal of Clinical Endocrinology and Metabolism,* 1972, *35,* 592.

Lucke, C., & Glick, S. M. Effect of medroxyprogesterone acetate on the sleep-induced peak of growth hormone secretion. *Journal of Clinical Endocrinology and Metabolism,* 1971, *33,* 851. (a)

Lucke, C., & Glick, S. M.   Experimental modification of the sleep-induced peak of growth hormone secretion. *Journal of Clinical Endocrinology and Metabolism*, 1971, *32*, 729. (b)

Mandell, A. J., Chaffey, B., Brill, P., Mandell, M. P., Rodnick, J., Rubin, R. T., and Sheff, R.   Dreaming sleep in man: Changes in urine volume and osmolality. *Science*, 1966, *151*, 1558.

O'Connor, J. F., Wu, G. Y., Gallagher, T. F., & Hellman, L. The 24-hour plasma thyroxin profile in normal man. *Journal of Clinical Endocrinology and Metabolism*, 1974, *39*, 765.

Parker, D. C., Morishima, M., Koerker, D. J., Gale, C. C., & Goodner, C. J.   Pilot study of growth hormone release in sleep of the chair-adapted baboon: Potential as model of human sleep release. *Endocrinology*, 1972, *91*, 1462.

Parker, D. C., & Rossman, L. G.   Human growth hormone release in sleep: Nonsuppression by acute hyperglycemia. *Journal of Clinical Endocrinology and Metabolism*, 1971, *32*, 65.

Parker, D. C., Rossman, L. G., Siler, T. M., Rivier, J., Yen, S. S. C., & Guillemin, R.   Inhibition of the sleep-related peak in physiologic human growth hormone release by somatostatin. *Journal of Clinical Endocrinology and Metabolism*, 1974, *38*, 496.

Parker, D. C., Rossman, L. G., & Van der Laan, E. F.   Relation of sleep-entrained human prolactin release to REM - nonREM cycles. *Journal of Clinical Endocrinology and Metabolism*, 1974, *38*, 646.

Parker, D. C., Sassin, J. F., Mace, J. W., Gotlin, R. W., & Rossman, L. G.   Human growth hormone release during sleep: Electroencephalographic correlation. *Journal of Clinical Endocrinology and Metabolism*, 1969, *29*, 871.

Pawel, M., Sassin, J., & Weitzman, E.   The temporal relations between HGH release and sleep stage changes in nocturnal sleep onset in man. *Life Sciences*, 1972, *2*, 587.

Perlow, M., Sassin, J., Boyar, R., Hellman, L., & Weitzman, E. D.   Reduction of growth hormone secretion following clomiphene administration. *Metabolism*, 1973, *22*, 1269.

Plotnick, L. P., Thompson, R. G., Kowarski, A., DeLacerdal, L., Migeon, C. J., & Blizzard, R. M. Circadian variation of integrated concentration of growth hormone in children and adults. *Journal of Clinical Endocrinology and Metabolism*, 1975, *40*, 240.

Sassin, J., Frantz, A., Kapen, S., & Weitzman, E. The nocturnal rise of human prolactin is dependent on sleep. *Journal of Clinical Endocrinology and Metabolism*, 1973, *37*, 436.

Sassin, J., Frantz, A., Weitzman, E., & Kapen, S. Human prolactin: 24-hour pattern with increased release during sleep. *Science*, 1972, *177*, 1205.

Sassin, J. F., Parker, D. C., Johnson, L. C., Rossman, L. G., Mace, J. W., & Gotlin, R. W. Effects of slow-wave sleep deprivation on human growth hormone release in sleep. *Life Sciences*, 1969, *8*, 1299.

Sassin, J. F., Parker, D. C., Mace, J. W., Gotlin, R. W., Johnson, L. C., & Rossman, L. G. Human growth hormone release: Relations to slow-wave sleep and sleep-waking cycles. *Science*, 1969, *169*, 513.

Stern, W. C., Jalowiec, J. E., & Morgane, P. J. Growth hormone and sleep in the cat. *Sleep Research*, 1974, *3*, 173. (Abstract)

Takahashi, Y., Kipnis, D. M., & Daughaday, W. H. Growth hormone secretion during sleep. *Journal of Clinical Investigation*, 1968, *47*, 2079.

Takahashi, K., Takahashi, Y., Takahashi, S., & Honda, Y. Growth hormone and cortisol secretion during noctural sleep in narcoleptics and in dogs. In N. Hadotani (Ed.), *Psychoneuroendocrinology*. Basel, Switzerland: S. Karger, 1974.

Vigneri, R., & d'Agata, R. Growth hormone release during the first year of life in relation to sleep-wake periods. *Journal of Clinical Endocrinology and Metabolism*, 1971, *33*, 561.

Weitzman, E., Nogeire, C., Perlow, M., Fukushima, D., Sassin, J., McGregor, P., Gallagher, T., & Hellman, L. Effects of prolonged 3-hour sleep-wake cycle on sleep stages, plasma cortisol and growth hormone and body temperature in man. *Journal of Clinical Endocrinology and Metabolism,* 1974, *38,* 1018.

Weitzman, E., Perlow, M., Sassin, J., Fukushima, D., Burack, B., & Hellman, L. Persistence of a 24-hour pattern of episodic cortisol secretion and growth hormone release in blind subjects. *Transactions American Neurological Association,* 1972, *97,* 197.

Wolff, G. & Money, J. Relationship between sleep and growth in patients with reversible somatotropin deficience (psychosocial dwarfism). *Psychological Medicine,* 1973, *3,* 18.

Zir, L. M., Parker, D. C., Smith, R. A., & Rossman, L. G. The relationship of human growth hormone and plasma tyrosine during sleep. *Journal of Clinical Endocrinology and Metabolism,* 1972, *34,* 1.

Zir, L. M., Smith, R. A., & Parker, D. C. Human growth hormone release in sleep: Effect of daytime exercise. *Journal of Clinical Endocrinology and Metabolism,* 1971, *32,* 662.

SLEEP AND MEMORY: EFFECTS OF GROWTH HORMONE ON SLEEP,
BRAIN NEUROCHEMISTRY AND BEHAVIOR

WARREN C. STERN and PETER J. MORGANE

Worcester Foundation for Experimental Biology
Shrewsbury, Massachusetts 01545 USA

The influence of various peptide hormones on brain
physiology and behavior has received considerable attention
in recent years. For example, much effort has centered on
the involvement of ACTH and its analogues on avoidance
performance (de Wied, 1969; Gispen, de Wied, Schotman, &
Jansz, 1971; Bohus, 1973) and brain protein synthesis (Gispen,
et al., 1971; Reith, Schotman, & Gispen, 1974).   Recently,
vasopressin and melanocyte stimulating hormone, among others,
have been shown to influence a variety of electrophysiological
correlates of brain function as well as behavior (Kastin,
Miller, Nockton, Sandman, Schally, & Stratton, 1973;
Zimmerman, & Krivoy, 1973; Bohus, see this volume).   We now
describe a series of studies investigating the possible
involvement of another pituitary peptide, growth hormone (GH),
in the regulation of sleep, and in the metabolism of brain
biogenic amines and brain protein synthesis.   The final
section of this paper presents the outline of a model of the
physiological basis for a sleep-memory relationship.

Relations Between Growth Hormone and Sleep

Takahashi, Kipnis, and Daughaday (1968) first described
the close association between the occurrence of slow-wave
sleep (SWS) and the subsequent rise in secretion of GH in
man, especially during the initial episodes of SWS stages
3 and 4.   For example, it was observed that in normal adults,
plasma GH levels usually rise from a concentration of 0-2 ng/ml
during relaxed wakefulness to a peak of 10-20 ng/ml or more

during SWS. This SWS-dependent release of GH has also been
reported to occur in baboons (Parker, Morishima, Koerker,
Gale, & Goodman, 1972) and in dogs which were sleep deprived
and then allowed to sleep (Takahashi, Takahashi, Kitahama, &
Honda, 1974). The dependence of GH release on the presence
of SWS rather than the time of day is demonstrated in
sleep-reversal studies in which displacement of sleep to
another portion of the day results in an immediate shift in
GH secretion to the new SWS time period (Sassin, Parker,
Mace, Gotlin, Johnson, & Rossman, 1969). Examination of
the 24 hour secretory pattern of GH in man generally shows
that the amount of GH released during SWS represents a
substantial majority of the total amount of GH secreted in
a 24 hour period. Interestingly, the biological significance
of the association between SWS and GH release is unknown,
as are the effects of GH on brain physiology and behavior.

One stable characteristic of sleep cycles in normal
adult mammals is that SWS always precedes the occurrence
of a rapid eye movement (REM) sleep episode. Therefore,
direct transitions from waking to REM sleep do not occur.
Since in man the initial SWS periods produce a pronounced
release of GH the possibility arises that the elevated
plasma levels of GH play a role in the triggering of
the subsequent REM episodes. We tested this hypothesis in
a series of experiments in cats and rats in which bovine GH
was administered intraperitoneally to subjects bearing
chronically implanted electrodes for sleep recordings.

Adult female cats received 3-4 baseline sleep recording
sessions of 7 hours duration followed by test days in which
intraperitoneal injections (given in random order) of 0.9%
saline (n = 7), 0.05-0.5 µg (n = 4), 50 µg (n = 7), 100 µg
(n = 7), 500 µg (n = 7), 1000 µg (n = 7) and 3000 µg (n = 2)
of bovine GH were given at the start of the recording sessions.
The percent of time spent in waking, slow-wave sleep and REM
sleep during the first 3 hours post-injection and the next
4 hour period are shown in Figures 1 and 2. During the
first three hours doses of 50-1000 µg of bovine GH produced
significant elevations in the amount of REM sleep, so that
REM sleep rose from a baseline level of 11.3% to 16.4-18.6% of
the total recording time. These GH effects (50-1000 µg
groups pooled) were also significant compared to saline
control values. The 3000 µg dose produced mainly waking
behavior. During hours 1-3 in the 50-1000 µg groups the
percentages of SWS and waking were not appreciably altered.
Thus, the effects of GH on sleep appear to be specific to
the REM state. By 4-7 hours post-injection, the REM
elevating effects of GH had terminated and some significant

EFFECTS OF BOVINE GROWTH HORMONE ON WAKEFULNESS
AND SLOW—WAVE SLEEP IN CATS (N = 7)
MEAN (—S.E.) PERCENT OF RECORDING TIME

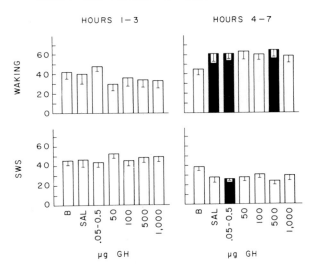

Figure 1. Percent of recording time spent in waking
and slow-wave sleep (SWS) during baseline (B) or after i.p.
injection of saline (SAL.) or growth hormone (GH). Solid
bars indicate significant differences from baseline values.
See Figure 2 for percentages of REM sleep.

increases in wakefulness were observed. Cats given a
subsequent series of control injections of either 50 or
500 μg of bovine thyrotropin showed no significant alterations in sleep-waking percentages in hours 1-3 or 4-7 (see
Figure 3). Since bovine thyrotropin and bovine GH have
similar molecular weights (20,000), the increase in REM
sleep seen after GH is not simply due to the i.p. administration of a high molecular weight peptide hormone.
    Studies on man of the relation between sleep patterns
and GH secretion often show a lag of several hours between
peak plasma GH values and the peak occurrence of REM sleep.

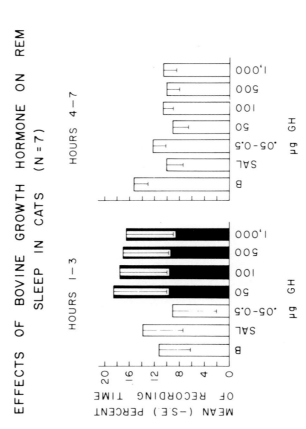

Figure 2. Percent of recording time spent in REM sleep during baseline or after i.p. injections of saline or growth hormone. See Figure 1 for percentages of waking and slow-wave sleep and for explanation of abbreviations.

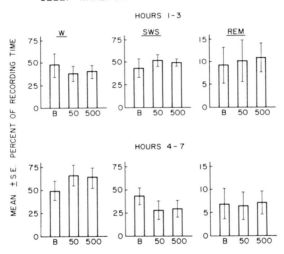

EFFECTS OF BOVINE THYROTROPIN (μg) ON
SLEEP-WAKEFULNESS IN CATS (N=6)

HOURS 1-3

HOURS 4-7

*Figure 3. Lack of effect of control injection of
bovine thyrotropin on sleep-waking patterns in the cats
employed in the prior GH study (Figures 1 and 2). The data
represent the percent of recording time spent in waking (W),
slow-wave sleep (SWS) and REM sleep during baseline (B)
and after i.p. injection of 50 or 500 μg of bovine thyrotropin.*

This delay might suggest that GH is not directly involved
in the triggering of the subsequent REM periods since it
would require that the action of GH could be delayed for
several hours. We, therefore, determined whether it would
be possible to demonstrate a similar lag in cats between
peak plasma GH levels and the elevation of REM sleep. Five
cats from the prior GH study (Figures 1 and 2) received, on
separate recording sessions, an injection of either saline
or 100 μg of bovine GH. Following these injections the
cats were REM deprived for the first 3 hours. The deprivation

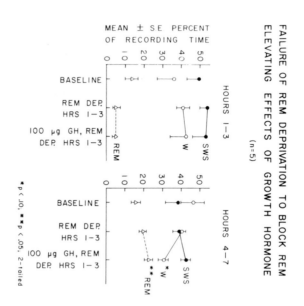

Figure 4. Comparison of the effects of i.p. injections of saline followed by 3 hour REM deprivation (REM DEP) or 100 μg of bovine growth hormone followed by 3 hour REM deprivation on subsequent sleep. Statistical analysis (paired t-tests) was performed only on the data obtained during hours 4-7 after injection for the REM DEP versus GH-REM DEP. The GH injected cats had a significantly greater amount of REM sleep in hours 4-7 after REM DEP than did the same animals when they received saline injections prior to REM DEP.

was produced by EEG monitoring and tapping on the side of the recording chamber at the start of each REM episode. Undisturbed sleep was then permitted for the subsequent 4 hour period. The results, shown in Figure 4, were that the prior injection of GH produced a significantly greater increase (p < 0.05, 2-tailed t-test) in REM sleep 4-7 hours after REM deprivation than was observed in the saline-REM

deprivation sessions. SWS, however, was not significantly
increased during the 4-7 hour period after GH-REM deprivation.
Thus, even when the REM elevating effect of GH is blocked
for 3 hours an increase in REM time still occurs in the
next 4 hour period. Perhaps a similar delay in the action
of GH on REM sleep also occurs in man, so that SWS continues
for up to 2-3 hours following peak plasma GH levels and then
the increase in REM sleep occurs.

We have also examined the effects of i.p. injected bovine
GH on sleep patterns in rats. Six normal adult male rats
were implanted with chronic cortical and hippocampal EEG
electrodes and were placed on an activity platform while
undergoing 24 hour baseline sleep recordings. The rats
were then injected with bovine GH (10, 200 and 1000 μg)
and bovine thyrotropin (500 or 1000 μg) in random order at
the start of each 7 hour recording session. The results
following GH administration, summarized on an hourly basis,
are shown in Figure 5. The REM sleep percentages showed a
clearcut time and dose response curve. GH at 200 μg produced
a marked elevation of REM sleep for the first 4 hours after
injection while the 10 μg and 1000 μg doses produced little
or no significant increases in REM time. The 200 μg dose
of GH produced no change in SWS occurrence at the 1-4 hour
time points when REM sleep was increased. This indicates
that the REM elevating effects of GH are not simply due
to a nonspecific increase in time spent asleep.

The results from the preceding cat and rat studies
with administration of bovine GH, as well as a recent
report using rat GH (Drucker-Colin, Spanis, Hunyadi,
Sassin, & McGaugh, 1975), all demonstrate that injection
of GH produces selective and time-dependent increases in
the amount of REM sleep. In addition to these studies there
are parallels between endogenous plasma GH levels and the
spontaneous occurrence of REM sleep. During early post-natal
development basal levels of circulating GH are much higher
than in adulthood. Young infants average greater than
50 ng/ml plasma GH during waking and sleep compared to
a peak night time level of 15-20 ng/ml in adults (Takahashi,
et al., 1968; Vigneri, & D'Agata, 1971; Shaywitz, Finkelstein,
Hellman, & Weitzman, 1971). The percentage of REM sleep
over a 24 hour period in infants is typically 4 to 5 times
that of normal adults (Roffwarg, Muzio, & Dement, 1966).
Conversely, in old age, REM time often diminishes to less
than half that of young adults (Roffwarg, et al., 1966;
Carlson, Gillin, Gorden, & Snyder, 1972). This diminution
has been correlated with a reduction or total absence of
the normal SWS release of GH (Vigneri, D'Agata, & Polosa,

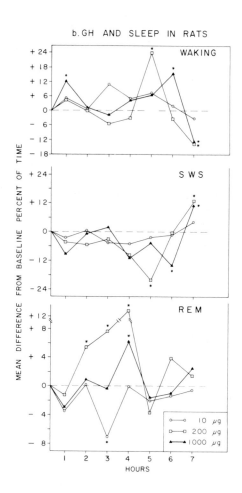

Figure 5. Effects of i.p. injection of bovine growth hormone (b.GH), given at the start of the recording sessions, on sleep-waking percentages in adult male albino rats (n = 6). The data is expressed as the change from baseline in the percent of recording time spent in waking, SWS and REM sleep. Mean baseline percentages for these states were 34%, 54% and

*12%, respectively. The peak increase in REM time seen after
the 200 µg dose of GH occurred in the absence of an increase
in SWS occurrence. Asterisks indicate significant differences
from baseline values for that time period.*

1971; Carlson, et al., 1972). This parallel between the
amount of REM sleep and the level of circulating GH during
the life span of man is noteworthy since there are no prior
experiments showing a possible mechanism which accounts
for the well known developmental pattern of REM sleep.
    If, as suggested by the results of the preceding GH
administration studies, endogenous secretion of GH plays
a significant role in triggering of REM episodes, then it
would be expected that the absence of GH would lead to a
marked diminution of REM time. Spies, Whitmoyer, and
Sawyer (1970) reported that ovariectomized and hypophysectomized rabbits had a 20-45% reduction in REM time compared
to ovariectomized rabbits with intact pituitary glands.
However, the effects of hypophysectomy on sleep in otherwise
normal rabbits was not examined. We, therefore, recorded
sleep-waking patterns from adult male normal and hypophysectomized rats following a 48 hour adaptation period. The
results, given in Table 1, show that the hypophysectomized
subjects had a nonsignificant reduction in percent of
recording time spent in REM sleep. However, compared to
normals the distribution of the lengths of the REM episodes
was considerably different in the hypophysectomized subjects
(see Figure 6). Normal rats had fewer short and more long
(greater than 4 minutes) REM episodes than the hypophysectomized subjects. Apparently, the absence of pituitary factors
is associated with a shortening or fragmenting of REM periods,
although total REM time is not drastically reduced. The

TABLE 1

*SLEEP-WAKING PERCENTAGES
IN NORMAL AND HYPOPHYSECTOMIZED ADULT RATS*

	Mean ± S.E. percent of recording time		
	Waking	Slow-wave sleep	REM sleep
Normal (n=6)	34.4 ± 2.9	53.7 ± 3.1	12.0 ± 2.1
Hypophysecto-mized (n=7)	42.9 ± 4.1	48.1 ± 2.7	8.8 ± 0.9

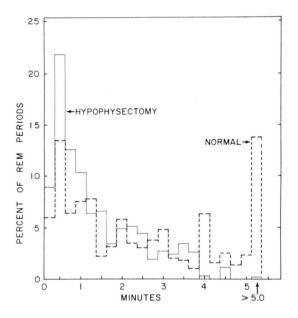

Figure 6. Distribution of the frequency of occurrence of different duration REM episodes in normal (n = 7 rats, 335 REM episodes) and hypophysectomized (n = 6 rats, 150 REM episodes) male adult albino rats. Data are expressed as the percent of the total number of REM periods which are of a given length. The distributions are significantly different for the normal and hypophysectomized rats (chi-square test, p < .001).

prior suggestion that the secretion of GH plays a role in producing REM episodes is not contradicted by the sleep data from the hypophysectomized rats. By analogy, other homeostatic regulatory systems, such as that controlling fluid intake, are responsive to a number of internal stimuli (oral factors, plasma tonicity, cellular volume). The absence of any one of these factors does not abolish the ability of the organism to regulate water ingestion since the other stimuli still exert their effects. A similar situation may exist in the case of the GH-REM sleep relationship. The presence of high plasma GH levels may be a sufficient, but not a necessary factor, for the occurrence of REM sleep. In the absence of GH other, as yet unidentified, physiological stimuli continue to promote the occurrence of REM periods.

Growth Hormone and Central Nervous System Neurochemistry

Surprisingly little is known concerning the effects of GH on any major neurochemical characteristic of the brain. In fact, there is only indirect evidence that the GH molecule, or a metabolite, enters the central nervous system. Using radioimmunoassay methods it was reported that normal and acromegalic humans contained measurable amounts of GH in the cerebrospinal fluid (CSF) taken from a spinal tap (Linfoot, Garcia, Wei, Fink, Sarin, Born, & Lawrence, 1970). To what extent this reflects the entry of GH into the neuronal or glial tissue of the brain is unknown, especially since the presence of other substances in spinal cord CSF (5-hydroxyindoleacteic acid) primarily reflects spinal cord physiology and is little related to brain CSF or brain tissue (Young, Lal, Martin, Ford, & Sourkes, 1973).

To help determine whether systemically administered GH does enter the CNS and whether it is distributed in a region-dependent manner we evaluated the uptake of i.p. injected ^{125}I-labelled rat GH into the brains of normal and hypophysectomized adult rats. The rats received 300 μC of ^{125}I-GH and were sacrificed by guillotine 30 minutes later. The brains were then dissected into the telencephalon, diencephalon, midbrain, pons-medulla, cerebellum, pituitary and pineal body. Peripheral tissue samples were taken from the liver, kidney, diaphragm and serum. The level of radioactivity in homogenates and in trichloracetic acid protein precipitates of each tissue sample was determined using liquid scintillation counting. The results, summarized in Table 2, show that, relative to background, appreciable levels of radioactivity were counted in each of the seven brain regions. The two areas examined which were taken from extra-blood-brain-barrier structures, the pineal and pituitary glands, had two to three times the counts as did the other regions of the CNS. This indicates that the blood-brain-barrier reduces, to some extent, the entry of

TABLE 2

UPTAKE OF ^{125}I-LABELED RAT GROWTH HORMONE INTO THE CENTRAL NERVOUS SYSTEM
AND PERIPHERAL TISSUES OF NORMAL (N) AND HYPOPHYSECTOMIZED (H) RATS

| | | Mean ± S.E. | | |
Tissue sample	n	nC/mg homogenate	nC/mg protein precipitate	Percent of homogenate radioactivity present in protein precipitate
Telencephalon				
N	5	175 + 30	32 + 5	18.7 + 0.2
H	3	256 + 151	48 + 23	18.7 + 0.1
Diencephalon				
N	5	216 + 61	39 + 16	18.1 + 0.3
H	4	193 + 94	34 + 14	17.9 + 0.1
Midbrain				
N	5	195 + 31	26 + 4	13.5 + 0.1
H	4	238 + 99	32 + 12	13.4 + 0.1
Pons-Medulla				
N	5	228 + 46	40 + 7	17.3 + 0.1
H	4	197 + 84	34 + 12	17.4 + 0.1
Cerebellum				
N	5	273 + 64	53 + 11	19.7 + 0.1
H	4	262 + 87	51 + 15	19.6 + 0.1
Pineal				
N	2	572 + 8	137 + 13	23.9 + 0.1
H	4	697 + 117	181 + 26	26.0 + 0.1

TABLE 2 (Continued)

Tissue sample	n	nC/mg homogenate	Mean ± S.E. nC/mg protein precipitate	Percent of homogenate radioactivity present in protein precipitate
Pituitary				
N	5	516 ± 158	157 ± 44	23.5 ± 4.1
H	-	---	---	---
Diaphragm				
N	5	14296 ± 8729	5003 ± 2733	35.0 ± 0.0
H	4	12979 ± 12477	4542 ± 3778	35.0 ± 0.1
Liver				
N	5	2368 ± 155	1141 ± 67	48.2 ± 0.0
H	4	2433 ± 628	1144 ± 290	44.8 ± 6.8
Kidney				
N	5	9042 ± 2521	4113 ± 1160	45.4 ± 0.8
H	4	8995 ± 3035	4111 ± 1200	45.5 ± 0.6
Blood (serum)				
N	5	2991 ± 348	825 ± 112	36.0 ± 0.0
H	4	3607 ± 480	1298 ± 149	36.0 ± 0.0

125_I-GH, or a metabolite, into the brain. However, there
do not appear to be any substantial differences in the ability
of the other brain regions (telencephalon, diencephalon,
midbrain, pons-medulla and cerebellum) to concentrate 125_I-GH.
The presence of endogenous circulating GH, as occurs in normal
rats, did not diminish the entry of 125_I-GH into the brain
since the normal and hypophysectomized values in Table 2
were comparable in most instances. The presence of radioactivity in peripheral tissues was much greater on a nC/gm
tissue basis than in the brain. Also, the association of
GH with brain and peripheral tissues appeared to differ
since the percent of tissue radioactivity bound to the
protein fraction of the peripheral tissue was 35-48% versus
only 13-25% for brain. The metabolic significance of this
difference, if any, is unclear.

Several lines of evidence suggest a link between brain
biogenic amines and GH release. There are many studies
examining the influence of dopamine and norepinephrine on
the secretion of GH in primates and rodents. Much of this
work is summarized elsewhere (Collu, Fraschini, & Martini,
1973; Muller, 1973), but it is worth pointing out that some
recent pharmacological and neurochemical evidence suggests
the presence of a serotonergic mechanism in the promotion
of GH secretion (Collu, Fraschini, Visconti, & Martini, 1972;
Collu, et al., 1973). One implication of such a mechanism
is that it provides a potential bridge between the major
extant theory of the neurochemical generation of SWS, the
serotonin hypothesis (Jouvet, 1972; discussed in Morgane, &
Stern, 1974), and the control of GH secretion. The serotonin
hypothesis of SWS is supported primarily by studies demonstrating that the interference with brain serotonin by
pharmacological means or by lesions of the raphe nucleus
(in which reside the perikarya of serotonin-containing
neurons of the brain) markedly disrupt SWS. Implicit in
the serotonin hypothesis is the yet to be demonstrated
relation that SWS is accompanied by an increase in serotonergic
activity. The concomitant involvement of the raphe-serotonin
system with the facilitation of GH release, as suggested by
Collu et al. (1972) would provide a neurochemical basis for
understanding how SWS produces an elevation of plasma GH
levels. Accordingly, a subset of the raphe neurons whose
activity generates SWS also activates the hypothalamo-
pituitary system responsible for GH secretion and increases
the release of GH-releasing factor which produces a rise in
plasma GH levels.

Most homeostatic regulatory organizations in the central
nervous system have, as an integral component, a negative

feedback characteristic by which the occurrence of a particular event, such as the release of a hormone, tends to inhibit the subsequent occurrence of that event. On the basis of the expectation of a negative feedback system one might suppose that GH would tend to depress brain serotonergic activity and perhaps other biogenic amines as well. Results from prior studies examining the effects of GH on polyamines in peripheral tissues demonstrate that GH decreases liver spermine and spermidine levels while increasing their synthesis rates (Kostyo, 1966; Russell, & Snyder, 1969; Raina, & Holtta, 1972). In neonatal rat brain, GH also enhances polyamine synthesis as judged by the stimulation of ornithine decarboxy-lase activity (Roger, Schanberg, & Fellows, 1974). Thus, indirect evidence exists for suggesting that GH administration might significantly influence brain biogenic amines.

We assessed the possible effect of GH on brain catechol- and indoleamines by injecting bovine GH (1.0 mg/kg, i.p.) or saline into normal rats and measured regional brain serotonin, 5-HIAA and norepinephrine levels .25, 1 and 3 hours later. The results, illustrated in Figure 7, show that GH produced significant and long lasting decreases in the biogenic amines and 5-HIAA in the diencephalon and pons-medulla, while not affecting telencephalic levels. In hypophysectomized rats, however, GH tended to increase the levels of these amines (Stern, Miller, Jalowiec, Forbes, & Morgane, 1975). This suggests that the presence of other pituitary factors can importantly influence the nature of the effects of GH on brain amines. In normal rats the decreased catecholamine levels following GH are also associated with a decrease in the stimulatory effect of d-amphetamine on general activity levels (Figure 8). GH administration can significantly alter the functioning of brain biogenic amines. The effects of exogenous injection of GH or of endogenous variations in plasma GH levels on the synthesis and release of brain biogenic amines remains to be studied.

Another major neurochemical aspect of brain function concerns the synthesis of macromolecules, especially proteins. A number of pituitary-peptides have been reported to influence brain protein synthesis. For example, ACTH fragments increase the rate of ^{14}C-leucine incorporation into protein by about 35% in brainstem slices (Reith, et al., 1974). Conversely, the absence of pituitary factors, as in hypophysectomized rats, results in a decreased rate of protein synthesis in the brain (Gispen, et al., 1971; Reith, et al., 1974). The involvement of GH in the regulation of brain protein synthesis is less clear. Indirect evidence from prenatal or neonatal administration of GH suggests that brain protein synthesis

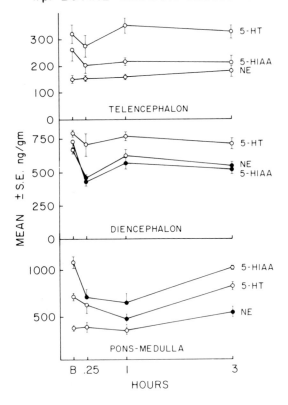

Figure 7.   Time course of effects of 1.0 mg/kg, i.p.,
of bovine growth hormone on norepinephrine (NE), serotonin
(5-HT) and 5-hydroxyindoleacetic acid (5-HIAA) levels in
three brain regions.   The abscissa represents the time
between injection of growth hormone and sacrifice.   Filled-in
points indicate significant differences from the saline
injected baseline (B) values.   (From Stern, Miller, Jalowiec,
Forbes, & Morgane, 1975).

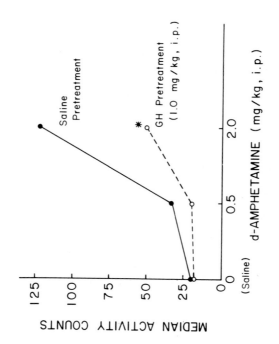

Figure 8

389

Figure 8. Effects of growth hormone (GH) on the stimulation of general activity levels by d-amphetamine in normal rats (n = 10). The rats were pretreated with either saline or GH and were then injected i.p., 30 minutes later with d-amphetamine at zero (saline vehicle), 0.5 or 2.0 mg/kg, i.p. The median activity counts of the 10 rats in each of the 6 drug conditions represents the activity in the 120 minute period following the second injection (saline or amphetamine). The asterisk indicates a significant difference from the saline pretreatment condition. (From Stern et al., 1975.)

is enhanced since increases in the number of neurons in the brain and in whole brain weight have been observed in GH treated rat pups (Zamenhof, Mosley, & Schuller, 1966). However, the reliability of this effect has been questioned (Diamond, Johnson, Ingham, & Stone, 1969; Croskerry, Smith, Shepard, & Freeman, 1973). In peripheral tissues, such as liver or diaphragm, GH clearly increases protein synthesis (Kostyo, 1968; Kostyo, & Nutting, 1973) as measured by elevated incorporation of radioactive amino acids into protein. These effects may last for up to 24 hours or more following a single dose of GH (Kostyo, & Nutting, 1973). In brain, increased levels of protein were also observed at two hours following an injection of GH in rats (Drucker-Colin et al., 1975). This effect could have resulted from increased protein synthesis and/or decreased catabolism of protein in the brain.

We employed a more direct measure of brain protein synthesis, the incorporation of a pulse-injected labelled amino acid into brain protein. Normal adult rats received an i.p. injection of bovine GH (1.0 mg/kg) or saline followed by an i.v. injection of ^{14}C-leucine (5 μC/300 gm) 20 minutes prior to sacrifice. The rats were sacrificed at 0.5, 3.0 and 6.0 hours following GH administration. The results, illustrated in Figure 9, show that 3 hours following the injection of bovine GH there is a significantly increased uptake, by about 40%, of ^{14}C-leucine into the homogenates of the brain tissue samples from the diencephalon and pons-medulla. The liver, however, does not show increased uptake of the leucine. The increased amino acid uptake in the brain after GH is reflected in a concomitant increase in amino acid incorporation into brain protein (protein pre-cipitated with trichloroacetic acid) three hours after GH. No significant increases in brain protein synthesis were observed 0.5 or 6 hours after injection of GH. The effect at three hours was due to the increased uptake of amino

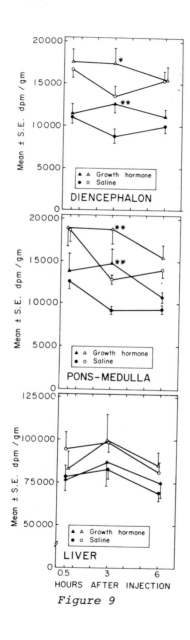

Figure 9

*Figure 9.   Effects of pretreatment with saline (n = 4
per point) or bovine growth hormone (n = 4 per point), i.p.,
on the uptake of i.v. injected ^{14}C-leucine into the brain
and liver of normal adult rats.   Open symbols represent dpm/gm
in tissue homogenates while filled symbols are counts present
in the trichloroacetic acid protein precipitates from each
tissue homogenate.   Asterisks indicate significant differences
in the level of radioactivity between the saline and growth
hormone treated groups for corresponding time points.   Three
hours after injection of growth hormone the two brain regions
examined, the diencephalon and pons-medulla, showed significantly increased uptake and incorporation into protein of
^{14}C-leucine when compared to the saline controls.*

acid pool and the protein precipitate was essentially
unchanged after GH.   Interesting, it is during the first
3-4 hours after injection of 200 μg of GH, i.p. (compared
to the 200-300 μg/rat dose in the present study) that REM
is markedly increased in the rat.   Thus, in a general sense,
there is a good correspondence between the post-GH time course
of increased REM sleep and elevated brain protein synthesis.
Whether there is a causative link between REM sleep and
brain protein synthesis remains to be determined.

Consideration of the results of the ^{125}I-GH uptake study
with the previously described effects of GH administration
on brain biogenic amine levels and protein synthesis provides
divergent lines of evidence supporting the view that GH does
enter the central nervous system and readily affects the
ongoing functioning of the brain.   The manner in which such
effects might have significance for memory, or other higher
order processes of the CNS, is discussed in the final section
of this paper.

The Sleep/Memory Interface: A Possible Role for Growth Hormone

We have previously discussed data which demonstrate that
the administration of GH can importantly alter sleep patterns
and several key aspects of brain neurochemistry, especially
protein synthesis.   To our knowledge, however, there is no
work on the question of whether GH plays a role in higher
order mental processes, such as memory formation.   A recent
investigation, reported that prenatal administration of
porcine GH to rats produced significant increases in learning
ability using brightness discrimination tasks when the
offspring were tested in adulthood (Sara, & Lazarus, 1974).

These data suggest that GH secretion, at least during the early developmental period, may predispose the CNS towards more rapid memory formation. Whether GH secretion during adulthood influences memory processes remains to be determined.

Based on the general observations that significant relations are likely to exist between sleep and memory function (reviewed in Stern, 1970; Greenberg, & Pearlman, 1974), biogenic amines and memory (Essman, 1970) and protein synthesis and memory (Glassman, 1969) and upon the fact that GH affects each of these processes (sleep, biogenic amines and protein synthesis) it might be hypothesized that GH secretion could also influence formation of long term memory. The framework of one possible set of interactions between sleep and memory is shown in Figure 10. The solid lines represent relations which have been reported to occur while the dashed lines represent hypothetical untested relationships. This schema can account for the observations that when a learning experience occurs there is a significant and specific elevation of REM sleep for the first 1-2 hours after the end of the training session (Lucero, 1970; LeConte, Hennevin, & Bloch, 1973; Hennevin, LeConte, & Bloch, 1974). What might be a mechanism mediating this learning-REM relationship? One possibility is that the learning process directly produces an increased release of GH (line "a" of Figure 10) or that when SWS occurs following the learning experience, while memory is still in short term or intermediate term storage, there is an enhanced release of GH (line "b"). If the post-learning release of GH is responsible for the increased REM time observed in rodents then one would expect that hypophysectomized rats would fail to show the post-learning augmentation of REM exhibited by normal rats. Hypophysectomized rats are known to be poor learners in the conditioned active avoidance tasks (Gispen, et al., 1971) similar to those used to demonstrate REM augmentation. It has also been reported that rats which are poor learners show little or no REM increase following the training session (LeConte, et al., 1973). It is thus quite possible that hypophysectomized rats would fail to show increased REM time following avoidance training.

The second major aspect of the schema of Figure 10 concerns the potential relation between the antecedent conditions which produce efficient memory formation, such as a normal level of brain protein synthesis and/or the occurrence of REM sleep, with the secretion of GH. Several studies, conducted primarily in rodents, provide results demonstrating that disruption of REM sleep shortly after a training experience impairs memory formation (see Greenberg, & Pearlman, 1974). Similarly, the inhibition of brain protein

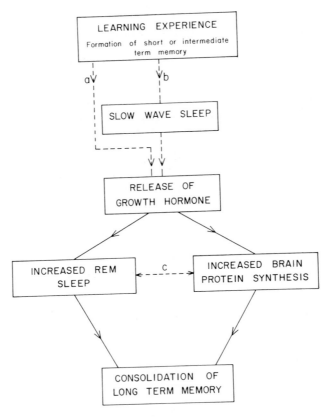

Figure 10. *Theoretical schema relating learning, sleep, and secretion of growth hormone to increased REM sleep, brain protein synthesis and the formation of long-term memory. Solid lines indicate relations for which supporting experimental data exist. Dashed lines represent hypothetical relations. See text for discussion of lines a, b, and c.*

synthesis with the antibiotic cycloheximide has been repeatedly found to block long term memory formation (Glassman, 1969). Since our initial studies, described earlier, have shown that the administration of GH increases both REM sleep and brain protein synthesis the possibility exists that endogenous GH release (as may occur during slow-wave sleep) plays a facilitative role in the development of new long term memories. The dashed line "c" in Figure 10 indicates the uncertainty as to the nature of the relation between brain protein synthesis and REM sleep. The GH produced augmentation **of both** REM and brain protein synthesis may represent two independent events which proceed in parallel with neither one necessarily depending on the other. There is also the possibility that the increased REM following GH may be the cause of the increased brain protein synthesis or, conversely, that the enhanced formation of macromolecules produces the increased occurrence of REM sleep. If GH secretion produces physiological conditions conducive to the consolidation of long term memory then post-trial injections of GH should enhance memory formation. At present, there has been no examination of this hypothesis.

In summary, several investigations of the effects of GH administration on sleep and central nervous system neurochemistry are described. We have tentatively outlined an as yet untested schema relating learning to the chain of events consisting of sleep--GH secretion--brain protein synthesis and REM sleep--long term memory consolidation. Future assessment of the involvement of GH and other pituitary peptides in brain function may reveal fundamental relationships between sleep and higher neural processes.

ACKNOWLEDGMENTS

Supported by grants HD 06364, GB 43529X and funds from the Worcester Foundation for Experimental Biology. We thank M. Miller, O. Resnick, W. B. Forbes, J. E. Jalowiec and J. P. Leahy for their valuable contributions.

REFERENCES

Bohus, B.   Pituitary-adrenal influences on avoidance and
    approach behavior of the rat.   In E. Zimmerman, W. H.
    Gispen, B. H. Marks & D. de Wied (Eds.), *Progress in
    Brain Research*. Vol. 39. Amsterdam: Elsevier, 1973.

Carlson, H. E., Gillin, J. C., Gorden, P., & Snyder, F.
    Absence of sleep-related growth hormone peaks in aged
    normal subjects and in acromegaly. *Journal of Clinical
    Endocrinology and Metabolism*, 1972, *34*, 1102-1105.

Collu, R., Fraschini, R., & Martini, L.   Role of indoleamines
    and catecholamines in the control of gonadotropin and
    growth hormone secretion.   In E. Zimmerman, W. H.
    Gispen, B. H. Marks, & D. de Wied (Eds.), *Progress in
    Brain Research*, Vol. 39. Amsterdam: Elsevier, 1973.

Collu, R., Fraschini, F., Visconti, P., & Martini, L.
    Adrenergic and serotonergic control of growth hormone
    secretion in adult male rats. *Endocrinology*, 1972, *90*,
    1231-1237.

Croskerry, P. G., Smith, G. K., Shepard, B. J., & Freeman,
    K. B.   Perinatal brain DNA in the normal and growth
    hormone-treated rat. *Brain Research*, 1973, *52*, 413-418.

Diamond, M. C., Johnson, R. E., Ingham, C., & Stone, B.
    Lack of direct effect of hypophysectomy and growth
    hormone on postnatal rat brain morphology. *Experimental
    Neurology*, 1969, *23*, 51-57.

Drucker-Colin, R. R., Spanis, C. W., Hunyadi, J., Sassin,
    J. F., & McGaugh, J. L.   Growth hormone effects on
    sleep and wakefulness in the rat. *Neuroendocrinology*,
    1975, *18*, 1-8.

Essman, W. B.   The role of biogenic amines in memory consoli-
    dation.   In G. Adam (Ed.), *The Biology of Memory*.
    Budapest: Akademiai Kiado, 1970.

Gispen, W. H., de Wied, D., Schotman, P., & Jansz, H. S.
    Brain stem polysomes and avoidance performance of
    hypophysectomized rats subjected to peptide treatment.
    Brain Research, 1971, *31*, 341-351.

Glassman, E.   The biochemistry of learning: An evaluation of the role of RNA and protein.   *Annual Review of Biochemistry*, 1969, *38*, 605-646.

Greenberg, R., & Pearlman, C.   Cutting the REM nerve: An approach to the adaptive role of REM sleep.   *Perspectives in Biology and Medicine*, 1974, *17*, 513-521.

Hennevin, E., LeConte, P., & Bloch, V.   Augmentation du sommeil paradoxal par l'acquisition, l'extinction et la reacquisition d'un apprentissage a reinforcement positif.   *Brain Research*, 1974, *70*, 43-54.

Jouvet, M.   The role of monoamines and acetylcholine-containing neurons in the regulation of the sleep-waking cycle.   *Ergebnisse der Physiologie, Biologischen Chemie, und Experimentellen Pharmakologie*, 1972, *64*, 166-308.

Kastin, A. J., Miller, L. H., Nockton, R., Sandman, C. A., Schally, A. V., & Stratton, L. O.   Behavioral aspects of melanocyte-stimulating hormone.   In E. Zimmerman, W. H. Gispen, B. H. Marks, & de Wied, D. (Eds.), *Progress in Brain Research*.   Vol. 39.   Amsterdam: Elsevier, 1973.

Kostyo, J. L.   Changes in polyamine content of rat liver following hypophysectomy and treatment with growth hormone.   *Biochemical and Biophysical Research Communications*, 1966, *23*, 150-155.

Kostyo, J. L.   Rapid effects of growth hormone on amino acid transport and protein synthesis.   *Annals of the New York Academy of Science*, 1968, *148*, 389-407.

Kostyo, J. L., & Nutting, D. F.   Acute in vivo effects of growth hormone on protein synthesis in various tissues of hypophysectomized rats and their relationship to the levels of thymidine factor and insulin in the plasma.   *Hormones and Metabolic Research*, 1973, *5*, 167-172.

LeConte, P., Hennevin, E., & Bloch, V.   Analyse des effets d'un apprentissage et de son viveau d'acquisition sur le sommeil paradoxal consecutif.   *Brain Research*, 1973, *49*, 367-379.

Linfoot, J. A., Garcia, J. F., Wei, W., Fink, R., Sarin, R.,
    Born, J. L., & Lawrence, J. H. Human growth hormone
    levels in cerebrospinal fluid. *Journal of Clinical
    Endocrinology*, 1970, *31*, 230-232.

Lucero, M. Lengthening of REM sleep duration consecutive
    to learning in the rat. *Brain Research*, 1970, *20*, 319-322.

Morgane, P. J., & Stern, W. C. Chemical anatomy of brain
    circuits in relation to sleep and wakefulness. In E.
    E. Weitzman (Ed.), *Advances in Sleep Research*. Vol. 1.
    New York: Spectrum Publications, 1974.

Muller, E. E. Nervous control of growth hormone secretion.
    Neuroendocrinology, 1973, *11*, 338-369.

Parker, D. C., Morishima, M., Koerker, D. J., Gale, C. C.,
    & Goodman, C. J. Pilot study of growth hormone release
    in sleep of the chair-adapted baboon: Potential as
    model of human sleep release. *Endocrinology*, 1972, *91*,
    1462-1467.

Raina, A., & Holtta, E. The effect of growth hormone on
    the synthesis and accumulation of polyamines in mammalian
    tissues. In A. Pecile & E. E. Muller (Eds.), *Growth
    and Growth Hormone*. Amsterdam: Excerpta Medica, 1972.

Reith, M. E. A., Schotman, P., & Gispen, W. H. Hypophysectomy,
    $ACTH_{1-10}$ and in vitro protein synthesis in rat brain
    stem slices. *Brain Research*, 1974, *81*, 571-575.

Roffwarg, H., Muzio, J., & Dement, W. The ontogenetic
    development of the sleep-dream cycle in humans. *Science*,
    1966, *152*, 604-619.

Roger, L. J., Schanberg, S. M., & Fellows, R. E. Growth
    and lactogenic hormone stimulation of ornithine
    decarboxylase in neonatal rat brain. *Endocrinology*,
    1974, *95*, 904-911.

Russell, D. H., & Snyder, S. H. Amine synthesis in regenera-
    ting rat liver: Effect of hypophysectomy and growth
    hormone on ornithine decarboxylase. *Endocrinology*,
    1969, *84*, 223-228.

Sara, V. R., & Lazarus, L. Prenatal action of growth hormone
    on brain and behavior. *Nature*, 1974, *250*, 257-258.

Sassin, J. F., Parker, D. C., Mace, J. W., Gotlin, F. W., Johnson, L. C., & Rossman, L. G. Human growth hormone release: Relation to slow-wave sleep and sleep-waking cycles. *Science,* 1969, *165,* 513-515.

Shaywitz, B. A., Finkelstein, J., Hellman, L., & Weitzman, E. D. Growth hormone in newborn infants during sleep-wake periods. *Pediatrics,* 1971, *48,* 103-109.

Spies, H., Whitmoyer, D. I., & Sawyer, C. H. Patterns of spontaneous and induced paradoxical sleep in intact and hypophysectomized rabbits. *Brain Research,* 1970, *18,* 155-164.

Stern, W. C. The relationship between REM sleep and learning: Animal studies. In E. Hartmann (Ed.), *Sleep and Dreaming.* Boston: Little Brown, 1970.

Stern, W. C., Miller, M., Jalowiec, J. E., Forbes, W. B., & Morgane, P. J. Effects of growth hormone on brain biogenic amine levels. *Pharmacology, Biochemistry, and Behavior,* 1975, *3,* 1115-1118.

Takahashi, Y., Kipnis, D. M., & Daughaday, W. H. Growth hormone secretion during sleep. *Journal of Clinical Investigation,* 1968, *47,* 2079-2090.

Takahashi, Y., Takahashi, K., Kitahama, K., & Honda, Y. A model of human sleep-related release of growth hormone in dogs. In M. C. Chase, Stern, W. C., & Walter, P. (Eds.), *Sleep Research. Vol. 3.* Los Angeles: Brain Information Service/Brain Research Institute, 1974 (abstract).

Vigneri, R., & D'Agata, R. Growth hormone release during the first year of life in relation to sleep-wake periods. *Journal of Clinical Endocrinology and Metabolism,* 1971, *33,* 561-563.

Vigneri, R., D'Agata, R., & Polosa, P. Growth hormone secretion related to sleep at different ages in man: Chronobiological and physiological implication. *II Progresso Medico,* 1971, *27,* 366-372.

Wied, D. de. Effects of peptide hormones on behaviour. In W. F. Ganong, & Martini, L. (Eds.), *Frontiers in Neuroendocrinology.* New York: Oxford University Press, 1969.

Young, S. N., Lal, S., Martin, J. B., Ford, J. M., & Sourkes, T. L. 5-Hydroxyindoleacetic acid, homovanillic acid and tryptophan levels in CSF above and below a complete block of CSF flow. *Psychiatria Neurologia Neurochirurgia,* 1973, *76,* 439-444.

Zamenhof, S., Mosley, J., & Schuller, E. Stimulation of the proliferation of cortical neurons by prenatal treatment with growth hormone. *Science,* 1966, *152,* 1396-1397.

Zimmerman, E., & Krivoy, W. Antagonism between morphine and the polypeptides ACTH, $ACTH_{1-24}$, and B-MSH in the nervous system. In E. Zimmerman, Gispen, W. H., Marks, B. H., & de Wied, D. (Eds.), *Progress in Brain Research.* Vol. 39. Amsterdam: Elsevier, 1973.

MEMORY AND SLEEP: NEUROENDOCRINOLOGICAL CONSIDERATIONS

ELLIOT D. WEITZMAN

Department of Neurology
Montefiore Hospital and Medical Center
The Albert Einstein College of Medicine
Bronx, New York 10467 USA

POSSIBLE INFLUENCES OF HORMONES ON MEMORY AND OTHER COGNITIVE FUNCTIONS

At the present time little is known about the role of hormones on memory processes during sleep. Although there is considerable evidence that certain hormonal deficiencies in man can lead to major abnormalities in cognitive functioning including disorders of memory, there is almost no information regarding hormonal effects on the normal short-term and con-solidation phases of memory function. However, it is not un-reasonable to consider that such mechanisms might exist. The profound effect of steroidal as well as polypeptide hormones on CNS neuronal cell metabolism and protein synthesis and the recent evidence that virtually all hormones have 24-hour sleep-wake secretory characteristics in normal man (Weitzman, Boyar, Kapen, & Hellman, 1975) certainly raises the possibil-ity that temporal phase relationships between sleep-stage patterns, hormonal availability, and memory processes might exist. In this report I will review some of the evidence in support of this notion in hopes that it might lead to produc-tive research efforts in this area.

Most present theories regarding CNS mechanisms of memory revolve about biochemical or electrophysiological events or combinations of the two. The biochemical area in which most work has been done concerns either a macromolecular theory of memory or one in which specific neurotransmitter neuronal systems have been implicated as mediating memory stage proc-

esses (Nakajima & Essman, 1973). The macromolecular theories
assume that mnemonic information is stored in an altered
macromolecular form from repetitive or even one trial infor-
mational input. The biochemical systems which have been implicated are changes in base sequences (purine and pyrimidine)
of RNA (Hyden & Egyhazi, 1962), changes in position of nucleotides of DNA or RNA (Gaito, 1961), or alterations of amino
acid sequences in proteins or glycoprotein molecules (Bogoch,
1968). These theories presume that such macromolecular
events then lead to alterations in neuronal functional activity either by altered enzyme induction processes or by
changes in critical membrane sites of the subcellular organ-
elles (such as an endoplasmic reticulum, mitochondria, golgi
apparatus or the complex pre- and post-synaptic apparatus).
These alterations are presumed to effect major changes in
control of frequency and rate pattern of neuronal discharge,
inhibitory-excitatory relationships, as well as neurotransmitter storage, release, and re-uptake mechanisms. Specific
neurotransmitters have been proposed as potential candidates
for memory processes and include acetylcholine (Deutsch,
1970), serotonin (Nakajima & Essman, 1973) as well as adrenergic biogenic amines (Roberts, 1970). The use of a wide
variety of non-specific and specific inhibitory drugs in animal learning studies have been a major technique in approach-
ing these biochemical CNS mechanisms (Barondes, 1970). Although in some cases these drugs have been found to produce
their presumed effect on "memory consolidation" by unexpected
and confounding ways (e.g., seizure discharges in the hippocampus after injection of actinomycin D [and puromycin] into
the hippocampus) (Nakajima & Essman, 1973), in others specific results have strengthened the hypothesis (e.g., cyclohexamide given subcutaneously almost completely suppresses
cerebral protein synthesis [94-97%], produces no seizure activity and significantly interferes with memory consolidation
processes [Barondes, 1970; Andry & Luttges, 1972]).

For our purposes in this discussion, the major point to
be made is that biochemical systems have been implicated in
memory functions which may be under considerable influence in
the CNS by a number of hormones. There is, of course, extensive evidence that all hormones will affect brain tissue metabolism in many different ways (Williams, 1974). However,
evidence that there are specific hormonal effects on biochemical mechanisms in relation to CNS memory processes is
meager. It should be emphasized, however, that with the exception of certain clinical pathological conditions, experimental work on the general issue of the role of hormones on
memory has been performed to only a limited extent.

There is now sufficient evidence to suggest that adrenocorticotrophic hormone (ACTH) may play a role in the acquisition of a conditioned avoidance response (in rats). In a
series of studies deWied (deWied & Bohus, 1966; deWied &
Witter, 1970; Bohus, 1970) and his group have shown that the
impaired acquisition of a conditioned avoidance response can
be restored to normal by ACTH and by peptide subportions of
the ACTH molecule, including α-melanocyte stimulating hormone
(α-MSH). These effects were shown in both intact and
adrenalectomized rats. They conclude that ACTH and related
peptides can act to influence the consolidation of memory.
Since we now know that ACTH occurs in a series of time dependent transient episodes of secretory bursts in relation to
the 24-hour sleep-wake cycle (see below), further studies
must be done to show that such pharmacological effects produced by long lasting pharmaceutical preparations can be
translated to a physiological temporal pattern of secretory
events.

Growth hormone (GH) has been reported to play an important role in the growth of the brain in fetal animals (rats)
(Clendinnen & Eayrs, 1961; Block & Essman, 1965; Zamenhof,
Mosley, & Schuller, 1966). In addition to an increase in
cell density in the cerebral gray matter, the subsequent
mature rat has been shown to have better performance and decreased extinction rates in a conditioned avoidance task. GH
causes an increase in the total RNA content in the cerebrum
of young, hypophysectomized rats. However, shortly after
birth there is little evidence that GH will alter brain
growth or significantly influence learning functions. There
is no clinical evidence that patients with acromegaly develop
significant alterations in cognitive function--although
alterations in affect and mood have been reported. Nor is
there any evidence that GH deficiency in childhood or adulthood is associated, in itself, with a cognitive or memory
disorder. Indeed, the specific metabolic function of the
daily transient and sleep related pulsatile releases of GH in
adult man is unknown (see below). Since it has been fully
documented that GH (in large doses and over prolonged time
periods) has strong stimulatory effects on the synthesis of
nucleic acids and protein macromolecules in many body tissues
(Kostyo & Nutting, 1974), it is possible that the transient
availability of GH could stimulate or play a permissive role
in such biochemical systems related to memory functions in
the brain. However, such considerations must remain purely
speculative at present.

Because of recent evidence that melatonin may be released during sleep in man (Pelham, Vaughn, Sandoch, &

Vaughn, 1973; Lynch, Wurtman, Moskowitz, Archer, & Ho, 1975;
Lynch, Wurtman, Moskowitz, & Weitzman, 1975) it is of interest to briefly review evidence that the pineal hormone may
have specific effects on brain function. It has recently
been reported that a single dose of melatonin given to two
patients with temporal lobe epilepsy was followed by a
slowing of the EEG, an increase in REM sleep, and a rise in
the convulsive threshold. Chronic administration of melatonin to two Parkinsonian patients produced improvement in
their mood and Parkinsonian symptoms (Antón-Tay, Diaz, &
Fernandez-Guardiola, 1971; Antón-Tay & Fernandez-Guardiola,
1973). In addition, in cats, deposition of melatonin into
the pre-optic area was reported to produce sleep with EEG
slow wave activity (Marczynski, Yamaguchi, Ling, & Grodjinski,
1964) and in chicks intravenous administration produced sleep
of 30 to 45 minutes (Barchas, DaCosta, & Spector, 1967;
Hishikawa, Cramer, & Kuhlo, 1969). Melatonin also prolonged
the sleeping time of mice when administered in a combination
of hexobarbital and melatonin (Barchas, DaCosta, & Spector,
1967). These and other data indicate that melatonin and
possibly other pineal substances may affect brain activity.
However, there is no evidence that memory function is affected by melatonin or pineal function.

Thyroid hormones have a major influence on both emotional and cognitive functions of the human brain. Profound
changes in short and long-term memory are seen in both hypo
and hyper-thyroid acquired conditions. In addition, prolonged hypothyroidism in infants and young children leads to
severe and permanent intellectual impairment (cretinism)
which can be partially reversed if recognized early and cor-
rected with thyroid medication. Anatomical studies of neuropathological changes have demonstrated that in such matura-
tional hypothyroid states, widespread abnormalities of the
axonal and dendritic arborization of neurons are especially
pronounced.

Thyroid hormones have been shown to exert important effects on protein metabolism, RNA synthesis and mitochondrial
respiratory enzyme function in many cells (Tata, 1974). One
of the clinical consequences of hypothyroidism and myxedema
is the loss of memory with generalized intellectual slowness.
In these cases the ability to consolidate or retain information is impaired and leads to a loss of memory for recent
events (Akelaitis, 1936; Asher, 1949). These specific memory
changes are a small part of a more global disturbance of
mental functions including apathy, lethargy, and slowness in
thought. Excessive somnolence may be present and, in some
cases, insomnia and irritability are seen, as well as psychotic

symptoms including delusions and hallucinations (Weiner & Ingbar, 1971). After two years of age acquired hypothyroidism is not irreversible with regard to mental functions (Smith, Blizzard, & Williams, 1957). It is also of some interest that administration of excessive thyroid accelerates the maturation of a number of CNS reflex, behavioral and EEG patterns in rats (Schapiro, 1968).

During the past two years, a series of reports have been published indicating that the tripeptide thyrotrophin-releasing hormone (TRH) may have significant behavioral CNS effects. Significant alterations in mood with an increase in mental clarity and alertness have been reported in patients with depression (Kastin, Ehrensing, Schalch, & Anderson, 1972; Prange, Wilson, Lara, Alltop, & Breese, 1972), schizophrenics (Wilson, Lara, & Prange, 1973) and in a child with a severe behavioral problem (Tiwary, Frias, & Rosenbloom, 1972). However, in a careful double-blind crossover study in depressive patients, Coppen, Montgomery, Peet, Bailey, Marks, and Woods (1974) have not confirmed the therapeutic action of intravenous TRH.

HORMONE PATTERNS DURING THE SLEEP-WAKE CYCLE IN MAN

Most of the hypothalamic-pituitary systems in man have been shown to have temporal patterns of secretion that are closely linked to 24-hour sleep-wake activity. The hormonal systems which have been studied include ACTH-cortisol, growth hormone (GH), prolactin, luteinizing hormone (LH) and follicle stimulating hormone (FSH) and thyrotrophic stimulating hormone (TSH). I will briefly describe the evidence demonstrating such 24 hour patterns primarily for ACTH-cortisol, LH and TSH since Dr. Jon Sassin at this Symposium will describe the sleep-wake relations for GH and prolactin. For a more extensive review the reader is referred to *Recent Progress in Hormone Research* (Weitzman, Boyar, Kapen, & Hellman, 1975) and *Chronobiological Aspects of Endocrinology* (Aschoff, Ceresa, & Halberg, 1975).

In 1964-1965 we found that the elevation of plasma 17-hydroxycorticosteroids (17-OHCS) during the latter half of the nocturnal sleep period was not a smooth gradual rise in hormonal concentration but rather was characterized by a series of episodic peak elevations (Weitzman, Schaumberg, & Fishbein, 1966). Utilizing a technique of measuring changes in plasma ^{14}C labelled cortisol specific activity, these episodes were shown to be due to newly formed (unlabelled) cortisol secreted into the blood (Hellman, Fujinori, Curti,

Weitzman, Kream, Roffwarg, Ellmann, Fukushima, & Gallagher,
1970). The finding of episodic secretion during the latter
half of the night's sleep was then extended to studies of the
24-hour pattern in normal adults who had a normal sleep-
waking cycle with 7 to 8 hours of regular noctural sleep
(Weitzman, Fukushima, Nogeire, Roffwarg, Gallagher, & Hellman,
1971). With sampling every 20 minutes, it was found that
episodic secretion was present throughout the entire 24-hour
period, and that the "circadian" concentration curve is actually the result of the temporal clustering pattern of episodic secretion.

Although we speculated at the time that the nocturnal
episodes might be related to the REM-non-REM sleep cycle,
other studies did not support a specific 1:1 relationship
between these secretory episodes and the short-term sleep
cycle, since when subjects were totally deprived of sleep for
one or two nights, the nocturnal episodes were not prevented
(Halberg, Frank, Harner, Matthew, Oaker, Granem, & Melby,
1961). When the sleep-waking cycle was acutely inverted a
significant delay in the re-establishment of the circadian
cortisol pattern occurred and a dissociation between the
sleep stage patterns and plasma cortisol concentration was
present (Weitzman, Goldmacher, Kripke, MacGregor, Kream, &
Hellman, 1968).

In order to evaluate the role of light and dark and visual perception in the 24-hour cycle we studied a group of
seven blind adult subjects, all without light perception
(five blind from birth, one had eyes removed at age 1, and
one lost all vision between ages 9 and 11) (Weitzman, Perlow,
Sassin, Fukushima, Burack, & Hellman, 1972). Cortisol was
secreted episodically in all of the blind subjects. Five had
a definite circadian pattern (low concentration in the evening and high in the morning). Two blind subjects had an
atypical pattern and did not clearly demonstrate a 24-hour
rhythm. There was no relation between the 24-hour pattern,
however, and whether the subjects had congenital or adventi-
tious blindness.

We have recently carried out a study of the effect of
large shifts in the ratio of natural environmental light and
darkness during seasonal extremes in the course of the polar
year on sleep patterns and 24-hour plasma cortisol and growth
hormone patterns (Weitzman, DeGraaf, Sassin, Hansen,
Godtlibsen, & Hellman, 1975). A group of seven healthy Nor-
wegian Air Force pilots were studied during four yearly seasons in an arctic environment (Tromso, Norway). No differences in total sleep or sleep stage percents were found for
any of the yearly seasons. A small but statistically signif-

icant increase in the mean plasma cortisol concentration and
amount secreted for 24 hours was found for the autumn-winter
seasons, as compared with the spring and summer. However, no
difference in the circadian curve of cortisol hormone pattern
was found. All subjects secreted growth hormone shortly
after sleep onset at night and no difference was found as a
function of season of the year. The choice of a relatively
stable group of Air Force personnel in our study decreased
the possibility of variable life styles producing deviations
of the diurnal routine of the sleep-wakefulness pattern.
Therefore, it does not appear that any seasonal sleep pattern
difference in man in the arctic is an obligatory direct re-
quirement of that environment, but rather suggests that, if
a change does occur, the effect is an indirect one mediated
through seasonally altered social and work schedules. The
clear consistent snychronization of the 24-hour cortisol and
GH patterns with the stability of the sleep stage patterns
and sleep waking 24-hour rhythm is in full agreement with the
concept that social and sleep cues are the dominant determi-
nants, in man, of circadian phase relationships.

We have carried out several studies investigating the
effect of altering the sleep-waking cycle on the 24-hour
pattern of cortisol secretion. In one study a group of
normal subjects was subjected to a two week 180° inverted
sleep-wake cycle, following one week of baseline measurements. In a second study, normal subjects were subjected to
a three week 180° sleep-wake cycle inversion, preceded by a
three week baseline, and followed by a three week reinversion
recovery period (Weitzman, Goldmacher, Kripke, MacGregor,
Kream, & Hellman, 1968; Weitzman, Kripke, Goldmacher,
MacGregor, & Nogeire, 1970). Both studies demonstrated a
delay of one to three weeks before evidence of inversion of
the circadian cortisol rhythm could be seen. Following
sleep-waking reversal, the characteristic pattern of a series
of peak elevations of plasma cortisol, occurring during the
later part of the sleep period, was disrupted. A significant
delay in the re-establishment of the circadian 17-OHCS
occurred, and a dissociation between sleep stage patterns and
plasma cortisol levels was present after sleep reversal.
Although considerable variability in the 24-hour rhythm of
urinary 17-OHCS took place during the three week inverted
portion of the experiment, a rapid reinversion (return to
baseline pattern) occurred within the first week (Weitzman,
Kripke, Kream, MacGregor, & Hellman, 1970).

We have also carried out a study of the effect of a prolonged 3-hour sleep-wake cycle (Weitzman, Nogeire, Perlow,
Fukushima, Sassin, MacGregor, Gallagher, & Hellman, 1974).

After one week of a normal control (baseline) period, seven healthy young adult subjects were subjected to a 3-hour sleep wake schedule (ultradian), which was adhered to for 10 days. Under this schedule they were allowed eight 1-hour sleep times, equally spaced throughout each 24-hour period. They were then allowed a normal nocturnal 8-hour sleep time for seven days. During all lights-out sleep periods, polygraphic definition of sleep stages and waking time was made. On the sixth 24-hour period of the first week (baseline) and on the eighth 24-hour period of the ultradian period, sequential 20-minute plasma samples were obtained by means of an in-dwelling intravenous catheter.

Despite significant sleep deprivation, a circadian pattern of total sleep time persisted throughout the 10-day ultradian condition. The distribution and amount of REM sleep time was most affected, with stages 3-4 sleep least affected. The time of maximum sleep was delayed by approximately six hours.

The temporal pattern of the secretory episodes of cortisol and the body temperature curves demonstrated a persistence of the 24-hour periodicity for all subjects during the ultradian condition. A 3-hour cortisol cycle was superimposed on the 24-hour pattern. This 3-hour cycle was entrained to the 3-hour sleep-waking cycle so that low plasma concentrations of cortisol were associated with the dark (sleep) period and high concentrations with the first hour after "lights on". No correlation could be demonstrated between a specific sleep stage and the subsequent release of hormone even though a correlation was present for total sleep. The persistence of a 24-hour sleep-waking cycle and cortisol pattern in spite of the attempt to disrupt these functions for 10 days demonstrates the highly resistant nature of these systems.

The 24-hour pattern of secretion of the gonadotrophin hormones is complex, as expected, because of the interrelated issues of maturation (pre-puberty, puberty, sexual maturity and post maturity), sex differences, menstrual cyclicity in mature females, and age-related factors with regard to sleep-waking cyclic patterns. Pre-pubertal children, pubertal boys and girls, and normal sexually mature adult men and women have been studied. There have been few studies of post-menopausal women and aged men and women. A most exciting finding has been that in pubertal boys and girls there is a major augmentation of luteinizing hormone (LH) during sleep periods (Boyar, Finkelstein, Roffwarg, Kapen, Weitzman, & Hellman, 1972). Shortly following the onset of sleep, and throughout the sustained nocturnal sleep period, the mean LH concentration was found to be 2 to 4 times higher than during wakefulness. Like other hypothalamic controlled pituitary hormones, the LH secretory patterns during sleep were characterized by regularly occurring secretory episodes. Although small irregular episodes can be recognized during waking times in the pubertal children, a 70 to 90 minute periodic secretion was most recognizable during sleep with an apparent association with the non-REM short-term sleep cycle. Most of the LH secretory episodes were initiated during non-REM sleep with termination in close temporal proximity to REM sleep.

In four pubertal boys (ages 14-15) who demonstrated the augmented nocturnal sleep (23:00-07:00) LH increase in concentration, acute inversion of their sleep-wake cycle (11:00-19:00) produced an increase in LH concentration during the day sleep period (Kapen, Boyar, Finkelstein, Hellman, & Weitzman, 1974). However, it was found that the mean nocturnal waking concentration was higher than during daytime waking in all subjects. This latter finding raises the interesting possibility that CNS regions responsible for LH secretion during nocturnal sleep might still exert increased control of LH release during the night when sleep was not present, and that it would require a more prolonged period than one day of sleep-wake cycle reversal to produce an adaptation of these brain regions to the phase shift.

The 24-hour patterns of LH for pre-pubertal children studied in our laboratories (ages 6-11) showed no difference in mean concentration for sleep compared with waking periods and the values were low (Boyar, Finkelstein, Roffwarg, Kapen, Weitzman, & Hellman, 1972). As pubertal maturation proceeds to sexual maturity, the waking LH concentrations increase and the peak values of the episodes of secretion approach those found in young adults. By sexual maturity, no differences were found between sleeping and waking LH concentrations in young adult men. In a group of normal men (ages 21-40) the 24-hour pattern (20-minute sampling) was characterized by a series of irregularly occurring secretory episodes but no difference was found in relationship to either the sleep-wake cycle or to sleep stages (Boyar, Perlow, Hellman, Kapen, & Weitzman, 1972).

Studies of the 24-hour pattern of LH secretion in adult women are, of course, complicated by changes in relation to the menstrual cycle. Following menstruation, the concentration of LH in the plasma progressively rises until the mid-cycle ovulatory period when the "LH surge" occurs and when plasma values are two or more times greater than those observed during other portions of the cycle. During the luteal

portion, LH concentration decreases for several days after
the LH surge and then low values are maintained through
menses (Ross, Cargille, Lipsett, Rayford, Marshall, Strott, &
Rodband, 1970). We have carried out 24-hour pattern sleep
waking studies in women (ages 23-27) during selected portions
of the menstrual cycle. During the earlier follicular phase,
the pattern of LH secretion was characterized by a sequence
of 10 to 15 secretory episodes during the 24-hour period
(Kapen, Boyar, Perlow, Hellman, & Weitzman, 1973). A consistent decrease in the plasma LH concentration was found during
the first few hours of the nocturnal sleep period for all
five women studied. When the onset of the first stage 2
sleep of the night was used as a reference point, a decrease
of approximately 33% in the mean plasma LH concentration was
present for the third hour after the onset of stage 2. This
clear decrease in LH concentration in the first half was followed by a rise in the latter half of the sleep period of the
night. Comparison was made with an age-matched normal male
group and no such pattern could be found for the men. In a
recent study, acute inversion of the 24-hour sleep-wake cycle
of women during the early follicular phase of the menstrual
cycle demonstrated that the early sleep period decrease in LH
concentration also accompanied the early sleep period of the
"day" sleep period (11 a.m.-7 p.m.) (Kapen, Boyar, Hellman, &
Weitzman, 1974).

During the past few years, several studies have reported
significant differences in plasma TSH concentration as a
function of time of day. In general, these studies have suggested that there is a 24-hour pattern with generally higher
concentrations in the late evening pre-sleep period and the
first few hours after the onset of nocturnal sleep. However,
when 24-hour measurements of plasma thyroxin were made, the
rapid fluctuations in concentrations did not appear to be
related to the 24-hour TSH pattern and specifically not related to the nocturnal TSH surge (O'Connor, Wu, Gallagher, &
Hellman, 1974; Pekary, Hershman, & Parker, 1975). We have
recently carried out 24-hour TSH measurement in collaboration
with Drs. Jack Oppenheimer and Martin Surks. Utilizing the
frequent sampling technique and polygraphic sleep stage
measurements, we have preliminary evidence in two normal
young men that a rise in TSH concentration occurred between
10:00 p.m. and 2:00 a.m. These data generally agree with the
recent reports outlined above.

SUMMARY

It is now clear that the hypothalamic-pituitary hormonal system functions in close temporal relationship with 24-hour sleep-waking function in man. Each system appears to have its own temporal organization and response to manipulation of the sleep-wake cycle. Since there is indirect but suggestive evidence that hormones have effects on biochemical mechanisms implicated in memory processes, it is possible that temporal phase relationships during the sleep-wake cycle might contribute to memory acquisition and consolidation processes. The availability of a humoral agent at the right time of the day, and at a time when CNS neuronal functions such as sleep and sleep stages are critically operative in relation to certain cognitive functions such as memory consolidation and/ or rehearsal processes, might significantly enhance the probability of these functions occurring. Certainly the evidence that hormones are often "permissive" to functional and biochemical processes would fit with this possibility. It is important to emphasize that there is no direct evidence to support such a temporal sleep-wake functional cognitive memory role for hormones. However, the theoretical potentiality for such a role can be considered and should be explored with appropriate experimental studies.

REFERENCES

Akelaitis, A. J. Psychiatric aspects of myxedema. *Journal of Nervous and Mental Disease,* 1936, *83,* 22-36.

Andry, D. K., & Luttges, M. W. Memory traces: experimental separation by cyclohexamide and electro-convulsive shock. *Science,* 1972, *178,* 518-520.

Antón-Tay, F., Diaz, J. L., & Fernandez-Guardiola, A. On the effect of melatonin upon human brain. Its possible therapeutic implications. *Life Science,* 1971, *10,* 841-850.

Antón-Tay, F., & Fernandez-Guardiola, A. Changes in human brain activity after melatonin administration. In D. C. Klein (Ed.), *Pineal Gland: Biochemistry and Physiology.* New York: Raven Press, 1973.

Aschoff, J., Ceresa, F., & Halberg, F. (Eds.) *Chronobiological Aspects of Endocrinology*. Stuttgart: F. K. Schattaner Verlag, 1975.

Asher, R. Myxoedematous madness. *British Medical Journal*, 1949, *2*, 555-562.

Barchas, J., DaCosta, F., & Spector, S. Acute pharmacology of melatonin. *Nature*, 1967, *214*, 919-920.

Barondes, S. H. Cerebral protein synthesis inhibitors block long term memory. *International Review of Neurobiology*, 1970, *12*, 177-205.

Block, J. B., & Essman, W. B. Growth hormone administration during pregnancy: a behavioral difference in offspring rats. *Nature*, 1965, *205*, 1136-1137.

Bogoch, S. *The Biochemistry of Memory*. New York: Oxford University Press, 1968.

Bohus, B. Central nervous structures and the effect of ACTH and corticosteroids on avoidance behavior. *Progress in Brain Research*, 1970, *32*, 171-183.

Boyar, R., Finkelstein, J., Roffwarg, H., Kapen, S., Weitzman, E. D., & Hellman, L. Synchronization of augmented LH secretion with sleep during puberty. *New England Journal of Medicine*, 1972, *287*, 582-586.

Boyar, R., Perlow, M., Hellman, L., Kapen, S., & Weitzman, E. Twenty-four hour pattern of luteinizing hormone secretion in normal man with sleep stage recording. *Journal of Clinical Endocrinology and Metabolism*, 1972, *35*, 73-81.

Clendinnen, B. G., & Eayrs, J. T. The anatomical and physiological effects of pre-natally administered somatotrophin on cerebral development in rats. *Journal of Endocrinology*, 1961, *22*, 183-193.

Coppen, A., Montgomery, S., Peet, M., Bailey, J., Marks, V., & Woods, P. Thyrotrophin-releasing hormone in the treatment of depression. *Lancet*, 1974, *2*, 433-435.

Deutsch, J. A.   The cholinergic synapse and the site of memo-
    ry.   *Science,* 1970, *174,* 788-794.

Gaito, J.   A biochemical approach to learning and memory.
    Psychological Review, 1961, *68,* 288-292.

Halberg, F., Frank, G., Harner, R., Matthew, J., Oaker, H.,
    Granem, H., & Melby, J.   The adrenal cycle in men on
    different schedules of motor and mental activity.
    Experientia, 1961, *17,* 1.

Hellman, L., Fujinori, N., Curti, J., Weitzman, E., Kream, J.,
    Roffwarg, H., Ellman, S., Fukushima, D., & Gallagher, T.
    Cortisol is secreted episodically by normal man.
    Journal of Clinical Endocrinology and Metabolism, 1970,
    30, 411-422.

Hishikawa, Y., Cramer, H., & Kuhlo, W.   Natural and
    melatonin-induced sleep in young chickens--a behavioral
    and electrographic study.   *Experimental Brain Research,*
    1969, *7,* 84-94.

Hyden, H., & Egyhazi, E.   Nuclear RNA changes of nerve cells
    during a learning experiment in rats.   *Proceedings of
    the National Academy of Sciences,* 1962, *48,* 1366-1373.

Kapen, S., Boyar, R., Finkelstein, J., Hellman, L., &
    Weitzman, E.   Effect of sleep-wake cycle reversal on
    luteinizing hormone secretory pattern in puberty.
    Journal of Clinical Endocrinology and Metabolism, 1974,
    39, 293.

Kapen, S., Boyar, R., Hellman, L., & Weitzman, E.   The re-
    lationship of LH secretion to sleep in women during the
    early follicular phase: effects of sleep reversal and a
    3 hour ultradian sleep-wake rhythm.   *Sleep Research,*
    1974, *3,* 169.

Kapen, S., Boyar, R., Perlow, M., Hellman, L., & Weitzman, E.
    Episodic release of luteinizing hormone at mid-menstrual
    cycle in normal adult women.   *Journal of Clinical
    Endocrinology and Metabolism,* 1973, *36,* 724-729.

Kastin, A., Ehrensing, R., Schalch, D., & Anderson, M.   Im-
    provement in mental depression with decreased thyrotro-
    pin response after administration of thyrotropin re-
    leasing hormones.   *Lancet,* 1972, *2,* 740.

Kostyo, J. L., & Nutting, D. F.   Growth hormone and protein metabolism.   In *Handbook of Physiology,* Section 7, Endocrinology, Volume 4, part *2.*   Baltimore: Williams and Williams, 1974.

Lynch, H. J., Wurtman, R. J., Moskowitz, M., & Weitzman, E. Daily rhythm in human urinary melatonin: correlation with sleep wake cycle.   *Federation Proceedings,* 1975, *34,* 424.

Lynch, H. J., Wurtman, R. J., Moskowitz, M. A., Archer, M. C., & Ho, M. H.   Daily rhythm in human urinary melatonin. *Science,* 1975, *187,* 169-171.

Marczynski, T. J., Yamaguchi, N., Ling, G., & Grodjinski, L. Sleep induced by the administration of melatonin to the hypothalamus in unrestrained cats.   *Experientia,* 1964, *20,* 435-436.

Nakajima, S., & Essman, W. B.   Biochemical studies of learning and memory.   In W. B. Essman & S. Nakajima (Eds.) *Current Biochemical Approaches to Learning and Memory.* New York: Spectrum Public, 1973.

O'Connor, J. F., Wu, G. Y., Gallagher, T. F., & Hellman, L. The 24 hour plasma thyroxin profile in normal man. *Journal of Clinical Endocrinology and Metabolism,* 1974, *39,* 765-771.

Pekary, A. E., Hershman, J. M., & Parker, D. C.   Characterization of the nocturnal TSH surge with a new high sensitivity radio immunassay for TSH.   *Clinical Research,* 1975, *23,* 129A.

Pelham, R. W., Vaughn, G. M., Sandoch, K. L., & Vaughn, M. K. Twenty four hour cycle of a melatonin-like substance in the plasma of human males.   *Journal of Clinical Endocrinology and Metabolism,* 1973, *37,* 341-344.

Prange, A. J., Wilson, I. C., Lara, P. P., Alltop, L. B., & Breese, G. R.   Affects of thyroxtropin-releasing hormone in depression.   *Lancet,* 1972, *2,* 999-1002.

Roberts, R. B.   Some evidence for the involvement of adrenergic sites in the memory trace.   *Proceedings of the National Academy of Sciences,* 1970, *66,* 310-313.

Ross, G. T., Cargille, C. M., Lipsett, M. B., Rayford, P. L., Marshall, J. R., Strott, C. A., Rodbard, D. Pituitary and gonadal hormones in women during spontaneous and induced ovulatory cycles. *Recent Progress in Hormone Research*, 1970, *26*, 1-62.

Schapiro, S. Biochemical and behavioral consequences of neonatal hormone administration. *General and Comparative Endocrinology*, 1968, *10*, 214-228.

Smith, D. W., Blizzard, R. M., & Williams, L. The mental prognosis in hypothyroidism of infancy and childhood. *Pediatrics*, 1957, *19*, 1011-1022.

Tata, J. R. Growth and developmental action of thyroid hormones at the cellular level. *Handbook of Physiology*, Section 7, Volume 3, Chapter 26, American Physiological Society, Washington, D.C., 1974.

Tiwary, C. M., Frias, J. L., & Rosenbloom, A. L. Response to thyrotrophin in depressed patients. *Lancet*, 1972, *2*, 1086.

Weiner, S. C., & Ingbar, S. H. (Eds.). *The Thyroid*. New York: Harper & Row, 1971.

Weitzman, E. D., Boyar, R. M., Kapen, S., & Hellman, L. The relationship of sleep and sleep stages to neuroendocrine secretion and biological rhythms in man. *Recent Progress in Human Research*, 1975, *24*, 399-446.

Weitzman, E. D., DeGraaf, A. S., Sassin, J. F., Hansen, T., Godtlibsen, O. B., & Hellman, L. Seasonal patterns of sleep stages and secretion of cortisol and growth hormone during 24-hour periods in northern Norway. *Acta Endocrinology*, 1975, *78*, 65-76.

Weitzman, E. D., Fukushima, D. K., Nogeire, C., Roffwarg, H., Gallagher, T. F., & Hellman, L. The twenty four hour pattern of the episodic secretion of cortisol in normal subjects. *Journal of Clinical Endocrinology and Metabolism*, 1971, *33*, 14-22.

Weitzman, E. D., Goldmacher, D., Kripke, D. F., MacGregor, P., Kream, J., & Hellman, L. Reversal of sleep-waking cycle: Effect on sleep stage pattern and certain neuroendocrine rhythms. *Transactions of the American Neurological Association,* 1968, *93,* 153-157.

Weitzman, E. D., Kripke, D. F., Goldmacher, D., MacGregor, P., & Nogeire, C. Acute reversal of the sleep-wake cycle in man: Effect on sleep stage patterns. *Archives of Neurology,* 1970, *22,* 485-489.

Weitzman, E. D., Kripke, D., Kream, J., MacGregor, P., & Hellman, L. The effect of a prolonged non-geographic 180° sleep-wake cycle shift on body temperature, plasma growth hormone, cortisol and urinary 17-OCHS. *Psychophysiology,* 1970, *7,* 307.

Weitzman, E. D., Nogeire, C., Perlow, D., Fukushima, J., Sassin, P., MacGregor, P., Gallagher, T. F., & Hellman, L. Effects of a prolonged 3-hour sleep-wakefulness cycle on sleep stages, plasma cortisol, growth hormone, and body temperature in man. *Journal of Clinical Endocrinology and Metabolism,* 1974, *38,* 1018-1030.

Weitzman, E. D., Perlow, M., Sassin, J. F., Fukushima, D., Burack, B., & Hellman, L. Persistence of the twenty four hour pattern of episodic cortisol secretion and growth hormone release in blind subjects. *Transactions of the American Neurological Association,* 1972, *97,* 197.

Weitzman, E. D., Schaumberg, H., & Fishbein, W. Plasma 17-hydroxycorticosteroid levels during sleep in man. *Journal of Clinical Endocrinology and Metabolism,* 1966, *26,* 121-127.

Wied, D. de, & Bohus, B. Long term and short term effects on retention of a conditioned avoidance response in rats by treatment with long acting pitressin and α-MSH. *Nature,* 1966, *212,* 1484-1486.

Wied, D. de, & Witter, A. Anterior pituitary peptides and avoidance acquisition of hypophysectomized rats. *Progress in Brain Research,* 1970, *32,* 213-218.

Williams, H. I. *Textbook of Endocrinology.* New York: Williams & Wilkins, 1974.

Wilson, I. C., Lara, P. P., & Prange, A. J. Thyrotrophin releasing hormone in schizophrenia. *Lancet,* 1973, *2,* 43-44.

Zamenhof, S., Mosley, J., & Schuller, E.   Stimulation of the proliferation of cortical neurons by prenatal treatment with growth hormone.   *Science,* 1966, *152,* 1396-1397.

THE EFFECT OF SLEEP ON HUMAN LONG-TERM MEMORY

BRUCE R. EKSTRAND, TERRY R. BARRETT,
JAMES N. WEST, and WILLIAM G. MAIER

Department of Psychology
University of Colorado
Boulder, Colorado 80302 USA

Sleep facilitates memory. There is no doubt about it. This effect was first demonstrated in 1924 by Jenkins and Dallenbach (1924) and has been replicated many times. We refer to this as the *sleep effect*. To be specific, the sleep effect refers to the fact that performance is superior when sleep occurs during the interval between learning and recall than when there is no sleep during this retention interval. In the prototype experiment, subjects learn a list of associations by the paired-associate learning method. Upon reaching a common learning criterion, the subjects are divided into two groups, sleep and awake. After a specified retention interval of either sleeping or being awake and carrying out normal waking activities, the two groups are tested for recall of the learned associations. The sleep effect refers to the fact that recall or memory is higher in the group which stayed awake. As we said, the sleep effect has been demonstrated many times. There is no argument about the reliability of the effect. There is an argument about why the effect occurs.

For the past six years we have been investigating the effects of sleep during the retention interval on human, long-term memory in an effort to understand why sleep facilitates memory. Our focus has been on trying to understand why forgetting occurs and our hope has been that an understanding of the sleep effect will help us to answer questions about forgetting. We would like to review our efforts in this regard and present data on a new phenomenon relating sleep and memory, a phenomenon which greatly complicates the picture.

THREE THEORIES OF THE SLEEP EFFECT

There are three major interpretations of the sleep effect, each one coming from an overall theory about memory and forgetting. The sleep effect is one phenomenon (perhaps the only one) of memory that all three theories have attempted to explain. For most other phenomena, the experimental paradigms used by the proponents of the three theories have been so different that there has been little or no direct comparison of all three theories. This state of affairs means that the sleep effect is somewhat like a common "battle ground" for the three theories. We have been trying to pit the theories against each other on this battle ground to see which one gives the best account of itself when it comes to explaining the sleep effect.

The first theory is decay theory. This theory says that forgetting is a matter of decay of the neurobiological traces that underlie learning. Presumably there is some ongoing, catabolic process that is responsible for the decay of the traces. As time passes, the catabolic process does its work and the result is forgetting. In order to account for the sleep effect, it may be assumed that the decay process, whatever it is, occurs at a slower rate during sleep than during wakefulness. It is a fact that general body metabolism is lower during sleep than wakefulness and so it is reasonable to assume that any neurobiological process could be taking place at a slower rate during sleep than during wakefulness. If the decay process is slower during sleep then, of course, we would expect to find the sleep effect.

The second theory is interference theory. This theory says that forgetting is caused by interfering learning. The most potent interfering learning is learning which takes place during the retention interval. It is known as interpolated learning (IL) and is the cause of retroactive inhibition (RI). The learning of the first task, the one which will be tested at the time of recall is usually referred to as original learning (OL). Forgetting takes place because the OL task suffers from the RI produced by the IL. In words, forgetting occurs because there is other learning taking place between the original learning and the memory test. If there were less learning taking place during the retention interval, it is obvious that this theory predicts that memory would be improved. This is, of course, how interference theory can account for the sleep effect. Going to sleep prevents interfering learning, so there is less RI, meaning better recall.

In 1924, when Jenkins and Dallenbach first demonstrated the sleep effect, it was believed that the very existence of the sleep effect "proved" that the interference theory was correct and the decay theory was wrong. Since time continued to pass during sleep, the argument was that the decay process, if it existed, would continue to operate. For this reason, it was assumed that decay theory would have to predict no difference in forgetting between sleep and awake groups. The first demonstration of the sleep effect was then taken as sort of a final proof that decay theory was wrong. Of course, now it is easy to see that all that a decay theory would have to do in order to account for the sleep effect would be to suggest that the rate of the decay process is slower during sleep than wakefulness. But in 1924 the times were in favor of the behaviorally-oriented inter- ference theory and decay theory was dealt a severe blow by the demonstration of the sleep effect. Today, with our interest in the neurobiology of memory, we can treat a decay hypothesis with more respect.

The third theory of memory is the consolidation theory. This theory, whose leading advocate is James McGaugh, one of our conference co-chairmen, suggests that there are neuro- biological processes which persist after the termination of a learning experience. Storage of information into long- term memory is dependent upon these processes. It is these processes that constitute the laying down of a physical representation in the brain of the learning experience. This is called the consolidation of memory. Treatments which presumably disrupt the consolidation process, such as electroconvulsive shock or seizure inducing drugs, are known to disrupt memory in a retrograde manner. Recent learning experiences are most affected presumably because the traces of these experiences have not yet consolidated. Presumably, because the consolidation has been completed by the time the convulsive treatment is given, older memories are not as affected. On the other hand, drug treatments which facilitate the consolidation process (neural excitants such as strychnine and picrotoxin), lead to improvements in memory. The consolidation explanation of the sleep effect would be that sleep facilitates the consolidation process. Such an account, however, predicts that the sleep effect will occur only if the sleep comes immediately after learning. Delayed sleep would not have a facilitating effect on the consolidation process because the consolidation would be completed before sleep occurred. This interpretation has received support because there have been at least three reports that delayed sleep is less effective than immediate sleep (Heine, 1914; Ekstrand, 1972; McGaugh & Hostetter, Note 1). This phenomenon will be referred to as the immediate-delayed sleep effect.

The Immediate-Delayed Sleep Effect

The importance of the immediate-delayed sleep effect should not be overlooked in this discussion because it is an effect which consolidation theory predicts and neither interference nor decay theory can easily account for. Both immediate and delayed sleep should reduce interfering learning during the retention interval and so according to interference theory both immediate and delayed sleep should result in a better memory than no sleep, but there should be no difference between immediate and delayed sleep. Likewise, a decay theory would predict that the rate of decay would be reduced during the sleep period regardless of whether the sleep came immediately after learning or was delayed for some time after learning. So the existence of the immediate-delayed sleep effect is a problem for the inter-ference and decay theories and a "cornerstone" of the consolidation theory. Ever since we demonstrated the immediate-delayed sleep effect for the first time in our laboratory (Ekstrand, 1972) we have been trying to understand it. We have completed four different experiments on the immediate-delayed sleep effect since our first experiment. We are sorry to report that not only do we not understand the effect, but we have failed on four subsequent occasions to replicate it.

The very first time we tried to produce the immediate-delayed sleep effect, we succeeded. There were just two groups. The retention interval between OL and recall was 24 hours. The immediate sleep group learned the OL paired-associate task and immediately went to bed for eight hours. They then got up and spent the next 16 hours awake carrying out their normal daily activities. At the end of this 16 hours of wakefulness the subjects returned to the laboratory and were tested for recall. In the delayed-sleep condition, the subjects learned the same OL task to the same criterion. Immediately after learning they were released from the lab and spent 16 hours awake. They then returned to the lab and went to sleep for eight hours after which they got up and were tested for recall of the OL task. The two groups differed significantly in the percentage of loss from memory (the number of pairs learned minus the number of pairs recalled divided by the number learned). Percent loss in the immediate sleep condition was 19.26% compared to a 34.07% loss in memory in the delayed-sleep condition. The superior memory (less loss) in the immediate-sleep condition is, of course, the immediate-delayed sleep effect.

This experiment, while demonstrating that immediate sleep is more beneficial to memory than delayed sleep, does not answer the question as to whether or not the delayed sleep is having any beneficial effect at all. To do so, there must be a condition in which there is no sleep whatsoever during the retention interval. This first experiment did not include such a condition because the retention interval was 24 hours and a no-sleep condition would thus have involved sleep deprivation. At this point in time we were now convinced that the immediate-delayed sleep effect was reliable and we set out to see if delayed sleep was having any effect compared to a no-sleep condition.

Our next three experiments all used essentially the same design, involving three retention-interval conditions (immediate sleep, delayed sleep, and no sleep) and a 14-hour retention interval. In the immediate sleep condition, Ss learn the OL paired-associate list and go directly to bed for the first 7 hours of the retention interval. They are then awakened and released from the laboratory for 7 hours of waking activity, after which they return and are tested for recall. In the delayed sleep condition, the Ss learn the OL list, leave the lab for 7 hours of waking activity, return and go to sleep for 7 hours, and then are awakened and tested for recall. Finally, in the no-sleep condition, the Ss learn the OL task and are then released from the lab for 14 hours of waking activity, after which they return and receive the recall test. It should be pointed out that in all these experiments there is a confounding of retention-interval condition with the time of day at which learning and recall take place. Immediate sleep Ss are learning late at night and are recalling in the early afternoon of the next day. Delayed sleep subjects are learning late in the afternoon and recalling early the next morning. No-sleep subjects are learning early in the morning and recalling late in the evening. This confound exists because we chose to have the subjects do their sleeping at the normal time of day and to be awake during the daytime. It would, of course, be possible to have subjects in all three conditions learn and recall at the same time, but this would introduce additional problems such as trying to get subjects to sleep normally during daytime hours. We obviously do not know what problems are introduced by test and time of day, although we can report that we have never observed significant differences in speed of learning of the PA task despite the fact that the

time of day is different. Of course there could be subtle
circadian rhythm effects, but there does not seem to be an
adequate way to control for these in this experiment without
introducing other problems.

The three experiments we have completed with this
design involved other variables, notably the degree of
original learning and the imagery value of the word pairs
in the list. These variables were of interest because we
thought they might interact with the retention-interval
condition variable but this never occurred so we will present
only the data for the retention-interval condition variable.
The means for percent loss in memory for the three conditions
in each of the three experiments are shown in Table 1. Also
in Table 1, we have pooled the data across all three experiments and present overall means for the three conditions.
There was a significant difference between the average of
the two sleep conditions (immediate and delayed) and the
no-sleep condition, but the difference between the two
types of sleep conditions (immediate vs. delayed) was never
significant.[1] Looking at the overall means, it can be seen
that the amount of forgetting was almost identical in the
immediate and delayed sleep conditions (23.47 vs. 24.56).   It
can also be seen that both sleep conditions are superior to
the no-sleep condition. To summarize these experiments we
might say that memory is facilitated if there is sleep during
the retention interval, but that it makes no difference
whether the sleep comes immediately after learning or immediately before recall. In short, there was no evidence of the
immediate-delayed sleep effect. Needless to say we were
disappointed and dismayed by these failures to find the effect
which we had seen in our first experiment but we have been
unable to find a methodological reason as to why we obtained
the effect in our first attempt but failed on our next three
attempts.

TABLE 1

*MEAN PERCENT LOSS AS A FUNCTION OF
RETENTION-INTERVAL CONDITION*

	Immediate sleep	Delayed sleep	No sleep
Exp. I	17.41	25.29	29.75
Exp. II	22.69	18.30	39.38
Exp. III	30.32	30.10	44.24
Overall	23.47	24.56	37.79

We decided that there was a possibility that the first attempt involved a sampling error, or that somehow the effect depended upon there being at least a 24-hour retention interval. The first study had used 24-hours as the interval while the three failures had reduced this interval down to 14 hours so that a no-sleep condition could be run without introducing sleep deprivation. So we went back and repeated the first experiment using the exact same lists, degree of learning, and procedures to see if we could find the effect again. Again there were just two groups (immediate or delayed sleep) and a 24-hour retention interval. The results were disappointing for the fourth time. There was a mean of 28% memory loss in the immediate sleep condition and only a 20% loss in the delayed condition. The difference was not significant, but it may be noted that this time there was numerically more forgetting in the immediate sleep condition than in the delayed sleep condition.

From this series of experiments we are forced to conclude that there is not a reliable immediate-delayed sleep effect. The results show that sleep during the retention interval facilitates memory (reduces forgetting), but it apparently makes no difference whether the sleep comes immediately after learning or is delayed. This, of course, is quite inconsistent with the consolidation interpretation of the overall sleep effect. The results are consistent with both the interference and decay interpretations.

On the basis of this series of experiments, we conclude that consolidation differences are not responsible for the differences in memory between subjects who sleep and subjects who are awake during the retention interval. This conclusion should not be taken to mean that consolidation processes do not play a role in human memory. The conclusion applies only to the particular experimental design and procedures we have employed, procedures which we feel are not particularly suited to the demonstration of consolidation effects in general. For one thing, the task involves many trials and takes many minutes to learn. Also, the subjects must usually reach a fairly high learning criterion before we consider the list to be "learned." Finally, after learning there is likely to be a fairly long time interval before the subject actually falls asleep. The subject must leave the learning room, go to his bedroom, undress, and get into bed, and then it is still likely that it will take an additional 15 to 30 minutes before actual sleep occurs. The time interval from the onset of the learning task to the onset of actual sleep can easily be 45 minutes to an hour. All this means that consolidation processes could have been

operating during learning and for some short time after learning, but that consolidation could have been complete before
sleep onset. In situations where the learning task is very
brief and where sleep could be introduced very quickly after
learning, it is quite possible that sleep would facilitate
the consolidation and lead to superior retention. Of
course, sleep might disrupt consolidation (see the paper by
Guilleminault in this volume). We are only suggesting that
consolidation is not a factor in the experimental paradigm
we have employed. Nevertheless, we do find a sleep effect
with this paradigm and so we conclude that the explanation
for this superior memory after sleeping is not to be found
in consolidation theory. Instead, we turn our attention
to the decay and interference theories.

The First-Half, Second-Half Effect

In attempting to distinguish between the decay and
interference interpretations of the overall sleep effect,
we have employed a paradigm which compares memory over the
first and second half of the night (Barrett & Ekstrand,
1972; Fowler, Sullivan, & Ekstrand, 1973; Yaroush, Sullivan,
& Ekstrand, 1971). The rationale for this paradigm centers
around the fact that sleep is not a unitary phenomenon, but
instead consists of several different stages that are,
at the extremes, dramatically different from a physiological
point of view. At one end there is Stage-4 sleep characterized by high amplitude slow waves (delta waves) predominating
in the EEG and at the other end there is rapid-eye-movement
sleep (REM sleep) characterized by a desynchronized EEG and
the presence of rapid eye movements in the electro-oculogram.
Compared to Stage-4 sleep, REM sleep appears to be much more
activated in character and much closer to wakefulness in
terms of physiological arousal. In contrast, Stage-4 sleep
seems physiologically most distinct from wakefulness.
Behaviorally speaking, however, in both stages the subjects
are asleep and are not capable of learning; therefore, both
stages would prevent interfering learning. In short, the
two types of sleep represent great differences in physiological activity, but no difference in the opportunity to learn
interfering material. The question we asked and have been
attempting to answer for over six years is whether or not
memory will be affected by the type of sleep that occurs
during the retention interval.

    Assuming that the decay rate would be higher when there
is substantial physiological activity than when this activity

is minimal, a decay theory would predict that forgetting would be less when the retention interval was filled with Stage-4 sleep than when it was filled with REM sleep. In contrast, the interference theory would be hard pressed to account for a difference of this sort. This theory would predict that both Stage-4 intervals and REM intervals would result in less forgetting than awake intervals (due to the prevention of interference by sleep) but there should be no difference between the two types of sleep since they both prevent interpolated learning equally well. In short, we felt that a comparison of forgetting between REM-filled and Stage-4-filled retention intervals would be a crucial test of the two theories.

The only problem remaining is how to produce experimentally these two types of retention intervals. After trying to manipulate REM and Stage-4 with drugs, and with deprivation (waking the subject each time he enters REM or Stage-4), we settled on a paradigm that involves much less intrusion into the normal sleep cycle. It involves comparing memory over the first and second halves of a normal 8-hour sleep interval. It has been known for some time that the majority of the Stage-4 sleep occurs in the first 4 hours of the night and the majority of the REM sleep occurs during the second 4 hours of the night. The other stages of sleep are more evenly distributed over the entire night. This means that a retention interval that is defined over the first half of the night will have large amounts of Stage-4 sleep and small amounts of REM sleep compared to a retention interval defined over the second half of the night.

Our design in the series of experiments we have completed on this effect consists of three conditions: first half, second half, and awake. In the first-half condition, the subjects learn the OL task (again paired-associate learning) and then go right to bed and are allowed to sleep undisturbed for the first half of the night. They then are awakened and tested for recall. This means that for this group, the retention interval should have high Stage-4 percentages and low REM percentages. The second-half condition involves having the subjects sleep through the first half of the night after which they are awakened and given the learning task. They then return to sleep for the second half of the night which is now the retention interval, and are tested for recall upon awakening. Thus, the second-half condition has a retention interval high in REM and low in Stage-4 percentages. Finally, the awake condition has a retention interval that involves no sleeping at all. The subjects come to the lab, learn the task, and then stay awake for the retention interval, and are finally tested for recall.

TABLE 2

*MEAN PERCENT LOSS AS A FUNCTION OF FIRST-HALF,
SECOND-HALF, OR AWAKE RETENTION INTERVALS*

	First half	Second half	Awake
Experiment I (Yaroush *et al.,* 1971)	14.01	31.82	38.26
Experiment II (Barrett and Ekstrand, 1972)	20.90	41.94	56.34
Experiment III (Fowler *et al.,* 1973)	18.86	35.55	48.24
Experiment IV (Fowler *et al.,* 1973)	20.76	34.44	42.04
Overall	18.63	35.94	46.22

The results from a series of four experiments involving these three retention-interval conditions are shown in Table 2 (percent loss means), along with an overall mean percent loss pooled across the four experiments. The results are quite consistent in all four experiments. Memory is best (forgetting is least) when the retention interval is filled with the first half of a night's sleep, next best when the second half of a night's sleep is the retention interval and worst when the subjects are awake during the retention interval. The difference between the first and second half was significant in each experiment, and the difference between the second half and the awake conditions was significant in all but the first experiment. Looking at the overall means, we can see that there is almost twice as much forgetting during the second half of the night compared to the first half. This difference defines the first-half, second-half effect and is very substantial. We can also see, however, that the second-half condition is superior to the awake condition, but by a smaller amount.

Our physiological recordings during these retention intervals have verified the fact that the first and second halves of the night are indeed filled with different amounts of REM and Stage-4 sleep but are equal in the percentages of the other sleep stages. Thus, we conclude that memory is better over a retention interval with high amounts of Stage-4 sleep than one with high amounts of REM sleep. This difference is consistent with the prediction from decay theory and inconsistent with the interference theory. The advantage of the second-half condition over the awake condition could be due to the prevention of interfering learning, but it could also be due to a lower decay rate during the second half of the night than during wakefulness. So we cannot conclude that prevention of interference by sleep is not involved at all in the overall sleep effect. But we can conclude that there must be something else going on besides reduced interference during sleep. We believe that this is a reduced rate of decay during sleep, particularly during slow-wave sleep.

The four experiments in Table 2 have used various procedures designed to eliminate alternate interpretations of the first-half, second-half effect. Experiment II eliminated time-of-day as an explanation by running all three conditions such that the retention interval occurred between 2:50 a.m. and 6:50 a.m. In all four experiments, there has never been a difference in speed of learning the OL list, so the effect cannot be explained on the basis of a simple degree-of-learning explanation. We have also used a procedure where first-half subjects are allowed to go to sleep before learning, but we awaken them as soon as they get to Stage 2, so the effect cannot be explained by the fact that first-half subjects were not awakened from sleep just before OL whereas second-half subjects were.

However, there is a problem of confounding that exists in all four experiments. The first-half subjects have had essentially no sleep at the time of OL whereas the second-half subjects have had four hours of sleep prior to OL. This also applies at the time of recall where it can be seen that first-half subjects are recalling after having had only four hours of sleep while second-half subjects have had eight hours. It is conceivable that the difference in the amount of prior sleep at the time of learning or recall could be producing the effect instead of the effect stemming from the type of sleep the subjects experience *during* the retention interval.

The Prior Sleep Effect

We have completed three experiments on the effect of prior sleep on memory and report the results for the first

time here. We had dismissed the prior sleep confounding in
our first-half, second-half experiments because in order to
account for the advantage of the first-half condition, one
would have to predict that 4 hours of sleep prior to learning
would have a *detrimental* effect on memory for something learned
after sleep. Our intuitions told us that this could not be
possible. If anything, we felt that the prior sleep would
facilitate memory for things learned subsequently because
we assumed that four hours of sleep would in some sense
"restore" the capacity of the brain for learning and memory,
if it would have any effect at all. We are sorry to report
that our intuitions were wrong, but we are happy to report
a very interesting phenomenon in its own right which we call
the prior sleep effect.

The question is, "Does sleep coming *just prior to* learning affect the subsequent memory for the learned material?"
The answer is unequivocally yes and the effect is such that
prior sleep *decreases* memory.

Our paradigm for demonstrating the prior sleep effect
is quite straightforward. We ask subjects to learn a paired-
associate list to criterion and to recall that list 4 hours
later. This 4-hour retention interval is filled with waking
activity in the laboratory (studying, reading magazines,
playing games such as Monopoly). The variable is whether or
not the subjects do any sleeping prior to learning the OL
task. Now we are manipulating sleep *before* learning instead
of sleep during the retention interval after learning has
taken place.

Our first experiment involved three conditions. The
prior sleep condition had four hours of sleep prior to
learning. Subjects in this condition came to the lab at
night and slept from 10 p.m. to 2 a.m. and then were awakened
and completed the OL task. They spent the next four hours
(the retention interval) awake in the lab and were then tested
for recall. The other two conditions involved no prior
sleep; the difference between them was the time of night of
the retention interval. In the awake-control I condition,
the retention interval was from 10 p.m. until 2 a.m.--subjects
came to the lab, learned at 10 p.m., stayed awake for four
hours and recalled at 2 a.m. The awake-control II condition
had the retention interval set from roughly 2 a.m. until
6 a.m. (this is the approximate time of the retention interval
in the prior-sleep condition). Subjects in awake-control II
came to the lab and were awake from 10 p.m. until 2 a.m. at
which time they completed the OL task and then remained
awake for the retention interval and were tested for recall
at about 6 a.m.

The results demonstrated a significant, although not a large prior sleep effect. Forgetting was 45.50% in the prior sleep condition, and 38.50% and 31.50% in awake-controls I and II, respectively. The average of the two control conditions was significantly different from the prior sleep condition, and the two controls did not differ significantly. In short, four hours of sleep prior to learning resulted in more forgetting than no sleep prior to learning. The most obvious place to look for an explanation was in the learning itself, but we could find no evidence whatsoever that prior sleep affected the rate of acquisition of the learning task. The prior sleep increased the amount of forgetting, but it did not affect the speed or the amount learned.

Our second experiment varied the amount of prior sleep and also asked the question whether or not it is necessary for the sleep to occur *immediately prior* to learning in order to demonstrate the detrimental effect of prior sleep on memory. The design is somewhat complex and is shown in Table 3. There are six different conditions coming from an incomplete 4 x 2 factorial design with two variables: (1) the amount of prior sleep (0, 2, 4, or 6 hours), and (2) the location of the prior sleep (either it occurred immediately prior to learning or it occurred 2-4 hours before learning). All Ss in all conditions reported to the lab at 10 a.m., and all learned the OL task at 4 a.m., spent the next four hours awake in the lab and were tested for recall at about 8 a.m. The differences among the six conditions were all introduced during the time between 10 p.m. and 4 a.m. These are described in the lower portion of Table 3. Conditions B, C, and D have 2, 4, or 6 hours of prior sleep, the sleep ending just at 4 a.m., the time of OL. Subjects in these three conditions, then, have just been awakened from sleep when they are asked to learn the list, although they have gotten dressed, gone to the bathroom, washed their faces, and performed a warm-up task before attempting the OL task. Conditions E and F, have received 2 and 4 hours of prior sleep, but the prior sleep occurred earlier in the evening, at least 2 hours before OL takes place. These subjects have been awake for 4 and 2 hours respectively when OL takes place. Condition A is simply the awake control condition which gets no prior sleep.

The results, again in terms of the mean percent loss in memory over the 4-hour retention interval, are shown in Table 4. Looking across the top row of the table, it can be seen that again there is a prior sleep effect--forgetting is greater in the three prior sleep conditons (B, C, and D) compared to the awake control (condition A). It can also be seen that the size of the effect decreases with increasing

TABLE 3

EXPERIMENTAL DESIGN FOR PRIOR SLEEP EXPERIMENT

	Amount of prior sleep (hrs.)			
Location of prior sleep	0	2	4	6
Immediately before OL		B	C	D
	A			
2 or 4 hrs before OL		E	F	Not run

For all six conditions, Ss reported to the lab at 10 p.m.,
learned the OL task at 4 a.m., and were awake from 4 a.m.
until 8 a.m. when they were tested for recall.

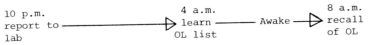

10 p.m.   4 a.m.   8 a.m.
report to ──────────────▷ learn ─────── Awake ──▷ recall
lab   OL list   of OL

Activities from 10 a.m. until 4 a.m. in the six conditions:

A: awake
B: awake from 10 p.m. until 2 a.m.; sleep from 2-4 a.m.
C: awake from 10 p.m. to midnight; sleep from midnight to
    4 a.m.
D: sleep from 10 p.m. until 4 a.m.
E: sleep from 10 p.m. until midnight; awake from midnight
    until 4 a.m.
F. sleep from 10 p.m. until 2 a.m.; awake from 2 a.m. until
    4 a.m.

amounts of prior sleep. The effect is largest with two
hours (condition B), decreases at 4 hours, and is no longer
present when 6 hours of prior sleep are given (the difference
between conditions D and A is not significant). Looking at
the bottom row where the control mean is repeated, it can
be seen that there is no prior sleep effect--the variation
among conditions A, E, and F is not significant. Memory
is not affected by the prior sleep unless the prior sleep
comes immediately before OL. Interpolating a period of
wakefulness between the prior sleep and the OL task eliminates
the detrimental effect of the prior sleep on memory for the
OL task. Again, in this experiment there was no evidence
for differences among any of the conditions in speed or degree
of learning.

TABLE 4

PERCENT LOSS AS A FUNCTION OF AMOUNT
AND LOCATION OF PRIOR SLEEP

Location of prior sleep	Amount of prior sleep (hrs.)			
	0	2	4	6
Immediately before OL	A 30.10	B 52.94	C 43.60	D 35.52
2-4 hrs. before OL	A 30.10	E 37.70	F 25.98	-----

Our third experiment sought to determine how much prior sleep was necessary in order to demonstrate the memory deficit. There were six conditions, each one involving learning at 2 a.m. and recall at 6 a.m. The retention interval was always filled with waking activity in the lab. The six groups consisted of 4 experimental groups that received different amounts of sleep just prior to OL ($\frac{1}{2}$, 1, 2, or 4 hours) and 2 different types of control groups that received no prior sleep. In the Normal control condition, the subjects never went to bed--they just stayed awake until 2 a.m., learned the list, stayed awake until 6 a.m., and then recalled. In contrast, the Stage-2 control condition defined sleep onset as the appearance of Stage-2 sleep, so Ss in this condition were put to bed and stayed there until the first signs of Stage-2 sleep appeared. They were immediately awakened for OL and then spent the retention interval awake. Instead of calling this a no-prior-sleep control, we might say that these subjects got perhaps one or two minutes of sleep. We included this condition to control for the fact that subjects in the prior sleep conditions do get to go to bed and fall asleep. For the experimental groups, the amount of prior sleep ($\frac{1}{2}$, 1, 2, or 4 hours) was measured from the onset of Stage 2 for each subject. This required us to physiologically monitor the sleep intervals and so the Stage-2 control condition also controls for the wiring and wearing of recording electrodes.

The results (mean percent loss in memory) are shown in Table 5. We can again see a prior sleep effect. This time the effect is of rather substantial magnitude, especially

TABLE 5

MEAN PERCENT LOSS AS A FUNCTION OF PRIOR SLEEP

		Amount of prior sleep (hrs.)			
0 (control)		½	1	2	4
Normal	Stage 2				
36.89	26.96	50.38	42.89	44.46	46.22

when the four prior sleep conditions are compared against the Stage-2 control condition. Analysis of variance showed that the variation among the four prior sleep conditions was not significant, that the difference between the two control conditions did not reach significance, but that the four experimental groups showed more forgetting than the average of the two controls. This means that as little as one-half hour of sleep, coming just prior to learning, can dramatically increase forgetting. The results also suggest that the amount of prior sleep, up to four hours, does not affect the size of the decrement in memory. Our previous experiment, however, did show that the effect was not present if the amount of prior sleep is increased up to six hours.

We have reached the following conclusions about the prior sleep effect: (1) the effect is reliable and can be fairly substantial in size--sleep immediately prior to learning increases forgetting; (2) the effect is present with as little as one-half hour of prior sleep and remains constant up to four hours of sleep and disappears with six hours of prior sleep; (3) the effect is present only when the prior sleep comes immediately prior to learning--a reasonable period of wakefulness (2 hours and perhaps less) coming between the end of the prior sleep period and the start of learning will prevent the effect from occurring; and (4) the effect cannot be accounted for in terms of different levels of arousal at the time of learning--all subjects are fully awake, have performed a warm-up task that itself is arousing, and there are not any differences in the speed of learning the OL task.

We obviously do not know yet what causes the prior sleep effect, but the above experiments give some valuable clues that invite speculation, wild though it may be. Based on these clues we feel that the effect implies that some neuro-biological event or process begins very rapidly after the onset of sleep, within a half hour or so, and that this

process affects the brain in such a way that it is less able
to store information. The observation that learning speed
is not affected by prior sleep suggests that we must distinguish between storage in long-term memory and storage in
a less permanent "working" memory. The prior-sleep effect
is an effect in long-term memory, not working memory, and
so we must suppose that the neurobiological process triggered
by sleep onset is one which blocks the transfer of information from working memory into long-term memory. We
speculate that sleep onset triggers a process that involves
changing levels of some biochemical substance(s) in the
brain. This biochemical substance is capable of retarding
transfer of information into long-term memory, but has no
effect on storage and availability of information in short-
term or working memory. The process and the level of the
critical substance is tied very closely to sleep onset,
beginning very shortly after sleep onset. The process stops
when the subject is awakened, but the unusually high levels
of the critical substance are present for some time after
awakening, but return to "normal" levels within two hours
after awakening. This would account for the 'fact that the
prior sleep effect disappears if the subject is awake for
awhile before attempting to learn. The prior-sleep effect
occurs because the subject having just awakened from
sleep, has high levels of the critical substance active in
the brain and this blocks long-term memory storage. If the
subject stays awake for awhile before learning, the level of
the critical substance returns to normal and memory storage
is not affected. Finally, remembering that the prior sleep
effect is constant in magnitude from one-half up to four
hours of prior sleep, but disappears after six hours of prior
sleep, we can try to pin down the critical process. This
effect of amount of prior sleep suggests to us that, not
only is the process and critical substance tied very closely
to sleep onset, but that the process is tied closely to the
first half of the night. This naturally leads to the
speculation that the process is correlated with slow-wave
sleep, particulary Stage 4 sleep.

Given all these clues about the underlying culprit in
the prior-sleep effect, and given the information we have
heard at this symposium about some of the neurochemical
events that take place during sleep, we would like to suggest
a major candidate for the culprit. This is human growth
hormone (HGH) which we have heard about in the papers by
Weitzman, Sassin, and Stern (in this conference). Its
release is tied closely to sleep, and seems particularly
correlated with slow-wave sleep. Levels of HGH rise quickly

after sleep onset and remain high for the first part of the night. Levels drop in the later part of the night and they drop after awakening. All of this, of course, may be a coincidence, but the correlation is too close to ignore. This suggests that it would be worthwhile to examine the effects of HGH on learning and memory. We would predict that HGH would affect long-term memory, but not acquisition or short-term memory. We hope that someone will do the requisite experimentation.

Why Does Sleep During the Retention Interval Reduce Forgetting?

In concluding, we must return to our original question and examine where we stand at this point in time with respect to interference, decay, and consolidation interpretations of the overall sleep effect. In the first place, we have already suggested that in the type of paradigm we use, consolidation does not appear to be a factor. This conclusion is based primarily on the failure to demonstrate a difference between sleep coming immediately after learning and sleep that is delayed for some time after learning. We feel that the superior memory after sleep is not due to improved consolidation.

We should point out, however, that our interpretation of the prior sleep effect, where we speculated that HGH might be involved, is basically a consolidation interpretation. This is so because it is quite likely that consolidation and transfer of information into long-term storage are two different ways of referring to the same neurobiological events. So, while we feel that consolidation is not involved when sleep comes after learning, it might very well be involved in memory effects produced by sleep coming before learning.

Next, let us return our attention to the decay and interference interpretations of the sleep effect during the retention interval. We felt that the first-half, second-half effect was a crucial phenomenon and that all of our experiments were in support of a decay theory. As we said earlier, the difference between memory over the two halves of the night cannot readily be accounted for by an interference theory, but it is what a decay theory would predict by assuming that decay rates would be slower in the first half of the night. Based only on our experiments demonstrating the first-half, second-half effect, we would have concluded that at least some and perhaps all of the effect of sleep during the retention interval is due to a reduced rate of memory decay during sleep compared to wakefulness.

Such a conclusion is not now warranted, simply because the prior sleep effect is an alternate way of accounting for the first-half, second-half effect. Second-half memory may be worse only because subjects in this condition have had prior sleep just before OL whereas subjects in the first-half condition have not had any prior sleep. Combining the results from all our experiments, it is the case, however, that the size of the prior sleep effect is not as large as the size of the first-half, second-half effect. Nevertheless, the difference in magnitude of the two effects is not great and it could very well be that if there were a way to eliminate the confounding from the prior sleep, we would find no difference between the first and second half of the night (no difference between REM and Stage-4 sleep). As is so often the case, crucial experiments turn out to be not so crucial after all. No difference between the first and second halves of the night, but both halves being superior to being awake during the retention interval would be exactly what an interference theory would predict. Jenkins and Dallenbach (1924) thought that they had a crucial experiment in 1924 which proved interference theory correct and decay theory wrong. About 50 years later, we thought we had a crucial experiment which proved that decay theory was correct and that interference theory was wrong (at least wrong about the sleep effect). The more things change, the more they stay the same.

FOOTNOTE

[1] The statistical procedure used to test for the differences among means in all the experiments presented in this paper was analysis of variance with orthogonal or nonorthogonal comparisons, and alpha = .05.

ACKNOWLEDGMENT

The research presented in this paper was supported by Grant Number MH 15655 from the National Institute of Mental Health. The paper was written at the Institute for the Study of Intellectual Behavior which is supported by the Graduate School of the University of Colorado.

REFERENCE NOTE

1. McGaugh, J. L., & Hostetter, R. C.   Retention as a
    function of the temporal position of sleep and activity
    following waking.   Unpublished manuscript, 1961.

REFERENCES

Barrett, T. R., & Ekstrand, B. R.   Effect of sleep on memory:
    III.   Controlling for time-of-day effects. *Journal of
    Experimental Psychology*, 1972, *96*, 321–327.

Ekstrand, B. R.   To sleep, perchance to dream (about why we
    forget).   In C. P. Duncan, L. Sechrest, & A. W. Melton
    (Eds.), *Human Memory: Festschrift in Honor of Benton J.
    Underwood*.   New York: Appleton-Century-Crofts, 1972.

Fowler, M. J., Sullivan, M. J., & Ekstrand, B. R.   Sleep and
    memory. *Science,* 1973, *179*, 302–304.

Heine, R.   Uber wiedererkennen und ruckworkende hemmung.
    Psychologie Forschung, 1914, *17*, 13–55.

Jenkins, J. B., & Dallenbach, K. M.   Oblivescence during
    sleep and waking. *American Journal of Psychology,* 1924,
    35, 605–612.

Yaroush, R., Sullivan, J. J., & Ekstrand, B. R.   Effect of
    sleep on memory.   II.   Differential effect of the first
    and second half of the night. *Journal of Experimental
    Psychology,* 1971, *88*, 361–366.

AMNESIA AND DISORDERS OF EXCESSIVE DAYTIME SLEEPINESS

CHRISTIAN GUILLEMINAULT and WILLIAM C. DEMENT

Sleep Disorders Clinic and Laboratory
Stanford University School of Medicine
Stanford, California 94305 USA

Sleep is generally a time of amnesia. It is not un-
common for a person to experience a nocturnal sleep period
of seven or eight hours as if it had lasted only a few
seconds. The usual explanation of this amnesic gap in the
lack of recognition of the passage of time is that there is
nothing to remember. Some people have also speculated that
sensory input to the central nervous system is blocked during
sleep. However, this latter notion may be regarded as un-
tenable in view of the abundant evidence that sensory input
evokes EEG responses during sleep and that information is
incorporated into mental content during sleep. With regard
to the former notion, it is now known that a great deal of
mental activity occurs in sleep which could add to our
memory stores--approximately two hours per night of vivid
and varied experiences that occur as dreams during REM periods
(the question of whether or not there is additional dreaming
in NREM sleep is moot, but is not necessary to our argument).
Not only are REM periods associated with vivid dreaming, but
the activity of the brain during this time appears to resemble waking function in many ways. The principle evidence
that dreaming occurs during REM periods results from the
fact that if one is aroused *during* (in the middle of) a REM
period, he will recall the dream experience quite easily and
with vivid detail. If awakenings do not occur during REM
sleep, dreams are generally *not* recalled the next morning.
A question we might ask is: do the memory traces of all
these complex, hallucinatory experiences just fade away, or
are they stored in a form that is inaccessible?

It has been found (Dement, & Kleitman, 1957; Dement, & Wolpert, 1958) that the amount recalled from a REM period awakening and the length of the corresponding REM period bear a relationship that is approximately linear for several minutes and then the dream recall tends to plateau. One hypothesis is that dream experiences produce short-term memories, but then the subsequent formation of permanent or persistent engrams does not occur. For example, a dream experience may persist in short-term memory for perhaps 10 minutes before dying out. This could explain why an awakening after 10 minutes of REM sleep generally elicits the same amount of recall as an arousal after 20, 30 or even 60 minutes of REM sleep. It is *as if* the "gate" between short-term and long-term memory closes during sleep. This principle cannot be directly tested during NREM sleep. However, Portnoff, Baekeland, Goodenough, Karacan, and Shapiro (1966) have presented data suggesting that a similar effect on memory processes may exist in NREM sleep. These investigators showed that verbal information perceived *just before the onset of NREM* sleep was not recalled during a later test of retention. When a lengthy period of wakefulness intervened between presentation of the material and the onset of NREM sleep, a fairly high level of retention was demonstrated. The Portnoff study focused on the duration of the interval between presentation of the test material and the onset of NREM sleep. The duration of NREM sleep was not controlled. Subjects were awakened at various times during the night according to a pre-determined schedule and were tested once in the morning for all material. Furthermore, in these instances where the sleep latency--the interval between presentation and NREM onset--was longer, the results were not compared to a waking control. The authors suggested from their results that "NREM sleep may impede the consolidation of memory traces."

Pilot Study

A study was conducted to test this conclusion in a more precise manner. Two male college students, ages 20 and 21, limited their sleep to two hours on the night before the experiments in order to facilitate daytime napping. Each experimental session began immediately after the noon meal and lasted about two hours. The subjects were prepared for standard sleep recordings. They reclined on a bed in a quiet, darkened room. Two-syllable words were presented at the rate of about one per minute and no words were presented twice (several hundred words were previously selected for presentation from *The Teacher's World Book of 30,000 Words* (Thorndike, & Lorge, 1944). When the subject heard the word, he was instructed to verbally repeat it out loud once, and not to think about it thereafter. In addition, the subject was told to relax and let sleep come without resisting, since falling asleep was, in fact, a goal of the study. The presentation of two-syllable words continued until the subject fell asleep as indicated by attentuation or disappearance of alpha rhythm in the electroencephalogram (EEG) and the appearance of slow eye movements in the electro-oculogram (EOG). Two arousal conditions were instituted, one 30 seconds after sleep onset and the other 10 minutes after sleep onset. At this time the subjects were asked to retrieve[1] as many of the words as possible. A single trial began with the presentation of the first word after an awakening. The mean number of successive words presented per trial was 6.5. This was approximately equivalent to a sleep latency of 6.5 minutes. Four to six such trials were conducted during each afternoon session and each subject was studied on five different days. When the data was pooled from both subjects, a total of 387 words were presented (see Figure 1).

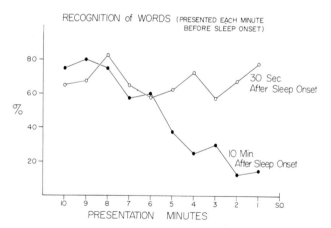

Fig. 1. Percent of words presented during the 10 minutes preceding sleep onset and recognized on a multiple choice test when the subject was awakened 30 seconds after sleep (white dots) and 10 minutes after sleep onset (black dots). There is no significant difference between the two conditions up to 6 minutes before sleep onset: a similar percentage of words is recognized. But between 5 minutes before sleep onset and

*sleep onset, there is a progressive decrease in the percent-
age of words recognized when the subject is awakened 10
minutes after sleep onset.*

Figure 1 shows the percentage of words recognized as a
function of the number of minutes prior to sleep onset that
a word was presented. These results indicate that words
perceived just before the onset of sleep are forgotten after
10 minutes of sleep but not after only 30 seconds of sleep.
On the other hand, words presented 5 to 10 minutes *before*
sleep onset persist in memory whether retrieval is tested
30 seconds after sleep onset or 10 minutes after sleep onset.
One interpretation of these results is that when words are
presented 5 to 10 minutes before sleep onset it is possible
to form relatively permanent memory traces; thus, the words
are retrievable even after 10 minutes of elapsed sleep. The
words presented just prior to sleep onset are still in short-
term memory when sleep onset occurs, and these do not go on
to long-term memory storage. Retrieval of the words is
possible after only 30 seconds of sleep, since these words are
still in the short-term memory.
The precise point in time at which the "gate" between
short-term and long-term memory closes is not certain. It is
possible that permanent memory traces are no longer formed
when a subject is very sleepy (almost asleep) but still
behaviorally awake. This formulation is extremely relevant
to the extensive clinical observations which will now be
reported.

*An Automatic Behavior Syndrome Associated With Excessive
Daytime Sleepiness.*

The complaint of Excessive Daytime Sleepiness (EDS) can
be subdivided into several well-known syndromes: Narcolepsy-
cataplexy, sleep apnea hypersomnia, the subwakefulness
syndrome, and the neutral state syndrome. These disorders can
be diagnosed with the help of nocturnal polygraphic monitoring
and specific chemical analysis of metabolites of neurotransmitters in the cerebrospinal fluid. These syndromes greatly
impair the social and family life of all our patients and
interact drastically with their ability to handle adequately
their professional activities. Daytime naps are not the
worst problem that face this patient population. A careful
analysis of the complaints of 80 patients presenting an EDS
syndrome has revealed that the most devastating experiences

during the daytime are related to a very abnormal state of consciousness best denominated as an "Automatic Behavior Syndrome" where amnesia appears to be the predominant symptom.

After becoming increasingly aware of this problem through our clinical experience, 60 narcoleptics, 5 neutral state syndrome patients, and 15 sleep apnea hypersomniacs were systematically questioned about the possible existence of an automatic behavior syndrome. This syndrome was not reported as part of the symptomatology by referring physicians nor has it been described in medical textbooks. All of the patients surveyed in these groups reported experiencing this syndrome. It can be clinically described in the following way: The patient first feels a certain drowsiness which initially he tries to fight by changing his position; if possible the patient will get up and move, go and drink a cup of coffee and/or open a window to have some fresh air. Very often this drowsiness occurs while driving, and the driver will open the window widely and will increase the radio volume. Following these initial actions, the patient becomes less aware of his actions and his performance deteriorates. Sometimes the feeling of drowsiness is un- noticed by the patient and progresses into an abnormal state of consciousness without the patient being actually aware of it. This inability to perceive the alteration of consciousness is, in fact, the rule. For several minutes to several hours the patient generally presents a complete amnesia. The notion of time is severely altered and most of these episodes would be totally ignored by the individual if objective traces of continuous activity were not there as proof. However, this activity is very often not adapted to the environmental demands and performance deteriorates. Actions which do not require skill are usually performed satisfactorily, although in a semi-automatic way. However, if a sudden and well-planned decision is required, frequently the patient will be unable to adapt appropriately to the new demand. The ability of the patient to express himself in a coherent, appropriate manner is also impaired. Simple answers to simple questions may not indicate the abnormal state of consciousness but attempts at complex answers are abortive. Sudden bursts of loud, inappropriate sentences may also occur during the course of the episode. The complete amnesia for these episodes by the patient may result in an underestimation of their frequency, but the objective results of this abnormal behavior and the awful feeling of continuous activity without control and remembrance of it produces considerable anxiety.

The following are clinical reports of patients presenting this automiatic behavior syndrome. These are patient histories obtained from taped interviews.

Case 1 (40-year-old male): "I always needed more sleep than anybody else in the family when I was a child. During my early teens, I had a tendency to fall asleep during the 2:00 class but it was not a real problem until I went to college. I had some irresistible sleep attacks at that time, particularly in the late morning and between 3 and 4 p.m. I struggled through college and terminated with a masters degree in business. I learned to take a very short nap--10 minutes long, as a mean--during my lunch hour and have succeeded in my field. I am now the director of an important sales department.

About five years ago the clinical picture changed. First, I began to experience a sudden feeling of weakness throughout my body when I was surprised or laughing. Nobody really noticed anything but I experienced that feeling more and more frequently. I never fell asleep but about 2 years ago I began to experience a sudden drop of my head and my upper arms when I laughed or was under stress. During the same period I found myself in very embarrassing situations. I would be talking with someone and suddenly would burst out with a very inappropriate sentence. I would see a very surprised look on the faces of my companions but I would not remember what I said. Other times, I would not be able to remember anything about a conversation and when brought back to reality by an insistent question I would not know what the conversation (talk) was about.

Recently, I had two very frightening experiences. I took my car to go back home near 4 p.m. I remember driving out and turning on the freeway. Then I had a complete amnesia. I found myself 70 minutes later somewhere in Oakland. I could not figure out where I was. The surroundings were entirely unfamiliar and I was completely lost. I could not and still cannot remember how I got there and what I did for more than an hour. I have no memory whatsoever of any event during that time. A similar episode occurred recently but the amnesic period lasted longer, about 100 minutes and when I 'came back' I was once again lost, with a complete feeling of disorientation. I had total amnesia of what happened during the last hour and a half and a complete loss of the notion of time."

Case 2 (38-year-old male): "I was diagnosed as a narcoleptic six years ago. I usually drive back home from Palo Alto to San Francisco. I remember that I left work at 4:30

p.m.; after that I only remember a few visual images, like in a broken movie. I remember that I drove on a dirt road--I do not know why; I do not know where. I found myself at 7 p.m., 2½ hours later at the dead-end of a dirt road in Golden Gate Park. I was seated in my car. The engine was turned on. The most frightening thing was that I could not remember anything that had happened during the 2½ hours that had passed."

Case 3 (38-year-old female): "I am working as an assistant in a doctor's office. I am usually left alone in the office between 12 and 1 p.m.; the other girl goes to lunch and I answer the phone. It is one of the worst periods of the day. I have a feeling of drowsiness which usually starts near 11 a.m. I try to fight it, I drink coffee and put water on my face. But I have downs (of attention) when I am left alone. The problem is that I answer the phone-- several patients have complained that I give completely inadequate answers. Sometimes I try to take a message and usually I know that someone called because I find a note on my desk. The message is usually absolutely unreadable and most of the time I have no idea of who called or what the phone call was about. But my numbers are very easy to read. When I go through one of these episodes, if I have been lucky enough someone has given me a phone number and then I have to call back to find out what the message was. I have no recollections of anything, but there is an obvious dissociation of what I can do during this state. Any number that I write is very rarely wrong but if I am able to read any words I wrote, which is seldom the case, the words never make any sense."

Case 4 (45-year-old male): "I started to need more sleep at night 10 years ago, but daytime sleepiness was not really a problem until 5 years ago. Two years ago, I developed a new symptom: I began to be very forgetful. I misplaced objects that I use every day. I then find them in the most incredible places. I put my watch in the refrigerator and my toothbrush in the mailbox. Everybody in the family is aware of these misplacements and they are subjects of amusement. The problem is more serious at work. I have to attend numerous meetings and I do not really fall asleep but I 'blank out.' Decisions are taken that I cannot remember. I am running out of excuses such as 'I was not there" because of vacation, sick leave, etc. and I am on the verge of being fired or being forced to retire because of my complete lack of memory. I try to concentrate and give great attention to these meetings. I usually remember

perfectly the beginning but progressively in the smokey room
I have the feeling that I don't perceive anything anymore.   I
completely lose the notion of time; I suddenly realize that
the meeting is over; it could have lasted for 30 minutes or
3 hours; it does not make any difference--it usually seems
very short.   The only solution that I have found is to tape
the meetings and listen to them later on, but sometimes I
do not realize that the cassette tape should be turned over.
The very frightening feeling is the complete absence of control
of my mind, and the existence of multiple 'blanks' throughout
the day."

        Numerous anecdotes of this type have been obtained from
our patients.   The forgetfulness has been confirmed by the
family; sometimes it is just a subject of jokes; sometimes
it leads to the loss of a job and long-term unemployment.
The automatic behavior syndrome seen during these "blank"
periods can also, unfortunately, lead to severe accidents
endangering the life of the patient as well as others.
        Several questions were raised by the discovery of this
automatic behavior syndrome associated with amnesia in EDS
patients.   The first issue was to eliminate the possibility
that the syndrome might be occurring in connection with
temporal lobe epilepsy.   Ten patients had a clinical EEG with
naso-pharyngeal leads.   No electroencephalographic abnormalities could be noticed on the recordings.   In two cases
the EEG was performed after sleep deprivation, also without
any positive findings.   In order to further explore this
automatic behavior syndrome, 26 patients were asked to
participate in three different experimental protocols.   Five
of the patients presented a "neutral state syndrome"
(Guilleminault, Phillips, & Dement, 1975), 20 were diagnosed
as REM narcoleptics, and one presented a typical sleep apnea
hypersomnia.   All patients had been previously diagnosed by
means of polygraphic monitoring and/or CSF measurement.   The
performance of these patients was compared to that of 17
normal controls of the same age group (40 to 60 years of age)
recruited through press and radio advertisement and were
simultaneously recorded.

Experimental Procedures

        All patients were drug-free for a minimum of 15 days
before the start of the experiment.   Three different experimental protocols were followed.   These protocols were designed
to provide information about the patients' ability to perform
throughout the day in quiet and eventually boring situations,

situations which favor the appearance of any "automatic behavior syndrome."

Protocol A: Five neutral state syndrome patients and one sleep apnea hypersomniac were hospitalized for four days and one adaptation night. EEG (C_3/A_2 - C_4/A_1 - O_1/A_2 - O_2/A_1) electro-oculogram (EOG) and chin electromyogram (EMG) were continuously monitored except for one hour each day spent in personal care. Respiration was monitored at night by means of two abdominal and thoracic strain gauges and two nose and mouth thermistors.

During the first 48 hour period, each patient had a strict nocturnal sleep schedule with bedtime scheduled from 2300 until 0730. During the daytime, each patient was asked to perform two different tests (each of them one hour long), repeated three times throughout the day: the Wilkinson Addition Test - WAT - (Wilkinson, 1968) given at 1100, 1530, and 2000 and the Light Stimulus Vigilance Test - LSVT - (Morrell, 1966), administered at 0900, 1330, and 2000. During the following 48 hours the patients were on an *ad libitum* sleep schedule and did not perform any tests. When awake, they would watch TV, read, play cards or talk with physicians and technicians. If the patients fell asleep during the first 48 hour period or at any time during the day (testing or non-testing period) they were permitted to sleep for 3 minutes--the time being controlled by poly-graphic monitoring--and then awakened (see Figure 2).

Seven normal controls of similar age group were asked to undergo the same protocol. Protocols B and C were simple variants of Protocol A.

Protocol B: Five narcoleptic-cataplectic patients followed this protocol. During the first 24 hour period after one adaptation night, the patients were continuously monitored on *ad libitum* sleep schedules but were asked to perform a one-hour WAT after each nap between 0800 and 2100. If a sleep episode continued longer than three minutes during the test, the patient was awakened by the experimenters. During the second 24 hour period, patients were allowed to fall asleep *ad libitum*, but were systematically awakened after a 10 minute sleep period and were asked then to perform a one-hour WAT.

Protocol C: Fifteen narcoleptics followed this protocol. After one adaptation night, the patients were continuously monitored for the next 58 hours. During Day 1 from 0700 until 2230 the patients were kept awake. They were asked to per-form WAT and a serial counting task (the Serial Alternative

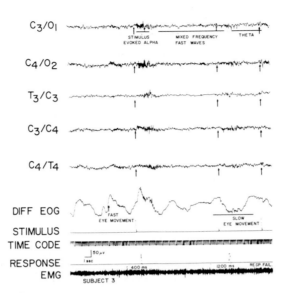

*Fig. 2. Example of micro-sleep characterized by a
burst of theta rhythm in the EEG, during the LSVT in a
"neutral state" patient. Slow rolling eye movements during
the micro-sleep contrast with fast ones recorded during
alertness. The patient did not see the bright, flashing
light positioned in front of his eyes during the micro-sleep
episode.*

Task - SAT - [Lubin, Moses, Johnson, & Naitoh, 1974]) in a
slightly different schedule than under Protocol B.   Each test
was broken into two 30 minute periods with a 15 minute break
between each 30 minutes.   WAT was given at 0930 and 1015,
1400 and 1445, 1830 and 1915; SAT was performed at 1145 and
1230, 1615 and 1700.   During Day 2, the patients were allowed
and even encouraged to sleep during each 15 minute break between tests (from 1000 to 1015, 1215 to 1230, 1430 to 1445,
1645 to 1700, 1900 to 1915).   During the testing periods
Day 1 and 2, the patients were systematically awakened
after two minutes of recorded sleep.   A total of eight
normal controls of similar age group (35-60) were asked to
undergo the same protocols as our patients.
Patients and normal controls were asked to fill out
questionnaires every day about their sleep and their symptomatology.   The Stanford Sleepiness Scale (SSS) was administered
every 15 minutes when patients and controls were not performing
and all subjects were systematically questioned about their
sleep time estimate each time they fell asleep (see Figure 3).

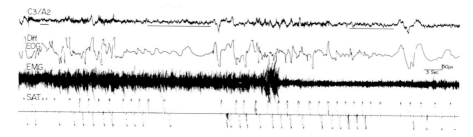

Fig. 3. Example of repetitive micro-sleep episodes in the polygraphic recording of a narcoleptic patient performing a serial counting task (Serial Alternative Task). Micro-sleep episodes are underlined. Slow rolling eye movements during micro-sleep contrast with the fast ones recorded during alertness. The patient stopped pressing the counter appropriately during the micro-sleep.

RESULTS

The performance of control subjects during each of the testing sessions was essentially normal; the error range in the WAT was approximately 6%. During LSVT the missed-trials were kept at a very low level (Guilleminault, Phillips, & Dement, 1975; Guilleminault, Billiard, Montplaisir, & Dement, 1975) and normal controls never stopped performing the SAT. Most subjects reported that the tasks were boring or of little interest but none of them at any time during the polygraphic recording presented any sign of an automatic behavior syndrome or reported any "blanks" or memory problems. Our patient poupulation had a very different level of performance. On any task, after the first 10 minutes of a testing session, performance deteriorated well below normal performance levels. During the WAT administration, patients suddenly would begin to perform inadequately, sometimes doing the same addition again and again, and at other times showing an increasing amount of errors (up to 30%). Some errors were not arithmetical errors, but resulted when one number or series of numbers was picked up in one addition and added to an addition which was located above or next to the addition considered. Sometimes there was a simple jump over one series of addition. The total number of problems solved by patient population was abnormally low compared to controls.

Patients often complained that they were cheated on the time allowance (one hour). They had the feeling that they had only performed for a short period of time and that the experimenters had reduced the testing period. This was not the case with our normal controls who usually were bored by the test and complained of an increase in the total duration of the test period. Patients and controls always denied any period of sleep during the testing condition.

During the SAT performance the discrepancy between the patient and normal population was also very obvious. The patients stopped pressing the counter suddenly, or pressed it inappropriately, forgetting to press the counter one finger after the other (the alternative task usually involves two fingers) and pressing with only one finger for a short period of time. The patients and normals denied the presence of sleep during most of the SAT and few had to be stimulated since the polygraphic recordings seldom indicated sleep episodes longer than 3 minutes. During the time when patients stopped performing adequately on the WAT or the SAT they appeared behaviorally to be motionless at their desk, eyes open but with a staring, empty (glassy) look, completely absent from the surrounding world. Concomitant with these episodes, micro-sleep periods lasting from 2 to 10 seconds were recorded on the polygraph. These short bursts were repetitive, often in close clusters, interrupting completely or disrupting performance. "Micro-sleep" is defined as a sudden, short-lasting burst of typical stage 1 slow-wave sleep as described in the Standardized Manual of Terminology (Rechtschaffen and Kales, 1968) and/or a short burst of "synchronous theta activity" recorded in central monopolar derivations (C3A$_2$ and C4/A1). During the LSVT, similar micro-sleep episodes were recorded associated with sudden loss of performance and non-recognition of the bright flashing light position one foot in front of the eye.

During the non-performance day periods when patients were allowed to have sleep *ad libitum*, these micro-sleep episodes were also noted, despite several daytime naps and the absence of specific performance tests. They usually appeared again in close clusters. In one episode, one of the patients was comfortably seated in an armchair and was supposedly participating in a conversation with a technician-- he suddenly burst out with an inappropriate sentence. This behavior correlated with polygraphic recordings of close cluster micro-sleep episodes. Similarly, one patient was accurately completing a questionnaire when he experienced some short repetitive "micro-sleep" episodes. During that time he wrote on the questionnaire one sentence which was barely readable and completely out of context. The patient had "no idea of what it meant and could give no reason for

writing it." He had a complete amnesia about the episode which
lasted "only minutes" (Guilleminault, Billiard, Montplaisir,
& Dement, 1975) (see Figure 4).

COMMENTS

Our patient population presents a syndrome where a
complete amnesia was closely related to repetitive close
cluster micro-sleep episodes. Our test situation confirms
that EDS patients may present sudden bursts of micro-sleep
which impair their ability to perform appropriately but
which allow them to pursue activities in between each micro-
sleep episode. Because of the short duration of each micro-
sleep period, the surrounding persons may not be aware of
the abnormal state of consciousness. The amnesia observed
during the test usually covers a longer period than the
duration of the micro-sleep episodes. Between the close-
cluster micro-sleep episodes, the activity may be pursued
in a more normal way, but the patients underestimated the
amount of time which had elapsed and many "blanks" in their
behavior existed. No long-lasting micro-sleep episodes
were recorded, but multiple clinical observations show that
the amnesia can cover several hours. In some cases where a
patient was particularly accurate, a notion of long-lasting
amnesia with a complete blank of several hours was tempered
by some vague images, as in a "broken movie," that the
patient could not relate to any rational situation. These
images had no temporal clue, no continuity, appeared to be
meaningless and were like floating ghosts in the "blank"
period. The patient who reported finding himself "at the
dead end of a dirt road in Golden Gate Park" had some vague
images of "being on a dirt road" previously. The expression
"broken movie" was his. He could not figure out why he had
been on a dirt road, where it was, or when it was. Perhaps
a larger number of our patients who claim to have a complete
amnesia for several hours in fact also experience these
floating images, but they are unable to rearrange in a
rational way these bits and pieces, which are left without
a temporal frame, and they may simply dismiss them because
they do not fit in their rational network.
Another question concerns what happens to the information
during this abnormal state and why patients deny any memory
trace of the events. During micro-sleep episodes a lack of
perception may exist, which is responsible for a non-
acquisition of information. The results obtained from the
LSVT seem to confirm this assumption. But micro-sleeps are

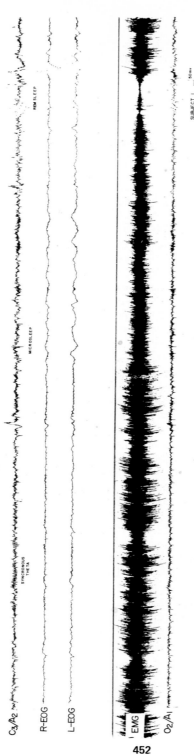

Fig. 4. Example of three repetitive micro-sleep episodes during a daytime polygraphic recording in a narcoleptic patient.

very short events and the absence of perception during these
periods can only account for a small amount of the total
amnesic period. Another component must also play a role in
the existence of the amnesia. Our patients obviously present
a retrograde amnesia and if we combine the results of our
pilot study on students and the findings on our patient
population, one could suggest that a certain amount of
information stored in the "short-term" memory pool cannot
be switched to the long-term pool because of successive
micro-sleep episodes.

The automatic behavior syndrome, and transient amnesia
which accompanies it, bear a resemblance to the amnesic
spells described in temporal lobe epilepsy. Brevity,
transiency, reversibility, and associated suspension of
memory are characteristics of both syndromes. But the
epileptic nature of the attack can easily be eliminated
in our cases on the basis of the clinical symptomatology
reported by the patients, the clinical observations and polygraphic recordings performed during the tests, the clinical
EEG recordings performed with naso-pharyngeal leads and,
in two cases, after sleep deprivation.

Perhaps some of the components of this syndrome are
more closely related to the "transient global amnesia
syndrome," first reported by Bender in 1956 and individualized
as a syndrome by Fisher and Adams in 1964. This syndrome
consists of the abrupt onset of disorientation due essentially
to a loss of the patient's ability to go from short-term to
long-term memory, with retention of a remarkable degree of
alertness and immediate responsiveness and a capacity for
fairly complicated short-term mental performances. This
syndrome is usually seen in otherwise supposedly healthy
patients in the sixth or seventh decade of life. It lasts
for several hours with a period of permanent amnesia corresponding to the duration of the attack plus a retrograde
amnesia, usually brief but in some cases lasting for several
hours. The etiology of this syndrome is still unclear, but
there is a valid suspicion in several cases of a transient
ischemia of the hippocampal fornical-hypothalamic system,
bilaterally.

However, the syndrome reported here differs by several
features. First, our patients are usually unable to perform
complicated mental tasks during these episodes. Catastrophes
happen because of the lack of intellectual control. Some
are humorous; others are costly--as in the case of the IBM
computer programmer who ran tapes and programs in such a way
that a $25,000 loss resulted (Guilleminault, Billiard,
Montplaisir, & Dement, 1975)! Second, our population is much

younger--the mean age is 40 years of age with a range from
28 to 60.   Third, the episodes are repetitive, a very infrequent
feature in the transient global amnesia syndrome and, last but
not least, the responsibility of the repetitive micro-sleep
episodes seem very well established in our EDS population.

CONCLUSION

From 1945-1960 the idea that "sleep was beneficial for
learning and memory" developed.   This idea led, in part, to
advertisements such as "learn during your sleep with a
cassette player."   But memory is a very complex phenomenon
and we are far from understanding the multiple steps involved
in storing and retrieving memories.   However, one step seems
absolutely necessary at the beginning of the memory process.
This is perception, and it appears that complex perceptions
may be impaired by sleepiness and sleep.   The next step in
the memory process--"short-term memory"--may still be
possible during sleepiness and it may allow a continuous
activity because the mark of the immediately preceding
information is still there.   Even if a micro-sleep episode
occurs the brain can still adapt its behavior to some degree.
This system could be compared to a film where a certain
number of frames are missing, but because of the speed of
the projection and our visual system, we are unable to "see"
the missing parts.   However, the overall quality of the film
is poor and we have a "feeling" that something is missing.
If the micro-sleep episodes are too long or too repetitive,
short-term memory will not be able to maintain an adequate
level of continuous function and the continuous fading of
perception will greatly impair the adaptation to the environmental demands.
    If the short-term memory functions, the repetitive micro-
sleeps may not allow the "gate" to open to long-term memory.
Lack of perception and perturbed long-term memory will then
result and be responsible for the complete amnesia reported
in our patients.   Therefore, information must have gone from
a short-term memory pool to another memory pool before sleep
occurs to observe a beneficial effect of sleep on the
retrieval process.

FOOTNOTE

[1]Retrieval or a modified form of recognition was routinely tested by showing the subject a list of 20 words in which were embedded the words that had been presented. The chance of being correct by guessing alone was usually around 1 in 3, but the subject was asked not to guess if possible. Only correct choices were tabulated.

ACKNOWLEDGMENT

This research was supported by National Institute of Neurological Disease and Stroke Grant NS 10727 and Research Scientist Development Award MN 05804 to Dr. Dement.

REFERENCES

Bender, M. B.   Syndrome of isolated episode of confusion with amnesia. *Journal of the Hillside Hospital,* 1956, *2,* 212.

Dement, W., & Kleitman, N.   The relation of eye movements during sleep to dream activity: An objective method of the study of dreaming. *Journal of Experimental Psychology,* 1957, *53,* 339-346.

Dement, W., & Wolpert, E.   The relation of eye movements, body motility, and external stimuli to dream content. *Journal of Experimental Psychology,* 1958, *55,* 543-553.

Fisher, C. M., & Adams, R. D.   Transient global amnesia. *Acta Neurologica Scandinavica,* 1964, *40,* 1-83 (Suppl. 9).

Guilleminault, C., Billiard, M., Montplaisir, J., & Dement, W. C.   Altered states of consciousness in disorders of daytime sleepiness. *Journal of the Neurological Sciences,* 1975, *26,* 377-393.

Guilleminault, C., Phillips, R., & Dement, W. C.   A syndrome of hypersomnia with automatic behavior. *Electroencephalography and Clinical Neurophysiology,* 1975, *38,* 403-413.

Lubin, A., Moses, J. M., Johnson, L. C., & Naitoh, P.   The recuperative effects of REM sleep and stage 4 sleep on human performance after complete sleep loss: Experiment I. *Psychophysiology,* 1974, *11,* 133-146.

Morrell, L.   EEG frequency and reaction time--a sequential analysis. *Neuropsychologia,* 1966, *4,* 41-48.

Portnoff, G., Baekeland, F., Goodenough, D. R., Karacan, I., & Shapiro, A.   Retention of verbal materials perceived immediately prior to onset of non-REM sleep. *Perceptual and Motor Skills,* 1966, *22,* 751-758.

Rechtschaffen, A., & Kales, A. (Eds.)   *A Manual of Standardized Terminology Techniques and Scoring System for Sleep States of Human Subjects.* Washington, D. C.: U. S. Government Printing Office, 1968.

Thorndike, E., & Lorge, I.   *Teachers World Book of 30,000 Words.* New York: Teachers College Press, 1944.

Wilkinson, R.   Sleep deprivation: Performance tests for partial and selective sleep deprivation. In L. Abt & B. Riess (Eds.), *Progress in Clinical Psychology* (Vol. 8). New York: Grune and Stratton, 1968).